THE GREAT
DRUG WAR

ALSO BY ARNOLD S. TREBACH

The Rationing of Justice
The Heroin Solution

THE GREAT DRUG WAR

By
ARNOLD S.
TREBACH

And Radical Proposals That Could Make America Safe Again

Macmillan Publishing Company
New York
Collier Macmillan Publishers
London

Macmillan Publishing Company
866 Third Avenue, New York, N.Y. 10022
Collier Macmillan Canada, Inc.

Library of Congress Cataloging-in-Publication Data
Trebach, Arnold S.
The great drug war.
Includes index.
1. Narcotics, Control of—United States. 2. Youth—
United States—Drug use. 3. Drug abuse—United States—
Prevention. I. Title.
HV5825.T743 1987   363.4'5'0973   87-7954
ISBN 0-02-619830-4

Macmillan books are available at special discounts for bulk purchases
for sales promotions, premiums, fund-raising, or educational use.
For details, contact:

Special Sales Director
Macmillan Publishing Company
866 Third Avenue
New York, N.Y. 10022

10 9 8 7 6 5 4 3 2 1

Designed by Jack Meserole

Printed in the United States of America

For Marjy

We're taking down the surrender
flag that has flown over so many
drug efforts.
We're running up the battle flag.

—PRESIDENT RONALD REAGAN,
   speaking in the Rose Garden

We has met the enemy, and it is us.

—WALT KELLY, *Pogo*

Contents

THE GREAT
DRUG WAR

1

The Scared Summer of '86

WHAT'S happening to us? And why is it happening now?" Randi Henderson asked. "It seems like George Orwell's *1984*."

It was actually 1986, near the end of a terrible summer, and she was asking questions that a number of journalists had been raising with me. Several things disturbed me about my discussion with Ms. Henderson. The most disturbing was the subject of the story the reporter was writing. Deanna Young, 13, of Los Angeles, had heard a sheriff's deputy give an anti-drug lecture at a church meeting. Deanna was impressed enough to go home, collect some cocaine and drug paraphernalia, and take it all to the police, thus accusing her parents of multiple crimes. The young girl, it seemed, had turned in two enemies of the state.

Randi Henderson's reporting became the cover story in the feature section of the *Baltimore Sun* on August 20. Her story commenced with a quote from Orwell's famous novel: "Hardly a week passed in which the Times did not carry a paragraph describing how some eavesdropping little sneak—'child hero' was the phrase generally used—had overheard some compromising remark and denounced his parents to the Thought Police." This was fol-

1

lowed by a quotation from Joyce Nalepka, a Reagan White House favorite and the leader of the National Federation of Parents for Drug-Free Youth, who applauded Deanna's actions: "We are in such a serious epidemic of drug use right now that it will take work at many levels. . . . This child did exactly the right thing."

I had been concerned about the direction of American drug-control activities for years. During the summer of 1986, my concern escalated to the first stages of real fright. That incipient fright was compounded by the fact that some of the reporters who called me for information seemed as scared for the country as I was.

It was a new experience for me to provide comfort to normally hard-bitten journalists. They asked for both information and assurance that somehow the country would endure and come through the hysteria. I particularly remember Ms. Henderson's personal concern because it seemed so heartfelt; it deeply affected me.

I want very much to answer her and everyone else who has been asking me recently why we are now in such difficulty over the drug issue. My previous answers have not, in my eyes, been sufficient. Now I would like to attempt better answers to those questions.

In this chapter, I will explain what happened in the scared summer of 1986, when the drug-war fever flashed higher than ever before. Then, in the remainder of the book, I will go back and describe the irrational forces that broke down our social defenses and allowed that fever to run rampant through the body of American society. Finally, I will suggest some measures we can take that might help to curb drug abuse in our families and in our nation, to preserve American freedom, and to make our country safe again.

WHY WE ARE LOSING: IN A NUTSHELL

There are several major reasons why, in my opinion, we have never won a war on drugs and why we are losing the great drug war of today.

We are losing the great drug war because our drug laws are irrational, based upon flawed scientific assumptions, and are out of touch with the desires of millions of Americans. Thus they cannot be enforced, even if we ordered all three million of our military troops and civilian police officers to devote themselves exclusively to that mission.

We are losing the great drug war because we delude one another into thinking that certain dangerous drugs, such as alcohol and tobacco, are less harmful than other dangerous drugs, such as heroin, marijuana, and cocaine. Yet diseases related to alcohol and tobacco kill approximately 500,000 Americans every year. According to official federal data, deaths from the most popular illicit drugs—heroin, cocaine, PCP, and marijuana—amounted to 2,177 in 1985. Wars based upon myths are doomed to failure.

We are losing the great drug war because we do not now have, and never had, the capability to manage a successful war on any drug. We should have learned that when we attempted, with the best of motives and for good reasons, alcohol prohibition several generations ago. Alcohol is a terrible drug because it incites people to violence. Today, approximately 9,000 murders and 23,000 drunken driving deaths (half the total of all murders and all drunken driving deaths) are related to alcohol use. As bad as alcohol is, however, most Americans concluded by the early Thirties that prohibition—with its massive crime and corruption as well as health problems caused by bathtub gin and whiskey—was worse. They were right.

We are losing the great drug war because our leaders, especially those now in the Reagan administration, have declared all users of illicit drugs to be "the enemy." Thus, they refuse to distinguish between drug use and drug abuse, between responsible drug use and compulsive, addictive use. The Reagan administration has, therefore, declared at least 50 million Americans to be enemies of the state because the most recent government surveys suggest to me that this huge number have tried an illicit drug in some form during recent years. A war waged intensively on 5 percent of our people will be a civil war that will tear the country asunder. This is starting to happen.

We are losing the great drug war because it does not deal with the most important problems related to drugs: abuse, crime, and corruption. Drug abusers (or drug addicts, terms I here use interchangeably) need help and treatment. It would not help our 12 million alcohol addicts or our 56 million tobacco addicts if they were disgraced, fired from their jobs, and declared enemies of the state. The same is true of the two-to-three million addicts of heroin, cocaine, marijuana, and other illicit drugs. The intensifying war on drugs keeps these substances in the black market, keeps prices high, and creates the conditions in which violent traffickers flourish and criminal addicts feel driven to victimize their innocent neighbors. Much of this happened during alcohol prohibition. Today, however, addict crime and the profits for traffickers are much greater—and so are police and prosecutor corruption.

We are losing the great drug war because, as so often happens in wars, hysteria and hate are dominating the public discussion. I have personally felt that hysteria and hate because for years I have been a somewhat lonely dissenter on American drug policy and have pleaded for more tolerance, for new thinking about drugs, and for radical new directions in national strategy, including legalization of some drugs. To oppose the excesses of the current anti-drug war is the same as having opposed the excesses of the McCarthy anti-communist war of the Fifties; then you were accused by the warriors of being soft on communism: now you are accused of being soft on drugs. My students at American University tell me that their friends ask them if it is true that I drive a Ferrari, purchased with the profits from my drug dealing. It is, in fact, a solid '76 Volvo—and it would not make much sense to be both a drug trafficker and an advocate of fundamental change in American drug laws and in the drug war. These are traffickers' laws and this is a traffickers' war because both the laws and the war ensure criminal markets and monopoly prices.

I am certain that my opposition to the drug war and its zealots will be interpreted again by some in the popular media and in scholarly research to mean that I view the illegal drugs as harmless as jelly beans—and that I propose selling them over the counter in candy stores. Yet, I view all mind-altering and addicting chemicals as potentially dangerous to many users. I believe that anyone who uses, say, heroin could well suffer serious physical and mental problems. I believe the same about some users of cocaine, marijuana, PCP, and all of the many new illegal designer drugs that keep hitting the eager American drug market. Anyone who reads this book and concludes that I just gave all of these drugs a clean bill of health had better take reading lessons again. I personally fear these drugs and I would fear the results if anyone I loved used them, especially if the use was regular and compulsive. My personal fear about those drugs, however, is not exclusive; I also fear the compulsive use of beer and cigarettes. My fears, though, do not lead me to support a war on heroin injectors any more than a war on beer drinkers. Nor do I feel impelled to go to the other extreme and seek relief in a wholesale repeal of the drug laws. I am opposed both to the extremism of the drug warriors and to the extremism of those who advocate repeal of all drug laws. The answers, for me and for a working democratic society, lie somewhere in the rational middle.

We must calm down and recognize that this hysterical war diverts us from seeking to accomplish realistic goals. The McCarthy war on every person on the left reduced our ability to deal with an enduring evil, Soviet espionage. The Reagan-Meese war on every individual drug user reduces our ability to help those Americans afflicted with the disease of drug abuse. That multitude of sick neighbors may reach the total of 70 million people if all addicts to illegal and especially legal drugs are counted. The design of programs to assist these unfortunate people should be the main target of our drug-control programs. To these new rehabilitation experiments the nation should commit billions of dollars and the best thinking of our most innovative treatment specialists. Instead, we devote billions to the enforcement of criminal drug laws while too many of our treatment experts, including leading medical doctors, are devoting their thinking to how they can fill beds in their chains of profit-making hospitals—even if some of the inmates have only had a few beers or smoked a few joints, so long as they have adequate health insurance. The same type of venality is true of too many government officials, academic scholars, and journalists: they know better but make conscious decisions to obtain money or power by playing the ever-popular and ever-profitable drug-war game. All of these powerful prostitutes must share the blame for the drugged chickens that came home to roost during the summer of 1986.

CRACK AND LEN BIAS

When 1986 began, relatively few people had heard of either crack or Len Bias. Soon both were to become tragic household words. They dominated headlines and national fears, often pushing aside such concerns as Soviet espionage, nuclear war, terrorism, poverty, and crime in the streets.

Crack may well have existed for decades in various quiet back rooms of the drug world. More widespread use of the drug was first noticed by a few experts during the Eighties. Public concern grew with stories of bizarre behavior by users, especially among our youth.

Few drug-abuse experts knew anything about the drug because it was, comparatively speaking, so rarely used. I certainly was ignorant. On April 24, I admitted as much to a nationwide television audience during a heated discussion on the "MacNeil/Lehrer Newshour." Susan Taylor, the editor of *Essence* magazine, shot back from New York that I certainly wasn't much of a scholar and that it was time to get hysterical about crack in order to save our children. Five weeks later, on another television interview show, Dr. Arnold Washton, a nationally renowned physician in the cocaine-treatment business, countered my plea for calm measures by declaring, twice, that we should get hysterical about crack. Dr. Washton had been quoted frequently in the media to that effect, declaring at times that "crack is the most addictive drug known to man right now" and that it caused "almost instantaneous addiction."

Virtually every major print and electronic media vehicle, including the most respected and influential, joined in the emotional stampede. The *Washington Post* commenced a news story on the drug with a report of a New York City youth who had stabbed his mother to death in a crack-induced frenzy. The prestigious paper gave no explanation of the details nor did it inquire into how many recent homicides were related to alcohol or handguns or the illegal drug trade. Reports were frequently made and repeated that females, including young girls, would go into houses where crack was sold, find that they were unable to stop taking the stuff, and would sell their bodies to man after man in order to buy more and more crack. The stories were never balanced with an inquiry into the extent to which drugs, mainly alcohol, and sex were intertwined in legal establishments known as bars.

Newsweek magazine seemed particularly hooked on the compulsion to run story after story on the drug, emphasizing the most sensational aspects of its impact on society and individuals. While it might be argued that such stories served the public interest by scaring off potential users, that was not always the case. One young, though mature, college student, with some modest drug experience, told me much later that after reading a story on crack in a March issue of *Newsweek*, "I had never heard of it until then but when I read that it was better than sex and that it was cheaper than cocaine and that there was an epidemic, I wondered what I was missing. I questioned why I seemed to be the only one not doing the drug. The next day I asked some friends if they knew where to get some."

One of the most hysterical issues of a major American publication in recent history was the June 16, 1986, *Newsweek*, which rivaled the sensationalism of *Reefer Madness*, the movie about pot in the Thirties. Editor-in-chief Richard Smith unburdened himself in a lead editorial entitled "The Plague Among Us," in which he compared the drug problem to medieval plagues and to the Japanese attack on Pearl Harbor. Mr. Smith saw all addictive drugs but now especially crack—"the . . . most addictive commodity now on the market"—as creating a crisis that threatened the survival of the nation. The drugs themselves, mind you, not the governmental and social reaction to them.

A few days later, on June 19, in one of those sad and unpredictable events that change the course of history, Len Bias died suddenly in his room at the University of Maryland. Bias was 22, black, a star basketball player at the university, liked and admired by his friends and those fans in his region who knew him, a nice American kid, a model of clean living. The Boston Celtics, one of the most prestigious teams in all of American sports, had drafted him to play in the National Basketball Association and he had just signed a rich contract. The kid even had a jersey number. Total strangers with no interest in basketball were elated for him. The young man from the other side of the tracks had his foot on the first step of the American glory trail.

Headlines in June suggested that crack might have killed Len Bias. Before the end of the month, another young black sports star, professional football player Don Rogers, died of a cocaine—many people heard that as "crack"—overdose. Coming on top of all of the previous hysteria, the tragic deaths of these two young Americans pushed the governmental and social leadership of the most powerful nation on earth into frenzied action in all directions at once.

Bills were tossed into legislative hoppers all over the country as if they were sandbags heaved onto dikes hastily erected to control a rampaging flood. Measures were proposed on both ends of Pennsylvania Avenue in Washington to demand mass random urine tests of government officials, to deploy the military to control drug trafficking, to impose the death penalty for certain homicides connected with drug sales, to water down the exclusionary rule so that evidence seized without a warrant and in violation of the Fourth Amendment could be introduced in drug prosecutions so long as the officer had good faith, and dozens of other, more repressive recommendations. It was a scary time to sit here in the middle of the national capital and sense my own government coming apart, losing its guts, blowing its cool, prostituting itself.

On July 10, Dr. Donald Ian MacDonald, the top operational federal drug-abuse official—the administrator of the Alcohol, Drug Abuse, and Mental Health Administration, or ADAMHA—held a major press conference on cocaine, which was reported in all the major media. The impression given by the television network anchormen and by leading reporters on national newspapers was that Dr. MacDonald had produced shocking new data proving that there had been an explosion in cocaine and crack deaths during recent months. In a typical front-page story in July, *USA TODAY* reported (in error, as it later turned out) that there had been 563 cocaine-related deaths during the first six months of 1986.

On July 15, it was dramatically revealed that armed American helicopter crews had arrived with their planes in Bolivia to transport local police on raids against cocaine laboratories in the jungles. Later, President Reagan said that the deaths of young Bias and Rogers had been important factors influencing his decision to send off other young Americans in uniform to get the drugs at the source. It was also revealed that our troops had already been secretly involved in such missions, in, for example, Colombia—and that more drug raids would be launched in other countries if the Bolivian attacks were successful. These overseas military drug missions were disturbing firsts in the long American anti-drug crusade. They pushed us all across a chemical Rubicon from which it will not be easy to return.

What do we know about the drug that has caused all this furor? Not much, even today; I can come up with only rudimentary information. What follows, therefore, are cautious observations.

Almost every major drug has been, at various times in our history, treated as a threat to the survival of the nation by some segments of society. Moreover, there seems nothing especially new about the type of chemical process that produced crack. Entrepreneurs have for eons sought to produce more potent forms of mind-altering drugs that could be transported more cheaply, be sold at a higher cost per unit, be appealing to different tastes, and produce more immediate effects. Fermented grapes and grains are effective for many millions of people. Distilling, however, produces spirits, sometimes called brandywine, that are more potent. Wine and beer create trouble for many people, but the greatest difficulty seems to come from the more concentrated distilled spirits of alcohol. The less natural the drug the more trouble for humans.

The same for opium. Smoking the dried powder that comes from the opium-poppy sap is both calming and potentially addicting—not nearly so alluring or dangerous, however, as using morphine, the main active ingredient in opium. Neither is as thrilling or as dangerous as diacetylmorphine, which could, for convenience, be called the essence of morphine plus a bit of vinegar-like acid; this concentrated and refined drug is also known as heroin.

Chewing the leaves of the South American coca plant produces, along with numbness of the mouth and tongue, a mild sensation of stimulation and good feeling. When chemists managed to isolate what might be called the essence of coca, the most powerful ingredient in the leaf, they produced a very potent white powder: cocaine hydrochloride. Largely ignored for years, cocaine, as it is usually called, suddenly became very popular to millions of Americans who now like to snort it through their noses.

For many thrill-seekers (and that is what is involved here), both the stimulation and the risks of the cocaine powder were enough. Then some bored souls decided to refine the powder further for smoking, which is *the* most rapid way to get drugs to the brain, being even quicker than injection. Thus, freebasing was born.

Traditional freebasing involves heating the powder with volatile chemicals, such as ether, which sometimes results in explosions and fires. This, apparently, is what injured comedian Richard Pryor several years ago. The preparation of crack is easier and safer. Cocaine powder is mixed with water and baking soda or ammonia. The result is a highly concentrated chemical that looks like bits of coagulated soap powder, often slightly off-white, about the size of large green peas. It is frequently smoked in a pipe and makes a crackling sound when lit. In some cities, it is known as rock or cooked cocaine.

A gram of cocaine, less than a teaspoonful, costs at least $100 in many communities. Crack pellets are sometimes sold for as little as $10 each in the same neighborhoods.

That this form of the drug is more addicting than powdered cocaine should come as no surprise. Any drug that is more refined and then smoked will be more potent than its less concentrated relatives.

However, it is premature and perhaps misleading to call it the most addictive drug now known. While I believe that anybody who tries this relatively unknown compound is a fool, my guess is that it is no more addicting than smoked tobacco or smoked heroin. I also believe, in passing, that anyone who uses either of those latter substances in any form is a fool. As with those dangerous drugs, however, some foolish people use crack and do not get hooked.

It is also misleading to view this as a plot to hook our children with a cheap drug, as many alleged experts and commentators have been doing. Those people susceptible to the allure of crack will often spend roughly as much as those who use cocaine powder. While the high of crack is immediate, it is also of short duration, perhaps a few minutes, necessitating repeated purchases for those at risk. Many adults with money and curiosity are users.

We do not know how many addicted customers there are out there. One is too many in my book, but if there is truly a national epidemic, I have yet to see the hard proof.

That hard proof would exist, in my eyes, in the records of federal agencies such as the Drug Enforcement Administration (the DEA) of the Department of Justice or the National Institute of Drug Abuse (NIDA) of the Department of Health and Human Services. When I heard and read the major news stories during July on the crack epidemic and related deaths, I was confused because they were inconsistent with my reading of the available federal data. My calls to officials in NIDA and DEA brought honest humility and responses like: We really don't know very much about crack but what we read in the newspapers. There is not even a separate listing for crack, they told me, in NIDA's authoritative Drug Abuse Warning Network (DAWN), which collects data on drug-abuse deaths and injuries. Crack injuries and deaths are listed under cocaine.

When I finally obtained a copy of the materials passed out at that sensational July 10 news conference, I discovered that Dr. MacDonald had made a disclaimer from the start to the effect that the federal experts had no new data on cocaine and crack. The disclaimer was not reported by the media. Why, then, call this a major news conference? Dr. MacDonald explained that he wanted "to underscore the great potential risk we know is involved in cocaine use." In the demagogic atmosphere of Washington at that time, this could have been interpreted as follows: we, the leading national medical scientists, have nothing new to tell you about the dangers of cocaine, but everyone else is getting press attention from crack, and we deserve some, too.

All during the public hysteria of the summer of 1986, the only complete annual DAWN data available was that for 1984, which showed 604 mentions of cocaine in reports by medical examiners. (A "mention" signifies that a medical examiner or coroner found indications of the drug in the body of a person who died suddenly from drug abuse, normally from an overdose. Coroners reporting to DAWN may provide mentions of up to three drugs for each sudden drug abuse death.) That was a significant rise above the 195 mentions of 1981, an increase that was heralded from one end of the country to the other. Even if each of those 604 mentions involved a death caused by cocaine, which is not the case, and as tragic as each death was, it is difficult to see the destruction of a nation of 240 million in 604 cocaine deaths when so many more of our people are being killed by other drugs, especially the legal ones.

Totally ignored in the cries to save our children from crack were the NIDA data which showed that the total number of children who died from cocaine in 1984 was eight. Yes, eight, from all forms of cocaine, including crack—and these at the time of the greatest hysteria were the latest complete data from the federal government, which also showed 14 mentions of cocaine for ages 18 and 19, and 273 for young people in their twenties, or a total of 295 mentions for all Americans under age 30. No data are available as of this writing, the fall of 1986, for this year. Thus all of the claims about the great rise in crack deaths *for the first months of 1986*, such as that reported by *USA TODAY* and other major media voices, were false. Even more significant, none of the leading government drug-abuse officials, who knew the claims for 1986 to be false, felt any responsibility to tell the public the truth during the scared summer of '86.

During that summer, preliminary information *was* available for 1985 on all cocaine deaths. The significance of this information was either ignored or reported in a misleading fashion by the government and the media. While the end of America from drugs was being declared, the number of known cocaine deaths in those preliminary figures had actually declined from 1984 to 1985. Because there had been a slight rise in recorded cocaine, including crack, *use* in those years, a fair headline might have been "Cocaine and crack use rise while deaths decline!" I would have settled for no headlines at all on the matter.

Now, in the fall of 1986, we have a full annual DAWN report for 1985. Final figures do show a continued rise in cocaine death mentions during 1985—to 643. That final toll represents a rise of only 6.5 percent over 1984. The total number of known mentions of cocaine in drug-abuse deaths of children (aged 10–17) remained tiny; during 1985, it dropped to seven for the entire country. Total mentions of cocaine in drug-abuse deaths for all young people up through the age of 29 was 285, a drop of 10 mentions since 1984. No press conference has been held to herald that drop.

In the great majority of all of the cocaine mentions, death apparently was caused by use with other drugs. The most common fatal chemical companion to cocaine was alcohol, which was cited in 224 episodes. More than likely, this is how the death of Len Bias will be listed by DAWN when 1986 reports are issued—because it turns out that the poor young fellow may not have died from crack at all, but perhaps from a combination of massive amounts of powdered cocaine and alcohol during an all-night celebration with his friends.

How many reported cocaine deaths have been laid at the door of crack, alone or in combination with other drugs? I have searched. My assistants have searched. We have gone through many government reports. We have quizzed government statistical experts. We have yet to discover one death in which the presence of crack was a confirmed factor. In time, I am sure that we will because it is such a potent and addicting drug, but up to now, we have not.

Thus, behind all of the public hysteria about the cocaine and crack epidemic destroying our nation, especially our young, during the summer of 1986, there was no evidence of an epidemic either in terms of rising use or rising deaths. Nor was there objective evidence of an epidemic of other illicit drug use in any of the surveys being issued by the very government leading the hysterical forward charge in the new great drug war. The significant NIDA survey of drug abuse among a randomly selected group of 8,038 household residents in 1985 showed, for example, that current marijuana use (at least once during the previous month) among youth aged 12–17 dropped from 16.7 percent in 1979 to 12.2 percent in 1985, while among young adults aged 18–25, it dropped even more sharply, from 35.4 percent to 21.6 percent. For cocaine, including freebase and crack, the figures for current use for youth aged 12–17 rose from 1.4 percent in 1979 to 1.7 percent in 1985. Young adults aged 18–25, those allegedly with too much money and few moral restraints, actually reduced current cocaine use from 9.3 percent in 1979 to 7.7 percent in 1985.

Such reports document serious problems of drug use, and perhaps abuse, which are, on the whole, either stable or declining. They do not document an escalating epidemic.

When reporters from major publications and networks called me for interviews, I kept pleading with them to look at such reports and not to put out more misleading stories that would feed into the hype and cause more hysteria in the country. (Some reporters, like Randi Henderson, needed no pleading, of course.) When they interviewed me, I would say, often on camera, "You people are taking an obscure drug, crack, and selling it to the kids of the country." My interviewers would wince when I said that. Some took it to heart.

Most did not. Drug stories were surefire moneymakers. For example, CBS put on a news program on September 2, "48 Hours on Crack Street," which hooked 15 million viewers, and, according to the Nielsen surveys, achieved the highest rating of any news documentary on any network in over five and one-half years. Network corporate officers and politicians knew the power of those ratings.

Despite the dominance of hysteria and negative drug-policy developments, the year 1986 was also witness to a few encouraging events. For the first time in the 14 years I have been involved in drug-policy studies, I observed the beginnings of a small but sturdy wave of open doubting about the simple common sense of the drug war. I sensed this critical movement in the worried questions of a few journalists like Randi Henderson and also in the constant requests from print and electronic media reporters to hear my point of view, even from those who went on to ignore it. I sensed it also in the number of newspapers that printed my columns, which I started to write several times a month in the summer of 1986, so outraged was I by the deceptions being foisted on the American public, and in the number of editorial writers who started to express similar thoughts. When, during August, the President, the Vice President, and approximately 70 White House staffers showed their devotion to the drug war by taking "voluntary" urine tests, the power of critical humor was brought to bear. The press corps began having great fun with reports on "jar wars." One veteran Washington journalist told me that he fully expected them to demand photo opportunities. Art Buchwald saw that the drug warriors were so extreme that they were funny and soon he was tearing them down with humor in his columns. Garry Trudeau's *Doonesbury* was even more caustic in its comic strip humor.

Pieces of what I would term honest reporting about the drug problem came recently from other seemingly surprising sources. DEA is the top drug-law enforcement agency in the United States, indeed, in the world. It is not known for its liberal views. At the end of the scared summer, DEA issued a special report, "The Crack Situation in the United States." This was a balanced and honest report, the type I would have expected from the physicians and academic drug-abuse experts at NIDA or other federal agencies, or even from major news organizations. Instead, the most objective report issued by the government on the subject of all the hysteria during 1986 came from the federal drug police. I must confess I was not terribly surprised that it had been written within the DEA because I have encountered a good deal of honesty and openness in my contacts with federal police agents and intelligence analysts. I *was* surprised that the report, once written, had been released by the Reagan administration.

Prepared by the Strategic Intelligence Section of DEA, the report concluded that the excessive media attention had created a "distortion of . . . the extent of crack use as compared to the use of other drugs." With massive amounts of powdered cocaine available, snorting was "the primary route of cocaine administration." Thus, crack was "a secondary rather than a primary problem in most areas." Indeed, in many areas, such as New Orleans, Chicago, and Philadelphia, it was barely a problem at all. In others, such as New York City, Detroit, and Boston, crack was usually produced locally and sold by small-time dealers in poor, minority group neighborhoods, with seizures almost always of tiny quantities.

At the time of the release of the report, Robert Feldkamp, director of public information at the DEA, observed, "There are 20,000 to 30,000 crack dealers in the greater New York area, all dealing in gram to ounce quantities, not the kind of dealers that DEA would normally target."

This honest reporting from inside the government was largely ignored by the government official most responsible for drug enforcement, Attorney General Edwin Meese III. Shortly after the DEA report was released, he urged the formation of 24 federal-state-local police crack task forces in major cities across the nation to deal with "a crisis of epidemic proportions in some areas." This idea of diverting the time and efforts of federal agents to pursue small-time street dealers and the talk of a crack crisis must have mystified the career, nonpolitical analysts in DEA who had just prepared the intelligence report.

CONFESSIONS OF A JOURNALISTIC JUNKIE

Further honest reporting on a related aspect of the drug problem came a few weeks later from, of all things, a Washington reporter. In its own way, the story by Adam Paul Weisman was even more surprising than the DEA report. Journalists rarely admit that they have abused the public trust and have irresponsibly hyped stories simply to enjoy the power of notoriety, the rush of fame, or as Mr. Weisman wrote, to feel "a journalistic orgasm in my brain." After the summer was over, Weisman confessed that as "a reporter at a national news organization" (which, I later found, was *U.S. News & World Report*) "I Was A Drug-Hype Junkie." This was the title of his article in *The New Republic* of October 6. The subtitle was "48 Hours on Crock Street."

The repentant journalist admitted that during the summer of 1986, he and his colleagues were guilty of "cooking figures and using alarmist headlines and prose . . . to convince readers that practically everyone they know is addicted to crack, and that they too are likely to be addicted soon." For national reporters in 1986, "the drug crisis in America is more than a story, it's an addiction—and a dangerous one. . . . We know the rush that comes from supporting these claims with a variety of questionable figures, graphs, and charts, and often we enjoy it. Blatant sensationalism is a high."

Weisman then went on to explain how his subsequent reflective review of the NIDA data along with a growing sense of guilt made him take the cure and come clean. His review of the facts brought him to the same conclusions that I reached: there is no epidemic

of illicit drug abuse destroying the country. He also found evidence
that the greatest drug threat in America today is alcohol. No surprise, no journalistic orgasm, no headlines.

Adam Paul Weisman, the recovering journalistic addict, finished his confession with some advice—"I'm clean now but I've
seen the depths of drug journalism depravity. A little education
has helped me kick the habit that once threatened to ruin my
career. Now I hope that I can help others avoid making the same
mistake I did. So if someone offers you drugs or the opportunity
to write a cover story about them, take a tip from Nancy Reagan:
just say no."

AN HONEST OFFICIAL'S DESPAIR

Another piece of critical reporting reached my desk as the awful
summer was almost over. This one came directly to me from a
federal official with many years of experience in the related fields
of criminal justice and drug abuse. It is nothing new for me to
receive dissenting reports from federal and state drug-abuse officials. Indeed, over the years in my role as a member of the loyal
opposition to the drug war, I have been given a good deal of encouragement by drug-abuse officials at all levels of government.

One night in November 1983, for example, I was relaxing at a
party in a Capitol Hill townhouse, just across the street from the
Supreme Court. Earlier in the day, I had given a speech critical
of government drug policy at a Washington conference. At the
party, I was startled by a stranger who approached and opened
the conversation by saying, "You *are* right, you know." When I
inquired about what, he went on, "The government *does* lie about
the scientific basis for its tough drug-control policies. It emphasizes
only negative scientific findings about illicit drugs and ignores benign evidence." At that point I suddenly remembered that the man
had been sitting in the audience when I had made such statements
in my speech.

The fellow then motioned me into a corner and told me quietly
that he was a federal drug police official and identified his agency.
He was disgusted, he continued, because his superiors ignored him
when he tried to do his job honestly: to weigh conflicting pieces of

information and to suggest the possible results of alternative paths of action. In almost every case, when his analysis suggested that new information about a drug and its potential use by human beings might call for a relatively gentle governmental response, leading officials would call instead for more rigid legal controls and for tougher police action. He pleaded with me to keep telling all sides of the truth, with all of its subtleties.

The communication from the official during the summer of 1986 was unique in my experience since it was in writing. It is a sad commentary on the repressive chill imposed by the orthodox national drug ideology that dissenting officials almost never put their doubts in writing. To protect himself somewhat, the official continued to remain anonymous and listed himself as "X." X sent his brief report—"The New Front in the War on Drugs: You"—to about 20 people whom he trusted. I had known X for years and observed that, while he believed most current drug laws made little sense, he attempted to work loyally within the current system, bringing a sense of reason and restraint to the field. Never had I known him to despair about eventually fashioning sensible compromises on national drug policy. He believed, as do I, that there must be laws that control drugs. The challenge is to design new, more humane, and more effective drug laws, not simply to throw out all of the existing ones without replacements. Now, this reasonable and responsible official *was* in a state of despair.

His despair arose from the fact that amidst all of the propaganda in the bills thrown in the congressional hopper during the summer, X saw in them for the first time in his experience the real probability of dramatic legal changes in the drug-war strategy of the national government. X explained, "For decades the prevailing view has been that our enforcement effort should target the highest level drug trafficker. The change is that now the government is going to go after the users—particularly you pot smokers." The reasons for this change:

The traditional enforcement approaches (suppressing the supply) on which the federal government is spending at least $2 billion per year obviously have not succeeded. The alternative to suppressing the supply is suppressing the demand. The traditional demand reduction approaches [treatment and education] have also failed and it is doubtful that they will ever succeed. The current demand for a solution to the drug problem, if it is sustained, is going to force the opening of a "new front" in the war on drugs to "come down hard" on the users, what an Assistant Attorney

General calls a "scorched earth" policy. That new front is you, whether you use drugs or not, because in the inspection of everyone's brain, no brain is above suspicion. This new front in the war on drugs will be intolerable to any person who values his or her freedom.

X was aware of the good intentions of the First Lady and of the sympathy she evoked, as when she appeared on nationwide television Sunday evening, September 14, with President Reagan, appealing for a reduction in drug use. At the same time, he saw chilling invasions of traditional values being proposed by the Reagan White House, by Attorney General Edwin Meese III, by Assistant Attorney General Stephen S. Trott (he of the scorched-earth policy), and by leading Reagan supporters in Congress. The startling new position that X saw and heard directly from this group of powerful national leaders, never before expressed so harshly in American history, certainly not during alcohol prohibition, was, "Demand will be reduced when a substantial onus is placed on the user—a real threat of criminal prosecution or the loss of one's job. They are giving voice to the view that it is the user who is the ultimate villain." While there is some simplistic support for this notion, the practical implications, X concluded, were simply unacceptable in a democratic society.

Because marijuana is the most popular illicit drug and because it stays in the system longer than most drugs, X observed, millions of occasional marijuana smokers, many of whom hold responsible jobs that they perform well, will be caught in the vast new urinalysis dragnet. They will then be given a choice—"treatment for drug abuse you don't need or losing your job." X predicted, moreover, that "It won't be long before the Rehnquist court is asked whether a positive urine test is probable cause to sustain a search for possession of illegal drugs." In the likely event that such searches are upheld by that conservative court, occasional pot smokers will then find themselves, in addition to being unemployed and unemployable, subject to the mandatory criminal sentences for possession of drugs now being proposed by the Reagan administration. If the war on drugs continues its present course, then, "it is likely that millions of successful, responsible, capable, patriotic American adults are about to become like the villages of 1960s Vietnam—destroyed in order to be saved."

BOOM MARKET: LOCKING UP CHILDREN

Another critical report during the summer of 1986 brought out new facts about a particularly ugly aspect of the drug war: the institutionalization of American children on false claims of drug and alcohol abuse. I was already aware of the excesses of one prominent group of anti-drug zealots in the treatment organization known as Straight, Inc. I had seen how Straight often locked up children who used pot and beer occasionally—or who were afflicted only with the normal though disturbing condition known as adolescence and who did not use any drugs. Straight, however, does not operate traditional psychiatric hospitals or professional drug-treatment facilities.

On May 20, 1985, the CBS network had revealed that a major drug-abuse treatment conglomerate, CompCare, had agreed to institutionalize some children who had no drug-abuse problems—simply to pick up a few new customers. Its facilities were directed and staffed by professionals, by physicians, psychologists, nurses, and social workers. The medical director of CompCare was Dr. Joseph Pursch, one of the most respected drug-abuse experts in the country.

On August 21, 1986, the ABC network show "20/20," hosted by Hugh Downs and Barbara Walters, demonstrated in greater detail than ever before how CompCare had institutionalized large numbers of children, simply in order to make money, by claiming that they were drug abusers. Such charges suggest that some of the leading drug-abuse experts in the country either do not understand the condition they are supposedly treating or do not care to know because in the present hysterical climate, these medical doctors are prepared to lock up virtually anyone brought to their doors if the relatives or the insurance companies have the price. They are enjoying the monetary benefits of a boom market because of the current fears about drug abuse and do not give a damn that they are taking away the liberty of multitudes of free Americans.

The ABC investigative reporters focused on hospitals operated by CompCare known as CareUnits. Television ads promote the services of CareUnits in many parts of the country by appealing to the natural concerns and fears of parents in today's emotional chemical climate. The main target of the investigation was the CareUnit in Jacksonville Beach, Florida, to which two local mothers had brought their teenaged daughters. Correspondent John Stossel explained, "The mothers say CareUnit willingly accepted them both. CareUnit said, 'Yes, we can help, we care.' " The transcript of that "20/20" investigative report continued:

CAREUNIT COUNSELOR: They care about the insurance, they care about the money. That's what they care about.

STOSSEL (*voice-over*): This woman's identity is concealed because she still works here as a counselor. She is one of several CareUnit employees who told us that CareUnit will take just about anyone, that kids as young as 10 are locked up and treated for being drug addicts and alcoholics, even if they're not.

CAREUNIT COUNSELOR: The vast majority of our kids are teenagers just experimenting with drugs, having a little bit of pot now and then, a drink now and then, a beer now and then, but they're not drunkies, they're not drug addicts, they're not anywhere near that, and they shouldn't be there.

CAROL JAMES, former counselor: I think in all the kids I saw, I saw one that I would term an addict . . .

STOSSEL: . . . Why are the parents then locking them up in a drug center?

MS. JAMES: Because I think that most of them are scared. We hear so much about this alcohol abuse, drug abuse. They're not seeing the kids' real problems.

STOSSEL (*voice-over*): Dr. Rob Pandina is a nationally known expert on drug and alcohol problems of adolescents. He says hospitals like CareUnit regularly misdiagnose the kids.

DR. ROB PANDINA, substance-abuse expert: They are prepared to treat the child for what it says over the door. If it says over the door, "This is an alcoholism and drug clinic," they are prepared to treat the child for that problem . . . whether that's the problem or not. . . .

CAREUNIT COUNSELOR: CareUnit is about getting anybody in there that has good insurance, whether they have a drug problem or not, keeping them in there as long as their insurance is good for and then discharging them when their insurance is done.

STOSSEL: Could they get out before their insurance expired?

MS. JAMES: I didn't know of any cases that did. I didn't know one that did. . . .

STOSSEL (*voice-over*): Now, I should point out that even critics say that some kids are helped at CareUnit. But they also say that money is what comes first.

(*On-camera*) Employees tell us they hold meetings here every morning that they call pep rallies. The boss's cheer is "Get the census up. We've got to fill more beds."

(*Voice-over*) Vacant beds are a problem facing lots of hospitals today. Cost-control measures have meant fewer medical and surgical patients, so many hospitals were losing money until companies like CompCare came along and said, "We can fill those beds." And they are filling them. Psychiatric and drug hospitals are a booming business. Five big for-profit chains control the field. CompCare alone has 160 CareUnits across the country, a quarter of them strictly for kids.

CompCare corporate executives refused to be interviewed by ABC so as to refute these serious indictments. In making that refusal, Mr. Stossel explained, "They told us we should be doing a story on drug trafficking. They said that's a more important issue than how they treat kids." Yet, as Stossel observed on the television program, "The experts warn, don't fix what's not broken. For example, simple drug use does not mean that your child needs hospitalization. Most kids experiment with drugs or alcohol. Only a minority become abusers. And while that is serious, treatment abuse is serious too. Only a few people want to talk about that. Certainly not hospitals like CompCare. They're riding high, enjoying national prestige."

Then, on the screens in millions of American homes during that hot August in the scared summer of 1986 appeared the image of the First Lady at a ceremony, with a man at the podium. The CompCare corporate executive declared: "It's an honor and a pleasure today to dedicate this Nancy Reagan CareUnit."

PART ONE

The common denominator is rotten behavior. Despite a wide range of geographic, social, and economic backgrounds, our young people today behave with stereotypical predictability. Like clones stamped out in some satanic laboratory, they share an underlying selfishness and similar ways of demonstrating it.

—PHYLLIS AND DAVID YORK AND TED WACHTEL, *Toughlove*

A Rotten, Satanic, Dying Generation of Youth?

2

War Orphan

ON TOP of the world. That's where Fred Charles Collins III was as he and his father, Frederick Charles Collins, Jr., and his mother, Teruyo Collins, drove up to a large unimposing one-story structure in the suburbs of St. Petersburg, Florida. It was approximately 10:00 A.M. on June 19, 1982. At the relatively young age of 19, Fred felt quite successful. While there had been a good deal of turbulence in his life during the previous few years, now almost everything seemed to be on track.

Soon, though, Fred's world was torn apart by his parents and by the well-meaning people in that building, organized as Straight, Inc., who were operating with the support of some of the most powerful people in American government, medicine, and drug-abuse treatment. This courageous young man eventually fought back and won a stunning victory over these powerful forces. In the process he revealed how destructive are many of the principles motivating our war on drugs and the new wave of cults dedicated to controlling the allegedly chemically crazed current generation of youth. Yet, the facts about Fred's unlawful imprisonment, escape, and eventual vindication have been largely forgotten. The tactics of Straight, Inc., have been promulgated to the world as the wave of the future in youth drug-control treatment. Lest, then, we visit this nightmare on millions of other young people and their families, the story of what happened to one American teenager is worth recalling.

I was fortunate that in this case the details of his story were made available to me in massive volume, much of it in sworn pretrial depositions and trial testimony from the law suit that eventually occurred. Moreover, Fred Collins, who believed he had a duty to expose the harshness of his treatment so as to save other youths, spent days as a guest in my house relating his story. Several of the people who had served as jurors in the subsequent lawsuit also agreed to talk to me or my assistants. We taped many of those discussions, which were then transcribed. Most of the direct quotations in this account come from those tape transcriptions or from the sworn depositions and trial testimony.

I spent months reviewing all of the written records and the transcripts of the many interviews that my assistants and I taped. I recognize that the story seems unbelievable in places and that Fred at times appears incredibly naïve. And I also recognize that there is another side to the matter: that of the passionate, sincere supporters of Straight, of which there are many. I came to believe that Fred was telling the truth. So did an impartial federal jury, as documented in two separate votes and also in later recorded personal interviews. What follows, then, is a summary of the true story of Fred Collins's incredible ordeal.

A HAPPY CHILDHOOD

Fred had been born on October 22, 1962, near the beginning of the so-called Dope Decade, in Washington, D.C. His mother was a native Japanese. His parents had met in Japan at a time when his father, a brilliant, well-educated man, was working there for the American government. Mrs. Collins eventually became a naturalized American citizen. Four years later, a second son, George, was born. Fred Senior (as I will occasionally call him, even though his formal name does have a "junior" attached to it) had good relationships with his sons in their early years.

"I had everything I wanted as a child. I was happy. . . . I lived in a beautiful neighborhood . . . a *big* house! The neighborhood is

... in Alexandria, Virginia, right next to the Mount Vernon Estate. In fact, my backyard was once . . . part of one of George Washington's farms," Fred recalled during one of our discussions.

In the seventh grade at Walt Whitman Junior High School, Alexandria, Virginia, Fred was placed in the Gifted and Talented Child program, played first-chair clarinet in the school orchestra, and after school one day in the summer following completion of that grade, he partook of his first drug—half a joint of marijuana—with his schoolmate, Robert,* in the woods that once were George Washington's plantation.

If the stories about the Father of Our Country growing hemp on his land are true, then there was an elegant historical congruence in the carefree actions of these two happy young boys on that hot afternoon. Of course, they were not thinking of the history of marijuana-growing at that moment. "All I remember about that joint is that I laughed for three hours afterward," Fred recalls. "I tried pot a few more times during that summer and during the next one. Robert told me that if I used pot the girls would think I was less of a nerd."

In the ninth grade in Mount Vernon High School, Fred encountered Mark, who was to become a close friend. "I met Mark through the video club when I was filming a play he was acting in. Then I became involved with the members of the Drama Club because they had good parties, went drinking after the plays. However, when I tried alcohol, I found I had no tolerance for it, would turn red in the face, and fall asleep after two beers. My new friends used to joke about it. They said I was a real lightweight or a wimp because I couldn't handle my beer.

"I found that I had a much greater tolerance for pot than I did for alcohol. . . . Pot agreed with me and beer did not. . . . [Yet] we sometimes would go for a month without smoking any. During those years, I probably smoked pot about twice a month during the school year and perhaps once or twice a week over the summer. None of us seemed to have any trouble with drugs."

Fred's eleventh grade was a rough year. By now, he was going through a hippie phase and grew his hair long, down to his shoulders. He began to fight with his father, now retired from the government with a pension and also working successfully as a real

* I will use only first names—sometimes fictional, sometimes real—when anonymity has been requested or when it seems otherwise appropriate. Whenever a full name appears, however, it is real.

estate agent, whom he viewed as a representative of the Establishment. By the twelfth grade, however, he started to change, began working on the grounds crew of the Mount Vernon Estate, saved money, and even bought an old car. Then, he cut his hair short, improved his grades, and began preparing himself for college. He achieved a 3.0 in his senior year, which brought his overall high school average up to a middling 2.5., high C, low B. However, he scored a very respectable 1135 on his Scholastic Aptitude Test. He applied only to one school, the Virginia Polytechnical Institute and State University, known as Virginia Tech, a good engineering school in rural Blacksburg, and was happy as a lark to be admitted.

TOUGHLOVE

As Fred was getting his life together, his younger brother, George, seemed to be doing the opposite. George started taking on a tough-guy image, in part by using drugs. He was extremely successful with girls, started ignoring school, and spoke often of dropping out. "I don't know if he really had a drug problem or not, while I know he did use a great deal," Fred recalls.

It was during this period that his parents encountered the new national movement known as Toughlove (usually spelled in all capital letters by purists), which emphasized the need for parents to group together in order to control their children, sometimes using very harsh measures. Mr. and Mrs. Collins began attending Toughlove meetings at the local high school. That Toughlove philosophy was a vital part of the operating policy of a new drug treatment organization, Straight, Inc., which appeared in the community during the late Seventies and soon gained two new enthusiastic supporters. This came about in part because the Collinses met parents at a Toughlove meeting who had a child in the Straight program.

Shortly afterwards, Mr. and Mrs. Collins began attending Sunday meetings of Straight parents at a church in nearby Annandale. Both organizations supported yet a third, the National Federation of Parents for Drug-Free Youth, which had the enthusiastic backing of the White House and, in particular, First Lady Nancy Reagan.

All of these new groups emphasized the need to reassert parental power that had been allegedly destroyed by the permissiveness of the Sixties. The new youth-control cults, then, tended to view virtually any form of private pleasure-seeking by young people as essentially suspect. In particular, sex and drugs were viewed as clear signs of degeneracy. Parents who were committed to these new groups paired the two activities and demanded both drug-free and sex-free children.

Fred Senior was deeply impressed by Dr. Miller Newton's book, *Gone Way Down*, which explained the Straight clinical philosophy. "That really opened my eyes," Mr. Collins said, "and I read that two or three times." The Straight official's book declares that any drug use by adolescents is evidence of a disease that impels insane behavior, and that parents must intervene forcefully or risk the possible death of their children from drugs. Not only did Mr. Collins read the book, he took direct action, as have so many other parents in recent years, on the basis of this and other extremist tracts. He made up his mind to put George into the Straight program and also, in line with Straight doctrine, decided to make the whole family drug-free.

Wine and beer had been frequently served in the Collins household up to this time. The elder Collins regularly had a martini before dinner. He did not originally consider alcohol a drug and his major worry was the use of marijuana by his sons, especially the younger boy, George. Mr. Collins apparently stopped drinking martinis in the house and told Fred that he, too, must stop using marijuana, as well as alcohol, both for himself and also to assist in the rehabilitation of George, who kept going downhill.

In January 1982, George was tricked into entering the Straight program in St. Petersburg, Florida. His parents had told him they were going to visit Disney World during the Christmas vacation period. Mr. and Mrs. Collins got George into the interview room by telling him they were visiting a real estate office.

Such outright lies by parents to their children are an accepted part of the doctrine of the new youth-control cults. They lie to us about their drug use, the dogma declares, so it is perfectly ethical for us to lie to them in order to save them from drugs and death. The drug-free parent leaders seem oblivious to the destructive impact of such practices on the feeling of trust that cements normal families together.

Fred's first real glimpse inside the program came a few months later in April 1982. He happened to see the last part of a brief documentary on Straight, which appeared on NBC-TV's "News

Magazine." The program featured an emotional and approving visit by First Lady Nancy Reagan to the very facility where George was being confined in St. Petersburg. Fred was appalled. "It scared me. I wondered what they were doing to George. I was hoping to see him and wondered what he would look like by then, but I didn't see him. That worried me more. It all reminded me of a Moonie cult."

Nevertheless, Fred's happy and successful academic work in the difficult first year of an engineering curriculum continued. He joined a respected fraternity, Theta Delta Chi, whose members became very much like a close family to him. They elected him house chairman. Fred had a good social life and achieved the top grade in chemistry of all 750 freshmen at the entire university during one semester, he claims. Also, Fred got an A– in calculus, an achievement of which he was quite proud. Fred's overall average for the entire freshman year was 3.2 on a four-point scale, a B.

While he had drunk beer and smoked pot during this year, these were occasional events. During the entire twelve months prior to June 19, 1982, the day of his illegal imprisonment by Straight, Fred claims that he had a maximum of 15 joints of marijuana. He did not use any marijuana at all during the last three months of the spring semester, just prior to the trip which brought him to that building in St. Petersburg. His last beer had been several weeks before the trip. Fred believed that he was following his father's wishes in his consumption of beer and marijuana, in that he was an occasional, responsible user, which he had always been, and that he did not use them at all in the family home. My review of the entire record leads me to believe Fred in these important claims as in so many others. I encountered no evidence that suggested he used more beer or pot than he claimed. Like so many of America's youth, he used marijuana and beer but he did so quite responsibly.

CAUGHT IN THE STRAIGHT TRAP

After final examinations, the plan was for the Collins family in Virginia to take a pleasant automobile trip to Florida, see George, and take in the beaches. The trip down was simply great, Fred recalls. He glowed under the praise of his father about his academic achievements. Such paternal approval was a new experience for the young man. Upon arrival, the happy family checked into a motel in the St. Petersburg area. That evening while his parents went to a meeting at the Straight facility, Fred took a pleasant swim in the motel pool, which caused a bit of redness in his eyes, a condition slightly aggravated by his contact lenses and which would greatly affect his life the next day.

Fred knew that early on that next day he had to undergo something called a sibling interview in order to see his brother, George, for the first time in months. Even though he had been bothered by his first view of Straight on that NBC documentary, he was not at all concerned about the interview.

Had Fred investigated Straight further, he might well have been deeply impressed by the fervent endorsements it has received from highly placed professionals and officials. These included Mrs. Reagan and the chief White House drug policy adviser, Dr. Carlton Turner. In addition, Senator Paula Hawkins (R-Fla.), chairwoman of the Senate Subcommittee on Alcoholism and Drug Abuse, was an outspoken supporter.

The most enthusiastic endorsements have come from Dr. Robert L. DuPont, a world-famous drug-abuse expert who has held a number of leading positions, including the presidency of the American Council on Marijuana; he was also founding director of the U.S. National Institute on Drug Abuse. At the First Annual Awareness Banquet of Straight, Inc., on October 17, 1981, according to a Straight brochure, Dr. DuPont had said: "To be blunt, I have spent 15 years working in the drug-abuse field, traveling to more than 20 countries and visiting hundreds of prevention programs. Straight, Inc., is the best drug-abuse treatment program I have seen. Lest there be any doubt that this is an accolade I have bestowed easily or casually, I can tell you that I have not said that about any other program."

Fred was not aware of these endorsements, however, as he strolled confidently in the door of that large, low-lying building in St. Petersburg with his parents, looking forward to seeing his brother. Just before walking in, he said to himself, recalling how his parents had tricked George, this *does* look like a real estate office! Fred was separated from his parents and led away by a blond-haired young fellow to a small reception room.

The young man's name was Jack Jeffrey Waldron. On this day, Jeff was 18 years old, a year younger than Fred, had not yet graduated from high school, and, as was brought out in the course of the later trial, his entire training in the profession of drug-abuse treatment consisted of five and one-half months as an inmate and staff-trainee in this Straight facility. He represented the epitome of the nonprofessional peer counselors so touted by the White House and by many leading national drug-abuse experts. Mr. Waldron bore the main responsibility for determining whether or not Fred Collins III would be locked up in this institution. Fred had not the vaguest idea that he was being so evaluated. He was asked a series of questions about family problems and his drug use, which he answered quite honestly. There seemed no reason not to.

"I told Jeff that I never believed that drugs were a major factor in my life. I told him, and wrote on the form they asked me to fill out, that I had tried pot, hash, alcohol, caffeine pills, and, once, laughing gas, nitrous oxide. When I asked how I should answer the question 'How long have you been doing drugs?' he said say five years, since I had first tried pot back then. I was apprehensive because it was very misleading, it looked like I had done them every day, but I wrote down what he said. Also, when I said 'caffeine pills' he wrote down 'speed' and said it was the same thing. [To most people in the drug-abuse field "speed" refers to amphetamines, sometimes the source of serious abuse. "Caffeine pills" normally evoke thoughts of relatively mild nonprescription compounds such as No-Doz.] Then, Jeff started to ask me a lot of things about my sex life, including if I had premarital sex in college. I said I had. Jeff retorted, 'How does it feel masturbating inside a woman?' At this point, I was starting to get angry and told him, 'My sex life is none of your damn business.'

"About then, three more young men, all rather large, came into the room and sat so that they blocked the door. Suddenly, I was scared shitless. I was sweating like crazy. I asked to see my dad but they said we had more forms to fill out. As I was doing them, they started to 'relate' to me, telling me about their bad drug and sex habits. They started to accuse me of being like them, that is, of having a terrible drug habit and perverse sexual habits. This went on for hours; I had lunch and dinner brought to me on a paper plate inside that small room under guard." Eventually Fred blurted out angrily, "You guys are crazy as shit. I don't have any drug or sex problems and I have a good relation with my family and if you get my father in here he'll straighten it out. I want to see my parents. Let me out. If I have a drug problem, then everyone at college must have a drug problem. I drink far less and I smoke far less than anyone there. I have good grades."

One of the young men replied, "You can't see your parents yet." It became clear to Fred that he was being kept in that room and if he attempted to leave, he would be forcibly detained. The young men have since testified that such physical restraint was standard Straight policy in sibling interviews and that their mission that day was indeed to prevent Fred from leaving that small room. The illegal imprisonment of Fred Collins had begun.

Why did he fill out that form about his drug use, as minimal as it was? Why did he not simply run out of there once he realized that these unarmed kids were holding him? What kind of a wimp was he, anyhow? Such questions have been raised about Fred's story, especially this part of it. I have no easy answers to those questions, except to say that many other young people were similarly taken in by these shocking tactics. Perhaps, indeed, shock was a major part of their power. Fred and other young people were traumatized by the impact of well-meaning authority imposed on them in an unexpected fashion and they acted almost like prisoners-of-war. Moreover, the guards often were strong and had the combined personal strength to beat down defiant inmates, which they did on numerous occasions.

Back at that first interview, Jeff Waldron brought his notes to Christopher Yarnold, 31 years old, who was on the executive staff. In the notes, Jeff had written, "I don't feel good about this guy. I don't believe him." Even though Mr. Yarnold had not yet even seen Fred, both went to Fred's parents in the lobby and told them, "Fred needs the program." His father disagreed with them, declaring that Fred had a good family relationship, and was doing well in school. Mr. Yarnold said he was going to talk to Fred directly. He spent fifteen minutes in the room with Fred and went back and told his parents, "I have found physical evidence of Fred doing drugs within the last 48 hours." Mr. Yarnold was a former priest with no professional education, save for a one-day session on alcoholism and on-the-job training in Straight, in the field of drug abuse. Nevertheless, as soon as Mr. Yarnold told Fred's dad of the physical evidence, and even though he had been with his son during most of the past 48 hours, the senior Collins did not ask what that evidence was. Instead, Fred's father told the stranger, "Take him in."

Before that fateful decision, the parents had been reminded of a fundamental Straight policy: if a sibling is using drugs, he or she must come into the program, or be emotionally and financially disowned; if not, the original child will be thrown out of the program. The doctrine was that when that child left the program he or she "would go down ten times as far." Often, it was stated that the discharged druggie child would surely die. This was the belief of many parents, including the Collinses. At this point, they believed that they had the choice of putting Fred in or taking George out and killing him. They chose the former.

The Collins parents were also influenced by a sincere concern for Fred's welfare. Despite all of the evidence of the fine manner in which their elder son was conducting his life, despite the fact that they had had no trouble with him about drugs or any other significant matter since the previous Christmas, despite the fine family relationship which had developed, these educated people chose to institutionalize their child on the basis of the judgment of two ill-trained strangers—because they now truly believed that Fred, also, must have a drug problem.

After seven to ten hours of being confined in that small room, of continually being told he was a drug addict, of having his denials met by the classic drug-abuse expert diagnosis that this was proof that he was "into denial," of being refused permission to go to the bathroom even once, Fred was near the end of his resistance. At this point, Chris Yarnold came back into the room and said, "Fred, I just talked with your father and he said that he's not going to give you any more money for school unless you sign yourself into the program." It is not at all clear if the senior Collins actually made that statement, but the news of it seemed to have been the final blow. Fred also wanted very much to see his brother after all those months, and he was also influenced by the fact that he was on vacation and hence would not miss school. He signed himself in at approximately 6:00 P.M. on the explicit assurance that at the expiration of 14 days he would be free to leave. He felt he could take almost anything for 14 days.

He was warned not to say anything to his parents, only to hug them and to tell them that he loved them. He was taken to them— literally taken, since from then on he was considered a "druggie," not to be trusted, and an "oldcomer" (an experienced inmate) had to hold him at all times, usually by the belt. Fred followed directions and hugged his parents and told them that he loved them. Mrs. Collins cried and Mr. Collins told his son, "I'm proud you signed yourself in." For reasons which can only be described as perverse and unfathomable, no other contact or discussion was allowed. Parents and son went along with this perversity.

In my mind, the behavior of all concerned here defied reason. Fred was not a drug abuser and his parents should have known it. So should the Straight staff who imprisoned him. The whole episode was in a sense pathological and unbelievable. That's the whole point of this recitation. It *is* unbelievable and pathological but that is what happens when irrational power is applied with great conviction to individual human beings: the will to resist of the victim is broken and he does and believes what he is told.

INSIDE THE STRAIGHT PRISON

Fred was taken into a room and made to take off all of his clothes, whereupon the Straight staff and "phasers" (yet another term for experienced inmates who were proceeding through the seven phases of the program) searched his clothes and his body, including all cavities, his anus, his mouth, and his ears. "I felt extremely degraded," Fred recalled, not surprisingly.

After this, he was taken into a large room about the size of a basketball court, in which were seated hundreds of other residents who were involved in a standard treatment session. Fred was introduced to the group as a newcomer who did not want to be there, but who had agreed to try the program for 14 days to deal with his drug problem. Then, Fred vividly recalls, the entire group turned toward him and said in unison, "We love you, Fred!" He sagged, put his head in his hands, and asked himself in despair, "What have I gotten myself into?"

The young man had gotten himself into a program that had been started in the Seventies by Florida parents worried about the drug-taking habits of their children, over whom they felt they had lost control. In many cases, of course, their fears were well justified. Straight parents made sincere and significant commitments to their new cause, including allowing their homes to be

used as residences where the "druggie" youth lived while undergo-
ing treatment. Most of the treatment program in each community
took place in a central facility, such as that large building in St.
Petersburg, to which the young people were brought every day
from their scattered so-called foster homes, which meant the residences of the Straight parents.

Straight, Inc., which by this time had facilities in several eastern cities, combined elements of a number of established drug-
abuse treatment programs, especially Alcoholics Anonymous and
the more rigorous residential therapeutic communities, such as
Synanon. Both of these program models emphasize the need to
confess one's failures before a group and for the group to confront
its members who are not being honest enough about those failures.
Essential elements of the famous Twelve Steps, which are the
heart of the AA program, involve participants admitting that they
are "powerless over alcohol," have come to believe "that a Power
greater than ourselves could restore us to sanity," have made "a
searching and fearless moral inventory of ourselves," and have
"admitted to God, to ourselves, and to another human being, the
exact nature of our wrongs."

As applied in AA, this philosophy is invoked in nonresidential
settings, normally in meetings that last one hour during a time of
day or evening convenient to the participants. Within therapeutic
communities, residents often spend many hours of rigorous confrontations, seeking to dig out confessions from other residents,
all aimed at getting the truth fully revealed and at creating an
honest atmosphere for change. Once troubled people enter AA or
a normal residential therapeutic community program, however,
they are free to leave at any time. This was not the case with
Straight, as Fred had already discovered. And there were other
vital differences.

Within a few days of arrival, Fred was taken to a pleasant
waterfront residence, a foster home run by Straight parents, and
placed in the care of John, an oldcomer who lived there. The oldcomer proceeded to educate his newcomer in the realities of Straight
and Toughlove. "John looked like the Hollywood example of a Nazi
Aryan type. Built like a lifeguard. He scared me more than anyone
else in Straight. He would tell me things like, you know, if you
try to leave, I'm gonna make your teeth eat the concrete, or something. He would poke his finger into my chest, just grind his teeth
and just yell at me and tell me the things he would like to do to

me if I tried to escape. . . . And this is all being thrown at me the first couple of nights. And of course every night before I would go to bed John . . . would say, 'Love ya, Fred!' . . . That was what they called Toughlove. It was brutality."

Fred discovered another hidden feature of the program in those first few days at the foster home: children were often institutionalized because they did not measure up to parental demands, whether or not they had drug problems. A second newcomer in that home was Tony, who had not used drugs, he claimed, for over a year before being committed. He was not as smart as his siblings and did not do as well in school. The parents diagnosed this as a drug problem. Straight agreed and accepted him without further question. Virtually any failing of a young person, Fred saw, Straight and its disciples traced somehow to drug use.

Total control of the residents in the early stages of treatment was the keynote of the program. Usually, Fred would spend the night in the home of Straight parents, often those who had a child in the program. He would be driven to the home under guard of his oldcomer. He would be walked to the car in the company of several oldcomers, at least one of whom had his hand through Fred's belt loop.

The homes were prisons. Under the direction of Straight staff and phasers, parents placed locks on windows and doors, installed alarm systems, and placed beds in such a way as to bar exits. Oldcomers slept on these beds so as to prevent newcomers from leaving their bedrooms, which were usually shared. Before going to bed, newcomers had to be watched even when they went to the bathroom, whether to use the toilet or to wash. If the oldcomer took a shower, he made his newcomers put their hands over the curtain rod and keep talking to him. Why? So he could know they had not left his presence and thus were not doing anything wrong, such as taking drugs or escaping. If a newcomer felt the need to leave the bedroom and go to the bathroom during the night, he was discouraged. Often Fred was forced to urinate in a jar kept in the bedroom.

The major activity of each evening in the Straight home was writing Moral Inventories, a sometimes wholesome concept borrowed from AA but invoked with quite a different impact. The oldcomers trained the newcomers how to write proper Moral Inventories, or MIs. It was important to confess guilt in the form of drug and alcohol use, or not being respectful to parents, and then for the resident to explain how he was going to improve. It helped if the newcomer made his guilt appear to be great, which meant his remedial measures then became more impressive. At first Fred tried to write truthful MIs and every day his oldcomer at the time, John, would confront him with, "This is bullshit, Fred!" Soon Fred learned to write a proper MI, especially since his meager food rations were often cut in half if he did not.

Fred usually got to sleep late at night, and had to get up early in order to be back at the Straight facility by 8:00 or 9:00 A.M. He became exhausted. Two nights a week, he got a maximum of four hours of sleep, often less than that.

The days were spent in the large warehouse-like Straight facility in St. Petersburg. For at least twelve hours on weekdays, and often half that time on weekend days, the residents went through a series of group sessions, or raps. In these raps, the males would be on one side of the large room and the females on the other. Even eye contact was forbidden between the sexes, although on many occasions, the group sessions were held jointly with both sexes present. If a female walked by the male group, it was expected that the males would cast their eyes downward.

A major feature of each rap was "motivating." The residents flailed their arms wildly about, moving their bodies frantically in their chairs, in order to get recognized by the group leader. The chosen person would stand and make confessions and "renouncements," often crying as he or she did so. These public confessions were usually about their "druggie pasts." It was common for residents to exaggerate their drug involvement so as to demonstrate the great progress they were making, as in the case of the Moral Inventories. At least half of the children and youth there, as far as Fred could tell, had been tricked into the program during sibling interviews. Almost all of this group simply did not have a drug problem so that public exaggeration was necessary. My independent research confirms the presence of large numbers of children in Straight who had no drug problems. I could not determine the precise percentage but came to believe that it was high.

In Rules Rap, the phasers discussed the rules of Straight and the Seven Steps (adapted from the 12 in AA and made more like absolute commandments than in AA) to a drug-free life. The top achievement was the Seventh Step, whose words Fred quoted as follows: "Having received the gift of awareness, I will practice these principles in all my daily affairs and carry the message to all

I can help." This meant that once a person was a Seventh Stepper, he or she had great freedom of movement but was in that seventh phase for life, and, as in many religions, was a committed missionary to help convert and thus save others.

In a separate rap for males only, the discussion was often about sex and how to avoid it. Sex and drugs were equated as destructive activities. The teaching was that if the young man had a sexual relationship with a girl and got pleasure from it and sought to repeat it, then sex had become like a drug to him. He was, as unbelievable as it sounds, told he was addicted to sex.

In "homes" or homes rap, residents were informed if they had earned the right to a visit to their own homes. Residents were coached to shout "Coming home!" and to rush into the arms of their parents, if they happened to be present, when granted this privilege. Despite all of the pressure and harassment, Fred made it to his fourteenth day in reasonably good spirits. He was right: he could take almost anything for two weeks. Fred stood up in homes rap that day and said that he wanted to go home, as he had been promised. The group turned on him harshly and informed him that no one left after only 14 days; 70 was the usual minimum. He was also told that he did not really want to "get straight," to really get rid of his "drug problem." From then on, Fred was depressed. He saw no way of breaking out of the main facility or out of the foster home. "I was scared to death!"

Much of his fear came from what he had been told and what he saw with his own eyes in regard to the punishment inflicted upon residents who fought the system. When residents defied the program while in the facility, a variety of physical punishments were imposed. It was common to have other phasers (of the same sex) simply sit on the offenders for minutes or hours until they were totally subdued and compliant. Fred was deeply affected, for example, by what happened to Keith, a young man who was openly defiant. Often Keith would walk toward one of the doors, all of which were constantly guarded, telling the Straight staff and upper-level phasers blocking his way to "fuck off." One time staff and phasers forced Keith into a bathroom, where Fred happened to be at the time, and proceeded to sit on him. Fred heard a loud crack and Keith yelled, "You've broken my ribs!" A staff member shouted, "Get back on his chest!" Some of the phasers did so. Later, it turned out that young Keith had suffered seven broken ribs and could not move his arm.

Still later, Fred heard, Keith left the program to go into a psychiatric hospital where he was diagnosed to be a schizophrenic. It appears likely that Keith suffered from this psychosis before coming to Straight, but Straight viewed all of his problems as stemming from drug abuse and were incapable of recognizing his mental illness or dealing with it. Instead, the Straight treatment seems much more likely to have aggravated that condition than to have helped it.

Leah Bright was quite sane but she also soon became defiant. She apparently did have a drug problem, which she recognized, and had entered the program voluntarily, with the encouragement of her parents. This 15-year-old girl was somewhat overweight and suffered from arthritis. Nevertheless, she was harassed during an exercise rap because she had difficulty doing the exercises and eventually simply refused to continue. Staff and other residents started to "marathon" her, which meant they continued to force her to conform, intending to keep at that process of coercion indefinitely, until she complied. She did not. Staff members ordered "a bunch of girls" to confront her and make her do the exercises. She fought back and was thrown to the ground. "And one girl stood behind me and took my hair . . . and pushed me down like doing a toe touch and then pulled me up by my hair. And by the time she was done with that, my head was numb."

The teenager was pulled in front of the group to be confronted. Leah Bright continued in sworn testimony, "And they took me to the front of the room and people would stand up and start telling me I was worthless . . . and I was so fat anyway I needed to exercise, and everything in the world. . . . And I started—you know, one boy, I flipped him off or shot him the bird. . . . And the next thing I knew, I was on the floor. And I looked up and Dr. Newton got up in my face and pointed his finger at me and said, 'I want this girl the fuck out of my group. . . .' He [had] grabbed me by the hair and threw me. But I didn't feel him grab my head or my hair because my head was so numb."

The man referred to was Dr. Miller Newton, the director of the St. Petersburg Straight program, whose books and methods have been endorsed by the Reagan White House. Indeed, Mrs. Reagan specifically recommended one of his books to the nation when she appeared on the CBS television network in January 1985 at the end of a program, "Not *My* Kid," that held up Straight methods as a model for treating youth drug abuse. Dr. Newton's performance demonstrating some of these new treatment techniques on Leah in 1982 took place in front of a group of approximately 600 young people, including Fred Collins.

Later, further treatment was ordered for the young lady by Dr. Newton: "This girl is to stay awake until after open meeting on Monday." Since this order was given on a Saturday, when this incident occurred, it mandated 80 hours of continuous marathoning by staff and other residents. The treatment order was carried out.

Special treatment was reserved for those who tried to escape or who actually did so and were recaptured. Very soon after he arrived, Fred's oldcomer, John, explained in great detail what had happened on his own escape attempt. John had been brought back by Seventh Step parents, apparently aided by a private investigator, "who brought him back in handcuffs," Fred told me. "And he explained to me that he was barefooted, dragged over the pavement. He was all bloodied and everything, and his hair was down in his face and they brought him up and confronted him before the group." Someone told him while he was before the group that he could leave, but that if he did the authorities "would put his parents in jail for kidnapping." This theme was often used to control defiant inmates, so it must be assumed that Straight leaders were aware of the fact that their actions raised serious questions as to whether or not they persistently committed wholesale violations of federal and state kidnapping statutes.

Fred became insistent on leaving when his brother, George, escaped from the St. Petersburg program on September 8. (George was later brought back to the program and stayed in it until he became a Seventh Stepper.) On September 10, 1982, "I told them that I didn't have a drug problem. And I just wanted to leave. The only reason why I was there was just because of my brother. . . . And [staff trainee] Joey Glaze . . . brought me in front of the whole group, and he told me 'We're going to make sure that you're never going to leave because we are going to ride your butt.' " To show they meant business, Straight pulled him from the second phase of the program, into which he had just recently advanced, and started him over on the first phase.

In some cases, these acts of humiliation before the group were punctuated by a standard tactic of a finger poked in the chest, or by a push back off his feet and into the group, or even by a punch. Fred suffered most, however, from what might be termed the ordinary activities of the program. "I was starving," Fred now claims. Whether or not this was literally true, he claims that he was always hungry and he was never fed enough. He had the huge appetite of a growing young man. Fred entered Straight a gangling 6 feet, 2 inches, 155 pounds. Within several months he had lost 20–25 pounds and looked like a concentration-camp survivor. He dreamed of food.

He was constantly constipated in part because what food there was consisted mainly of starches and some meats, and only rarely fresh fruit and vegetables. Also, he found it virtually impossible at first to move his bowels while he was being watched, and he *was* watched almost every minute of his imprisonment. Later he succeeded at times in moving his bowels while under supervision.

First phasers had severe limits on the times when they could avail themselves of restrooms while a rap was in progress. On a few occasions, a "bust-ass" rap would run into the early morning hours, after an already long day. It was common to see young men and women, by the hundreds, sitting for hours of "treatment" in a large room, motivating by flailing their arms so they could stand up and confess, while many of them were sitting in small pools of their own sweat and urine. Fred both saw this in others and suffered that humiliation himself. The rooms were often hot and stuffy both from the heat of the climate and also from body heat of the large number of emotional persons present. Inmates sometimes vomited, hyperventilated, and fainted. Rarely did residents see the sun or have exercise in the open air. Many, including Fred, took on a sickly skin pallor. In these unsanitary and stressful conditions, some of the girls reported vaginal infections and missed or delayed periods.

Despite his deteriorating physical and mental condition—or perhaps largely because of it—at one point Fred Collins started to believe he really did have a drug problem and that the Straight program was needed to save the country. One evening in mid-October, he was reading a novel which dealt in part with mind control and it suddenly dawned on him that he had probably been brainwashed.* Fred started to fear that the apparent brainwashing

---

* While the charge of brainwashing may seem overly dramatic, Fred was probably correct. After reviewing a draft of this chapter, Professor Barry Beyerstein, Department of Psychology, Simon Fraser University, British Columbia, wrote me that Straight's techniques seemed similar to those of the Chinese Communists in dealing with United Nations prisoners of war during the Korean War. Dr. Beyerstein explained: "The parallels with Straight's methods are striking. Contrary to widely held opinion, the Chinese (as opposed to the North Koreans) relied very little on physical abuse to achieve conversions and they

would continue and would never stop, and that he would never get out from under its spell. At various times during the previous several months, Fred had been so depressed as to be suicidal in his thoughts and he wondered how he could kill himself. Depression is sometimes described as anger turned inward. Upon achieving the brainwashing insight, his anger turned outward. He would become a good con and work the system to the limit, appearing to be a committed Straightling. But in actuality he started to think about how to escape.

This was difficult since he had no money or personal identification and had been kept in incommunicado detention during the entire period, except for two brief visits with his parents when they traveled to Florida. No mail or telephone calls were permitted in or out of Straight. Had he been held in a jail or prison for serious criminal violations, such detention would be deemed a violation of his constitutional rights. Such practices were normal in Straight, however. He had no idea, then, if he could count on anyone to help in his escape because he had been cut off for so long.

On October 28, 1982, Fred was transported under guard and in extreme heat in the back of what appeared to be a U-Haul trailer to the airport. The private chartered plane took him, along with over 100 other Straight youths originally from the northern Virginia area, to Dulles Airport. Again under continuous guard, he went to the new Straight facility in Springfield, Virginia, not far from his home. At approximately 9:00 P.M. he was transported under guard, with several other Straight children, to his new place of imprisonment. As in the past, down in Florida, this was the home of Straight parents, that is, adults who had a child in Straight and who had become fully committed to the Straight theology. In this case, Fred Collins's new place of confinement became his own luxurious home in Mount Vernon, Virginia.

---

had considerable success. In light of the P.O.W.'s performance, Fred's ability to resist to the end and escape are truly remarkable.

"The Chinese used techniques that Straight seems to have lifted wholesale. The group criticism sessions, self-confessions, etc., are particularly similar. What is most insidious about them is that many P.O.W.'s went along with these procedures thinking they would just play-act to achieve some small reward (such as an increase in rations or a letter from home) while secretly maintaining their previous political convictions. What was found was that this is very difficult to do—behaving in a way contrary to one's beliefs is very likely to cause the beliefs to shift in the direction of the behavior. Numerous studies in social psychology support this. . . .

"It seemed to me as I read your account that someone at Straight had read the literature on brainwashing and systematically set out to apply it."

Home is where the heart is. This had been Fred's home for
fourteen years and where virtually all of his memories of childhood
and family and friends were centered. He had been away from this
beloved place since Easter vacation the previous April. When he
returned after that absence and the most traumatic months of his
life, he found that his parents had converted that home into a
prison, under the guidance of Straight staff utilizing written instructions prepared by the organization. Locks had been placed on
all exterior doors and on many of those inside the house. The same
was true of the windows. On the door of his own bedroom, his
father had installed an electronic alarm system. The doorknob had
been turned around so that the key could only be used from the
outside. Most of his old belongings and mementos had been taken
out and placed in the hall. A Straight staff member supervised the
security of this locked institution, which, as far as I can determine,
contained three inmates including Fred.

ESCAPE

On the third night at home, at 3:30 A.M. on October 31, 1982,
Halloween, Fred pulled off his escape after 135 days as a prisoner.
He threw a table through a window and jumped out to the waiting
car of a friend, Lorna, whose father is a retired FBI agent, whose
brother-in-law is a Montgomery County, Maryland, police officer,
and whose brother is a correctional officer. Lorna had come to his
rescue after he had made a frantic telephone call to her in a moment
when he briefly got out of the hearing of his guards. The two young
people sped off into the night to freedom. They went to her brother,
who took them to the Groveton Police Station in Alexandria where
Fred reported his escape. Fred believed that his father and the
Straight staff would report the matter in such a way that the police
might be persuaded to recapture him. He left the police station
and went underground with the help of his fraternity brothers in
Theta Delta Chi, who took him in and showed him the first true
love and care he had experienced in many months. When he called
Mike, his fraternity Big Brother, Mike immediately drove over in
the middle of the night and took Fred back to his house. Fred
started to feel somewhat more secure again at 5:00 that morning
when he arrived at Mike's home.

For weeks, Fred acted like a hunted criminal or an escaped POW behind enemy lines. Five hours after he escaped, his father and Straight staff members showed up at the house where he was staying. His fraternity brothers lied and protected him, while he hid upstairs in a big commercial-style clothes dryer. Fred Senior urged his friends to call as soon as they saw his son because "Fred is chemically dependent and I fear for his life. We want very much to get him back into Straight." There is every reason to believe that the elder Collins was sincere in making this preposterous plea, and believed that only Straight could save him. The same seems to be true of Straight staff and other parents who supported efforts to recapture young Fred Collins. The sincerity of such destructive beliefs makes them all the more difficult to deal with rationally and humanely.

From members and alumni of his fraternity, money and offers of help poured into the safe houses to which Fred was spirited. Also, his fraternity friends kept offering him pizzas and other rich food which he had been missing so much. He found he could not even touch alcohol or marijuana and he remained quite paranoid. He trusted nobody except known fraternity brothers. Why did he not simply go to the police and ask for protection? Fred's answer: in Florida he had been led to believe that the police would simply hold him until Straight came to pick him up—and that Straight controlled many police agencies.

During this period of fearful hiding, he stayed for a while with David, a young man who recently had been the president of his fraternity, at his home in northern Virginia. To reassure Fred, David allowed him to keep a 30.06 rifle, a very powerful weapon, in his possession. One day, a man in a white coat came into the house and told Fred that he was there to pick up some furniture. Fred leveled the rifle at his chest and said, "You're from Straight, aren't you?" The terrified stranger asked, "What the hell are you doing?" David happened to come into the room from a side door, saw the scene, and tackled Fred, screaming, "He's here for the furniture, Fred!" Later, Fred said, "I was going to blow him away. That's how nuts I was. . . . I look back and honestly think I was insane."

When Fred was telling me about this event, he became very emotional and it might appear that he was engaging in hyperbole. Yet I believe that instances of true insanity periodically appeared in this tale, and not only on the part of Fred.

Fred realized that he had to take some more rational action to deal with his disabling fear of being forcibly kidnapped back into Straight and also with the real possibility of that event. He finally decided to seek legal advice. (Why in the world did it take him so long? Perhaps because he was a traumatized 19-year-old who truly had been brainwashed and who never had even contemplated asking a lawyer for help for any purpose.) One of his fraternity friends took him to his sister, who was a young attorney in Baltimore. When she heard Fred's story, she became furious that such practices could take place in this country. She also realized that she could not do the case justice. She told Fred that in her opinion the only lawyer for this case was Phil Hirschkop. The young lawyer called Mr. Hirschkop's office and made an appointment for Fred.

Phil Hirschkop is a trial advocate, a civil libertarian, and a fighter for unpopular causes. He is a successful lawyer whose firm owns a group of townhouses converted into stylish offices in a fashionable section of historic Alexandria. Mr. Hirschkop built a major portion of his practice by handling the litigation of cases referred to him from all over the country by attorneys who had tried in vain to settle these matters. Thus he is a lawyer's lawyer. A man of medium build and slightly graying hair at the age of 46, when Fred met him, he had a pugnacious reputation with judges and opposing counsel. He was the chief counsel in many of the cases that arose out of the peace movement during the Vietnam War. In his Pulitzer Prize-winning book, *Armies of the Night*, Norman Mailer described Mr. Hirschkop in those peace movement cases as being "built like a young bull." Mailer continued in admiration: "A perfect fullback. His physique spoke of the ability to mount a good second effort, which was the term in football this season for being able to drive hard with the ball, and when stopped by tacklers, able to drive forward again before the whistle blew." I had met Phil in the early Sixties when he was still a law student and I was an official of the National Legal Aid and Defender Association. I was not surprised that he had turned out as Mailer portrayed him.

The first meeting between Philip Hirschkop and Fred Collins on the afternoon of November 5, 1982, was significant for them and for the country. Fred related his situation to Mr. Hirschkop and to his younger associate, David Fudala. Both attorneys had listened to far-fetched tales before from potential clients. This one seemed beyond the pale of possibility in America.

At first, Fred's demeanor and story seemed too bizarre to be believed. "He was frightened to death that Straight and his father were both going to kidnap him," David Fudala later recalled in one of his many reflective discussions with me. The attorneys started to put this skinny, disheveled visitor to the standard lawyer's test. Tell us the significant dates, times, names, and events, precisely as they happened; don't leave anything out. Even though Fred had been through traumatic months involving imprisonment at the hands of his own parents, as well as other destructive physical and emotional stresses, he was able to respond in such detail that the experienced lawyers started to believe he might be telling the truth.

Both lawyers soon became outraged that such actions could be carried out in this country with such high-level official and professional medical support and open endorsements. Phil Hirschkop also found himself becoming emotionally involved as a parent of teenage children himself. "Who's going to protect the children? It could have been my son!" he thought then and still does. At some point during that meeting, Phil started to take on the role of the father-protector Fred had lost. He even growled protectively once, to Fred's delight, contemplating the potential of a new Straight kidnapping attempt, "I was a Green Beret!" (And so he was, having been in the first unit created by President Kennedy.)

I was touched by the emotion both Phil and young Fred still showed when they talked about these events to me several years later. Fred had been at the point of emotional collapse. Phil had been overcome with emotion that a decent young kid, who indeed could have been one of his own children, had been so brutally treated by a cult operating with the active support and collaboration of the boy's own parents—and all for no reason.

Phil Hirschkop called the Straight office in Virginia and the senior Collins, telling both that Fred was now represented by counsel, that he was to be left alone, and that if attempts were made to recapture him, Phil would immediately see to it that kidnapping warrants were sworn out against them. (There seems solid grounds for that threat and I wonder why no criminal justice official has arrested Straight officials for kidnapping. Florida officials considered doing so but did not, apparently because they believed both the involved parents and the Straight staff were sincerely trying to help the victims. Perhaps also it is not politically popular to seem to be on the side of "druggies" and against the drug warriors. It is difficult to imagine, for example, the Reagan Department of Justice arresting Straight leaders on kidnapping warrants.) Both Mr. Hirschkop and Mr. Fudala thought that would be the end of their involvement. They had not contemplated that the case would demand so much more effort from them.

Their temporary involvement stretched into several years. Within a few days, they had to respond to a criminal complaint and a warrant for destruction of property sworn out by the senior Collins against his own son. Fred had caused some damage in the house when he made his escape and, on the advice of Virginia Straight program director Melvin Riddile, Mr. Collins brought criminal charges and thus gave Fred the only criminal record he ever had. (Later at the trial, Phil Hirschkop asked, "You say you love your son. You think having your son arrested is expressing love, Mr. Collins?" The father replied, "Yes, I do. It may be a tough kind of love, but I believe it's the kind of love he needed at the time.") Phil defended Fred in that matter, which involved a settlement: Fred paid his father $75 for the damages incurred during his escape, and his father agreed to drop the criminal charges and to allow his son the right to come to the house and take most of his belongings.

Within the space of a few months, therefore, Fred Collins had become a war orphan. The American war on drugs had created a situation in which this successful college student and citizen could not live in his own house, could not visit his father or his mother or his brother, and could expect no financial support to continue his college education. As the new youth-control dogmas of Toughlove and Straight mandated, the young man had been cut off from his family, emotionally and financially. He was in intense emotional pain. Hanging over him, moreover, was the real threat that he might be kidnapped back into the Straight prison.

Phil wanted to sue the elder Collins, but Fred insisted that, despite everything, he still loved his father and under no circumstances would he participate in a suit against him. Within several months Mr. Hirschkop filed a civil suit against Straight, Inc., claiming that it had visited upon Fred Collins the civil wrongs of false imprisonment, intentional infliction of emotional distress, and assault and battery. Many months went into investigations, the taking of extensive sworn depositions from potential witnesses, and hearings on pre-trial motions. Because this case involved what is known as diversity of citizenship—in technical legal terms, Fred

was a citizen of Virginia and Straight was a corporate citizen of
Florida—it was possible to invoke the jurisdiction of a federal
court.

THE TRIAL BEGINS

At 10:00 A.M. on May 9, 1983, the case of *Fred Collins* v. *Straight,
Inc.* commenced in the United States District Court for the Eastern District of Virginia (Alexandria Division). The courtroom in
downtown Alexandria was small, stuffy, and sometimes affected
by street noise. The presiding judge, the Honorable Albert V.
Bryan, Jr., was a conservative, no-nonsense jurist who seemed to
take special pleasure in controlling hard-fighting advocates such
as Phil Hirschkop. Lead counsel for the defense was Ronald L.
Goldfarb of the firm of Goldfarb, Singer, and Austern of Washington, D.C. Over the years, Mr. Goldfarb had earned a solid reputation as a civil libertarian and an advocate of humane treatment
of prisoners. In addition to his lawyering, he is an award-winning
author of books that extol the need for protections of the rights of
the accused. For example, his book *Ransom* (1965) called for reform of the American bail system so that no person would suffer
the injustice of punishment before an impartial tribunal had rendered a verdict of guilty. In defending Straight, it is quite possible
that Mr. Goldfarb was simply carrying out the canons of legal ethics
which declare that all clients are entitled to competent counsel.

It also appears, however, that Ronald Goldfarb sincerely believed in the rightness of the Straight program both in general and
in this particular case. That is the impression Phil Hirschkop got
as the lawyers went through pre-trial skirmishes. He became personally offended over some remarks that Mr. Goldfarb made to the
press. Mr. Hirschkop told me bitterly, "It's almost like Goldfarb,
protector of rights, represents a whole group of people that says
when it comes to drugs, civil rights don't count." By the time the
trial actually started on that May morning in 1983, the lawyers
were poised at each other's emotional throats, illustrating the schism
created by the drug issue in traditional civil libertarian ranks.

A jury of seven people was quickly chosen from a panel of local
citizens, six regulars and one alternate in case of an emergency.
The six regulars who actually decided the case were, on the whole,

mature, well-educated, and middle class. They seemed precisely the type of people who might well support any program to control defiant young drug users.

The trial dealt with two key questions. First, did Straight hold Fred in custody improperly and thus imprison him falsely? That was the formal legal issue which the jury had to decide. False imprisonment is a centuries-old civil wrong, which Judge Bryan explained to be "restraint of one's liberty without any sufficient cause and against [one's] will." Actual force was not essential. If Fred was "under a reasonable apprehension that force will be used unless he willingly submits . . . it is false imprisonment." Nor was "malice or ill will or wrongful intention" necessary, only that Straight did accomplish the wrongful act of imprisonment.

Second, was Fred a drug abuser or an addict? That question was not a central point in the formal pleadings, technically speaking, but in actual fact it dominated the trial. It would indeed seem logical to say that if this second question were to be answered in the affirmative, then the charge of false imprisonment would be impossible to sustain. That conclusion was by no means certain, however, because both law and medicine are confused about how to define the condition known as drug addiction and also about the legal rights of people classified as addicts.

Fred's lawyers sought to show that Fred was a well-adjusted young man and loving son with a good family relationship who used alcohol and other drugs occasionally but not abusively, and who was imprisoned without just cause and against his will. At the same time, Phil Hirschkop argued to the jury, even "if Fred Collins was a heroin addict they had no right to kidnap him or hold him against his will" because he was an adult.

The lawyers for Straight sought to show, in the words of co-counsel John J. Brandt, "that the Collins family, who had two sons, was invaded by [the] curse of alcohol and drug abuse," and that during that initial sibling interview in June 1982 "there was revealed deep drug involvement by Fred Collins," who thereupon voluntarily entered the program for treatment. "The evidence will show you," Mr. Brandt also told the jury, "that Straight is the most successful drug rehabilitation program in the country."

Dr. Newton, the director of this highly successful program, filed an affidavit that put forth Christopher Yarnold as its designated expert who would explain how Straight diagnosed chemical dependency. In the actual event, Mr. Yarnold's testimony demonstrated the profound ignorance of some of the alleged leading experts on drug abuse in America. During the course of taking sworn pre-trial depositions, lawyers Hirschkop and Fudala brought out that diagnostic expert Yarnold did not know the name of the active ingredient in marijuana, did not know what laughing gas was, and had only the vaguest idea of how drugs interacted with human health and behavior. On the witness stand during the trial, this state of ignorance was again demonstrated by Mr. Yarnold. When asked if he knew at the time of the intake how the hallucinogenic factor in drugs worked, he replied, "No. All I knew was drugs affected people." In my opinion, that remark was a fair representation of the level of sophistication of Mr. Yarnold and of most Straight experts.

Mr. Yarnold also reiterated that it was his decision to commit Fred to the Straight institution—and then explained the physical evidence he had found that confirmed his professional diagnosis that Fred Collins was a drug abuser. "I'd diagnosed that—in my interview with Fred, his eyes were red," Christopher Yarnold testified. "Mr. Yarnold, are you telling these seven good people, you can look in someone's eyes and tell that they've been smoking marijuana?" asked attorney Hirschkop. "You can look in someone's eyes and tell that they've been smoking marijuana, yes," replied Straight executive staff member Yarnold. Phil Hirschkop then asked Chris Yarnold to come down and look in Fred's eyes right then, during the trial, for any indication of recent drug use. Mr. Yarnold did so and found no indication of dilation or redness, thus no hint of recent drug use.

Then Mr. Hirschkop brought out that the Straight executive had not noticed that Fred was wearing contact lenses that day in court, nor had Mr. Yarnold noticed it on the day of the sibling interview. Mr. Yarnold admitted that he knew that contact lenses could make eyes look dilated. (There was no mention of Fred's swim in the pool the night before the sibling interview which might also have contributed to red eyes. Fred believes that the combination of the swim plus the contact lenses might have given his eyes a dilated, red appearance during the interview, which he would have explained if asked at the time.)

Another important factor in the diagnosis of the chosen Straight expert was that Fred denied his drug problem, which, as in *Catch-22*, was taken as impressive evidence that he had one. "Fred was into denial, which is an indication that he didn't wish to be there and recognize his drug problem," Mr. Yarnold testified. In some cases, of course, denial is a major part of the addiction syndrome, but when used simplistically, as it was here, this symptom could be used to slap half the world into institutions.

Also important was that Fred had admitted to using a number of drugs, especially marijuana, even though he had not used it in the three months before the interview. On the witness stand, after intensive cross-examination, Mr. Yarnold delivered this conclusive pronouncement: "Anybody that is using a drug that is mood-altering has a problem. Okay. He has a problem. From now until eternity, Fred will be chemically dependent." Several jurors later recalled in discussions with me and my research assistants that they were deeply and negatively impressed by this dogmatic testimony of Straight, Inc. executive Christopher Yarnold.

WAS FRED COLLINS AN ADDICT?

However, the clash of values in this unique case, and by extension in the country, was brought out most dramatically in the testimony of the two psychiatrists presented as expert witnesses by each side. The dominant official view of adolescent drug abuse, which is strongly supported by the White House and many medical and social leaders, was represented by Dr. Robert L. DuPont, Jr., who was a paid consultant to Straight. He is a preeminent spokesman for that view—the world's heavyweight champion, in the eyes of many people—hence his testimony made this contest, in a very real sense, a trial not only of one narrow case but of a whole philosophy, one that controls much of American drug treatment today.

On the core issue in this case, Dr. DuPont testified that in his expert opinion, Fred Collins definitely was "a pathological user" at the time he "voluntarily" entered Straight. When asked how he would define a pathological user, Dr. DuPont replied, "Use of drugs in a pattern that is recklessly disregarding the real interest of the individual. There were at least two striking examples of that in that year we are talking about. One of these was his inability to continue on INH [a medicine which had been prescribed by a doctor] because he chose to drink instead, and the other was his risking his financial support to go to college and choosing marijuana instead. I considered both of these sick, pathological, and evidence of drug dependence."

That was the considered scientific judgment of one of the leading drug abuse experts in the world. That conclusion involved ethical and factual issues about which there were clear conflicts in testimony. Fred had been advised by his school's medical center to take the medicine INH (which is a brand name for the drug isoniazid) as a precaution after he had a positive TB test. This is a commonly used medicine in such situations. Fred claimed that he was told by medical personnel that it was acceptable if he drank moderately, that he did so, that he also kept taking the medicine, and that he experienced no difficulty from the medicine or, as it later turned out, from tuberculosis. His father's version was that adopted by DuPont. So also was Fred Senior's version of the ultimatum on marijuana and financial support for school, as we have seen.

In other words, there was a conflict in the testimony as to whether Fred's father had ever told him that he would be cut off financially and emotionally, in line with Toughlove and Straight ideology, if he ever used drugs or alcohol in any quantity. And there was a conflict as to the precise instructions of the school's medical personnel about the taking of INH and the moderate use of alcohol. In each case, Dr. DuPont came down against Fred although the doctor never took advantage of the opportunity given him to examine Fred.

Even had the facts been precisely as Dr. DuPont claimed, his invocation of mental disease on the basis of this behavior graphically demonstrates why many people who are not physicians have come to believe that there is precious little science involved when many doctors solemnly pronounce that a given person is suffering from the disease of drug abuse. Too often, the diagnosis is made entirely on the basis of the doctor's personal feelings about drug use (or, in some cases, as we have seen earlier, on the basis of the doctor's desire to obtain customers). In this case, citizen Robert DuPont might have said he strongly disapproved of citizen Fred Collins's behavior, and then there would have been no major problem. When, however, psychiatrist and drug-abuse expert Dr. DuPont made the supposedly scientific diagnosis that patient Collins was diseased on the basis of secondhand evidence, then serious questions should have been raised, which indeed they were at the trial.

There are standards by which fairly objective and impartial judgments may be made as to whether an individual is suffering from the disease of drug abuse. Some of the most authoritative have been formulated by the American Psychiatric Association. The primary APA diagnostic criteria for cannabis, or marijuana, abuse are "intoxication throughout the day; use of cannabis nearly every day for at least one month; episodes of cannabis delusional disorder." A related standard is "impairment in social or occupational functioning due to cannabis use." As Phil Hirschkop read these and other tests of cannabis pathology to Dr. DuPont in the course of the cross-examination, the physician admitted that none of them applied to Fred in any clearly significant manner.

Then how in the world did one of America's best-known drug-abuse treatment experts make a public scientific diagnosis that Fred Collins was a sick, pathological abuser of drugs? In the end, when pressed by Philip Hirschkop, Dr. DuPont retreated once again to the position that Fred violated the disputed agreement with his father not to smoke marijuana while in college—and thus rested his medical case primarily on a factor having little to do with the actual abuse of drugs.

The majority of the jury, according to juror Louis A. DeSanti, who holds a Ph.D. in political science, simply did not feel that the evidence showed Fred to be drug dependent. Moreover, they distrusted Straight's primary expert witness. "DuPont's tie-in with Straight was obvious," Dr. DeSanti observed in an interview with one of my research assistants after the trial was over. "He seemed to bend his testimony to protect his client. We believed Dr. Egan; he gave what appeared to us [to be] good professional advice."

James Harold Egan, chairman, Department of Psychiatry, Children's Hospital National Medical Center in the nation's capital, provided a different professional vision of the universe of youth drug taking and of the medical status of one young man. Dr. Egan's vision has a fair number of scientific and lay supporters, but it is ignored by most major political and scientific policymakers today.

"I think Fred had a number of devices that he used to defy authority. They were rather typical adolescent ones, I must say; letting his hair grow very long and wearing used, beat-up old clothes and getting an A one semester in a course and getting this supreme pleasure of getting a C the next semester, to sort of thumb his nose at the teacher, the equivalent of what many adolescents do as they attempt to become autonomous adults, which is to break away from the family by defying its norms, so that if the parents say, 'I hate rock music,' they buy three more rock records and play them very loudly." According to Dr. Egan's view of the whole universe of adolescent behavior, therefore, this conduct was "very normal."

Even if Fred had continued to smoke marijuana in defiance of the ultimatum allegedly issued by his father, Dr. Egan, unlike Dr. DuPont, would not have seen that form of adolescent risk-taking as necessarily a clear sign of drug dependency. "It depends on the motive for the risk-taking. If, for example, one takes the risk because one has a compelling need, an internal need for the drug, then one would say that the risk-taking is dependent on the drug. With a number of young people that I see, the drug is merely the instrument or the pawn in a battle with their parents, and not the problem itself," Dr. Egan stated on the witness stand.

Think of the global implications of that statement. The youth of America were not going to hell in a chemical handbasket. There was a venerable theme to the new and scary youth drug scene. Kids were fighting with their parents as they had since the beginning of time, as today's parents fought with their own parents a generation ago. Only the weapons in the ancient power struggle were somewhat new. Different chemicals, for example.

On the basis of having examined Fred for several hours (which Dr. DuPont never bothered to do) and of having read most of the important records, Dr. Egan stated flatly on the witness stand, "I do not think that he was at the time or now chemically dependent on any drugs." In making this diagnosis, the physician apparently closely applied the APA criteria that Dr. DuPont largely seemed to ignore. Even though Fred did occasionally use drugs, he was not regularly intoxicated, and he was functioning well academically, socially, and personally. "Let me be very frank," Dr. Egan interposed in the midst of a question being put to him on the stand. "Were I to have seen him as a patient in my office, I would not have referred him to a drug rehabilitation program." The next question was, "Do you think he needed any treatment for drug abuse at all?" The immediate, firm response was, "No."

In Dr. Egan's opinion, Fred was not only a "typical college student," he was "perhaps above average on most dimensions," particularly in regard to his independence and ability to endure difficulties. Dr. Egan was impressed that after the Straight episode, Fred persevered, got himself back into college on loans, and rose from being house chairman to being elected the president of his fraternity. "I think it's rather extraordinary and a sign of quite a healthy young man . . . who is not showing signs of deterioration from chronic drug abuse."

Young Fred Collins, the above-average achiever, did show signs of deterioration, however, from another source, in the eyes of Dr. Egan—and that was from the experience of going through the treatment program of Straight, Inc. He developed a number of neurotic symptoms stemming from the program that was supposed to cure him and save his life from a disease that, in fact, he did not have. He became depressed, fearful and anxious regarding involvement with women, and had recurrent, haunting dreams of being chased. The worst damage was done when his own family applied the Straight-Toughlove dogma to Fred. Dr. Egan thus concluded that he was most deeply wounded "by the serious estrangement from his family, the sense that he was in essence on his own, that he had been abandoned emotionally, interpersonally, financially, that each time he sees a father and son on the street, for example, he is emotionally overcome. He says he feels like an orphan, and at one point told me that he wishes, in fact, that he had been. That it would be much easier. And then, you know, [he] broke down and wept."

FRED WINS TWO JURY VERDICTS

At 12:18 P.M. on the fourth day of the trial, Thursday, May 12, 1983, the case went to the jury of six citizens, the alternate having been excused shortly beforehand. The jury was most influenced by the solid evidence that Fred, at 19 legally an adult, had indeed been imprisoned against his will. Had the jury believed him to be a true drug abuser, they might have doubted his ability to object to his imprisonment. That issue did not arise, however, for the six citizens did not believe that the evidence showed Fred Collins to be a drug addict. To the surprise of all concerned, the jury took very little time to deliberate, reaching a unanimous verdict by 3:15 P.M.

While the verdict was in favor of plaintiff Fred Collins on the claim of false imprisonment, for some reason the jury decided to find for the defendant on the claims of intentional infliction of emotional distress and assault. After having rendered such a speedy verdict, it was then the turn of the members of the jury to be surprised. Judge Bryan announced that this was a bifurcated trial and that there would be a separate trial on the issue of the extent of damages. This took place on May 24 and 25.

At that trial, Phil Hirschkop asked for two kinds of monetary damages for Fred Collins. First, compensatory damages, which are tied to actual and future projected losses: to pay him for his suffering and time lost from school, for his medical expenses to treat his mental and emotional distress, and to assist him in paying for his education. Second, punitive damages, to punish Straight by the seemingly indirect route of paying Fred additional money, on the idea that this civil "fine" would persuade the wrongdoers to stop harming children. In the proof of punitive damages, the law allows relatively wide leeway to bring in other cases of misconduct to demonstrate that this was not an isolated misstep but one piece of a larger pattern. Attorneys Hirschkop and Fudala sought to prove to the jury that both types of damages were needed in this case, especially the second.

They attempted to do so primarily by bringing in as witnesses young adults who, like Fred, were forcibly detained against their will by Straight. Arletha Schauteet, for example, had visited the St. Petersburg facility for a sibling interview to visit her brother on October 23, 1981, ten days short of her eighteenth birthday. She was kept against her will until April 21, 1982, when she managed to escape. At nearly midnight on April 25, her mother came to the door of the friend's house where she was hiding and told her emotionally that her brother would be terminated from the program if she did not return. Her mother grabbed Arletha by the arm and started dragging her toward a car. Two adult men and a woman, all strangers to the young girl, joined in the violent kidnapping, which involved thirty minutes of battling, and then they forced her into the car and drove her back to Straight. Despite the familiar routine of confrontation over her alleged involvement in drugs and sex, Ms. Schauteet stood her ground and insisted that there was no reason to keep her imprisoned.

After many hours of such harassment, the young girl was taken into Dr. Newton's office. On this occasion, the Reagan White House–endorsed expert told her that if she persisted in saying that she was being held against her will, "the state of Florida would take over and they would put my mother in jail for kidnapping." At one point, Arletha's brother was brought into a rap where she was being confronted and the treatment specialists "let him yell at me, too, like everybody else and call me names and tell me how much he hated me." When the pleas of friends on the outside prompted a Detective Brown from the local Sanford police department to call Dr. Newton, the girl was released later the next day.

The story of Arletha, then, demonstrated practices existing before Fred arrived. Hope Hyrons's ordeal took place after Fred left and at a time when Straight executives were telling the world that the Collins case had prompted them to make major changes and also to clear up some minor administrative oversights. On January 19, 1983, Hope, then 18, went to the St. Petersburg facility for a sibling interview so that she could visit her brother. She had held a student internship at the Seminole County sheriff's office and had some knowledge of her legal rights. Hope Hyrons persisted in refusing to sign herself in during the familiar scenario when she was told that the event had become an intake interview. In this case, though, a new twist was added. This young girl was told that not only would she be cut off from her family in line with Straight-Toughlove doctrine, but also that she would be cut off immediately. If she persisted in her refusal, her parents would simply leave her there in St. Petersburg, over a two-hour drive from her home in Longwood. She stuck to her legal guns and her parents carried out the Toughlove threat. Young Hope Hyrons was forced to walk and hitchhike alone to the home of her aunt and uncle in Longwood.

Approximately one month later, her mother apparently relented and picked her up in the family car to visit a doctor. At a gas station, her father and two strange men got into the car. She was restrained by the men and told by her father that she was being taken back to Straight. Soon, she found herself in the intake room where she was again forcibly restrained as she struck at her captors and fought to get out of the room. The young law-enforcement intern told the three or four girls that they were violating her legal rights. A man came into the small intake room and said, "I hear someone in here has a problem with their legal rights." "Yes, I do," replied Hope Hyrons. According to Hope, Dr. Miller Newton replied, "Well, I don't give a damn about your legal rights." A Florida social services official did, however, and helped secure the release of Hope Hyrons within two days.

(The cases of Ms. Schauteet and Ms. Hyrons received considerable publicity in Florida. Both retained lawyer William A. Leffler of Sanford, who commenced proceedings against Straight and Miller Newton. Months after Fred's victory, Straight settled both claims out of court. Mr. Leffler said that the settlements were "handsome" and that both of his young clients were "very happy.")

Unlike the two young people just described, Jeffrey McQuillen, a Canadian and 19 at the time of entry on April 5, 1983, testified that he *had* a drug problem and that he *voluntarily* entered the program in accord with an agreement he made with his parents. He entered the newer facility in Springfield, Virginia. However, almost immediately the young man announced that he wanted to leave. His requests were denied. He repeated them after the fourteenth day and again was refused. In addition, Straight staff then put a rope through his belt loops "and started tying me up and leading me around like a little monkey."

On April 23, he was led from the foster home where he was kept at night and into a car by his oldcomer, Bob, and driven toward the Straight facility. As the car was moving slowly in a traffic jam in suburban Maryland approaching the Woodrow Wilson Bridge, Jeffrey McQuillen managed to break partially free. Bob grabbed one end of the rope which was still attached to the prisoner, and grabbed onto his leg, screaming at him. The two young men fought on the side of the road. Jeff ran away with Bob in hot pursuit. Finally, young McQuillen lost his pursuer as he raced across the huge bridge, with the Straight ropes trailing from his body. Jeff eventually managed to hitchhike back to his native country.

Thus, the stories of Arletha Schauteet, Hope Hyrons, and Jeffrey McQuillen demonstrated that Fred Collins was only one among many young people abused by Straight, Incorporated. As I relate their stories and go back over their sworn testimony at the trial, my own sense of outrage starts to take over again. I have worked so hard to make sure that all of these facts are correctly set down here that at times I forget to insert my own emotions and I also forget that others may read them in disbelief. Let me assure anyone who has that feeling that this testimony was allowed to go into the public record of the trial without rebuttal by Straight and with only minimal cross-examination by defense counsel John Brandt. Therefore, this shocking and, in my opinion, unrebutted testimony had a strong impact on the jury in their assessment of punitive damages.

At 10:32 A.M. on May 25, the jury retired to commence its

deliberations, which were much more heated than the first time. The lone woman juror wanted to do precisely as counsel Ronald Goldfarb urged in pleading for a "Toughlove verdict"—an award of one dollar. She felt that Straight was doing vital work which should not be curtailed. Psychologist William Watson later told me that he believed that a substantial penalty had to be imposed, perhaps in the neighborhood of $100,000. Louis DeSanti found himself "100 percent pro–Fred Collins." He thought Fred was "a regular guy" and that he had been severely hurt by Straight and by his parents.

The most forceful juror seemed to have been Robert H. Hartzell, who was a relatively high-ranking federal civil servant—chief, Division of Administrative Services, Administrative Office of the United States Courts, located in the nation's capital across the river from northern Virginia, where he lives. Like any citizen of that district, Mr. Hartzell is expected to serve on juries in those cases in which he has no professional involvement. An open-faced, short, likable fellow in his late fifties at the time I interviewed him in his comfortable office a few blocks from the White House, Hartzell is a secure inhabitant of Middle America, with roots in traditional values. He was utterly appalled at seeing drug users face to face at the trial. It seemed to him that he had been "transported to a foreign land" because in his world, to his knowledge, people did not use drugs like marijuana. "I don't think I really believed that people took dope until I sat in that courtroom. I'd read it . . . but . . . I don't know if this will make any sense to you, I believed it but I didn't *believe* it. . . . I've come to realize that I've lived all my life rather sheltered. . . . A Mr. Straight."

While he was appalled at the revelations of drug use, Robert Hartzell was even more disturbed by the tactics of Straight, Inc. "I found myself angry. . . . I had concluded that . . . regardless of what their motives were, if not nipped in the bud, [their tactics] were the seeds of destruction for a nation. If you allow a little thing here that is the antithesis of democracy, a little thing there, a little thing here, you really have the deterioration of democracy in the incipient stage. And then the first thing you know you can't stop it anymore. And this business of scooping people up off the street, and just being so convinced of their rightness in the matter that they just scoop 'em up off the street and take 'em away!"

At times during the testimony, however, Hartzell had wavered and felt that if Straight had to use some harsh tactics to help the users beat their drug habits, then "You're darn right. Use them. Whatever it takes! But then you hear about locking them up without authority to do so, and then you hear about at least questionable practices from the standpoint of mental and physical abuse, and you get a little scared because, if you want to be honest about it, you *know* that that self-righteous organization can be convinced that you're . . . whatever . . . and they got the answer for ya, and God is on their side, so there can't be anything wrong with scooping you up off the street, and the first thing you know, you're scooped up because you're a Lutheran, or you're scooped up because you're a Methodist . . . or an alcoholic. . . . Now, some people, you'd be surprised, I think, at the number of people who think . . . this country will never come to that just because you scoop up an addict off the street."

Robert Hartzell, however, thought differently. To him, the time to protect liberty was at the first sign of a serious threat—and the actions of Straight represented just such a threat to his traditional concepts of American freedom. He was annoyed that some of his fellow jurors did not see that the proper thing to do was to stand up on your hindlegs and shout that such behavior is not allowed in this country. That is what he did when it came down to assessing damages. He felt that the Straight leaders and all those who believed as they did had to be sent a strong message. That is why his initial position was an award of $500,000 to Fred Collins. The single woman stood by her one-dollar award. Juror DeSanti sided with Hartzell and wanted a high award against the organization.

"A look of shock fell over the faces of attorneys for both sides as the decision was read in a stuffy, packed courtroom," said a newspaper account. The verdict: $40,000 in compensatory damages and $180,000 in punitive damages, a total of $220,000.

HOLLOW VICTORIES

The message that the jury sought to convey to Straight with this large award was not heard, however. The lesson that Dr. Newton took from the verdict was, "It certainly will open the door for people with 25 bucks and an unemployed attorney to come after us." The defiance implied in that declaration has been carried out in practice. After months of searching through records, reports on visits, and correspondence, I have yet to find solid proof of major changes in Straight's practices. Complaints against various Straight facilities around the country continue, as do passionate claims of successful help from supporters.

Moreover, the Collins case did not even deal with the rights of children who have not reached adulthood. The legal protection of their rights in relation to their parents is very weak. While some states are increasing that protection, only rarely is it possible for an American child to protest institutionalization ordered by a parent, even when the child is not mentally ill. One of those rare cases occurred roughly three months after the verdict in Fred's case. A mother in Albuquerque, New Mexico, hired two private detectives to abduct her 16-year-old son, Charles, who used drugs of which the parent did not approve. The detectives shackled the young American citizen in leg irons, and drove him 1,700 miles across numerous state lines to the St. Petersburg Straight facility, which took him in on September 3, 1983. Charles was lucky because he was able to get his case into a Florida circuit court where a judge ordered his release because proper legal procedure for a commitment had not been followed. Also, the judge found no sound evidence that Charles was a drug addict or abuser. Thus, it was plain that young Charles had been abducted.

Straight national executive director William Oliver fumed, "How can a parent *abduct* their own child? . . . A parent has a right to place, detain and restrain a child short of abuse. . . . Parents have the right to take an unwilling child to a dentist or a school or anywhere else that the parent feels is in the best interests of the child." Because the law on this matter is so vague, in most cases and in most states, Mr. Oliver's sweeping claim of parental power is, as a practical matter, sadly accurate. Clearly, then, we have reached that point in our national history when serious consideration must be given to new laws that create explicit protections for the rights of children against their own parents and, moreover, against those who would treat them for diseases which they do not have.

Until that reform occurs, we must still deal with the harm caused by present practices. Individual court cases are not the best methods to protect our children, even those who have reached adulthood. Although Fred Collins is now approximately $80,000 richer, after paying all attorneys' fees and expenses, he considers his victory to have been a hollow one. "Money is no comparison to a family. You can't buy back your parents' love."

Fred spent the Christmases of 1982 and 1983 away from his family and utterly depressed. The young man looked forward to spending the Christmas of 1984 with his own family in an attempt to re-establish a relationship. When he returned to the family home shortly before Christmas day, he found his brother, George, now a Straight Seventh Stepper (in the most advanced phase, out in the community) to be a drug-free but hostile human being. For the first few days, though, events went relatively smoothly. Then his father discovered upon reading a newspaper that Fred had told some reporters of his hopes for a family reconciliation.

An argument ensued over the unwanted publicity, and he left his house and came to mine for a few hours. I had spent a good deal of time with Fred over a period of months in the course of conducting research on this book and I suppose that I had taken on a touch of the father's role that Phil Hirschkop had assumed at times. On this occasion, my attempts to comfort him were to no avail. I could see that this young fellow's mental and spiritual health were still damaged by his unbelievable ordeal.

Fred Collins was again cut off from his family and more deeply depressed than I had ever seen him to be. For several years, he remained an orphan of the war on drugs.

Between December 1984 and December 1986, despite repeated attempts, I was unable to find Fred nor was I able to contact him through his family. They refused to speak to me on the telephone nor would they answer my letters asking about Fred's welfare. I was worried about him—and them.

Out of the blue, Fred called me in early December 1986. He told me that he had just discovered my letters lying about his parents' home. They had never told him about the letters or about my frequent attempts to contact him. Fred told me that he was doing well, that he had completed his undergraduate work and was pursuing a master's degree at Virginia Tech. The young man claimed that he was reconciled with his family but that they simply did not talk about their ordeal with Straight.

The matter has never been faced or resolved.

I remain worried about him and them.

3

The Hidden, Happy News About Our Young

AFTER POT PARTIES at night, kids would go to the manhole and shine a flashlight down on the decomposing corpse . . . for kicks." So wrote Peggy Mann in a highly influential article, "The Parent War Against Pot," in 1980. The popular writer was describing a situation in which a 15-year-old Cleveland-area boy had been murdered and his body stuffed down a manhole; it remained there known to perhaps 100 teenagers but not the police for six months. While admitting that this was "hardly a typical story," Ms. Mann felt it important enough to report and to connect with today's youth and marijuana in the public mind. She quoted the boy who revealed this story as saying to a doctor that he had to get into a "drug removal center" because "I suddenly realized how pot can make you do crazy things."

LIBELING OUR YOUTH

Even though I have serious questions about the motivation and the tactics of the current crusade for drug-free youth, that criticism, nevertheless, does not fully deal with the alleged serious condition of this drugged generation of youth. There has been a great deal spoken and written by governmental officials, leading medical authorities, and respected authors detailing the terrible deeds today's youth commit and the horrible maladies they suffer. They have been recently portrayed as infinitely worse than previous generations—lost, rotten, dying, and slaves to marijuana and other drugs.

To read the actual words of these experts, such as Ms. Mann, whose dire descriptions dominate public images, is enough to make any concerned American adult wonder how we have spawned such a self-destructive generation and to be almost thankful that they are, as the drug warriors say, dying off faster than any other group of our people. A comprehensive theory about the behavior of our current bad crop of youth is provided by Phyllis and David York, the originators, promoters, and marketers of Toughlove ideology, consultations, workshops, books, pamphlets, newsletters, T-shirts, and a whole line of related merchandise. Promotional material handed to me at the Toughlove sales booth in the Atlanta convention center during a White House–supported conference in April 1985 stated that within the space of a relatively few years, since the mid-Seventies, the movement has grown to over 1,400 groups in North America, Europe, Korea, and Australia.

To these disciples throughout the world, and to the general public, the Yorks have explained in their best-selling book, *Toughlove* (1982): "The common denominator is rotten behavior. Despite a wide range of geographic, social, and economic backgrounds, our young people today behave with stereotypical predictability. Like clones stamped out in some satanic laboratory, they share an underlying selfishness and similar ways of demonstrating it." We have already heard Fred Collins, one victim of the treatment which sometimes results from this philosophy, describe it as brutality. It might also be described as a rationale for hate of a whole generation of children, starting with one's own.

Nevertheless, armed with that satanic-clone vision of today's "troubled teens," the Yorks in their book discarded the well-established concept they had been taught in their training as professional drug-abuse counselors and family therapists: look for many of the roots of drug and alcohol abuse in family dysfunction. According to the Yorks, that makes no sense today because the selfish behavior of most of these kids comes from within themselves and from the fact that they are so often "stoned." Phyllis then told about the behavior of the kids she grew up with as a teenager in the early Fifties, when she "also felt the influence of the growing youth subculture. But drag racing, drinking, and balling in the backseat were considered the limits of outrageous teen behavior in that decade." Well, not exactly the limits, even for a nice Jewish girl in New York City, because, as *Toughlove* declares, without a hint of embarrassment or regret, "When she was a teenager she smoked pot, tried cocaine, sniffed heroin, and occasionally drank."

However, Phyllis York claimed that there was "a big difference" between her drug use and other shenanigans and "what is happening today." For example (writing in the third person about Phyllis), the Yorks said, "she liked the feelings she got when she used pot and cocaine and if she were a kid today she feels that she'd abuse these chemicals." The implication, of course, is that Ms. York somehow managed to use highly addictive illegal drugs ethically, occasionally, and responsibly! Why cannot young people sow their wild oats in that way today and then later become more responsible citizens, even going into the youth-control business as adults? Partly because they are more rotten than Phyllis and her friends were, but also because "at one time drugs were part of 'limit breaking' and the 'new consciousness,' but as the years have passed they have simply become part of the culture."

In other words, when the Toughlove Mother was a young girl, her profound deviance was much more understandable and less destructive because it was pioneering—and also because it involved greater effort in finding drugs. The kids today are selfish satanic clones because more of them are involved in the same activities and it is easier for them to obtain drugs. If the Yorks have demonstrated a significant difference here, I have failed to appreciate it. Nor did my undergraduate students whom I forced to read *Toughlove*. They were outraged to think that any adult would believe that it is part of the accepted culture for the majority of youth to fornicate in the backseats of cars, and also to use marijuana, cocaine, heroin, and alcohol. I can state categorically that any teenaged boy or girl who was involved in all of those activities today would be considered a deviant by most of the young people I know. That is why Phyllis York and her nice teenaged friends of the Fifties—held up almost as role models by the Toughlove gurus—were "rotten" themselves in the eyes of many of my students. Moreover, having personally known the teenagers of both the Fifties and the Eighties, in each case from the vantage point of an adult, my anecdotal impression is that, on the whole, I can discern no qualitative difference in the rottenness quotient of these two generations.

Thus I found it relatively easy to dismiss the impressionistic arguments about comparative qualitative degrees of rottenness put forth by such nongovernmental propagandists as the Yorks. More troubling, however, were the quantitative arguments from official sources, especially those that said the death rate of our young people today was worse than in the past. If there is one set of figures that seems to be reliable over much of the world, it is that relating to deaths, and I am still enough of an old-fashioned American to trust that my government will not purposely distort simple statistical fact. For that reason, I was deeply concerned by statements issued by the federal government which pointed with alarm to the death rate of our youth. For example, President Reagan's own apparently definitive *1984 National Strategy for Prevention of Drug Abuse and Drug Trafficking* declared flatly: "During the past 20 years, the health of all Americans has been improving, with one notable exception. The death rate for young Americans between the ages of 15 and 24 is higher than it was 20 years ago. Alcohol and drug abuse are the major contributors to these unnecessary deaths." That is a powerful indictment from the nation's leader of the harshness of the drug habits of this generation of our youth when compared with those in the past.

Such precise statements from seemingly unimpeachable sources about the adverse health consequences of horrible drug habits, especially those involving illegal chemicals, abound in the recent writings of many drug-abuse experts. Marsha Manatt wrote in *Parents, Peers, and Pot II* (1983), a book funded and distributed by the federal National Institute on Drug Abuse, of how Dr. DuPont had been going about the country inspiring the parents' movement with the new, true biological facts about drugs. He appeared, for example, in Texas to speak before the Texan's War on Drugs Committee, including Ross Perot, the leader of the war. "Robert DuPont . . . had a tremendous impact on the group," Dr. Manatt wrote. "His historical overview of the rise in marijuana use among teenagers from 2 percent in 1962 to 60 percent in 1979, and his revelation that young people between the ages of 18 and 25 are the only age group in the country with a rising death rate . . . helped the committee understand the epidemic seriousness of the drug problem."

There you have it, the fatal connection—American children are smoking marijuana at a record rate and they are dying at a record rate. Dr. DuPont also stated in his Texas speech: "If young people do not smoke pot, they simply do not use any other illegal drug; to reject marijuana is to reject the whole drug culture." Many members of the public interpret these statements to mean: stop our kids from smoking pot and thus save them from death.

Dr. DuPont expanded on these points in his 1984 book, *Getting Tough on Gateway Drugs*. In addition, he cited a whole host of teenage problems that were "strongly associated with drug use," including higher rates of suicide, motor vehicle accident deaths, pregnancy, and lower Scholastic Aptitude Test (SAT) scores.

Therefore, the proponents of current policies make repeated claims that there is solid statistical support for their position that this generation of American youth is being destroyed by drugs.

SEEKING THE TRUTH ABOUT YOUTH

For several years, numerous assistants and I have been engaged in a quest to find support for that position. We have gone straight to the source of every major claim of impending youth collapse—to the heads of the White House Drug Abuse Policy Office, DEA, NIDA, ADAMHA, and Dr. DuPont's American Council on Drug Education, and to all of the major agencies that compile health and census data. In some cases this search has taken the form of critical articles challenging the authorities, in effect, to put up or shut up. In other cases it has involved personal visits, persistent telephone calls, and letters. We have found most of the alarmist position to be as solid as a child's sand castle.

For example, on November 2 and 9, 1983, a nationwide media attack on the allegedly growing problem of youth drug abuse in two parts, called "The Chemical People," was launched through 300 PBS stations and 11,000 local meetings. Mrs. Reagan appeared on both programs as the host. At no point during either program was any mention made of the good news about our youth. For example, marijuana use had already started to drop during 1979 and 1980, the last two years of the Carter administration. In 1979, 16.7 percent of all youth aged 12–17 stated they had used pot at least once in the last month, the definition of current marijuana use. The federal figure for 1982 was 11.5 percent, a drop of almost one-third in a few years! Recently, there has been a change in the federal government's line: there has indeed been a drop in marijuana use and it has been brought about directly by the Reagan administration and the parents' movement.

The good news on the death rate has been totally ignored, as of this writing, in public declarations by the Reagans and all federal drug-abuse officials. It is true that while death rates for all groups were steadily dropping, the death rate for youth aged 15 to 24 increased from 106 deaths per 100,000 in 1960 to 129 in 1969, a rise of 22 percent. No expert has ever explained that rapid, fatal spurt, and for good reasons—it may well be unexplainable. By the early Eighties, happily, it had simply gone away. By 1982, the rate had dropped to 105, the lowest in history, and by 1983, to 96 deaths per 100,000, the first time that it had fallen below 100. The overall health of the nation is improving wonderfully. A child born in 1900 had a life expectancy of 47 years; in 1983, despite the cries of the drug alarmists and current high levels of illegal drug use, that expectancy at birth had risen 60 percent to 75 years.

It is immoral for our leaders to ignore or pervert these data for selfish purposes. Such actions can only lend weight to the suspicion that these leaders are deliberately hiding good news about our youth because it does not fit their political game plan about drugs, which requires a high level of public hysteria and alarm.

One of my research assistants has persistently called the major agency offices asking for explanations of these distortions. In most cases, as with the staff of Dr. Ian MacDonald at ADAMHA, the response was that they would get back to us—or, later, in exasperation, "These facts are commonly accepted by everyone; please do not bother us any more for documentation." Early in 1985, a junior staff person at the White House drug policy office responded to one of these calls—for data to support the bad news about kids— with a petulant *Catch-22* response that may hold a portent of the future: we are not sure if the youth drug situation is improving or worsening, the person said, but if it is getting better, the administration and the parent movement caused it; if worse, we need more funds to fight the problem!

We did find discouraging pieces of information in the federal data about our youth, some of the worst concerning deaths from intoxicated driving. There is no doubt that auto accidents are the leading cause of death among young people aged 15 to 24. Alcohol and other drugs seem to have played a role in approximately half of all these deaths in recent years, approximately 10,000 youngsters annually thus being the victims of improper use of chemicals. But there are no reliable indicators as to the rate of drunk-driving deaths among youth in most past decades. For many years, the leading cause of death for young people has been motor vehicle accidents. However, any claim that this generation of American kids is significantly worse than past ones on this score is simply unsupported by the facts we uncovered.

Indeed, those facts seem to point in the opposite direction. The overall motor vehicle death rate for youth 15-24 peaked in 1970 (47 per 100,000), commenced dropping in the Seventies, and then declined way down to 35 by 1983, almost the lowest in recent history. So also does it appear that *intoxicated* driving deaths by our youth are dropping, although the precise extent is not yet known. Today's generation of youth may well be safer drivers than those in the past, an improvement that began to take shape long before Mr. Reagan came to Washington. Declining highway deaths may well have been caused by numerous factors such as laws requiring seat belts and a 55-mile-per-hour speed limit. Nevertheless, the Reagan administration, prodded by such new groups as Mothers Against Drunk Driving (MADD) and Students Against Drunk Driving (SADD), is making major efforts to curb drunk driving by young and old. All are to be commended for their worthwhile work in this area.

YOUTH SUICIDES: WHY SO MANY?

There are precious few signs of improvement, however, to be found in the data on the youth suicide rate, which almost tripled in the thirty years between 1950 and 1980.* At least 5,200 youths be-

* In 1950, the rate of suicides for ages 15–24 was 4.5 per 100,000 of population; in 1980, 12.3.

tween the ages of 15 and 24 commit suicide every year, according to the Centers for Disease Control, a federal agency in Atlanta. There is no doubt, moreover, of a relationship between the taking of depressants, such as alcohol, heroin, and barbiturates, and an increased risk of suicide. It is a grim, vicious circle. Often, people who are depressed to start with take such drugs to relieve their depression, and for a while they feel better. Over time, these drugs tend to increase depression in many users, however. In some cases, they deliberately use those drugs to end it all. Suicides among British heroin addicts, for example, have been approximately 20 times the expected rate compared to the total population. Therefore, any young person who is regularly taking depressants should be watched, humanely controlled, and helped to the greatest extent possible.

All of which leads us to the broader and more important question. Has the increased youth national suicide rate been *caused* by an increase in drug taking? The drug-war zealots assume the cause-and-effect connection immediately, and also give the impression in their literature and speeches that drug-induced suicides are a major threat to large numbers of American young people. For example, a recent issue of *Epidemic*, published by the Straight, Inc., National Development and Training Center in St. Petersburg, had a bold red headline on the first page: "SUICIDE." The story fairly screamed, "Drug use left unchecked is a terminal disease—it kills." Dr. Richard Schwartz, a George Washington University medical school professor and the medical director of the Springfield, Va., Straight, supported the hysteria by (1) repeating the misleading information about the rise in the death rate of young people, which I have already shown to have changed, and then (2) stating the true facts about the general rise in youth suicides.

My belief is that only a part of the increase in the suicide rate may be due to increased alcohol and drug use. As tragic as each individual suicide is, official records reveal a small total number of drug-related youth suicides for the nation. Data from the Drug Abuse Warning Network (DAWN), the major federal source for such information which operates under a contract administered by NIDA, documented only 25 such suicides in 1984 among all of the children in this huge nation, that is, for all ages through 17. (Adulthood is normally considered to begin at age 18.) Another 34 drug suicides were listed for ages 18 and 19, and 258 for ages 20 through 29.

The total is 317 documented drug-related suicides among the entire American population through age 29 during 1984. DAWN data for 1985, when an epidemic was allegedly in process, showed a drop in drug suicides through age 29 as compared to the previous year; the total was 279 for 1985.

Because DAWN information comes from a limited number of medical examiners (77 in 1984) located in large metropolitan areas, and is not a scientific sample, and because suicides are often hidden from public view, one might speculate that this number should be greatly inflated to arrive at the true number of youth suicides with drugs. However, that process of inflation would be pure speculation. On the basis of what we now know, we can reasonably conclude that this generation of youth is not killing itself off with drugs, however much leading drug-abuse experts, congressmen, police officials, and the media may shrilly suggest that they are.

Perhaps, however, there is a form of death wish involved in much youth drug taking that ends in deaths, even those that appear accidental. While that may be the case, the actual number of *all* documented drug-related sudden deaths in this nation of millions is also relatively small. The total known dead in all age groups during 1984 for all drug-abuse incidents—accidental, suicide, and unknown causes—was 3,486. The total number of children—ages 6 through 17—who died from all of those causes was 54. For ages 18 and 19, the total was 79; and for ages 20 through 29, 1,068. Thus, the total known drug-abuse overdose deaths for all our people up through age 29 in 1984 was 1,151. The figures for 1985 in these categories were slightly less, with a total of 1,137 such deaths of children and young adults. In the entire country, 52 children between the ages of 6 and 17 died from all forms of drug overdoses during 1985.

I say again that each of those deaths was a tragedy and that there were probably more deaths from drug overdoses than appeared in the records, but those figures are the best and most reliable we have. Whenever I bring up these comparatively low figures to proponents of the drug war, whether in the media or in professional debates, the usual response is to disbelieve their existence or their accuracy.

As for the means used by youths to commit suicide, every objective study suggests that most tormented people rarely use drugs. Most youth, like older citizens, in their moments of extreme despair turn to poisons, gases, hangings, and especially to firearms.

In an authoritative article, federal research scientist Jeffrey Boyd, M.D., wrote in the *New England Journal of Medicine* of April 14, 1983, that the recent rise in the suicide rate was almost totally attributable to a rise in suicides by handguns. All other suicides, taken as a group, actually declined. Illegal drugs were not even mentioned by Dr. Boyd. He suggested not greater controls on drugs but (1) greater controls on handguns which might well reduce the number of suicides and (2) a reduction in the carbon monoxide content of domestic gas. The latter measure had resulted, he said, in a reduction in the suicide rate in Britain. Such calm, sensible suggestions, even when made by governmental experts, are generally ignored in discussions of youth and drugs because they do not fit into the prevailing hysterical public mood.

If drugs and alcohol are not the causes of the great rise in youth suicides, what are those causes? A review of much recent literature by specialists in the subject convinced me that, up to now, science has provided no clear answer and most honest experts are not blaming illegal drugs. My students, who are experts in a sense, insist that the greatest cause of the rise in adolescent suicides may be found in the great rise in stress placed upon our youth today as compared to years past. I report this with mixed feelings because I thought my world as a youngster was full of stress. Yet my students protest with some vehemence that the world imposed on them by adults contains distressing economic insecurity, terrorist explosions and hijackings, the smell of war everywhere, the threat of nuclear incineration pressing ever more closely from two superpowers who are being more warlike than ever—and in the face of all this, the youth are told that they must excel at their studies and at a lot of other endeavors and do it all without drugs or alcohol. You adults want us to face these anxieties and horrors drug-free, they say, while you slop up all the prescribed and non-prescribed soothing syrup you can!

It is a wonder, they continue, their voices rising, that *more* young people do not commit suicide. Whether or not my students are correct, it seems certain that those who blame the rising suicide rate of our young people on drugs are simply guessing, and probably incorrectly.

One could even work up a good argument that the use of certain drugs in some circumstances will ease psychic pain and prevent suicide. A young depressed person using a depressant like alcohol may be helped by a switch to marijuana, as outrageous as that sounds, because the latter drug tends to reduce depression for some but by no means all users. One mature addict I met, whose case is discussed in detail later, said that he suffered from emotional and metabolic deficiencies and was suicidal as a youngster; accordingly, he argued that he should have been maintained on powerful narcotic drugs under the watchful eyes of a physician starting at age 15. I have no idea if his claims were accurate. However, I do know that some treatment experts, who believe in drug-free therapy for most of their patients, have told me that they nevertheless saw that some of their patients were kept functioning for a good part of their lives only by their licit or illicit drug use.

The best cures for suicidal tendencies are joy, love, and human warmth, which are also the best cures for drug abuse. Yet drugs play a role in both preventing and causing suicides. My guess is that today drugs probably prevent as many youth suicides as they cause, but the exact causal relationships in youth suicides remain unclear in my mind.

SAT SCORES

When I dug into the welter of often confusing facts about all of the other supposed products of drug abuse by our youth, I came up with even more questionable causal connections. Consider Scholastic Aptitude Test scores, for example. In 1963, the verbal national mean average was 478 and the mathematical was 502. Starting in 1964, there was a significant drop in both national averages, which continued until 1981 when they had declined to 424 and 466. Why? During this period, there had been a rise in illegal drug use, especially marijuana, and there were those who were quick to lay the blame, as we have seen, on drugs.

However, the drug alarmists managed again to ignore much of the impartial evidence. An authoritative and comprehensive study on the decline in SAT scores was released by the College Entrance Examination Board in 1977. While not certain of the reasons for the decline, the panel eventually concluded that the most likely cause was the inclusion of greater numbers of formerly excluded people in the educational process. *In other words, not drugs but democracy and economic opportunity may well have been the most powerful reasons for the drop in scores; the population of test-*

takers had changed. As minorities and previously disadvantaged people improve at the educational game, a rise in all SAT scores seems probable. That general rise has already started to occur. The SAT scores for college-bound seniors in 1985 had risen to a national verbal average of 431 and a national math average of 475.

Of course, if any young person smokes marijuana during the school day, that youngster may well do poorly in school and also on the SAT. Marijuana, however, does not offer a new, special threat to the education of our children. Any intoxicant tends to interfere with the learning process. A child who drinks beer or his aunt Matilda's sherry at recess will be equally at risk of failing. Marijuana, then, is not the issue, nor is any other illegal drug; keeping a clear head while learning is. Nor are children the only ones in danger of not learning due to intoxicants. The use of any intoxicant—whether stout English beer, fine Amontillado sherry, or Maui Waui pot—by anyone so as to interfere with education or work is a perfect example of drug abuse.

It is possible, on the other hand, for people, young and old, to use marijuana and alcohol responsibly. I have met dozens, perhaps hundreds, of students over the past three decades who claimed to have used them during the evenings and on weekends to relax and enjoy themselves. Of their use, of course, I have no documentary proof. All I know is that many who made such claims did superbly on examinations and went on to brilliant professional careers. Moreover, I have met many people, not necessarily my own students, who alleged that they would never have made it through school without the regular use of marijuana or other chemicals to calm the enormous anxieties attendant upon the educational process. The existence of those successful drug-calmed students flies in the face of most of the orthodox dogma about the universally destructive effects of drugs. It is even conceivable that the number of young people helped through school by the responsible use of alcohol and drugs may be roughly equal to the number hindered in attaining their educational goals because of the irresponsible use of such chemicals.

I fear that these statements will be misinterpreted as an endorsement of student drug and alcohol use. I wish students would not use any intoxicant and am deeply concerned about those who become dependent. At the same time, I must honestly report my conclusions about the factual connections I have studied.

TEENAGE PREGNANCIES

Even weaker factual connections exist between drug abuse and teenage pregnancies. The new puritans of the drug-free youth movement actually place a large part of the blame for our huge number of teenage pregnancies on the improper use of drugs. The truth is that our young girls are not being sexually corrupted by drugs and alcohol; rather, both our boys and girls are being harmed by adult-imposed ignorance, prophylactic lies, and conflicting messages about sexual behavior and drugs. Within the space of a few days on their bedroom television sets, our young people can watch Hawkeye get sloppy drunk with the whole MASH gang and then engage in a happy mutual seduction with an eager nurse in the supply room; Mrs. Joanna Springsteen, playing a 17-year-old lifeguard, make a voluptuous display for two hours on a beach with her nipples periodically poking through her T-shirt, which display is interrupted only when the precocious child goes to bed with her boyfriend; and in between it all for thirty seconds a public service ad from the National Federation of Parents for Drug-Free Youth telling kids to just say no to drugs.

Based on a major study of teenage pregnancy in advanced countries, the Alan Guttmacher Institute reported in 1985 that the United States leads the developed world in teenage births, abortions, and pregnancies—and is the only such country in which teenage pregnancy has been increasing recently. Black teenagers constitute a major part of the problem for the U.S., but even if only whites are considered, the pregnancy rate for this country is considerably higher than most others. The researchers found the lowest teenage pregnancy rates in those countries with the most liberal attitudes toward sex as well as the greatest amount of honest information, such as frank education courses, and confidential availability of birth control devices. In other words, when youngsters were taught how to be responsible participants in sex, pregnancies were reduced. It all had nothing to do with drugs but rather with replacing ignorance with information and assistance. Indeed, Holland, which has the most liberal attitude on drugs of any Western country, also had the lowest teenage birthrate of all of the countries studied: 14 per thousand girls aged 15–19, compared to 96 for the United States.

The authors of the report observed that "none of the other [countries] have developed official programs designed to discourage teenagers from having sexual relations—a program innovation that is now advocated and subsidized by the U.S. government." That program, of course, is not effective.

"American teenagers seem to have inherited the worst of all possible worlds regarding their exposure to messages about sex," concluded the Guttmacher researchers. "Movies, music, radio, and TV tell them that sex is romantic, exciting, titillating; premarital sex and cohabitation are visible ways of life among the adults they see and hear about; their own parents or their parents' friends are likely to be divorced or separated but involved in sexual relationships. Yet, at the same time, young people get the message good girls should say no. Almost nothing they see or hear about sex informs them about contraception or the importance of avoiding pregnancy." *Thus there are striking similarities between the twin drives toward drug-free and sex-free youth—and between their perverse products.*

More recent reports on black teenage pregnancies illustrate that ignorance is not the main part of the problem. In many poor ghetto communities, teenage girls pick up a great deal of information from their mothers and from their friends—and also values that encourage teenage pregnancy in some circumstances. Many young black girls get pregnant to have somebody to love, to keep their man, or to achieve success at a personal task. It is a sad situation that should cause all decent people, of all races, to be deeply concerned.

Yet to suggest that drugs caused or were a major factor in the current pregnancy epidemic among American youth of any race is to turn reason and the evidence on its head.

MARIJUANA: ASSASSIN OF YOUTH?

Both reason and the evidence are securely upside down when it comes to marijuana. Marijuana is increasingly proclaimed as the major cause of the downfall of our youth. In her foreword to Peggy Mann's *Marijuana Alert* in 1985, the First Lady went even further when she declared that the book was "a true story about a drug that is taking America captive." Not only our youth, but the whole country. That book is one of the latest and most sophisticated examples of marijuana-scare literature. By mentioning only the research that tends to show marijuana's unique harmfulness, Ms. Mann implies that science has documented that the drug has spread over the country almost like a new nerve gas, paralyzing its people, especially youth.

Ms. Mann had the full cooperation of Reagan administration drug-policy officials in gathering material for her book. It has been treated by them as the definitive word on the drug. Since its publication, some of those officials have gone even further in finding new dangers from marijuana. Dr. Ian MacDonald alleged in 1986 that there was a connection between marijuana use and AIDS— the connection being that intravenous drug users often get AIDS and many of them started their drug careers with marijuana. Dr. Carlton Turner added fuel to the fears of 1986 by stating at various points during the year that there were new dangers in the increased potency of marijuana, in its connection with AIDS, and— a startling new claim—in a causal link with becoming homosexual. The story was broken by *Newsweek* reporter Margaret Garrard Warner, who wrote that Dr. Turner had said that he saw many homosexuals in drug-treatment centers. Ms. Warner had asked Dr. Turner, "Weren't these men maybe gay first?" The leading White House expert on drugs, especially marijuana, replied, "Oh, no, the drug came first." Dr. Turner later heatedly denied that he ever said that pot "caused" young people to become gay and went on to explain that he meant that the use of drugs caused them to lose "inhibitions against everything."

A balanced review of all the authoritative research during the past century documents no distinctive harm from marijuana. Its addictive threat comes from the fact that it is an intoxicant, but any intoxicant taken compulsively presents possible dangers to young people. Its threat to physical health comes from the fact that it is absorbed in the form of smoke, but any smoke, even from corn silk or chopped parsley, taken regularly into the body could eventually cause serious harm to some people.

Every major impartial official study—ranging from the *Indian Hemp Drugs Commission Report* in 1894 by British and Indian experts to the National Research Council report, *An Analysis of Marijuana Policy*, by American specialists in 1982—reached roughly similar conclusions: marijuana presented some danger to the people who used it, but the actual level of harm was consistently exaggerated and control measures were frequently too harsh. Thus there is a long history of rational official studies on marijuana existing side by side with periodic official revelations of alleged new dangers suddenly discovered.

When dealing with the public, some government medical experts often act as does Ms. Mann in her writing: they choose to mention only those scientific conclusions which support their personal point of view. In a pamphlet aimed at the general public— "For Parents Only: What You Need to Know About Marijuana"— NIDA stated, "In one study on humans, it was found that smoking five joints a week over time is more irritating to the air passages and impairs the lungs' ability to exhale air [more] than smoking almost six packs of cigarettes a week." I cannot count the times that this precise claim has been thrown at me in debates.

On December 6, 1982, I had the opportunity in a public debate at American University to ask Dr. William Pollin, who had signed the foreword to that pamphlet in his then-capacity as director of NIDA, why he did not warn the public that the objective research findings were inconclusive, fragmentary, and often contradictory. I read from his own testimony before a congressional committee in which he had cited that famous joint-to-pack comparison and then followed it with this caution: "This comparison, while widely quoted, needs confirmation by independent studies." I also read to him sections of a report from the American Medical Association's Council on Scientific Affairs which reviewed research on the impact of these drugs on lung tissue and functioning. That report cited one study with laboratory mice that showed tobacco to be more carcinogenic than marijuana, another with just the opposite results, and then concluded, "the degree of comparability of marijuana and tobacco smoke in pulmonary effects is still debatable." In other words, science could not honestly tell if tobacco or marijuana hurts the lungs more.

Then I asked Dr. Pollin why his agency had not simply told parents that while marijuana carried definite risks, science had not demonstrated that this drug was worse than tobacco. I also asked why he signed his name to a document that revealed only one side of the scientific findings while telling the parents of the country that this one side constituted the full scientific evidence. The director of the leading federal research agency on drug abuse responded that in light of the apparent disposition of the government during the Seventies to downplay the dangers of pot, perhaps now it was leaning in the other direction and exaggerating them.

Nevertheless, NIDA has consistently issued objective statistical reports through the DAWN system, which is based not on laboratory research but on actual deaths and injuries resulting from the abuse of drugs by real human beings living in American society. (These reports are to be distinguished from those based on a wide variety of secondary sources, such as those by the Surgeon General which estimate 350,000 tobacco deaths and 150,000 alcohol deaths each year, and which include mainly deaths from organic diseases caused by long-term use.) During 1984, as I noted earlier, DAWN reported 3,486 drug-abuse deaths, primarily overdoses, which involved the nonmedical use of any substance. As is the standard procedure, the pathologists listed the drugs—normally more than one—found in each of the bodies which seemed to have some connection with each death. These "mentions" were then tabulated into a national profile by DAWN staff.

There were a total of 7,623 mentions for that whole year. The drug with the greatest number of mentions (1,131) in 1984 was "alcohol-in-combination." This is a curious listing because DAWN reports on deaths from alcohol only when found in combination with other drugs in the body of a person who died suddenly. In any event, this method does not distort the truth because that friendly drug was still duly put at the top of the list by the medical examiners. Coming immediately behind in the lethal national rankings were heroin, cocaine, codeine, and quinine. Valium was in seventh place with 279 mentions; Darvon, with 237 mentions, was in eighth place; Tylenol, with 180, was in tenth place; and aspirin, with 121, in fourteenth. Marijuana, with eighteen mentions, was near the bottom of the list in forty-second place, and figured in .50 percent of the deaths. Thus, a medical examiner felt it important to mention marijuana in one half of one percent of the drug overdose deaths encountered, amounting, by my calculations, to 17 fatalities for the nation in the latest official compilations.

For a period of several years, I have asked the DAWN staff about the meaning of such mentions of marijuana. DAWN staff are not aware of a single instance in which marijuana, though found in the body of the deceased, was deemed to have been the principal cause of death. While these rankings have varied somewhat over the years, the overall comparative picture of drug dangers has changed little. That picture is similar to the one presented by other sources of vital statistics and by other experts, such as perhaps the leading authority on marijuana in the country, Dr. Lester Grinspoon of Harvard University Medical School.

While there has been a national obsession with controlling marijuana, and while the war on drugs primarily nets marijuana offenders, there is unimpeachable pathological evidence that our youth and adults are in greater danger from many other legal drugs, some of which are totally uncontrolled by the law. As far as I can determine, it is almost impossible to take a fatal overdose of marijuana, even though such claims are often made by drug-war zealots. After several decades of massive marijuana use by an officially estimated total of 61,940,000 Americans at least once in their lives, it is as yet impossible to identify a single overdose, accidental, or suicide fatality caused primarily by marijuana use when there have been many such deaths identified from abuse of such substances as Darvon, Valium, Tylenol, and aspirin! It is solid evidence such as this, issued by the Reagan administration and always ignored by the Reagans and ridiculed by their supporters as misleading, that leads me to the conclusion about the safety of marijuana as compared to other commonly used substances. As actually used by the great majority of consumers, marijuana appears to be one of the least toxic drugs that human beings take.

This is not, however, an endorsement of marijuana. It has many dangers. First, it is an intoxicant and for some people it is potentially addicting. Second, when smoked, it is probably at least as organically harmful as tobacco smoke and in time I predict there will be documented deaths from its persistent use, although perhaps not from overdosing on it. Because very few people use marijuana as compulsively as perhaps 85 percent of smokers use tobacco—56,000,000 smokers fix 20 times a day or more—the number of cancer and heart disease deaths from marijuana should be minuscule compared to tobacco. Those deaths, though, will occur.

IS MARIJUANA A GATEWAY DRUG?

 My greatest objection to marijuana is that it involves smoking. My personal fear is that if I ever used it, the habit of smoking might lead me back to tobacco and not on to heroin or cocaine, as the gateway-drug theorists claim. That theory is also sometimes described as the escalation theory. However it is labeled, it does not make much sense in reality. Just about as much sense, in fact, as the statement by the heavy drinker who said he was going to quit drinking water since he found that he got in trouble when he took bourbon and water, Scotch and water, and gin and water; water was the only common factor. So water was clearly his real problem.

Nevertheless, there are few ideas so commonly accepted by all of the drug-war and marijuana-scare proponents as the escalation or gateway theory. Since he became attorney general in 1985, Edwin Meese keeps repeating the theory, almost as a testament to his faith. In its 1986 report, the President's Commission on Organized Crime declared flatly, "While many beliefs about marijuana have been proven wrong by subsequent research, this concept has been affirmed." The warrior medical experts seem to imply that there is something in the chemical structure of the drug that sucks many young occasional users through that gate and on to harder drugs and into the whole drug culture. Thus if that gate is kept closed to our youth, then that illegal culture is never entered. However, except in the imaginations of a few people, there is no identifiable element that makes the illegal drugs, on the whole, significantly worse than the legal ones.

In fact, many of those unfortunate people who feel impelled to use and then to abuse mind-altering drugs often do not distinguish between legal and illegal substances. Certain drug addicts may specialize in taking heroin and to that extent they are involved in a criminal subculture. When heroin runs dry, however, they will turn to alcohol or prescribed methadone or Valium, all legal. Many of these addicts tried marijuana before they tried heroin but pot did not impel them to heroin. Their drive to alter consciousness with chemicals led them to both and they chose the former because pot is often the easiest drug to find, even more available to many young people than beer. Repeated studies have documented, though, that the first mind-altering chemical most young people use is alcohol. On the basis of such irrefutable evidence, we could postulate that the major gateway drug for millions of our kids is not pot, but alcohol, that alcohol leads to all drugs, and that therefore we should have a war on alcohol, starting with a new prohibition law. Other research suggests a similar role for tobacco, thus raising the possibility of another prohibition law based upon a different gateway drug.

I find little support for the gateway theory as applied to pot in any of the data issued by the government, including the massive surveys of residents of households put out periodically by NIDA. To me, they prove conclusively that (1) pot smoking usually leads only to more pot smoking; (2) many young people smoke pot a great deal, then get bored with it, and cut down or stop totally; (3) a minority of pot smokers move on to harder drugs or continue to smoke pot along with those more potent chemicals. I can find no evidence of a causal link between, say, pot smoking and heroin injection or cocaine sniffing in these surveys.

I searched for clues on the gateway theory in *The National Survey on Drug Abuse: 1982*, based upon detailed personal interviews with a scientific sample of over 5,000 people, which concluded that the great majority of marijuana users smoke it only occasionally as children (12–17 years) and also as young adults (18–25). What about the young kids who seem preoccupied with pot during some phases of their adolescence? While this can lead to terrible problems for a small percentage of children, the report saw even this kind of use as not harmful to the great majority. "A particularly intensive level of marijuana use often represents a passing phase in the marijuana use career," according to *The National Survey*, which then explained that many " 'occasional' users quit entirely" and that "many 'intensive' users drop back to moderate levels of consumption."

If the escalation theory worked for large numbers, then the percentage of users would be higher for other drugs, especially the illegal ones and especially for older users. The opposite was true.

Results of the larger 1985 household survey of drug use were similar in respect to the gateway theory, in my opinion. Projections were made of the total number of people in the United States who had ever used an illegal drug and of those who were current users (who had used it at least once in the 30 days prior to the survey). It was estimated that 61,940,000 people had used pot and that 18,190,000 were current users. Yet there were only 5,750,000 current users of cocaine and the number of current heroin users was so small (less than .5 percent of the sample) that estimates were impossible. I do not mean to downplay the problem of heroin and cocaine—only to point out humbly that if the marijuana gateway theory made any sense, then many more of those 61 million who had smoked pot would have gone on to those harder drugs.

These comprehensive federal studies document the continued existence in America of the responsible, controlled use of marijuana. Millions of our children and young adults are sufficiently in control of their minds and bodies to use marijuana for months and years—and then to make significant changes in their patterns of use as a matter of personal choice. Those changes rarely entail moving on to harder drugs.

It could be that for many of these young people marijuana may well work more as a filter than a gateway. Dr. Dale Beckett of Surrey, just south of London, has spent over two decades in the medical front lines treating heroin addicts and other people with drug problems. He found that as many adolescents struggle with the agonies of that stressful period they reach for some form of a chemical crutch. The physician believes that many potential addicts are able to calm their anxieties with minor drugs such as marijuana in moderate doses. "However, if personality defects are so great that minor drugs do not help him enough then it is possible he will try heroin," Dr. Beckett wrote. "It seems that the presence of minor drugs may actually filter off some adolescents who, if they were not available, would be likely to use narcotics from the start." Viewed in this novel light, the wide availability of marijuana may well be a positive force for society. The Beckett theory stands the escalation theory neatly on its head.

Whether it is a gateway or a filter, marijuana is smoked mainly by adults. Only about one in seven of current American marijuana smokers is a child, according to that NIDA household survey in 1985. Smokers between the ages of 12 and 17 accounted for 14.6 percent of the total of current users.

One of the few facts put forth by the drug alarmists that I found to be absolutely true is that illegal drug use has indeed risen since the early Sixties. Back then, approximately 2 percent of youth had ever used an illegal drug; that figure peaked at 68 percent in 1979. The rise is conventionally trumpeted as an epidemic of crisis proportions. And yet we have seen that our children are not dying in huge numbers from these drugs and also that their death rates are at a historical low and life expectancy at a historical high. There is reason to believe that this generation of our youth, along with the rest of the population, are using great quantities of illicit drugs but that their physical and mental health, on the whole, are not being seriously harmed by those drugs. At the same time, too many of our young people are tormented by the disease of drug addiction and deserve all of the help that society can muster. Those young people in need of treatment will not be helped, however, by wild claims that the entire generation is being destroyed by illegal chemicals.

NONDRUG THREATS TO OUR YOUTH

The public furor over drugs diverts national attention from the fact that this is the healthiest generation of youth in our history and also that many threats to our children come from other, more innocent-appearing sources. Parents and other family members, for example. Surgeon General C. Everett Koop spoke recently of the rising "epidemic of family violence" as evidenced by an increase in *reported* cases of child abuse and neglect from 500,000 in 1976 to 850,000 in 1981. Because so many cases are unreported, he put the total number of 2,000,000 annually in each recent year.

Documented cases of actual murders by parents of their children are, thankfully, of much smaller dimensions. Yet such cases do exist and thereby support the existence of a brooding and generally ignored threat to the safety of the nation's children and young people. A special computer run of FBI crime reports, performed at my request, came up with the distressing data that during 1983 alone, 408 American children up through the age of 14 and 93 aged 15–24 were murdered by their parents, a grisly total of 501 known victims.

Overall homicide rates from all assailants for children and young adults are rising at an epidemic rate. The increase for young white men in the age group 15–24 years is startling, from 3.7 per hundred thousand in 1950 to 15.5 in 1980. The comparable figures for young black men show a less dramatic rise but, at the same time, a more disturbing situation: a rate of 58.9 in 1950 and 84.3 in 1980. Thus 84 out of every 100,000 young black men in the country were murdered in 1980. In many of these murders among both races the use of alcohol and drugs played a role, but usually by reducing the inhibitions of the older assailants and not by directly harming the young victims.

In 1984, according to the FBI, 2,060 young people up through the age of 19 were murdered; another 5,527 in their twenties were also homicide victims; thus, a total of 7,587 Americans under the age of 30 were killed by other Americans, mainly by relatives and friends. The comparable figure for drug-abuse deaths, as we saw, was 1,151 that year. The principal means by which Americans kill one another is the firearm. The leading choice of firearm murderers is the handgun. Even though President Reagan was very nearly one of those handgun victims, and has never, as far as I know, been harmed by drugs, there is no national war on homicides in the family, on handguns, or on any of the other instruments and activities that constitute a much greater threat to the health and safety of Americans of all ages than drugs.

Great threats to our children and young people come from accidents involving any one of a thousand ordinary objects and activities, which normally get only passing mention in the press. The U.S. Consumer Product Safety Commission is a relatively new agency that is just beginning to develop methods of collecting information on deaths and injuries. Even from its incomplete files, between 1981 and 1985 it appeared that there had been a total of 34 deaths of American children due to suffocation from ingesting toy balloons. While that is a seemingly insignificant number, it is 34 more than I could discover for marijuana.

Swimming provides another innocent example. During 1985, the CPSC recorded 337 deaths of young people up to the age of 24 in swimming pools, and another 249 in swimming accidents elsewhere.

Another threat to the health and welfare of our youth is found in a combination of poor diet and lack of exercise. The pace and pressures of daily life combined with the recent boom in the number of fast-food outlets has meant that children and adolescents are eating more hamburgers, pizzas, french fries, and milkshakes. Those billions of McDonald's hamburgers boasted about on the golden arches are not being sold to laboratory mice. In addition to consuming huge quantities of fatty and starchy food, the average teenager takes in an average of seven hours of television a day. Even though the nation seems to be going through an exercise craze, some experts claim that, among young people, vigorous athletic activity is more and more restricted to a small group of youngsters who are seeking careers in sports.

The documented results are disturbing. An examination of 360 elementary schoolchildren recently in Jackson County, Michigan, discovered that 98 percent had at least one major risk factor for heart disease. High blood pressure was found in 28 percent, excessively high levels of cholesterol in 45 percent, and a combination of three or more risk factors in more than 50 percent. When Dr. Gerald Berenson of Louisiana State University autopsied children who had just died in automobile accidents, he found that some of them had both high cholesterol and fatty deposits in the arteries that could well lead to heart attacks. In the recent report of the National Children and Youth Fitness Study researchers told of how they had measured the thickness of the skin and fat in 8,800 youths and compared the results with past records. Professor Lloyd Kolbe of the University of Texas concluded, "In our representative sampling of kids from fifth to twelfth grade, we found that both boys and girls were significantly fatter than those studied in the Sixties."

In 1986, the Center for Science in the Public Interest, in the nation's capital, reported on precisely how unhealthy the fast-food craze was becoming. Burger King's Double Beef Whopper contains 12 teaspoons of fat. A small order of Chicken McNuggets at McDonald's contains nearly twice as much fat as that hamburger. A triple cheeseburger from Wendy's contains 15 teaspoons of life-threatening grease. "America is the world's greasiest greasy spoon," wrote columnist Colman McCarthy in reporting these facts. He continued, "It is also the nation where the swallowed fat is part of the reason that heart or blood-vessel diseases killed more than 980,000 people in 1983."

Even though these nondrug threats to our youth are significant, they do not change the claim that this is the healthiest generation of youth in our history. These threats are cited, not to contradict that position, but to bring balance to the discussion about the relative dangers of drug-taking and other activities.

When I compare pot, homicides, guns, television, toy balloons, hamburgers, swimming, and lack of exercise, a protest may well be made that I am comparing apples to oranges, that the comparisons make no practical sense. I admit that these activities, objects, and events are very different but they have a commonality in that they all have an impact on the health and lives of millions of our young people—and they could, and do, pose a threat, sometimes of a fatal character. A child killed by an angry parent, by a handgun in the hand of a friend, by the negligence of adults in a swimming pool, or by a piece of a swallowed toy balloon should be mourned as much as one killed by an overdose of a drug.

4

Do Not Corrupt Any More American Youth

THE PRESIDENT . . . AMERICAN UNIVERSITY . . . DLR SOONEST, DLR MASSACHUSETTS AT NEBRASKA AVENUE WASHINGTON, DC 20016
AFTER HEARING YOUR REPRESENTATIVE ARNOLD TREBACH ON TELEVISION NOVEMBER 27, 1984, I STRONGLY SUGGEST YOU CLOSE YOUR DOORS IMMEDIATELY. DO NOT CONTINUE TO CORRUPT ANY MORE AMERICAN YOUTH.
SAMUEL P. NORLEY
11-4 ASPEN WAY
DOYLESTOWN PA 18901

The president of my university, Richard Berendzen, sent that telegram on to me with a nice handwritten note that I was not to worry, that academic freedom was alive and well at American University. A copy of the telegram and the note were placed on the School of Justice faculty office bulletin board, where both drew numerous comments, mostly humorous. In some respects, however, I was not amused at all. In fact, I was more worried than amused.

CAN YOUTH STAND TO
HEAR DRUG DISSENTERS?

I have developed a thick skin over the decades in which I have supported a number of unpopular causes. Criticism comes with the territory. Much of it has been harsher than that contained in the brief telegram from a stranger. What bothered me was that it had hit a sore spot, one close to home, as it were.

Two questions illustrate the nature of the worries that make that spot in my psyche sore. First, to what extent will anyone, but especially young people, feel emboldened to try a drug or to use one regularly because they hear my arguments that the illegal drugs are no worse than the legal ones, that the enforcement of the drug laws hurt our people more than the drugs, and that irrational drug laws should be reformed? Second, what will happen to drug habits when and if those drug laws are actually reformed?

A linchpin in the continued support of existing methods is the belief that a relaxation of the tough criminal law approach will provide a signal to the young that society approves of the use of formerly banned substances. Once that occurs, the belief continues, clean-living American kids as well as many adults are apt to go on a drug orgy, and the number of addicts to such substances as marijuana and heroin and cocaine will rise geometrically to proportions never before even contemplated. "We'd have 60 to 100 million cocaine users," said Dr. Pollin of NIDA in 1984, implying that many of them would become addicts, not simply occasional users. This is also the position of a host of other experts.

Those expert supporters of existing methods also argue that *even talking about* the defects in current laws give a cue to the young that they may defy them with impunity. Mixed signals on drugs are the road to chemical disaster for our children, they declare. Such verbal laxity allegedly destroyed the past social consensus against illegal drug use and thus caused the drug epidemic that commenced in the Sixties. This widely accepted position was forcefully stated on the television program that so upset Mr. Norley of Doylestown. The program had been the Cable News Network show "Crossfire," which featured two hosts: rock-ribbed conservative commentator and former Nixon speechwriter Patrick Buchanan ("on the right") and liberal Tom Braden ("on the left").

After I had talked about the failure of current laws and the need to relax some of them, Mr. Buchanan declared that my proposals sounded like, "We have lost the war on drugs. Let's surrender."

The other guest on the program, Jeffrey Harris, a former federal prosecutor and also until recently a high-ranking official in the Department of Justice and one of the architects of the Reagan drug war, then observed that he was appalled that a university teacher would tell students "that sort of line," and that they would thereby feel encouraged to try prohibited substances. Mr. Harris declared that my ideas and my reform proposals would result in my students becoming addicted and ending up "on a heating grate down near Constitution Avenue, being wards of the society."

Later, Mr. Buchanan joined in. "Arnold Trebach says 'throw in the towel.'" Mr. Harris added, "There are people in this country who refrain from using those drugs, who might otherwise be induced, simply because it is [now] against the law. Why do you think you had the explosion in cocaine? One of the reasons is because at fashionable Hollywood parties, you see cocaine use, and you hear of it, and you see pro football players, the role models in this community, condoning it. Now, if the government, in addition, were to condone it, you would have an explosion of use."

After the show was over, and we were all chatting in the studio, both Mr. Buchanan (who reentered the White House a few months later to become Mr. Reagan's director of communications) and Mr. Harris iterated their concern that I was misleading impressionable young people and that I was making them think it was perfectly fine to try any of these illegal drugs. Indeed, they implied that my ideas were a positive incitement to drug abuse. They reached me. As I walked out into the cold streets of Georgetown that night, I was troubled. Then the telegram came.

NED'S RESPONSE

To ease my concern arising from confrontations such as these, over the years I have asked my students individually and through anonymous questionnaires about the impact of free and open discussion of drug policy issues in my classes upon their own personal use of drugs. Their answers have taught me a great deal.

These courses are part of a curriculum I developed in the School of Justice at American University, entitled Drugs, Justice, and Public Policy. Like the school itself, the courses evolved out of a basic concern with controlling crime. Soon the inquiry broadened beyond crime and into many other aspects of the drug universe, with the major emphasis on thinking out better laws and public policies. Even though I frequently tell my students that I am not a treatment professional, inevitably a few of them in every class come to me for detailed and personal discussions on drugs. In some cases they are seeking advice, in other cases, giving it. This is especially true of the addicts. In almost every large class there seem to be one or two of them and they are always testing what I—an innocent in terms of actual drug use—say against the deep and painfully acquired knowledge of their own experience.

Ned, for example, who was a student of mine some time ago, is very much on my mind as I write this because he gave me a great deal of education in the process of learning from me. This young man is a perfect example of how stereotypes about drug abusers are distorted. Ned is white, comes from a good upper-class home, and has two fine parents. He is well-dressed, intelligent, decent, and a thoroughly nice fellow. I really like him. Yet he has been a serious drug abuser, starting at the age of thirteen. He has used heroin and such a wide variety of other drugs and narcotics that at times I am forced to ask him for the spelling of some of the chemicals he casually mentions. Ned was once arrested and brutally handled by the police of the District of Columbia just after he had made an illegal purchase of drugs on the street.

The young man has suffered other degrading experiences, including treatment in some of the most well-known psychiatric facilities for drug abusers in the nation's capital. His parents stood by him and saw to it that as he fought to become free of drugs he was provided with the most expert care that money could buy. Yet Ned is very bitter about his treatment at the hands of some of the doctors and staff in these famous and expensive facilities because he feels that these medical experts simply did not understand what he was going through. While some of the physicians and professional staff were truly helpful to him, many of them made him feel unworthy, as if he were a piece of social garbage. This demeaning attitude is not universal on the part of drug-abuse treatment staff—although it is quite common.

A psychiatrist once burst out to him, "How can you do this to your parents?" Ned later remarked, "The guy just didn't have the vaguest idea how I felt or what kind of help I needed or how to reach inside me to help me. This was typical of the lack of knowledge of many of these medical experts. They tried to convince me that I was evil or that I had a character disorder."

In my courses, Ned never heard me state that I knew the *proper* way of treating addicts. Rather, he heard me expound on many of the ideas in this book and in my previous one dealing with the history of narcotic addiction control in Britain and America. On balance, I said, the British approach was more accepting of the basic human decency of drug addicts and of the doctors who treated them, sometimes with the drug of their dependence. While I mentioned with approval some American doctors, most of my favorable examples came from Britain.

In part, the better situation in Britain comes about from the laws which allow doctors greater freedom in prescribing drugs for maintenance of addicts. In part, it comes from culturally ingrained habits of respect for people who are different.

One day, Ned heard me describe the work of British psychiatrist Dale Beckett, who has specialized in the treatment of heroin addicts. Beckett does not believe in the venerable notion of an addictive personality—a clinical concept accepted by many leading physicians—but he does believe that many of his addicts share certain personality or life-history characteristics. Typically, the addict was a male, who did not have a stable or positive relationship with a supportive father during his formative years. If the father was present, he tended to implant feelings of guilt and inferiority in his son, often without consciously meaning to do so. As the young man struggled through the uncertainty of adolescence, he felt incapable of dealing with that stress unsupported by some type of chemical relief. I then explained Beckett's filter theory—for many young people, marijuana acts as a filter to keep them away from harder drugs, rather than as a gateway to those more potent substances—and also the belief of this unconventional physician that heroin, while not without its dangers, is a relatively gentle drug, as compared to, say, alcohol and barbiturates. For those young people in psychic agony, then, the taking of heroin is, in a sense, a fairly rational form of self-medication.

While it may seem bizarre to call heroin gentle and heroin taking rational, Beckett's observation was that it seemed to do less harm to his patients than many other drugs. Moreover, for a desperate person who might well have sunk into a psychosis or committed suicide, there was a certain level of logic to treating oneself with that feared drug instead.

It is not important, at this point in my tale, whether one agrees with these theories or not. What *is* important here is that Ned walked into my office shortly after that class, revealed the secret of his past, and said, "I feel as if you have been talking about me. Finally, I feel that *someone* understands what I have been going through." It was then that he poured out his story, including the fact that he had eventually been treated with methadone and had been off all drugs, including the prescribed methadone, for the past 18 months. He hated methadone and said that it had, as another addict told a reporter recently, "tried his soul." Even though Ned had been hooked on heroin, and knew deeply just how powerful a chemical it was, compared to methadone he found it to be a gentle drug—the chemical did not cause him great physical or mental distress—and believed that had the American doctors been allowed to treat him with heroin, his detoxification would have been more rapid and his recovery less disturbed.

Ned was struggling terribly to regain some sense of his own worth, of a sense of normalcy, of how to do ordinary activities in an ordinary, upwardly mobile social situation. He was still in distress but he was functioning and he was making it, coming out the other end of the addiction tunnel.

Another day, he came into the office and said, "Taking this class is like a religious experience." To my derisive barnyard response, he persisted in his position, explaining that for the first time in his life, after going through years of treatment and counseling, he was stunned, happily so, that he could sit in a class which did not even claim to teach treatment methods and learn so much about what he had been suffering through for more than ten years. He felt for the first time in his young memory that he wasn't a total loser, that there were other people like him, that he was a decent person.

Near the end of that semester, he told me that just recently he had gone through some terribly depressing days, especially after visiting some of his friends from the past who were not straightening out their lives. He was tempted on those days, he said, to turn to his old reliable cure for depression. He did not. "Taking this class has helped me stay off heroin this semester," Ned stated flatly. Again, I protested that the classes were not designed as treatment nor did I claim any ability in that arena. Ned simply reiterated his position.

When I cross-examined him, Ned scoffed at the idea that the teaching of drug dynamics, history, law, and policy options could induce drug use, even though I sometimes advocated the use of heroin and other drugs in the treatment of addicts. He recognized that method as one choice among many in a comprehensive array of treatment options, all based on the humane notion that many addicts were decent people. Ned observed, "I think every heroin addict should take your courses and I believe that more of them would be helped to stay off drugs."

He then recalled another day when I had read from the British Rolleston Report of 1926 that in cases of heroin and morphine addiction, permanent cures were rare and relapse was the rule. Ned said, "I walked out to my car practically jumping up in the air and clicking my heels over that." I then related the story of the addict in England who had walked into my room using those same words as the opening lines to an embarrassed confession that he had indeed relapsed. Why, I asked, did those thoughts give Ned such comfort? After all, they talk about persistent relapses. Why did they not make him pessimistic?

At first, Ned looked at me a bit askance, as if to say, *you* are the professor who uttered those words in class; *you* should know what impact they might have on me. Ned then explained that they made him understand that he was not totally odd, that he had relapsed many times and so had many other people. He was not a monster, not a failure, not without hope. Indeed, he had a great deal of hope . . . now. That new hope, I suspect, was the product of several positive factors: Ned's growing maturity, the knowledge gained in drug-policy classes, and, while he sometimes downgraded it, the treatment he received from drug-abuse professionals. It is likely that the first factor was the most powerful.

SYLVIA'S RESPONSE

Like Ned, Sylvia had surprised me some months previously when she stated that the study of drug policy had been an important positive factor in helping her cope with a set of personal problems, including drug use. The dimensions of Sylvia's drug problems were small compared to Ned's, but they were real and frightening to her.

The drug she liked most was cocaine. "The intense feelings of pleasure and well-being that I experienced from cocaine were without equal," Sylvia explained. Until recent years, she always had been given the drugs by friends. Not too long ago, she herself bought two grams from a neighbor. "I used just over one gram, sharing it with friends, over the next year. It was great to keep me awake as I studied and wrote papers. . . . My grades were very high. I felt logically that if I used less than a gram of coke a year for studying and social occasions, and I did not experience a compulsion to use it, I should not have a drug problem," Sylvia said. (There are 28 grams in an ounce. Some heavy users snort a gram in an evening.)

Because by now she was a student of drug abuse, she knew that she would be considered a chipper, a nonaddicted user of addicting drugs. Teaching about chippers or mentioning them in the mass media or in books like this makes those who adhere to the dominant drug ideology uncomfortable. Promulgating the concept of controlled use of such dangerous drugs is seen by those who support the drug war as a form of seduction of the innocent, the equivalent of saying, hey kid, try this drug, it won't hurt you. Yet Sylvia had been, like the great majority of users, a cocaine chipper.

She also had been taking Valium. Sylvia had been using this prescribed, highly popular, and quite legal drug on rare occasions, especially during times of special stress in her ordinarily driven life. Then suddenly she got into severe financial difficulty. She increased her use of Valium to cope with her increased anxiety and deepening depression. It was about this time that she came to me in a state of near-collapse and told me the whole story, including her use of cocaine and Valium.

University teachers have two major routine responsibilities to their students. They must, first, show up regularly at classes and provide objective scholarly information. They must, second, appear regularly at their offices for what are known as counseling hours. During those hours, and often at other times, it is expected that students will ask advice on a wide variety of topics, both academic and personal, and that the professors will respond as best they can. When Sylvia came to me, I was functioning both as an objective scholar and as a counselor. My two roles overlapped because the topic of discussion fit into both.

My first bit of advice to her was that in her distraught state, she simply had to start seeing a mental health professional regularly. I cautioned her that I had no qualifications to provide treatment. She responded that she was seeing a psychiatrist already who was quite helpful. However, she felt she wanted to talk to me about her personal approach to drugs against the backdrop of all the information about chemicals and altered states of consciousness she had been studying in my classes.

I told her that at that point the greatest problem I saw was her almost total loss of self-esteem due to her financial crisis. In my opinion, that damaged ego could, if not repaired, lead her on to some very serious difficulties with the drugs. I urged her to work with her psychiatrist on recognizing deep down that financial reverses do not really convert a winner into a loser, that even the best of us strike out now and then, and that she was still decent and good.

Because cocaine was not vital to her but could become a major and possibly destructive crutch at this time of crisis, I asked if she believed she could give it up totally. When Sylvia said she believed she could stop, I then asked her simply to stop using it. Don't laugh. She did. Not only did she stop, Sylvia also gave away her last full gram to a surprised but appreciative friend, who was already a user.

By this stage, however, Sylvia was taking up to 60 milligrams of Valium per day, which worried me greatly. Yet the medicine was helping her cope with enormous anxiety and depression. Even though it seemed possible that she was developing a dependency on the drug, I suggested that it would be a bad idea to stop suddenly. Rather, it seemed to me, she had to accomplish two goals before she attempted to reduce the dosage. She had to build up her self-esteem so that she felt like a decent person again, and also she had to obtain a deeper understanding of the dynamics through which the Valium had come to play a major role in her life.

Sylvia listened to my concerns about the regular use of Valium but originally was unimpressed. She was taking the "medicine" on the advice of a doctor through a prescription and it did not fit into the same category of a "drug" like, say, cocaine. In her mind, Sylvia equated Valium "with milk and my arthritis medicine—a staple of life." Thus she was quite comfortable taking my advice to continue it but not at heeding my concerns about coming to grips with its role in her life. (Remember, again, that Sylvia came to me and sought my advice, which I gave replete with humble reservations that I did not view myself as a treatment expert.)

During one of the classes that semester, we happened to study Andrew Weil's *Chocolate to Morphine*. Like his earlier books on drugs, this one dealt not only with pharmacology but also with the more important concepts and ideas about the interaction between human beings and chemicals. One of the most powerful of those ideas was: *"Any drug can be used successfully, no matter how bad its reputation, and any drug can be abused, no matter how accepted it is*. There are no good or bad drugs; there are only good and bad relationships with drugs."

Upon hearing such a revolutionary proposition from a medical doctor, a student might take a policy lesson from it—namely, that if true, it destroys any honest rational basis for most American drug-control strategies during this century. A student might also take a personal lesson from it: this Harvard-trained doctor just gave me permission to play around with any drug I want. Whoopee! However, Sylvia took a personal lesson of exactly the type that Weil intended: it suddenly dawned on her during one of the classes that she had a bad relationship with Valium. To come to grips with her use of Valium, in addition to her weekly visits to the psychiatrist, she started attending local meetings of Alcoholics Anonymous and Narcotics Anonymous.

When Sylvia told her story at one of her first meetings, "The entire room seemed to turn on me! I was told that I was an alcoholic because Valium was cross-addictive with alcohol (a conclusion I continue to take issue with), that the Valium had been what permitted me to stop my infrequent cocaine use, and that I should commit myself to a detox center to withdraw from Valium." Sylvia declared that under no circumstances would she enter an institution. However, she did accept the need to ask her psychiatrist to assist her in setting up a detoxification schedule for the Valium. She was becoming more determined to stop using the drug and she also felt better about herself. While she refused to accept most of the NA-AA philosophy, especially the idea that she was diseased because she had a problem with a drug, she did find the concern of the members helpful—that and the serene principle that a higher power had a hand in her life.

Over a period of a month, Sylvia worked her Valium down to

five milligrams per day. Near the end of the month, she told me that she was going to go off totally the next day and thanked me for my help. Again, I was surprised because she had not informed me about her reduction in use. Sylvia said after she had stopped Valium totally, "I find a small calmness is growing in a spot that has been functioning only on feelings of panic and fear. Although nothing in my life has changed dramatically, I am a lot more at peace with myself and the world around me." It is significant that the ideas of Andrew Weil, who does not fight the responsible use of drugs and is therefore reviled by the drug-free youth zealots, provided major support for Sylvia in her struggle to become drug-free.

Recently, Sylvia wrote, "My friends and classmates . . . seem to have found new patterns, mostly healthy, in dealing with their drug use . . . whether it is alcohol, cigarettes, or dope. Once the mystique is unwrapped from the entire drug area, the compulsion to use drugs to enhance life can be viewed dispassionately, and constructive alternative behaviors can be evaluated and accepted. There is something very right about approaching drugs with un-biased information as to the dangers or even the lack of danger of each class of drugs and method of administration. Young people today do not seem to reject drugs merely because they are against the law. However, we do frequently seek to alter our consciousness."

My reporting of what Sylvia said and much else in this chapter is quite immodest—for which I hope I will be mercifully forgiven in light of the need to answer the charges so often made about the dangers of an open approach to drug-policy research and education. Moreover, I hasten to point out, at the risk of being redundant, that my function as a scholar, a teacher, and a writer is not to create drug-free students or citizens but to be honest and comprehensive. I continue to be surprised that so many of my students and listeners have used the information I have provided as the basis for reducing their intake of drugs. I assure everyone who will listen that I am only barely aware of the dynamics at work that have created that happy result. However, this positive, though unplanned, experience has convinced me that the venerable democratic ideals about freedom of information apply also to drugs—and that only by telling the whole truth about them in all education programs and in governmental statements to the general public will we ever achieve balanced and civilized methods of living with the unavoidable presence of drugs in society.

RESPONSE OF AN ENTIRE CLASS

Some of my students have been strengthened in their determination to continue the use of drugs after taking my courses. One wrote on an anonymous questionnaire which I distributed to an entire class several years ago, "I am a good student and I work hard. But I do take a lot of drugs—always have. I started using drugs five-six years ago. All through high school I was on the honor roll, and my grade-point average is still very high. This class has taken away a lot of my worries that I'm abnormal or that it is going to catch up with me. Coincidentally, this school year I have been cutting down on my use of narcotics—but this was not a conscious effort. This class has made me feel better about myself, and I am more aware of what problem drug [use] is."

I have no idea who this student is but I would want him or her to be aware that I am concerned that a significant point might have been missed. There is always the danger that any psychoactive drug can indeed "catch up" with a user, especially one who persists in taking the substance regularly.

However, it should be added that one of the responses of this anonymous student was that the information presented in the class had no effect on the actual extent of his or her drug use. In this response, the student fit within the parameters of the majority profile of the students I surveyed that semester. Out of 112 students, 71 returned completed questionnaires. Of those 71 students (mainly undergraduates in their late teens and early twenties), 85.9 percent checked that "no effect" answer.

Only 2.8 percent, two students, said it worked so as to increase their use. Neither of those two explained the dynamics of that increase. It was not at all clear, moreover, that either had actually increased their own drug use but apparently both feared that the information might have that effect on others.

Typical of the comments of the great majority was this observation: "I don't believe for one second that anyone could say they increased drug use as a result of this class. It's a ludicrous assumption that just because you learn something you go out and do it." Another wrote, "Open and honest discussion does not lead to greater drug abuse, but rather demystifies the topic and thus removes one of its greatest appeals." This last was in response to the question as to whether or not such information should be presented in high schools. Like this student, the majority believed high school classes should adopt this open content, rather than use the scare tactics most of these college students faced back when they were in high school drug courses. Another responded, "As with sex education—teaching and understanding are one's own best protection. You must know the facts to make decisions and this [high school] is the time decisions are made."

One student wrote that such classes should be presented in high school, "because high school students (and junior high students) make their decisions based on what they learn from their friends, and their own ignorant perceptions of society and the world. For these kids to make the right decision, they need knowledge and access to counseling or books. Most important, kids should be told they do not need to feel guilty if they don't take drugs, *and* they shouldn't feel proud if they do take drugs (and believe me high school kids are *damned* proud of their drugs), and of course they shouldn't feel guilty if they experiment with drugs."

The responses to the question asking whether other students in the class appeared to have increased or decreased their drug use were almost uniformly "no effect." One added: "Although I do not think that many people's existing habits were changed, I feel that the course had a preventive quality. People are comfortable with their old habits and have rationalized them over and over. However, at least I will rethink my participation in drug use and I doubt that I will take on any new habits. They're not worth it!"

Eight students, 11.3 percent of those responding, reported that they decreased drug use as a result of taking my courses. One of those explained, "In these classes real objective knowledge is given, not harmful lies that students spot a mile away. . . . It leads us to define what is a drug problem and what is not. I cut down when I became objective." Another of these students was moved to make an even more dramatic personal response. He explained that the information had the effect of reducing his drug use "100 percent," and added, "Every student should be privy to this type of information. It could be the difference between life and *DEATH!* It made me realize that even if a drug is legal, it can be harmful and that abstinence is the best policy."

While the reaction of this student may seem extreme, it *is* one possible type of response that may be evoked by an objective, nonhysterical presentation of the known facts about drugs. When I tell my classes that the dangers of the illegal drugs are exaggerated, I nevertheless relate all the dangers that *are* known, including that of potential addiction. When I explain that the legal drugs are greater killers than the illegal drugs, I balance that statement with a full recitation of the dangers of both legal and illegal chemicals. While these facts argue against current drug laws and wars—and against wholesale invasions of traditional rights to save the nation from a mythical destruction by illegal drugs—they do not argue for an untroubled snort of cocaine with a teenager's morning Wheaties. Since I believe, and teach, that all drugs carry many dangers, one sensible reaction is to conclude, as did this student, that a life free of all illicit and licit mind-altering chemicals is the only way to go. Few students reach such a conclusion, but those of my students who do have come to that position on the basis of a balanced appraisal of the facts and not because of propaganda.

On the whole, it is difficult to find evidence that these youngsters, generally from middle-class or affluent backgrounds, many with ample funds to spend on luxuries, were corrupted by association with a professor who severely criticized dominant drug ideologies and policies.

THE ALASKAN EXPERIMENT

It is even more difficult to find reliable evidence to support the current dominant position about the potential impact of a relaxation of the drug laws upon the number of users and abusers. Certainly, drug laws must have some impact on behavior. It is possible, moreover, that the full legalization of such drugs as, say, marijuana and cocaine might well reduce the price, increase availability, and result in a rise in use—and abuse.

On the other hand, as Sylvia pointed out, drug laws do not greatly affect the drug-taking behavior of many young people. There is an almost perverse quality to the impact of drug laws.

The fact that a drug is illegal increases its allure because many young people are seeking symbols with which to outrage conventional society. Legalization may reduce the defiance value of the drug.

During the Seventies, there were two important experiments with various forms of what might be called legalization of marijuana. While neither involved total withdrawal of criminal penalties, both went beyond the decriminalization (penalties for personal possession reduced to fines as for traffic tickets) which was implemented in eleven American states in the same decade. One experiment took place in Alaska, the other in Holland.

The Alaska experiment was not designed as such. It grew out of the prosecution of an adult for possession of marijuana. In 1975 the Court of Appeals of the state of Alaska, the highest court ruling over one of the last American frontiers, stated in the *Ravin* case that marijuana did not constitute a public health problem except in the case of persons driving under its influence. To reach that unconventional official conclusion, the justices did their homework and reviewed virtually the entire body of conflicting research on the subject, much of it mentioned in this book. While they did not decide that marijuana was harmless, nor did they condone its use, the justices agreed with those authorities who saw it as one of the least harmful drugs human beings use, which is, of course, my position. Accordingly, the court held that the right of privacy in the state constitution invalidated those laws that prohibit possession of marijuana in the home for personal use. Thus, Alaska became the only state in the union and one of the few places in the world where possession for personal use was almost totally legal, not simply decriminalized. (Sales of marijuana and possession of large amounts remained illegal.)

Another citizen attempted to convince the court to apply the *Ravin* ruling to cocaine possession in the privacy of the home. The Alaska high court refused to do so in the *Erickson* case of 1978 because it saw a much greater public health threat from cocaine. The court, however, took that occasion to observe that on the basis of its review of scientific information, cocaine was probably less dangerous to society than alcohol!

The massive harm caused by alcohol had been well-documented in official studies in Alaska. Accordingly, a local-option law was enacted in 1980. A citizen, who also happened to be a state trooper, was convicted of violating that law which had been adopted in the small village of St. Mary's prohibiting possession of alcohol. The convicted man, Hugh Harrison, appealed, using the principles of the 1975 decision on marijuana. While the high court had held that the evidence on marijuana had demonstrated that it was "a relatively harmless drug," the vast body of data presented in this case had clearly "established a correlation between alcohol consumption and poor health, death, family violence, child abuse and crime." Accordingly, the Court of Appeals ruled in *Harrison* v. *State* on August 31, 1984, that the overall public danger of alcohol was so much greater than that of marijuana that it upheld the Alaska local-option law on alcohol prohibition but left undisturbed the constitutional protection on the right to personal possession of marijuana in the home.

Drug and alcohol use, for a wide variety of reasons, has always been higher in Alaska than in the rest of the country. Yet according to Dr. Bernard Segal, director of the Center for Alcohol and Addiction Studies at the University of Alaska, there is no conclusive proof that legalization affected use, since there was no good evidence about the extent of use before 1975. There do seem grounds to suggest that Alaskan youth are using less compulsively than those in the lower forty-eight.

One of Dr. Segal's studies found that approximately 4 percent of Alaskan students used marijuana every day in 1982. National surveys showed that 6.3 percent of all American high school seniors used it daily that year. Thus, Alaskan children who can often literally reach out and touch marijuana in the home, where its possession is legal, have not, as a group, become destroyed by its presence.

THE DUTCH EXPERIMENT

The Dutch actually set out to attempt a courageous experiment in drug-policy reform. I was able to observe it myself during July 1977 and again in September 1986. My last visit was particularly dramatic because I left my own country during the scared summer of 1986 and went to another that seemed as if it were in some distant, more peaceful galaxy. The Dutch have not solved their drug problems but they have gone further in rational control than any nation of which I am aware. They have consciously adopted a series of peaceful compromises and have rejected the idea of a war on drugs.

During the early Seventies, they commenced seemingly risky reforms that were based upon a view of drug use quite different from that held in America and most European countries. The Dutch saw marijuana "as a stepping-stone to hard drugs" but not, according to Frits Rüter, Director of the Institute of Criminal Law at the University of Amsterdam, because of the qualities of the drug itself. Rather, Professor Rüter explained, it was because the law forced marijuana "into the criminal sphere in common with hard drugs and . . . it was sold in the same place and frequently by the same dealers." Through changes in the substantive law and detailed written guidelines for police and prosecutors, the Dutch set about to break that connection. The legal reforms reduced penalties for simple possession of pot and increased them for large-scale dealing. Yet possession and small sales of marijuana still remained, technically speaking, illegal. It was the sophisticated use of police and prosecutorial discretion that made the difference.

Indeed, these experiments could not have worked without the strong support of enforcement officials. It was disorienting for me, after talking to so many American police, to be sought out by police leaders at an Amsterdam conference in September 1986 and to be told how much they believed in the use of discretion in allowing possession and small sales of marijuana—while vigorously pursuing organized crime figures and large traffickers who were involved in the trade of any drug, including marijuana. Such was the outspoken position expressed to me by, for example, two of the highest police executives in the Netherlands: W.F.K.J.F. Frackers, Inspector-General, Dutch National Police, and G. F. de Gooyer, the head of the National Criminal Intelligence Service. Both saw themselves as committed police leaders who could be more effective by taking a calm, flexible approach to the drug problem, which had to commence with distinguishing between marijuana and harder drugs. Both resented the attitude of the police of other nations, including those from the American DEA, who saw them as soft on drugs. They were not soft, they told me; they were smart. I agree with them.

I have seen with my own eyes how "house dealers" in youth clubs are allowed to sell marijuana and hashish and also how coffee shops all over Dutch cities sell these products right off the menu. The symbol of a marijuana plant on a sign tells the public that the products are for sale inside. The key is moderation and control, not prohibition and repression. I saw a coffeehouse with a marijuana plant painted on its sign within sight of the Ministry of Justice building in The Hague, the seat of government for the country. Any youth can walk in at any time and make a purchase under the eyes of the police. At the same time, I saw that the coffee shops were usually half empty and the youth centers were busy mainly on weekends. One American told me that he lived in Holland for six months near both a school with teenaged students and a coffeehouse that sold marijuana. He never saw a single student in the coffeehouse during school hours.

While Dutch criminal-justice and drug-abuse experts are independent characters and openly disagree on many things, there is almost universal agreement among them—including police leaders—that they have largely solved the marijuana problem. Their optimism and my personal observations from wandering the streets and coffeehouses of Dutch cities are supported by objective survey research. The use of marijuana by Dutch youth has dropped since the Seventies. Today, it seems to be substantially less than in those countries—especially West Germany, Norway, and the United States—that have undertaken a campaign to castigate the Dutch with the objective of forcibly enlisting them in the war on drugs.

Although the statistics are by no means precisely comparable, those collections of data that are available suggest dramatic contrasts. For example, NIDA reports for 1983 stated that 5.5 percent of American high school seniors interviewed said that they used pot daily. In 1985 the prestigious Foundation for the Scientific Study of Alcohol and Drug Use, located in Amsterdam, released a study of use throughout the country. A total of 1,306 residents between the ages of 15 and 24 were interviewed in 1983, with the great majority in the 15–19 age category. Seven youngsters replied that they used pot or hashish daily—one-half of one percent of the 1,306 young people who had full access to these drugs without fear of legal sanction. This rate was less than 10 percent of the rate for the United States where marijuana remains illegal and where the government is waging a war against use of the drug, especially by youth.

I do not know if that low comparative rate would be supported precisely by other studies today. I do know that the youth of the Netherlands have not been harmed by one of the most tolerant drug policies of any country in the world.

Dutch seem to have created a good model for the ...ve not gone to war on drugs and have been tolerant ...lave used them. They took away from youth the ... of marijuana as a symbol of defiance. Most important, ...ether they planned to or not, they succeeded in making pot a boring subject to most of the youth of the country.

FORMAL DRUG-EDUCATION COURSES

When the inquiry moves on to the impact of traditional drug-abuse education, we must all prepare ourselves for a disappointment. My courses, remember, do not fit into that category because I am not *attempting* to affect personal behavior but to provide a broad, objective education in an area of study, as would a teacher of history, government, or chemistry. It would seem logical that after decades of preventive drug education in the public schools, and more recently in the armed services, we would have some concrete ideas of the impact of such education, now a cornerstone of White House drug-control strategy. Yet the evaluations indicate no clear pattern in the impact of this vast array of courses upon students.

Scores of evaluation studies of hundreds and hundreds of educational programs in recent years have come up, in a sense, primarily empty. There is little evidence that the great majority of the courses had any significant impact on behavior or attitudes regarding drugs for most of the involved students. It is not that the findings were negative, but rather that they simply have been inconclusive. This means that after spending hundreds of millions of dollars we have not the vaguest idea if all of the effort in drug-abuse education is doing anything at all, save taking up time, making work for teachers and students, and making parents feel better because their children, they hope, have in some manner been inoculated against drug abuse.

There are a few exceptions to this pessimistic conclusion, all based upon telling children facts which are true and which ring true to them. In 1984, the Rand Corporation reported on a series of educational programs that apparently cut the number of cigarette smokers significantly in the groups studied. The programs provided "methods for resisting pressures to smoke: how to 'say no' gracefully. The reasons for wanting to 'say no' are illustrated by the short-term effects of smoking, such as bad breath, discolored teeth, and increased carbon monoxide in the blood, rather than by long-term health effects that tend to seem uncertain and far in the future to most young people." The authors of the Rand report concluded that such honest programs could be applied to education aimed at curbing the use of illicit drugs.

Other evaluation studies have reached the conclusion that good preventive drug-abuse education results not in the nirvana of abstinence but in the oft-despised reality of controlled use. One study covered three groups of grade-school students, two given different types of drug education, and the third, the control group, no drug education at all. Over a period of two years, the researchers found that both of the drug-education groups had increased their drug use as compared to the control group. In reporting on this in 1983, psychologist-pharmacologist Dr. Oakley Ray (a Vanderbilt University professor; chief, Mental Health and Behavioral Sciences Unit, Nashville Veterans Administration Hospital; author of one of the best-selling textbooks in the field) stated, "Drug education increased drug use. In contrast to that, students in the two drug programs were *less likely* to show extreme increases in the amount and type of drug use compared to the control group.

"To put it another way, when control-group students did increase their drug use, they were more irresponsible in their use. . . . If you give information about drugs, drug use will increase— but it will probably be safer drug use." Dr. Ray concluded, "Abstinence rarely succeeds, rehabilitation is at best marginally effective. The only choice is to teach safe drug use as well as alternatives to drug use."

Another expert who believes in the reality of controlled drug use is Norman Zinberg, perhaps the leading research specialist on that topic. He is director of psychiatric training, Cambridge Hospital, Harvard Medical School; author of the pre-eminent study on controlled drug use, *Drug, Set, and Setting* (1984); and, as it happens, the academic mentor and friend of his former student Andrew Weil. For a period of time, Dr. Zinberg's ideas on the need for detailed research to better understand the nature and the dynamics of controlled use were accepted by some policymakers. Even leading White House and cabinet officials for a brief time, while President Carter was in office, acknowledged in a major report that it was "not particularly distressing" that adolescents would experiment with drugs—and recommended that education and prevention efforts be "primarily focused on moderating the effects of drug taking."

However, unpredictable swings in style and political considerations prevail. Today, controlled use is out of style in Washington and the words have been virtually censored out of official policy statements, except to condemn the idea. President Reagan's *1984 National Strategy for Prevention of Drug Abuse and Drug Trafficking* declared that certain terms indirectly promoted drug use and henceforth their utterance would be discouraged. Included were "responsible use" and "recreational use" of drugs and alcohol. The President stated definitively, "Research tells us . . . that the phrase 'responsible use' does not apply to drug experimentation by America's youth. And so far as the 'recreational use' of drugs is concerned, I've never in my life heard a more self-serving euphemism by those who support drug use. There is nothing recreational about those children whose lives have been lost, whose minds have been ruined."

Such chilling attempts at thought control by the official priests of chemical orthodoxy were pushed to new extremes by President Reagan's organized crime commission in 1986 when it made this sweeping recommendation: "No federal, state, or local government funds should go directly or indirectly to programs that counsel 'responsible' drug use or condone illicit drug use in any way. Laws in certain States which 'decriminalized' the possession of marijuana constitute a form of such condonation, and should be reconsidered."

The emotional conflict of views on this one subject illustrates why we as a nation have such enormous difficulty in formulating effective national policies about drugs, including what we should teach our school students as well as what we should tell adults. There simply is no agreement among the leading experts about many of the most elemental facts. It is almost as if the law of gravity was periodically declared null and void by a new presidential science adviser who hated to see fruit fall from apple trees— and as if many of the leading physicists in the country hastened to agree with him and to apply for governmental research grants to prove the repeal scientifically justified.

In light of this factual disarray and disorder, what should responsible teachers tell students about responsible use? What about at least one hundred other points on which there is similar fundamental disagreement? The resolution of the conflicts should affect both the style of teaching and the substance of what is taught. My solution is to tell all sides of the conflicting professional disagreements, along with my own interpretation, and to let the students decide where they stand personally. However, in virtually all school drug-abuse education programs, the kids are told prophylactic lies: any use of these illegal drugs will harm you terribly. Often, they tune out the entire lesson, including a factual discussion of real dangers.

RESPONSE OF ONE ADULT STUDENT

There is another dimension to this discussion: the impact of a balanced and open review of all of the known facts, without censorship, not simply on the drug-taking behavior of our youth but also of our adults. I humbly offer myself as a brief case study on this important matter.

To start with, I was like Ned and Sylvia in that I was surprised that the study of an academic subject had so much influence on my personal life. I was not at all prepared for that internal result.

In the early Seventies, when I started to ingest drug knowledge, like many American male professionals, I smoked cigars, drank Scotch and Irish whisky, and consumed great quantities of coffee. It never occurred to me that my tame use of legal substances could in any way be connected to my studies of national policy regarding the control of such chemicals as heroin, cocaine, and marijuana—and of the enormous crime problems associated with them. As it happened, I never had any interest in the illegal drugs. To be polite to a friend once, I took two or three drags on a joint of marijuana, with boring results. My involvement with drugs remained focused on those that were legal. Periodically, I would seek to kick the tobacco habit but without success, and also, I suspect, without any firm commitment to stop.

Then a series of events over a period of four or five years helped me develop a deeper understanding of the nature of drug dependence and the dynamics of how human beings relate to drugs. One day, for example, a part-time graduate student, who was also a full-time probation officer, brought one of his probationers into the seminar as a guest speaker. The guest, a recovering heroin addict, asked me if I minded if he lit a cigarette. The probation officer interjected, "Don't worry. The professor is probably going to light a big cigar, as he usually does."

I declared proudly, "The joke's on you! Since last week, I have quit. It was rough, but I have gone and done it!" Then, embarrassed, I said to our guest, "Forgive me. Here I am bragging, and yet complaining about how tough it was to quit tobacco . . . and you have kicked heroin. I'm really sorry."

The addict replied, "That's okay. Don't apologize. I have beaten heroin, but I haven't been able to beat these damn things."

I had read that for many people tobacco was a more powerful addiction than heroin but I had never heard anyone, face to face, say that this was the case, sitting there, looking dolefully at a cigarette he had just lit. As we talked during that meeting of the seminar on drug policy, he compared the way in which heroin hooked onto you and the way in which tobacco did. "Heroin and tobacco. They work the same," he assured us. I had heard such ideas. Now, I started to believe them.

Those hard-won insights provided both great intellectual excitement and intense personal discomfort. It was good to start to understand a subject of research deeply. It was distinctly discomforting to think that my habit of enjoying a quite legal and respectable, even dignified and manly, wonderfully odorous Brazilian Mandarim Pai six to eight times a day, day in and day out, could in any way be compared to the illegal activities of a street junkie. My habit and his, I discovered, were more alike than different.

Patience and maturity were important in trying to overcome my habit. So also was the lesson that Ned learned about heroin—relapse was part of the process. Indeed, Ned has recently impressed upon me that as he reflects back on it, his relapses were not so much failures as vital parts of the dynamics of growth. Without the periodic relapses, without the occasional balm of his drug, he might have been in much worse shape, and the process of change would have been impossible. That is not conventional expert opinion, but it makes sense to me. And it describes what happened to me. Soon after my braggart's speech in the seminar, I was back on my Mandarim Pais, every day.

For years, my dentist, Jesse Caden, had been warning me that cigar smoking, while not as dangerous as cigarette smoking, carried enormous risks of mouth, tongue, and throat cancer. After a period of years, he started to tell me that he was concerned about the condition of my mouth. At about the time that I was increasing my involvement in the study of drug policy, Dr. Caden was becoming more and more ominous with his warnings. During one visit, he told me that in his opinion some of the tissues in my mouth were precancerous, a phrase I had never heard before that moment. It meant, he explained, that the tissues were on the verge of developing cancer. That worried me but, like most tobacco addicts, not enough to stop me.

Along with knowledge of drug-human dynamics and relationships, I was gaining an understanding of the superiority of natural methods to control emotions and consciousness. I started to appreciate the immense optimism which lies at the base of that understanding. If it is seen that drugs are only triggers to changed emotions and different levels of consciousness, then the real power is not in the chemicals but in the mind and body of each individual human being. Naturally induced changes are more difficult to create which is why many people resort to the quicker action of drugs, that is, quicker for the inexperienced or immature person. Once a person builds only a few, rudimentary pathways into the subconscious mind, however, a hint of the power lurking there is unlocked.

I started to believe that my happiness or unhappiness, my sense of ease or unease, depended less on external forces than on my maturing sense of self-control or self-power. That sense of personal power was severely tested when I saw my first wife through almost a year when she was dying of breast cancer. All through that year of agony, which mercifully ended on October 7, 1976, I smoked many cigars, but kept thinking of quitting. During that period, my wife would often urge me to stop the habit, and I never smoked in her hospital room or near her bed at home. My determination to quit was growing, but I kept on smoking.

Later in another seminar meeting, I was about to light up my usual cigar at the beginning of class. One of my students, Barbara Giniger, a young lady who looked as if she was about to get slightly green about the gills at the prospect of yet another session under a cloud of cigar smoke, asked sweetly, "Do you *have* to?" It was a courageous action. One does not lightly come between an addict and his fix. The gentleness and, at the same time, the directness of the question had its impact and hit home in my growing sense of power over my habit. I said, "Of course, I don't *have* to." And for the first time in memory, I waited several hours for my next fix and did not become terribly uncomfortable. Uncomfortable, but not terribly.

Months later, I was talking to another lady in a social situation. We were having a glass of wine together and I was enjoying myself. I started to unwrap a cigar and asked, "Do you mind if I smoke this?" She actually replied, "Not if you *have* to." This time, I became slightly defiant. After all, this was a social setting. I was not imposing my smoke on students, who could not complain too vigorously. I lit up and blew the smoke about the room. It was a great cigar. I remember it well. Tobacco is a wonderful drug. If it was not, 56 million Americans would not smoke it every day. Those people, approximately one-fourth of our entire population, are not crazy—only addicted.

As I smoked we talked. I observed that one of these days I wanted to give these things up, to stop completely. She, an experienced administrator of an alcoholism treatment center, replied: "I can give you the same advice we give alcoholics. You will quit when it is more important to you to stop smoking than it is to continue smoking."

My response was, "You have reached me. This may be my last cigar." I finished it and it was, at approximately 2:00 P.M., February 27, 1977. I have not had a puff of tobacco smoke since that moment. I still consider myself a tobacco addict albeit a nonusing one. I have internalized the lesson from Weil about bad relationships with drugs. My bad relationship is with tobacco and I now realize that the only way in which I can control that drug, in which *I* can be in charge and not a chemical, is never to use it. I cannot be a tobacco chipper, which I would dearly love to be.

My victory was the result of a long series of events, insights, and forces. All of them were brought to bear in a voluntary, tolerant fashion. Had the government demanded that I give up my harmful habit, the most destructive, I suspect, on the face of the earth, it would have had a fight on its hands, even if it had threatened arrest and imprisonment. I quit when I was ready and able, not when a police officer, a judge, or a doctor ordered me to do so.

With tobacco gone, I increased my exercise. Five-mile runs through the hills of Rock Creek Park became within my lung and aerobic capacity, easily so, if I may brag a bit more. Hard whiskey seemed inconsistent with regular exercise. Because I felt in control of alcohol, though, I kept using other forms, especially white wine. My caffeine consumption, however, has not changed dramatically.

My ability to concentrate became much greater. For the first time in many years, I wrote a new book, then many articles, and now the book you have in your hands.

In 1979, I married the lady who gave me that crucial bit of advice on making choices. There is much happiness all around me.

My unplanned insights were not the only factors in producing all of these positive results but they were powerfully important forces. Even had I gone in for other drugs, that is, drugs other than tobacco, I believe that those insights would have helped me create patterns of controlled use as I now do with alcohol.

I now believe more than ever that if our governmental and social leaders were to provide a wide array of honest information about drugs and consciousness, and if they then combined that often-conflicting information with a more tolerant law-enforcement policy, millions of our people would be helped to make similar positive improvements in their own lives. So to those who believe that we corrupt our youth, or our adults, by telling them the whole range of "truths" about drugs, my self-education of the last 14 years would say, no, they are very wrong. A free society *is* corrupted when national leaders make major policy decisions on the basis of a rigid refusal to consider the full spectrum of scientific and public opinion about an issue that so directly affects the personal lives of its citizens.

PART TWO

The Warriors

We, as parents of all nations, must say to our local law-enforcement officer, "If my child, my loved one, or my friend breaks the law by using illicit drugs, please arrest him or her."

—DR. THOMAS GLEATON, National Parents' Resource Institute for Drug Education (PRIDE)

Those people are operating up there in their own little Valhalla wilderness thinking everything is beautiful, knowing they got away with it, but we will see what happens next year.

—WILLIAM RUZZAMENTI, California Campaign Against Marijuana Planting

You have a choice: you give up your drugs, or you seek employment elsewhere. And one of the ways to do it [screen out drug users] is a urinalysis.

—DR. CARLTON TURNER, The White House

Neither the law of the land nor the law of nature supports the notion that petty government officials can require people to excrete on command.

—JUSTICE WILLIAM BRENNAN, The Supreme Court

5

The First Lady's Crusade for Drug-Free Youth

LIFE has been a light shining from your soul," sang the handsome, bright-faced young man in the sweatshirt emblazoned "America's Pride," as he looked into the First Lady's eyes. Steve Courtney, 17, of Overland Park, Kansas, handed Nancy Reagan a single red rose. She returned his gaze and wiped away tears. The sincerity of her commitment to this cause shone in her face and in her words, as she told the 2,000 youths and adults in the audience, her voice choked with emotion, "We depend on you. We need people who are clear-eyed, clear-minded. . . . I'm so proud of you and I love you." Someone in the audience shouted, "We love you, too!" Others joined in with thunderous applause and "We love you, Nancy!" Behind her on the stage, the first ladies of 15 other nations beamed and glowed in the warmth of this impressively emotional moment. The whole scene created an unforgettable image of the powerful impact of the crusade of America's First Lady on her country's youth—and potentially, now, on the youth of other countries.

AMIDST THE ARMY OF
ANGRY PARENTS

In order to understand the nature of this unquestionably worthwhile effort—for every decent person must certainly be in favor
of the ideal of drug-free youth—it would be instructive to look at
the content of the occasion where Steve Courtney gave Nancy
Reagan that red rose. It was April 25, 1985, at the International
Conference on Drugs, presented by the National Parents' Resource
Institute for Drug Education, Inc. (PRIDE), in the Grand Ballroom
of the Georgia World Congress Center in Atlanta. The speakers
and their ideas provide revealing insights into the parents' movement for drug-free youth, the international crusade which the
American First Lady has joined and now leads and through which
she has captured the imagination and good wishes of much of the
civilized world. I had come to Atlanta to witness personally this
crusade in action.

Later, that evening on the same stage the image I saw just a
few feet in front of me was that of Captain Kirk of *Star Trek*
booming out inspirational leadership messages from the bridge of
the Starship Enterprise. The reality was actor William Shatner,
proclaiming, "We have just begun to fight!" He ended his talk with
this pledge: "I want you to know that I will fight with you all the
way!" Mr. Shatner had been appointed the official spokesperson
for PRIDE during the year ahead and he had just started doing
his job.

When Captain Kirk and the First Lady both speak emotionally
in support of a cause, especially a good cause, my inclination is to
want to believe them. All of the events in that impressive modern
building were presented so well, moreover, that the dramatic staging served on its own to virtually assure agreement by all members
of the audience, including me. I felt like the Grinch who stole
Christmas when I resisted that seductive atmosphere of total ad-
ulation by forcing myself to adopt an attitude of detachment.

And yet, viewed objectively, Mr. Shatner's major message was
one of the leading prophylactic lies of the dominant youth-control
cultists: it is impossible for any youth to use any drug without the
near certainty of serious, even fatal, harm in virtually each and
every case. "I am happy to join you in declaring there is no such

thing as responsible drug use!" As the state-of-the-art electronic
speakers bathed us all in that message, there were cheers of emotional approval. "Responsible drug use is an attack on the health
of the youth of the country by the illegal drug industry," which is
"an international conglomerate with enormous resources." Then,
he declared, "We are no longer willing to let the illegal drug industry provide information to our children."

Such themes dominated the conference. It was a fight between
good and evil, and evil was represented by the criminal drug culture spawned in the Sixties and now perpetuated by a powerful
global conspiracy which seduced youth by minimizing the dangers
of drugs so it could grow rich by selling illegal chemicals to un-
suspecting victims. The drug lobby, and its allies, had to be fought
without quarter in order to save America's children, who could not
be expected to resist the blandishments of the drug merchants on
their own. Individual families and parents, moreover, were also
powerless on their own to educate their children about drugs or
to simply set rules and enforce them, without support from a network of parents—and from the agents of the criminal law.

Before the drug issue became an obsession of almost all of the
national press and media, perhaps the most prominent voice in the
field of drug reporting had been the *Reader's Digest*, which hails
itself as "the world's most read magazine." The leading marijuana-
scare writer for the general public, Peggy Mann, credits Dan
O'Keefe, the "brilliant senior staff editor" of that magazine, as the
person who "first awakened my interest in the damaging effects
of marijuana." The *Digest* helped fund the PRIDE conference, and
its work was everywhere in evidence.

The press office prominently displayed a news release from the
magazine headlined " '*Parent Power*' *Offers Best Hope Against
Drug Epidemic*." The release then declared, "An army of angry
parents is mobilizing around the world to go after the drug dealers
who have been going after their children, and according to a special
report appearing in many international editions of the May *Reader's Digest*, this is a force to be reckoned with. All across the globe,
national parent groups are joining together in the face of the inability of governments and police alone to combat the enormous
power that drug racketeers have wielded for so long. . . . Advises
Marsha Manatt, PRIDE co-founder, the international movement
must not repeat mistakes made in the U.S. such as concentrating
too exclusively on heroin and taking it easy on 'soft' drugs like

marijuana and hashish. 'You *must* focus on cannabis as a gateway drug,' she says. 'If youngsters say no to pot and hashish, they say no to the whole culture.' "

While I had heard these and related distorted ideas many times before, I had never heard them said to my face and repeated hour after hour, while surrounded by decent people who believed them with all their hearts and souls. Like Robert Hartzell at the trial of Fred Collins, I felt that I had been transported to another planet. The heavy air of that planet stifled me. I did not sleep well while there and did not for days afterward. Hatred of any drug user, any person who supported more liberal drug laws, any person who opposed the drug war and the drug-free dogma, any person who raised questions about the perversion of science to support that dogma—these hatreds were palpable forces in that air. That planet provided no breathing room for traditional American beliefs in restraint, balanced appraisal of conflicting ideas, freedom for dissenters, and constitutional rights.

During my time in attendance, I heard no dissent raised about any idea expressed from the podium (save for a few minor exceptions) nor did I read about any dissent in reports on the proceedings. It all resembled a massive religious meeting more than anything else I have ever experienced. As no one raises debating points with a clergyman conducting a prayer service in a house of worship, so none was raised in this politically oriented assembly. Even the existence of another respectable ideological side was not acknowledged. The Devil does not deserve a hearing in the same room with those who have heard and believe the Word of the Lord.

Twice before in my lifetime I remember feeling roughly similar fears for the survival of American democracy and freedom: during the McCarthy communist-hunting investigations of the Fifties and during the civil rights struggles which came to a head in the Sixties. During the latter era, as a federal civil rights official I spent weeks on investigations in the Deep South and saw firsthand how the assault on integrationists destroyed the freedom of all citizens in many communities. There was comfort, though, in the fact that many powerful national governmental and social leaders openly opposed the unbalanced zealots who were willing to burn the Bill of Rights in order to save the country from their favorite devil— in one case, the communist menace, and in the other, racial mongrelization. While there is some opposition at high levels of power to the drug-war zealots today, the strength of high-level support for extremism is frightening.

During the conference, Mrs. Reagan was asked by a reporter to comment on the fact that her husband's administration was cutting federal funds for drug-abuse treatment programs once again as it had done in the past. Mrs. Reagan said she did not see how her activities had anything to do with such mundane, practical issues. "I'm talking mother-to-mother," she replied. "I don't get into the other."

If the First Lady's high-visibility leadership in the drug arena is not a vital part of the overall federal drug control and treatment strategy—"the other"—then what is it? The answer is that it is anything that its supporters want it to be, part substance, part shadow, part private, part governmental, and all a splendid public relations vehicle for the Reagan White House, which is what it was originally designed to be. The "other" is also federal government funding of this event and the claiming of credit for major achievements by staging it. There was undeniable evidence of heavy governmental involvement in the conference and at the same time of a desire to present it as if it was simply a private meeting of mothers. Now you see the hand of the government. Now you don't! That was the hand of a mother. And what cad could deny that a mother knows what is best for her children?

The April 1985 conference was actually two conferences, both supported heavily by federal funds, as have been similiar parent conferences before and after this one. The initial event in 1985 was entitled "The First Ladies' Conference on Drug Abuse," which was scheduled for April 24 in the White House and April 25 in Atlanta. On April 24, Mrs. Reagan and the First Ladies of 17 other countries met in Washington to hear Dr. Carlton Turner of the White House explain national drug strategy; Joyce Nalepka, president of the National Federation of Parents for Drug-Free Youth, tell about the parents' movement; and other adult leaders lay out national policy directions. The importance of Mrs. Reagan to the entire federal program was underscored by Dr. Turner when he declared, "She has been our point man in this fight." A reporter who was present observed, "At times the morning session sounded as if it were as much a testimonial to Nancy Reagan as it was a skull session for trading ideas and searching for what she called a 'common understanding among nations of the drug problem.'"

The only young person on the program held at the White House, and the only one with an admitted drug problem, was 16-year-old Robin Page, listed as "Graduate of Straight, Inc., Drug Rehabilitation Center," who spoke on "Why I Used Drugs—Why I Stopped." While Ms. Page was apparently helped by the treatment she received at Straight, as other young people have been, no questions were raised about the dark side of the organization.

The second day of the First Ladies' conference merged with most of the events of the PRIDE meeting in Atlanta, at which only fifteen of the other First Ladies were present. I was able to attend it because it was touted as a meeting of private citizens that was open to any member of the public willing to pay the registration fee. However, when I sought to take one of the many vacant seats in the front rows of the huge ballroom, I was stopped by white paper signs on them saying "Reserved for DEA."

As on the day before in Washington, the first substantive speaker was Dr. Turner, whose speech was entitled, "We Are Winning the War on Drugs." The White House drug-policy adviser gave a victory report replete with tales of new laws, seizures, and drug law convictions, with the result that 10,000 more bad guys were in prison. That's why the prison population is going up, he bragged. Yet Dr. Turner could provide little in the way of concrete evidence that these measures had been successful in stemming the overall influx and use of drugs. Dr. Turner did make one claim now often stated by drug-war leaders—that the recent drop in reported marijuana use by youth was due mainly to the drug-control efforts of the Reagan administration and the parents' movement. He pointed with pride to the survey figures which showed, he stated, that daily marijuana use among high school seniors dropped during the Reagan years.

It is possible, of course, that the drop was created in part by those efforts, for which appropriate credit should be given. However, my view is that we know very little about the reasons for mass swings in drug preferences, whether for a particular brand of beer or for a specific illegal drug.

Dr. Turner also stated that a goal of communist drug dealers in Latin America and elsewhere was to destroy American democracy. Those who dealt in drugs from any country were such despicable people that "in some cases I personally believe the death penalty is warranted," the presidential adviser declared. He did not mention that only 13 repressive countries have the death penalty for drug trafficking and that no Western democracy does.

THOMAS GLEATON: ARREST MY CHILD

Several of the major ideological leaders of the parents' crusade dominated the remainder of the day. Each talked in kindly terms about the need to save children around the world from drugs. Each seemed blissfully unaware that the programs proposed might have little impact on drug abuse but could well serve to repress many traditional democratic values and freedoms.

The director of PRIDE and chairman of the conference, Thomas J. Gleaton, who holds a doctorate in education and is a professor of physical education at Georgia State University in Atlanta, explained how PRIDE was formed at the university in 1977 "to provide education and training for parents who wanted to fight back against the commercialized drug culture." Soon, Dr. Gleaton continued, the internationalization of the parents' movement began. By 1983, representatives of 17 countries came to the PRIDE conference. By 1984, 34 countries attended. At this conference, over 50 were present. "The internationalization of the parents' movement has become a reality," Dr. Gleaton declared proudly. To that international audience, he repeated a powerful theme of the American parents' crusade: "In nearly all cases, prevention fails when it does not address the gateway drug—*cannabis*—and instead concentrates on treatment of 'end of the road' drugs—opiates and cocaine." As he uttered those words, I noted not a smile, not a questioning look, not a doubting comment around me. The huge audience was quiet, deadly serious, determined, seemingly united: fight marijuana and conquer the drug menace.

Unfortunately, Dr. Gleaton said, the worst mistakes of the American experience, especially decriminalization of marijuana, are being repeated in other countries, usually by the inaction of enforcement officials. "The result of this *de facto* legalization is a legal muddle that supports increasing drug use. If possession and use of an illegal drug is condoned or excused, the primary cause of the drug epidemic is ignored—the user." Having laid out this simplistic explanation for the rise in drug use, Dr. Gleaton then propounded one of the most repressive principles in the drug-free dogma: "We, as parents of all nations, must say to our local law-enforcement officer, 'If my child, my loved one, or my friend breaks the law by using illicit drugs, please arrest him or her.' "

Thus there was complete support for the logic of the law. Not a single person in the entire conference seemed capable of the venerable American exercise of raising questions about the simple horse sense of the laws. Not a single person seemed capable of asking if the classification of the drugs into legal and illegal was more an hysterical action from decades past than a matter of current objective science. Not a single person seemed to understand that the genius of America lay in periodically challenging irrational laws. All seemed to accept the extraordinary notion that we Americans should actually applaud the act of calling in the police to arrest our children and other loved ones if they so much as smoke a marijuana cigarette, which is, technically, still a crime in most of the United States. Not a single person pointed out that many experts find the gateway theory without factual foundation.

Not a single person raised questions, moreover, about the ideas put forth by the next speaker, Jean-Michel Cousteau, eldest son of the famous ocean explorer Jacques Cousteau. Jean-Michel narrated a film, "Snowstorm in the Jungle," produced by his famous father. The film dealt with cocaine trafficking in South America. To me it all seemed out of place in a conference on drug education for youth. Even more bizarre was the vivid showing of how some doctors in Peru were dealing with cocaine addiction among Peruvian youth: the equivalent of a brain lobotomy. Right there on the screen in Atlanta before 2,000 parents and young people was patient 29, aged 16, "deemed irrecoverable" and going under the knife as a last resort. And there was Jean-Michel Cousteau clucking in a kindly voice as if to say how sad but to exorcise evil spirits one must do some cutting. My skin crawled and I tried to block out the images on the screen but everyone else there seemed to accept the idea of operations on the brains of addicted children as one of the exciting new technologies for the future. Sadly, Jean-Michel tells us, patient 29 relapsed a year later.

MARSHA MANATT: NORML AS DEVIL

Thomas Jefferson was surely churning in his grave as Dr. Gleaton and Mr. Cousteau spoke. The venerable Virginian and his fellow conspirators of 1776 were kept churning by the two appearances of Dr. Marsha Manatt that day. The main villain in creating the drug culture, she said, was the "pro-drug lobbying organization" NORML, the National Organization for the Reform of Marijuana Laws. The reason nice kids in her neighborhood started "partying with pot" was because "they were indoctrinated by a popular culture all around them." That culture was apparently created in large part by NORML, but also very much by its allies in "the powerful world of the commercialized glamorization of drugs." Those dope profiteers included the purveyors of drug-oriented comic books, movies, and magazines, especially *High Times.* Also part of that evil world were "major, reputable corporations," which marketed such pro-drug products as Opium perfume, eyedrops for smokers through ads in *Seventeen* magazine, and Weil's book *From Chocolate to Morphine.* (I am not making any of this up. These are her precise arguments.) This world was allowed to develop in the recent past by irresponsible adults, who "distorted and twisted the fundamental and noble conception of civil rights into the 'personal right' to illegally use mind-altering drugs." The good news of the 1980s, according to Dr. Manatt, was that parents were fighting back "against the merchants of greed who manipulated and exploited . . . the young. . . . But we still have a long way to go, for the criminal syndicates are powerful and increasingly violent."

Thus all those who oppose the current parents' movement are smeared with the same violent, criminal brush. You are either with us and for strict enforcement of all current laws or you have joined the camp of the traffickers and the pushers.

However, in such mass, emotional indictments, scant attention is paid to facts which would seem to call for rational distinctions between pushers and protesters. While NORML, for example, has many supporters who *are* decidedly pro-pot, it has many, like me, who are anti-pot. For most of its brief existence since 1970, the organization has repeatedly declared, as its official policy statement explains, that it "is strongly committed to the concept that growing up should be drug-free." This remarkable congruence of ideals is never mentioned by the zealots of the parents' movement. Thus NORML has pushed not pot for youth but reform of the laws through legal means so that adults would be freed of criminal controls on a drug that millions of them have used largely without apparent harm.

Moreover, it is highly likely that the sudden, unexplainable interest in pot by millions of decent American citizens might have preceded and accounted for both the existence of NORML and of the pot partying of our teenagers. The possibility of that congruence never seems to have dented the consciousness of the intellectual leaders of the parents' movement, such as Dr. Marsha Manatt. Nor has it occurred to them how destructive it is to teach our youth that writings and public appearances by ideological opponents are part of a criminal conspiracy and thus must be suppressed—and not allowed into the marketplace of ideas, a development which Jefferson saw as the supreme method for weighing conflicting versions of truth in a democracy. It is sad that the White House supports a movement that teaches children to hate freedom while it is teaching them to hate drugs.

A MAN OF OUR TIME: GABRIEL G. NAHAS

Many of the most extreme proposals to combat the drug menace with minimal regard for traditional American values and rights came from Gabriel G. Nahas, M.D., Ph.D., professor of anesthesiology at the College of Physicians and Surgeons of Columbia University and a consultant to the United Nations Commission on Narcotics. He is the chairman of the Scientific Advisory Committee of the National Federation of Parents for Drug-Free Youth and the chief medical advisor to PRIDE. Because of Mrs. Reagan's close links to these two related organizations, Dr. Nahas must be rated as one of the most influential physicians in the country in terms of setting the tone and philosophy underlying current American drug control strategy. During World War II, he was a heroic member of the French underground and received the Legion of Honor medal from his own government's leaders and the Medal of Freedom from President Truman.

The doctor began doing research on the pharmacological and biological impact of marijuana in 1969. In 1972 he published his first book laying out the dangers of the drug, *Marijuana: Deceptive Weed.* Dr. Nahas burst fully upon the national scene on January 25, 1974, when he issued a press release to announce the results of a study he directed at Columbia University. The release claimed startling new discoveries that "habitual marijuana smoking weakens the body's immune defenses against disease." To the world he announced that he had proudly stuck his flag into the virgin sand of this new scientific island: "The findings represent the first direct evidence of cellular damage from marijuana in man."

The press release—unusual in itself as a method of announcing the results of scholarship—was remarkable on two other counts. First, it revealed breathtaking scientific ignorance when it stated that the marijuana smokers studied in the research claimed "that they did not use any other mind-altering drugs." Yet the very next sentence admitted, "They drank alcoholic beverages and smoked cigarettes, as did the members of the control group." No marginally literate student would dare to refer to alcohol as anything but a mind-altering drug, and many experienced researchers view tobacco in the same light. Also, there is scientific evidence that both of these latter drugs could account for some depression in the activity of the immune system. Second, the medical scientists leaped with similar recklessness from the laboratory to the legislature. "The new biochemical evidence . . . has led Dr. Nahas to call for a thorough reappraisal of the findings of the National Commission on Marijuana . . . which might lead to marijuana legalization," the press release declared.

The reports of that official commission in 1972 and 1973 had stated that while marijuana posed potential health hazards, they were not so serious, especially when compared to other drugs such as alcohol, as to require continued total prohibition. (Despite a Big Lie created by drug-war zealots, neither that commission nor any other responsible research or lobbying group during the past century has ever concluded that marijuana was harmless.) The commission had, therefore, recommended decriminalization for personal use as a moderate, compromise position. Appointed by a conservative president, Richard Nixon, chaired by a conservative, and staffed by a full range of experts who conducted wide-ranging reviews of all medical and legal evidence, that commission and the reports it issued had been viewed as balanced and authoritative by many impartial observers. Suddenly, on the basis of one narrow study of a relatively few subjects, the major recommendations of the commission were called into question to the accompaniment of massive media coverage on the front pages of newspapers and on major network television news shows. Subsequent works by Dr. Nahas, such as his *Keep Off the Grass*, aimed at the general public, also received a good deal of media attention, although he often complained that there was a conspiracy of silence about his research.

His publications also produced other results which he, like the leaders of the parents' movement, find intolerable, even criminal: widespread criticism. No drug-abuse scholar in recent history has been the subject of such scathing commentaries in the scientific journals. A review in *The New England Journal of Medicine* described his work as "psychopharmacologic McCarthyism that compels him to use half-truths, innuendo and unverifiable assertions." In *The Journal of the American Medical Association:* "examples of biased selection and . . . omissions of facts abound in every chapter." In *Contemporary Drug Problems:* "meretricious trash."

On the other hand, Dr. Nahas has received encouragement from many physicians, funds from governments, and strong support from the parents' movement and the White House. At the PRIDE–White House banquet on April 25, just before Captain Kirk spoke, every person, including me, was handed a six-page brochure entitled "A Man of Our Time: Gabriel G. Nahas, M.D., Ph.D," which laid out his life story including his persistence in revealing the dangers of marijuana in the face of vicious attacks against him by other researchers. Most of these scholarly attacks were laid at the door of apparently conspiratorial action by members of NORML. Dr. Nahas was particularly distressed by a review of one of his books in *The New England Journal of Medicine* on December 20, 1984. That "prestigious publication" had actually called upon Dr. Andrew Weil ("whose own books are recommended by *High Times* magazine") to write the review—with predictable results. The brochure observed, "It is sad when a major medical journal acts as spokesman for the commercialized, criminal drug culture."

Also handed out that day had been a companion eight-page brochure: "A Drug Policy for Our Times—1985, a Position Paper of P.R.I.D.E.," the principal author of which was Dr. Nahas, with the assistance of Drs. Gleaton and Schuchard, among others. It had been presented earlier that day by Drs. Nahas and Gleaton at a special press conference, which I witnessed from a front-row seat. In a calm and kindly fashion, these two men explained to perhaps 25 members of the American and foreign press, not a policy aimed at helping youth cope with the many real dangers of drugs but rather how to reorganize democratic societies around the world in the name of producing drug-free citizens of all ages.

In the process of laying out the major ideas of the position paper, Dr. Nahas stated that up until the 1960s "social taboos" had operated to inhibit almost all people from taking illicit drugs. The taboos had been destroyed by "social theoreticians" who had caused great harm in recent years by their permissive ideas that nations should teach their people "how to live with drugs, how to use them for pleasure in a responsible fashion, without abusing them." He went on to say that while this might be possible, in many cases, with alcohol and tobacco, it was impossible with the illicit drugs, which, unlike the legal drugs, almost always produce "neuropsychotoxicity," defined as "a temporary impairment of brain function." The permissive social theoreticians, he continued, did not understand this greater organic and mental impairment created by the illicit drugs, such as marijuana (alleged, with a straight face, to be seven times more addictive than alcohol), cocaine, and heroin (both 14 times greater). These same theoreticians are largely responsible for destruction of the social consensus against illicit drugs during the past two decades and thus they are also responsible for recent drug epidemics.

THE NEW CHEMICAL GULAG

According to Dr. Nahas, there is no need to adopt the "very harsh methods of repression" of the communist-bloc nations—meaning, I assume, summary executions—for we can look rather to more enlightened models of control which, during recent years, have been "sucessfully implemented in Japan, Taiwan, and Singapore," all three of which countries being described as "Asian democracies." The experience of the latter country is especially important to democratic nations. The basic assumption of the Singapore model, in accordance with the advice of leading scientists and the United Nations, is that "since there is no medical cure for drug dependence, the only effective measure is to suppress the drug as much as possible, treating it like an infectious agent, and to rehabilitate the addict through quarantine until he is able to lead a drug-free life." Addicts are spared the stigma of a criminal conviction because they are simply arrested, given a urine test, and, if they do not pass, are placed in the rehabilitation center without the formality of a trial. So there you have it: The solution. It worked in Singapore, Dr. Nahas declared, and within a few years a raging heroin epidemic was stopped in its tracks and the number of addicts reduced from approximately 13,000 in 1977 to 6,000 in 1983, an unvalidated claim which, indeed, had been made by officials in Singapore.

I sat there through that performance stunned. This was America talking to the world. The First Lady of our democratic nation was still in the building along with the First Ladies of other countries. This was a White House meeting. This presentation was being made by the meeting's most honored medical expert. Yet, the content of the solution offered the world was so full of scientific errors and legal horrors that I held my breath, for I barely knew where to start asking questions or if I could do so without declaring how utterly mad I thought both Dr. Nahas and Dr. Gleaton were. They were offering quick-fix police-state solutions to a delicate and distressing problem requiring patience, toleration, humane treatment options, and adherence to the principle that even suspected drug users, like suspected robbers, had rights in a democracy.

These two widely respected experts with advanced degrees might just as well have said that they had a simple, handy-dandy cookbook for a drug-free and right-free world. If there is no medical cure for addiction, how in the world do treatment personnel rehabilitate an addict once he has been confined in this new chemical Gulag? How do you suppress drugs? Our massive police-military efforts have failed miserably to do so. And the notion that the illicit drugs had been proved to be more addicting than alcohol flew in the face of every piece of objective research I had encountered in the past 14 years. How can anyone refer to Taiwan and Singapore as democracies, when both are highly regimented societies? While I was reorganizing my thoughts, the press sat for the most part quietly, accepting the whole frightening scheme, except for a few mild questions.

Finally, I managed to say in a quavering voice, "There are perhaps one million heroin and cocaine addicts [in the United States]. . . . Are you suggesting that we consider locking them all up without judicial process?" Dr. Nahas's long answer started with the observation that the number of "heroin addicts and consumers" must be closer to 5,000,000, thus confirming my concern that any user of an illicit drug, not only an addict, might be subject to involuntary quarantine under this scheme. He then stated that giving addicts methadone was no cure since it substituted one addiction for another. The only answer is abstinence. We have many such drug-free programs already in this country. "These programs are all the same . . . all successful." The physician included Straight, Inc., in that category, citing it as an example of the best approach yet discovered anywhere in the world. In addition, we would have to start thinking about more extensive efforts that would require an involuntary "prolonged period of quarantine" for many more users and addicts—he did not estimate how many—which might start with people in certain elements of society—the army and the schools, for example—where controls were already accepted. If we don't lock these people up, Dr. Nahas explained, they will continue to take drugs.

Writer Peggy Mann, sitting among the other reporters, was asked by Dr. Gleaton for her opinion of the Singapore method. She indicated that it seemed to work very well and that it had cured a large number of addicts. "I think it's a very interesting program to look at," Ms. Mann observed.

Dr. Gleaton explained how various elements of this model have already been applied in several American communities, especially the use of urine tests to check up on illicit drug use, to discover, as he called them, "contaminated persons." In one Arkansas school system, for example, students who had been involved in growing and using marijuana were met by a demand from parents that urine tests be administered to students who appeared intoxicated. Failure of the test meant suspension. Dr. Gleaton noted with approval that there was a good, strong tendency in the country to move toward manadatory urine tests in schools, government, industry, and the armed forces "with an option for the person who's involved in drugs to stop taking or to go into treatment or to take their place in the jails." The professor made no distinction between users and addicts. Evidence of any illegal substance, including marijuana, in the body was sufficient. No mention was made of the existing gridlock in our criminal justice system and of the bulging conditions of our prisons.

At the instant the press conference was over, I attempted to rush out of that room. It seemed an unhealthy, unclean place to be. Dr. Nahas came rapidly in my wake and handed me a copy of a guest editorial he had published in the *Wall Street Journal* on February 13, 1985, which explained those "successful" Asian programs. I thanked him but said that I had already read it and that I had published my own guest editorial in that paper some months previously that was 180 degrees away from his. Then I put my arm on his shoulder and in an attempt to be kind said, "Dr. Nahas, I know your work and I respect it. It's like religion, though. Listening to you talk is like a Catholic listening to a sermon from an orthodox Jew, or vice versa."

He put his glasses on and came close and read my name tag. Suddenly, he pulled back as if he had come in contact with old Beelzebub himself. "I know you!" he said in a shocked voice. Responding as if that remark were a compliment, I said, in a friendly way, "Why don't we sit down sometime and have a talk?" He said "Yes," but in such a manner that the thought flashed through my mind that he would do so only if he could secure my imprisonment first.

During the next day at the conference, Dr. Nahas looked at me several times with deep distrust, indicating no desire for a chat. Finally, he approached and said, to the best of my recollection, "This program which you find so distasteful"—remember, I had merely raised a few basic issues—"is based on fifteen years of scientific study and mathematical formulae. *Your* ideas are very damaging. When I fought with the French underground, the American troops I met were drug-free." Gesticulating now with two fingers, together, that kept coming down on my forearm, he continued, "*You* caused all this to change! *You* are responsible for this epidemic of drugs in America!" I replied that harsh methods like his had dominated drug enforcement during this century and they had failed; now, his side wanted more and more of the same repression that failed. Later, of course, I thought of other bright answers I should have shot back at him but didn't.

A few weeks after the conference was over, I had another opportunity. I was called, out of the blue, by a producer of "Firing Line," the discussion television show chaired for 20 years by conservative columnist William F. Buckley, Jr., and asked if I would appear for a taping on May 22. I readily agreed. To my surprise, the other guest was Dr. Gabriel Nahas. During that show, Dr. Nahas repeated the positions he had stated in Atlanta. Dr. Nahas became particularly incensed when I pointed out that he seemed to bend scientific objectivity when it came to his, and my, favorite drug, alcohol. Drinking a few glasses of wine was civilized, I observed, while smoking a few joints of marijuana was not only criminal but so extremely dangerous to the health of the entire society that involuntary quarantine was necessary. The comparison made the French hero livid with rage. Several times, he threatened to walk off the set in the middle of the show, so furious did my questions and observations make him. I felt sorry for the man in personal terms because he seemed so sincere and so distraught—and at the same time I believed it necessary to challenge openly his ideas that did violence to democratic values and scientific facts.

After the sound recording had stopped, and the producer was rolling film just to have a background to show the credits, Dr. Nahas stood up and made an impassioned speech to the dumbfounded studio audience, shook his fingers vigorously in my face, accused me again of causing the drug epidemic, and said he refused to shake my hand—he simply could not! Mr. Buckley leaned back in his chair as he often does, smiled slightly, and raised his eyebrows at me, looking past the lecturing physician, as if to ask: why is he doing this when the show is over? Is he out of control? I looked back at Mr. Buckley with a similar quizzical message. When he had finished, Dr. Nahas started to storm off the set with his microphones still attached. Mr. Buckley managed to catch him just in time to disengage them from his lapel.

THE FIRST LADY AND THE PARENTS

When Mrs. Reagan accompanied her husband into the White House on January 20, 1981, there was little in her past history to suggest that she might get involved with the difficult issue of drug policy. Her major involvement with a social issue had been her strong support of the Foster Grandparents Program, a private organization that offered help to children. During her first year in Washington, few members of the general public knew or cared about that. Nancy Reagan was and is a rich, classy lady. She acted like one, once she arrived in this capital city. A former aide was quoted in *Time* magazine on the royal Reagan scene: "There is a little element here of Louis XIV's French court and *les précieuses*—the affected ladies. She had a certain liking for witty, amusing, well-dressed men who were willing to walk three paces behind and carry the purse." Yet she acted no differently from scores of other rich Americans; it was all so much a matter of position, timing, and image.

Believing quite sincerely, and perhaps quite properly, that the White House could use some internal dressing up, she called mainly upon her rich circle of friends who dipped into their petty cash funds and produced $800,000 to redecorate the private rooms in the fine old mansion. Mrs. Reagan's magic touch worked again when she arranged to get $209,000 worth of china donated to the cause of matching dishes at huge state dinners. While these events were transpiring, the country was going through a minor depression and millions were out of work. Although her husband, "the great communicator," was doing splendidly on Capitol Hill and in the media, the press printed withering stories on the rich, frivolous First Lady. The new White House china became a standing joke among Washington reporters, and through them, among the people of the country. Mrs. Reagan read these often spiteful stories and was deeply hurt.

Nancy Reagan has said, "That first year was a terrible year." In addition to public humiliation at the hands of the press, "There were all those personal things that happened." On March 30, 1981, the President was shot and seriously wounded. In 1982, her stepfather, to whom she was deeply attached, died. A small cancer was removed from her lip. The First Lady's emotional and physical health seemed adversely affected; her weight dropped from 114 to 104 pounds. She began to look frail, almost sickly, as if a strong wind would blow her over the heads of her cordon of Secret Service agents.

Thus, before the end of President Reagan's first year in office Mrs. Reagan was in a personal and political slump, even, some might have said, in a depression. Then someone on her staff came up with the idea of supplanting the bland image of the Foster Grandparents Program with the more robust vision of a massive effort to help control youth drug abuse. It has been alleged that the campaign was designed by political operatives to rehabilitate a political disaster area in the White House—the frivolous, loser image of the President's wife. There is no doubt in my mind, however, that a basically decent and sincere First Lady then pitched in tirelessly to further an important cause that reached the hearts of millions.

"We're in danger of losing our whole next generation," Mrs. Reagan told leaders of the National Federation of Parents for Drug-Free Youth (NFPDY) on November 9, 1981. They had been invited to the White House as part of the beginning effort to get the First Lady involved in a serious project. The danger came primarily from marijuana, according to parents at this meeting. Marion McClatchy, a member of the NFPDY board from Rosemont, Pennsylvania, explained that her son started smoking the drug at 12, and by the time he was 16, she and her husband decided that marijuana was the reason they were losing him. He was 21 at the time of that White House event and the parent-organization board member reported that he was then fully estranged from the family and that they did not even speak with him. Marijuana caused this estrangement, it was reported. "If we'd had the information then we have now, we wouldn't have lost our child," Ms. McClatchy told the First Lady and the other parents. This false claim—the loss of a generation primarily to marijuana—was to be repeated time and time again by Mrs. Reagan and by the parents' movement.

When her staff allied the First Lady with the parents' movement, they created a union of immense benefit to all directly concerned. Mrs. Reagan conferred greater national and international status on the movement and she, in turn, found herself as the spiritual leader of a grassroots political force that is utterly elemental in the essence of its power: that of a mother who believes that evil people are menacing her young.

That movement had started years before the First Lady began looking for a serious involvement. It was spontaneously and almost simultaneously created in many separate communities, primarily in the South, during the Seventies by groups of middle-class parents concerned about the puzzling behavior of their children, especially regarding the use of marijuana. While the parents had lived through the Dope Decade of the Sixties, and some of them had tried pot, most were repelled by the legacy of that permissive era which they believed was reflected in the strange drug preferences of their young. One of the most important small streams that eventually became an international flood tide began flowing at 1:00 A.M. on a hot, muggy August night in 1976, according to Peggy Mann's book, *Marijuana Alert,* in the backyard of the Atlanta home of Marsha and Ron Manatt. At that hour the Manatts were crawling around in the wet grass after the end of a birthday party for their 12-year-old daughter, Kathy. The children had been acting strangely and the parents were suspicious, for good reason. To their shock, they found dozens of marijuana butts, empty beer cans, and empty bottles of "Mad Dog 20/20" wine, which is 20 percent alcohol.

All responsible parents must share the shock and dismay of the Manatts at these discoveries. Clearly, they had to take some action. There will, however, be serious disagreement among many responsible parents as to what that action should have been.

At this point, many parents, then and now, would have called in their child and laid down the law: here are the rules of this house, or else. Those rules would have been laid down regardless of how harmless or harmful other people thought the substances or activities were—and probably without even talking to the neighbors. Young lady, you are not allowed to smoke pot or drink alcohol. While we are at it, you have been eating too many fatty foods. Cut way down on hamburgers and french fries. Because of this party, you will be grounded (no recreational excursions out of the house) for the next month. On weekends, you will be allowed out but with us and under our supervision. Why? Because I told you so. But my friends told me that none of that stuff will hurt me. I do not control your friends but I do control you. Please go to your room and study. *Now!*

In the overwhelming majority of cases, I suspect, this approach has worked. Criminologists know that the most powerful correctional forces in the world are loving parents who both provide positive examples and also say "no" at the appropriate times to their children. Such parents are more important and more powerful than all the community institutions and police forces and governments combined. I firmly believe in that venerable form of parent power—and in that healthy element of the current parents' movement that exercises it.

Marsha Manatt did not rely on that form of individual parent power alone in dealing with her daughter. Like other parents around the country at the time, she also invoked another venerable American tradition of direct action and launched a campaign to reorganize the world around her. She went to the neighbors to find out what they knew and to seek their support for common action. Then she sought to organize them, the schools, and the police into a massive campaign to keep the children under constant surveillance. Virtually all of the children in the community were grounded for a month. The police were encouraged to watch more closely places where young people were known to sell and exchange drugs, such as parking lots, and to make arrests. Marsha Manatt Schuchard, who holds a Ph.D. in English from the University of Texas, also sought to straighten out the misinformation about marijuana which she felt was confusing the children and parents of the country. Too many teachers and experts treated it as harmless, she believed, in some cases even conceding its positive benefits as a medicine. On March 17, 1977, she wrote Dr. DuPont, who was then director of NIDA under President Carter, stating that the government was giving confusing messages about pot and that it failed to differentiate between adult and juvenile use. Robert DuPont was so impressed that he made a trip to Atlanta.

"I don't mind saying that it was parent power that changed my attitude about marijuana. That trip to Atlanta was what really opened my eyes," he related to Peggy Mann. Dr. DuPont then called Tom Adams, director of NIDA's Pyramid Project, which DuPont had set up in 1975 to provide assistance to community anti-drug abuse groups. Adams introduced Manatt to Dr. Gleaton at nearby Georgia State University, who had been running the Southeast Drug Conference at his school since 1975. All four of these key actors agreed that most professionals downgraded the role of parents and especially the allegedly true health hazards of marijuana, now being documented in the new research. (Many drug-abuse scholars, including me, see no significant new dangers documented in the new research.) They agreed, as Peggy Mann wrote in *Marijuana Alert*, that "since there was such a dearth of accurate information about marijuana, a new organization would be formed to collect and disseminate such information"—PRIDE. Thus, the marijuana obsession was built into the movement from the start; other drugs have always been secondary.

PRIDE conferences commenced in 1978 and have been a vital gathering ground for the parents' movement. Speakers always reinforced the alleged new evidence showing the massive health threat posed by marijuana to children. If a debate has occurred on the issue at any such conference, I have not discovered it. Parent groups proliferated around the country with the help of federal funds and leadership from NIDA and other agencies, under the aegis of the Carter administration. At the 1980 PRIDE conference the National Federation of Parents for Drug-Free Youth was formed at the initial suggestion of Dr. Gleaton. Federal support continued into the Reagan years, especially through NIDA under the new director, Dr. Pollin, before Mrs. Reagan became involved. Reliable estimates of the actual number of local parent groups have been difficult to find. I have seen reports of numbers ranging from 4,000 to 9,000. Some critical investigative reporters, such as Tom Seay of *The Drugs & Drug Abuse Education Newsletter*, have suggested figures only in the hundreds. Whatever the actual number, there is no doubt of their great combined political power.

THE BIBLE OF THE PARENTS' MOVEMENT

Parents, Peers, and Pot, one of the most powerful products of this alliance was, in Dr. Gleaton's words, "the bible of the parents' movement." It had been suggested by Tom Adams, funded by NIDA at the direction of Robert DuPont, and written under contract by Marsha Manatt. First published in 1979 during the Carter administration, a second enlarged edition was published in 1983 under Mr. Reagan. It set out the basic philosophy of the movement in terms of the allegedly new, more reliable drug knowledge and also provided numerous examples of political activism to secure compliance with that dogma at all levels of society, starting in local communities and schools. More than a million copies have been distributed free by NIDA, and it has been translated into several other languages.

I assigned Marsha Manatt's second edition of her bible, *Parents, Peers, and Pot II* (1983), to my university classes on drug policy as required reading because, like most university teachers, I want my students to be exposed directly to a wide variety of views. Students normally welcome that diversity and conflict in assigned readings. Nevertheless, in this case, my students complained bitterly to me in class about being forced to read the brief 160-page paperback book. They had just completed high school within the past few years, they said, and this was a complete distortion—they used more pithy expletives—of what high school students were really like and of proper ways of dealing with their drug problems. Their mass complaints were to no avail. The reading assignment stuck.

Along with many of the students, however, I was shocked at the total lack of balance exhibited in this publication, which the American government and its drug experts have presented to the world as an official version of Truth about drugs, parents, and youth. The publication is so one-sided that it can be justified only if it were indeed seen as a narrow religious tract, the presentation of theological dogma, not facts. In its present form, it is government-funded propaganda and thus raises serious legal and constitutional issues.

This bible taught, for example, that marijuana was always harmful, even fatal, for young people. This conclusion was based firmly, it alleged, on new "credible biological" research, information that was taught in school classes established at the behest of parents' groups, and which became the basis for the elders' "non-negotiable position on drugs." It was absolutely crucial that the other side of this issue and all others never be presented. Hidden at the bottom of a page which reproduced a pamphlet passed out by a Nebraska group was a sentence that illustrates how well they had learned their anti-democratic lesson: "It's wise to interview speakers first to see if their views are compatible with recent information." Acceptable recent information was the work of such experts as Drs. Gabriel Nahas or Robert DuPont. No mention was made of the vast body of knowledge in major studies in numerous countries over the past century that plead for more gentle social approaches to marijuana use.

The book argued for the need to enforce relentlessly the criminal drug laws without regard for appeals to technicalities such as legal rights or to ideas about avoiding giving children criminal records whenever possible. Civil liberties lawyers were referred to in negative terms because they sought to "stir up students to protest their loss of 'Constitutional rights' " (the quotation marks around the last two words were in the original). Pointed to as a superb role model is the school principal who called the police whenever students were found with drugs: "I make two phone calls and the second one is to the parents," bragged Bill Rudolph of Atlanta's Northside High School.

Some of the harshest criticism was saved for those professionals who advocated teaching children about the reality of moderate or responsible drug use. Even though there is a massive body of research knowledge which supports the concept that most minors, like most adults, use most drugs, legal or illegal, responsibly, that very idea is treated with derision by the parents' movement. In one case, reported in this bible with pride, a professional association was persuaded to rewrite its version of the truth to please the aroused parents. At the behest of Principal Rudolph, psychologist Robert Margolis worked with the Georgia Psychological Association to develop a new position paper on adolescent marijuana use that eliminated the idea of responsible use from the policy statements of that organization.

It may seem a subtle point but, I submit, it is perfectly acceptable for parents to demand that their children be drug-free or that organizations, including NORML, declare that growing up should be drug-free, but it is either incompetence, lack of integrity, prostitution, or all of the above when professional organizations deny the possibility of moderate use of drugs by minors under some circumstances.

This prophylactic lie is the equivalent of the position virtually every social leader took years ago in regard to sex education: telling children about the reality of sexual relations and about contraception only encourages them to copulate, which is a crime in many states for unmarried people. In effect, just say no to sex. Most sensible social leaders have come to believe in recent years, however, that many children get happily and eagerly involved in all forms of sexual activity, including intercourse, regardless of what adult society tells them.

A rational compromise is to teach them a realistic set of moral options: you are quite capable of controlling your impulses; there are many sound, practical, and ethical reasons for abstaining from sex; sex brings responsibilities; if, however, you feel you must engage in intercourse, one responsibility is to prevent conception and disease. The same thoughts apply to understanding the dynamics of alcohol and drug use: you do not have to use these chemicals, not even a glass of beer; the best highs are natural highs such as religion or athletics, but if you feel you must use drugs, be very cautious; never use drugs whose content you do not know; never use with addicts or while driving; never use during the school day; and never use every day.

The drug-free zealots argue that children should hold off on learning about responsible sex and drugs until they are adults. That is, as I have argued, perfectly appropriate as one option for many children, but it is not the only option for all children. Nowhere in the drug-free dogma, moreover, has any expert explained how these young people will magically become responsible participants in sex and in mind-altering experiences, either with or without drugs, when they become 18 years of age. Indeed, the parents' movement provides no guidance for children who are young adults—say, 19 to 25 years of age—to understand and achieve such moderate and controlled behavior. One likely result of the current parents' movement will be more people of all ages who are ignoramuses about all mind-altering experiences, with or without drugs, as well as sex.

A frank exposition of this traditional position on sex and drugs was put forth by Dr. Herbert London, a dean at New York University, during a panel debate which later appeared as an article in the December 1985 issue of *Harper's* magazine. I had been arguing that society should approach sex and drug education in roughly the same spirit and that responsible participation should be one rational option that is contemplated and taught, at least for children who are also adults. Even for them Dr. London objected, declaring flatly: "You say no, and you know full well the kid's going to engage . . . anyhow. But it's desirable to say no; the hypocrisy is desirable."

Most children are raised today in this spirit of hypocrisy, of prophylactic lies. When they become adults, it is no wonder that they have difficulty suddenly shifting gears and dealing honestly with an adult sexual partner or with any type of drug. There is thus the likelihood that many of the parents of the drug-free youth movement today are themselves confused about the dynamics of their own sexual and drug appetites.

None of the sages leading the drug-free movement has observed, moreover, that the spiritual message is strikingly negative: the highest value is bestowed on the activity of *not* taking chemicals. Even more disturbingly, this movement seems destined to produce youth who might possibly be drug-free but who also will be utterly hostile to the great American traditions of toleration, dissent, and open debate. Free of drugs and free of democratic values.

Some insight may be gained into the repressive values being taught by the spiritual leaders of the alliance between the Reagan White House and the parents' movement by looking at a relatively insignificant but typical incident involving one ideological opponent, me. Jean-Marie George, an assistant producer for the CBS News "Nightwatch," was attempting to obtain a balanced audience for an hour-long, nationally televised debate on the legalization of drugs, which was to be taped in Washington on the evening of May 9, 1985. Dr. Robert Baird of Manhattan was set to argue firmly and politely against the proposition, and I, for it with certain qualifications. As was usual, the producer called a variety of organizations on all sides of the issue and asked them to send a representative for the audience, with the promise that questions could be asked of the debaters. On all other issues during the previous five years—ranging from nuclear war to energy to Soviet relations—she had found governmental and private agencies eager to have staff members in the audience so that their points of view would be represented in the questioning. But not this time. Not on this issue.

Every federal agency flatly refused to send an official, including the DEA, the FBI, the State Department, and the White House Office of Drug Abuse Policy. It was as if an order had been handed down from the top that debate was not allowed—so uniform and uncompromising were the responses. Then Ms. George called Joyce Nalepka, president of the National Federation of Parents for Drug-Free Youth. The producer later told me, "She shocked me so! She burned my ears off!" Ms. Nalepka shouted that she would never appear in the same room with "that man" (this writer) or with any other who held such ideas about drugs, especially not with NORML officials, who had already agreed to appear in the audience. In a cold, strident voice, she insisted on being given the assistant producer's name, as well as the names and telephone numbers of everyone in the chain of command above her. Then President Nalepka, friend of the First Lady, spent the next several days calling higher-ranking CBS officials demanding that the program not be put on the air and questioning the motives of the network in doing so. (Ms. Nalepka failed in her repressive mission.)

After Ms. George had told me this story, I observed, "It seems to me that when you push these parent groups a bit, they become like cultist hate groups." "You bet they do," replied the traumatized young woman.

REGAL VISITS TO FRED'S PRISONS

Mrs. Reagan has made numerous visits to treatment centers. The First Lady has been particularly impressed by the sight of young drug addicts telling their own stories. She had never wept in public until she started those visits. "It began last winter," she wrote in a national woman's magazine in 1983, "with my visit to Straight, a drug-treatment program in Florida. It is one of a growing number of rehabilitation programs in the country in which drug-addicted children and their parents pull together, with professional guidance, to try to straighten out their truly tragic lives." She described the scene in which perhaps 350 teenagers were sitting on one side of an enormous room and 650 mothers, fathers, and foster parents on the other. The children stood up, one by one, and told how they had fallen into the trap of drugs. "As each child finished revealing a story, he or she would be crying, spilling out feelings of enormous guilt. . . . By the end of the meeting, after two and a half hours, I was expected to make a comment. My voice was trembling and tears were rolling down my cheeks. I was upset . . . but . . . I said what I felt. 'I'm so proud of you and I love you, too.' "

This was the session George Collins attended and that Fred later saw on the NBC television network and described as resembling a Moonie cult. Later, he learned that much of that crying was staged, as we saw, and that many of those children had no real drug problems and were virtually kidnapped into that institution. Mrs. Reagan was oblivious to all of that. Now the First Lady goes from victory to victory in her own anti-drug crusade.

The political rehabilitation of Mrs. Reagan has been a huge success. She is viewed now as a great asset to the Reagan White House and to all of the causes it supports. Her drug-abuse trips during the 1984 campaign were timed to produce the greatest political rewards for the Reagan-Bush ticket. In Washington, she is seen to be an independent power in her own right and not simply on drug abuse issues. Throughout the country, there is a huge reservoir of general good feelings toward her personally, some of which emanate happily from those citizens who, like this writer, strongly oppose much of the content of her projects. *Time* magazine conferred upon her the distinction of a cover picture with the caption "WHITE HOUSE CO-STAR—Nancy Reagan's Growing Role." By early 1985, when that cover appeared, it could have been said that Nancy Reagan's success story had reached historic dimensions.

Shortly after her triumph at the First Ladies' conferences in Washington and Atlanta, Mrs. Reagan accompanied her husband to the economic summit of the seven great democracies of the world in Bonn, West Germany. While he was facing up to disharmony and controversy at the Bitburg cemetery and in economic discussions with democratic leaders, she visited leading officials in several European countries and even had an impressive audience with the Pope in Rome. On numerous occasions, she seemed close to tears, especially when she visited drug addicts in treatment centers. She won the hearts of the people and leaders of Europe as she had in America. No reporter dared to write about the White House china or the rich and frivolous First Lady of 1981.

Even though she was not at the Bonn meetings, her subject somehow became part of the discussions. All of the leaders agreed that more coordinated action in dealing with drug trafficking was needed. A surprised and happy President observed with a smile, "Never have I seen all my summit partners so united and determined on a single subject." Secretary of State George P. Shultz cogently observed, "We have picked up another assignment which was unexpected. It wasn't on our agenda, particularly. It emerged from the discussion by the heads of state on this subject, and it may well be that one of the most important people to this meeting is not here—namely, Nancy Reagan."

A few weeks after the First Lady's European triumph, the CBS network aired the results of a detailed investigative report into the dramatic rise in the institutionalization of American youth, not at the hands of nonprofessional organizations such as Straight but in some of the country's best hospitals. One young man was shown who had been diagnosed by doctors as an alcoholic and then had been institutionalized for this alleged disease. In fact, he was not an alcoholic at all but was suffering from a mental illness—and now, years later, was just starting to recover from the ill effects of both his actual disease and from the improper medical treatment. Moreover, CBS investigative reporters had sent an adult male and a 15-year-old girl, posing as father and daughter, to a number of mental health institutions. The "father" told about symptoms similar to Fred's—occasional marijuana use, defiance, and denial by the girl that she had a drug problem. In all but one case, these institutions, which apparently operated under the general supervision of medical doctors, diagnosed the girl as a drug abuser and took in the new customer.

One of the hospitals was a unit in that major drug abuse conglomerate, CompCare. Its medical director, Joseph Pursch, M.D., is one of the most respected drug-abuse experts in the country.

When the story was aired on the network on May 20, 1985, Dr. Pursch was shown declaring he was shocked that a doctor did not examine the girl and prevent her entry into one of his units. That distress should be widespread since the number of children in locked psychiatric wards has risen from 10,764 in 1980, just before the start of the Reagan years, to 48,375 in 1984, an increase of 350 percent. Much of this rise was due to alleged alcohol and drug abuse. Those figures cover only 230 accredited hospitals and disregard entirely the use of imprisonment by the new wave of non-professional institutions such as Straight, Inc.

The thrust of the criticism in the CBS story, and in a subsequent treatment of the subject on Phil Donahue's show, was that some members of the medical profession were unethically seeking vast profits by cashing in on public fears about drugs—and in the process indelibly staining the reputations of thousands of our youth with a psychiatric hospital record. A later show on ABC during the scared summer of 1986 documented further how CompCare sought only to fill beds in its profit-making hospitals. There has been little discussion in the country, however, about how much of the fear that laid the basis for this abuse has been heightened or even created by the extremist crusade of the First Lady and the parents' movement.

Mrs. Reagan took Princess Diana on a regal visit to a drug treatment facility in the Washington suburbs on November 11, 1985. It was, of course, to Straight, Inc., in Springfield, Virginia, where a typical show with a cast of hundreds was presented and was reported to the world by an army of media people. Children stood up and told shocking tales of their abuse of drugs and of how they were seeking to get straight again. One Straight father, Mike Kirsch, told Diana that all six of his children were drug users. "Now am I hearing right? You have six children?" asked the somewhat startled Princess of Wales. "Six druggie children," Mr. Kirsch replied. "All on drugs?" Her Highness persisted. And Mr. Kirsch persisted in his affirmative answer.

No member of the press pointed out that the Straight definition of a "druggie" would cover most of the human beings on earth including virtually the entire royal family. Nor did anyone bring up the inconvenient fact that Fred Collins had last been imprisoned in this very facility, had sued successfully for damages, and in the process had documented in sworn testimony how destructive this extremist organization was for many children. Rather, the White House, through its chosen instrument, the First Lady, was allowed to foist the lie upon visiting royalty—from a country which excels in the gentle treatment of real hard-drug abusers—that one of our most harmful drug-treatment programs was a model for the world.

6

The Drug Warriors and Their Impossible Mission

I NEEDLED Barry Inman because I beat him back up the hill from the big marijuana garden. Even though my lungs were close to bursting and I was gasping for breath, I could not resist saying to the good-natured young officer as he reached the crest shortly after me, "I thought you young guys would set an example so as to encourage the rest of us." He just smiled and shrugged his shoulders as if to say, Hey, we're not in a race.

THE REAL REAGAN DRUG WAR

It was August 6, 1985, the second day of the largest nationwide marijuana-cultivation crackdown in American history (and, as it happened, the fortieth anniversary of Hiroshima). The day was hot and dry. The long line of vehicles had kicked up the dust on the dirt road as we wound our way up the mountain earlier that morning and the taste of the stuff was in our mouths. We were in the beautiful and remote hills of Mendocino County at a spot perhaps 140 miles north of San Francisco.

He could have gone by me easily, of course, as we all dug our feet in for traction on that rutted old logging road which rose steeply for approximately a quarter of a mile from the plateau where the illegal crop had been secreted. Barry was 22 years old and seemingly in splendid condition, but he was weighed down somewhat by his AR-15 semiautomatic military rifle (*not*, a senior officer had just pointed out, a potentially fully automatic M-16, as the press often reports) and a huge machete.

Moreover, the crew-cut reserve policeman from the nearby town of Ukiah had spent the morning hiking through these hills to fix the location of the garden and had just used that machete to assist in cutting down the 220 marijuana plants that had been discovered. The young man had stopped to take a breath and to wait for a fellow officer halfway up the hill, when I passed him.

Reserve Officer Inman is a true frontline soldier in the American war on drugs, the real one, the war that finds young men with badges and weapons out in the streets and hills enforcing the policies of older men, who, as often as not, are confused about the reasons that impelled them to seek a military solution in the first place. Moreover, like virtually every civilian or military drug-enforcement officer I have encountered during the past 14 years, he seemed decent and well-motivated, the type of fellow you would want in the next foxhole during a battle—and about whom one often develops a sense of parental protectiveness, which creates outrage at the very thought that his life might be risked by high-ranking leaders who would send him out on foolish missions.

The California campaign in which he enlisted involved the greatest application of armed force to enforce the drug laws on American soil in our history. My trip to California at that time was part of an attempt to see the American drug war with my own eyes and to hear what the major participants, especially the police, have to say about its successes and failures. I came away from these excursions into the front lines of enforcement all over this country with greater respect for the personal courage and commitment of our police and even greater disdain for our drug laws and for the political leaders who continue to impose such an impossible mission upon the many fine men and women of American law enforcement. The situation in the hills of California provided especially revealing insights into why seventy years of drug enforcement have failed and into the great danger to freedom presented by massive, military-style enforcement of the drug laws—even when the action is being carried out by essentially well-meaning, good-natured enforcement agents.

The California anti-marijuana battle had been going on for several years and had gained wide notoriety—as had the allegedly superb variety of sinsemilla (marijuana without seeds) which Yankee ingenuity and frontier adventurism has created in these hills within less than a decade. I had made arrangements with lawyer Ronald M. Sinoway, a leader of the legal counter-attack on the drug war with an office in the tiny crossroads town of Miranda in southern Humboldt County, to be in this region during early August. It was then, Ron Sinoway had told me, that the harvest would begin in some fields and when CAMP, the California Campaign Against Marijuana Planting, would launch its third year of military-style activities. I had no idea that I would find myself in the middle of a nationwide police-publicity blitz, utilizing the CAMP program as a model to capture the attention of much of the world.

However, on Monday, August 5, Operation Delta-9 (the major active mind-altering ingredient in marijuana is delta-9 tetrahydrocannabinol, sometimes called THC and sometimes delta-9) was launched involving marijuana-destruction raids in all 50 states by 2,200 federal, state, and local law-enforcement agents. Their immediate objective was to eradicate as many as 250,000 plants in three days. Attorney General Edwin Meese III, who opened the campaign by viewing a raid in the Ozark National Forest, explained the broader purposes of the campaign during an Arkansas news conference: "increasing the cost to drug traffickers and eradicating marijuana crops in the United States." He added, "We are sending a strong message, both to the domestic producers of marijuana and to the source countries outside our borders, that the U.S. government takes very seriously the need to attack the production of this drug." The chief law-enforcement officer of the nation promised that no observed marijuana plant would survive on the land of the United States. Thus, Mr. Meese was responding to skeptics who doubted the nation's ability to curb marijuana cultivation significantly—and most particularly to those officials in foreign source countries, feeling the lash of U.S. criticism, who accuse the Americans of being more lenient on their own growers.

The attorney general was proclaiming a venerable theme since the first comprehensive American drug law, the Harrison Narcotic

Act, was passed on December 17, 1914, in part to convince other nations that the United States would do its share in carrying out the new global drug-control order first formulated in the Hague Opium Convention of 1912. The basic concepts of that new law seemed quite logical and relatively easy to enforce. All civilized nations would agree that certain drugs, too harmful for general use, would be restricted by international treaties and national laws to medical purposes only. Regulations would be imposed on the growth, production, and sale of these particularly dangerous drugs in all nations. Eventually, it came to be accepted that some drugs— such as heroin and marijuana—were so attractive to potential abusers that they would be totally prohibited, even in medicine.

Difficulties in enforcement of the global order arose almost immediately. Moreover, fundamental questions were soon raised about which drugs deserved condemnation and prohibition, and which did not. Millions upon millions of basically decent people have regularly violated the drug laws of over 100 nations during the past seven decades. In America, as in other countries, the government responded by announcing periodically that it meant it, it *really* did, and that it was going to war against drugs. In some instances, these wars were announced by Presidents, sometimes by village mayors or chiefs of police.

Another curious habit, especially during the past two decades in America, has been that of declaring victory in the war on drugs— followed at a decent interval by the declaration of a new war, either by the original alleged victor or by one of his successors in office. Early in his administration, for example, President Nixon launched the first modern, massive war on drugs and by September 11, 1973, felt emboldened to declare, "We have turned the corner on drug addiction in the United States." It has turned out, of course, to be a much longer corner than he envisioned. This did not stop President Carter and especially President Reagan from declaring new wars and announcing at least partial victories.

Ronald Reagan's administration has made the greatest effort at enforcement of the drug laws in American history. No rational observer can fault him or his leading officials on the score that they did not try to make the drug laws work in our nation and around the world. A review of only those elements of his drug-control work involved with police, intelligence, and border interdiction reveals a massive commitment of will, money, equipment, and people. Even though I have long been a critic of drug wars, I was awed by a simple reading of the programs that have been developed by Mr. Reagan's drug-war grand strategists. Before his first year in office was over, those strategists convinced Congress to amend the *Posse Comitatus* Act of 1878 so that the military forces could be used for the first time to assist civilian officers in the enforcement of the drug laws by providing equipment, training, and information—although the amendment did not authorize direct military enforcement of those laws. Also in December 1981, the President issued an executive order that directed the entire federal intelligence community, in particular the CIA, which usually deals only with foreign analyses, to provide guidance to civilian drug-enforcement agencies. During the next month, another executive order by the attorney general placed the FBI director in overall charge of the DEA and gave the FBI concurrent jurisdiction with the DEA in the enforcement of the federal drug laws.

Each of these actions demanded major political skill and fervent commitment to the cause of all-out enforcement of the drug laws so as to overcome major traditional obstacles. For decades, for example, the FBI has developed the habit of steering clear of the sometimes dirty business of drug-law policing and its great monetary temptations. Within a few months, the immense political power of Ronald Reagan had not only brushed aside that reluctance but had also thrown the elite FBI fully into the front lines and top echelons of drug enforcement. Yet these major accomplishments were only the beginning.

In response to urgent requests from leading officials and citizens to deal with a crisis in drug trafficking and related crime, in January 1982 President Reagan created the South Florida Task Force under the direct leadership of Vice President Bush for the purpose of coordinating all enforcement elements in the region: federal, state, local, and military. Out of the experience in south Florida grew the National Narcotics Border Interdiction System (NNBIS), which was given the mission of coordinating all efforts against drug trafficking over any American border. So also out of the south Florida experience came the establishment of twelve other Organized Crime Drug Enforcement Task Forces (OCDEs) that soon covered the entire country. The El Paso Intelligence Center (EPIC) was expanded to provide better tactical intelligence support to the major federal and state agencies involved in drug-law enforcement.

Operations have been mounted under the direction of the Vice President and other leading officials that have all of the look and feel of major military operations, especially in the Caribbean and the waters around Florida—as well as in northern California. Navy and Coast Guard ships and planes, aided by Air Force AWACs and Navy E2C electronic surveillance planes, have thrown up blockades to interdict drug-smuggling boats from South America. Combined air, sea, and ground operations have taken place in the Bahamas. To listen to a Coast Guard officer in the Executive Office Building right next to the White House in Washington, to the Vice President's staff director, and to young Coast Guard sailors in Miami, and also to read service newspapers with martial headlines ("Drug War D-Day") is to be aware of the presence of highly trained professionals who believe they are fully at war with drug traffickers and users. The connection between drug traffickers and radical terrorists in South America has lent reality to the war mentality.

In order to impress upon his warriors the seriousness and commitment of their commander-in-chief, President Reagan conducted an unprecedented White House ceremony on June 24, 1982. Attending at his direction were 18 federal agency heads, the Vice President, military leaders, the commissioner of the IRS—and there without need of orders, one assumes, the First Lady. The President explained that he wanted everyone to know of the new massive and coordinated federal strategy to control drugs, especially marijuana, and he hoped these efforts would erase "the false glamour" that surrounds it and other drugs. His concluding charge was: "We're rejecting the helpless attitude that drug use is so rampant that we're defenseless to do anything about it. We're taking down the surrender flag that has flown over so many drug efforts. We're running up the battle flag. We can fight the drug problem, and we can win."

A major objective in this battle plan is to cripple organized crime, which is so often involved in drug trafficking. The regional task forces have gone after major crime figures and have secured many arrests and convictions. Under the leadership of Rudolph W. Giuliani, U.S. attorney for the Southern District of New York, new working arrangements were made with Italian authorities and indictments have been secured of the chiefs and sub-chiefs of whole Mafia families. To aid in the prosecution and more severe punishment of organization criminals and especially to ease forfeiture of their assets, the Reagan administration was able to persuade Congress to pass the Comprehensive Crime Control Act of 1984.

More money and people were devoted to the federal drug enforcement effort. The total drug-enforcement budget (not including treatment and prevention) for fiscal year 1985 was more than $1.4 billion, almost a 100 percent increase over that of 1981, the last Carter budget. The FBI hired 1,000 new agents to work in the related fields of organized crime and drug trafficking. Many of the new, and the old, staff have solid educational backgrounds and are dedicated, highly trained police professionals. (Some of my former students, I have discovered, are involved in DEA and FBI drug-enforcement activities. How could they *not* be well-educated and competent police officers?)

The bill that finally emerged from that fateful summer of 1986 added even more money and power to the national effort to control drugs under the leadership of Mr. Reagan. Signed in late October, the Anti-Drug Abuse Act of 1986 provided a vast array of new resources, including $1.7 billion in additional funds for that fiscal year. Save for the death-penalty provision, which liberals killed, most of the major drug-warrior proposals were enacted in some form. Drugs were formally declared a national security problem, which gave additional support to the use of military power to control trafficking. Moreover, money was given for more civilian police officers and for additional military aircraft in drug enforcement. For the first time, a mandatory minimum sentence was provided in the case of a conviction in a federal court for simple possession of any illicit drug, including marijuana. The first conviction for possession would draw a mandatory fine of $1,000; the second, 15 days in jail and $2,500. On the treatment side, several hundred million dollars were provided for new rehabilitation programs, but these were minor themes in the law.

There is more, much more, to the entire historic effort of the Reagan administration in the field of drug enforcement. Its work represents the culmination of repeated courageous efforts by American police and military officers in the seven decades that have passed since the Harrison Narcotic Act went into effect on March 1, 1915.

In most significant respects, however, all of those efforts have failed. Perversely, America's governmental, military, and police leaders act as if the opposite were true, as if the story of drug-law enforcement involved a long string of victories, interrupted only by occasional defeats—instead of just the other way around.

Yet the persistent, massive use of police and military power in drug enforcement continues.

ORIGINS OF THE WAR
AGAINST CALIFORNIA
MARIJUANA

The northern California anti-marijuana program started in 1983 at a time when the level of marijuana planting and associated violence from growers seemed to be beyond the resources of local law enforcement. Humboldt County Sheriff David A. Renner had observed in 1983, "You can't send four people to 1,500 plants guarded by you don't know who. . . . It was a year ago or more that we would ride through southern parts of Humboldt County and they would just see us and snicker." Fourteen northern California sheriff's departments followed DEA leadership and worked together that year. At an extra cost to the federal and state governments of $1.6 million, 524 raids were made which resulted in the arrest of 128 people and the seizure of 64,579 plants worth at least $130 million wholesale.

The CAMP report on 1983 expenses contained a laconic footnote: "Includes $500,000 for U-2 cost." Indeed, the DEA did contract with NASA for the use of the famous spy plane, which did fly some marijuana-search missions over American territory in California, with some success and a lot of ensuing outrage. For a variety of reasons, the missions apparently were not continued beyond 1983.

CAMP '83 was proclaimed a success by its organizers. Even so, it was clear that the surface had just been scratched, especially in Humboldt County, which has been portrayed by many observers as the world center of high-quality sinsemilla production. The DEA marijuana coordinator for California and the operational field commander of CAMP, William Ruzzamenti, in particular, seemed to be fairly spoiling for the campaign to begin again, his appetite only whetted. "The problem in Humboldt County is so gigantic that it could be an exaggeration to say that we got 10 percent there. But we learned a lot from Humboldt County—and I can tell you, they can expect more up there next year in the way of manpower and everything else," he said in late October 1983. The feisty DEA official then predicted, "Next year, with the resources of the federal government and the state, we will get rid of marijuana in Humboldt

County. Those people are operating up there in their own little Valhalla wilderness thinking everything is beautiful, knowing they got away with it, but we will see what happens next year."

Because of the successes of 1983, 37 sheriffs signed up for the 1984 campaign, during which only 398 sites were raided but with a much higher yield per site. As a result, 158,493 plants were seized and 218 arrests were made. The extra costs contributed by the federal and state governments amounted to $2.3 million. Mock diplomas were printed at the State Printing Office in Sacramento for presentation at the post-season banquet. They were headlined "Bud Buster Award" and declared they were to be given to officers in recognition for "having turned the tide in the 'war on drugs' " by eradicating "$325,000,000+ worth of the dreaded killer-weed sometimes known as 'sinsemilla.' . . . all accomplished while working to the haunting refrain of 'Ride of the Valkyries.' You are a charter member of the million-pound club and have earned the title of BUD BUSTER EXTRAORDINAIRE and may now proudly proclaim: 'We came, we saw, we kicked grass!' " (Those who saw *Apocalypse Now* will recall that the "Ride of the Valkyries" was played by the helicopter-borne American assault troops to terrorize the Vietnamese enemy.)

Before coming to California in the summer of 1985, I called the DEA office in Sacramento to arrange an appointment with the field commander of these grass-kicking, high-spirited police, William Ruzzamenti. He and his staff could not have been more cordial and he readily agreed to see me for dinner when I was in the state. I found Mr. Ruzzamenti to be a thoroughly engaging and idealistic fellow, an opinion shared on a personal level by many of those in active opposition to the powerful force he leads. As it happened, I was in Ron Sinoway's office in Miranda, talking to him and his legal colleague, Melvin Pearlston, just before leaving for my drive to Ukiah and our dinner appointment. As I rushed out of the office toward my car, civil rights lawyer Sinoway said, "Give him my best regards. He's really a nice guy . . . for a zealous drug warrior! Remind him that there was nothing 'personal' about the fact that I made him a personal defendant in that suit."

When I transmitted those greetings, Bill Ruzzamenti replied a few hours later as we chatted over a beer in his room in Ukiah, "Oh, I know there's nothing personal in it. I don't mind being sued for twenty million, or a hundred million dollars, whatever it is. My wife told me to just write him a check. Anyhow, Sinoway was nothing until I came here and started CAMP. I made him what he is today!"*

Mr. Ruzzamenti does not joke, however, about his views of the harm caused by drugs, the dangers to the public created by marijuana growers, the vital need for CAMP, and his commitment to use every legal weapon in the American arsenal to pursue pot cultivators and their allies relentlessly. To Bill Ruzzamenti this *is* a war, a just and moral one, and he is on the side of right. After fifteen years as a federal narcotics agent, this well-groomed, slightly built, idealistic Californian, then in his late thirties, knows that he is doing precisely what his personal morals tell him he ought to be doing. He had seen the ravages caused by drugs to parents and children and concluded that his calling would be to get rid of the drugs and put people in jail who were dealing in them.

CAMP, with his active encouragement, regularly compiles and promulgates stories of violence by anyone connected with marijuana growing, whether on public land or on the grower's own plot. The releases make good copy and are regularly picked up by papers all over the country and in other nations as well. That persistent scary publicity accounts in part for the fact that the news of my impending trip was greeted with trepidation and warnings from my family and friends. I, too, was somewhat fearful and felt the apprehension I remembered that accompanied me on trips into the Deep South when I was a federal civil rights official in the early Sixties. The basis for my fear about California was exaggerated, as far as I can now tell. Northern California in the mid-Eighties is quite different from Mississippi and Alabama in the early Sixties.

Neither Bill Ruzzamenti nor any police leader I met in California, however, believes that the dangers of violent growers and their ilk are anything but very real. Mr. Ruzzamenti welcomes a growth in public fear about the dangers of drugs and of violent growers. Even sensational journalism which exaggerates those dangers is accepted as a just weapon in a necessary and harsh war. He believes that the press also overplayed the danger of the chemical herbicide Paraquat being sprayed on Mexican marijuana in the Seventies. "It was a hysteria situation which the media created—and we went right along with it because that's what killed the marijuana business in Mexico," he told local writer Ray Raphael,

---

* The suit is explained in the next chapter.

who related the conversation in his book *Cash Crop* (1985). "Now we would certainly hope that we would create a similar media event that would kill the marijuana cultivation here. I think we'd be silly to miss the opportunity." While the Mexican marijuana business has risen profitably from the dead, if it ever really was in that state, there is no doubt of the willingness of the DEA and CAMP to play upon the fears about drugs that may be generated, however hysterically, by the press. Mr. Ruzzamenti also favors the future use of Paraquat on American marijuana fields, a weapon which the DEA shelved temporarily in 1983 in the face of a NORML suit because of its environmental impact. (The DEA began using other herbicides in September 1985.)

Moreover, the field commander appreciates the practical and psychological impact of helicopters in this war. "The helicopters have provided us with a sense of superiority that has in fact established a paranoia in the growers' minds and has kept us from getting involved in violence with the growers. . . . When you come in with a helicopter there's no way they're going to stop and fight; by and large they head for the hills, and we don't get a confrontational situation," he explained.

Emboldened by what they saw as previous successes, the drug warriors made major plans for more of the same in 1985. A press release explained the continuing nature of the police commitment: "This year, seven CAMP teams, each consisting of 12 to 25 trained special agents and volunteers from participating agencies, are conducting raids in 38 California counties during the prime marijuana cultivation season—a 14-week period from July 15 to October 18, 1985." The approved procedure is for CAMP pilots to fly fixed-wing small aircraft, not helicopters, at heights of 1,000 feet or more over areas thought likely to have marijuana gardens. When I originally drove into this vast, open country, stretching as far as the eye can see in many areas, I doubted that it was possible for airborne observers to find a significant number of marijuana plants hidden in its distant reaches. Both police and defense lawyers, to my surprise, agreed that experienced officers can readily spot the plants either by direct observation or from photographs. From the air, I was assured, marijuana has a distinct shiny green color that fairly calls out, "Hey, look at me! I am illegal!" Even with the aid of a magnifying glass, I could not pick out the miscreant plants in photographs used successfully in some criminal cases, so I merely offer this as agreed-upon expert opinion.

Once the plants are sighted, the police then must scour maps to determine the precise location and ownership of the property, which may be a difficult and tedious task. If it turns out to be public land or private property for which consent may be secured, then no search warrant is necessary. Otherwise, a search warrant is obtained to authorize a raid on private property. Then one of the private helicopters CAMP has under contract for the duration of the summer campaign each year (seven in 1985) comes into play. The helicopters transport the raiders to the often inaccessible sites selected by illegal growers to make their valuable crops difficult to find. Frequently, the troops must do a great deal of hiking on the ground in order to reach the garden since the helicopters must find an open area on which to land. An advance party of three to four agents "secures the site" by checking for booby traps and armed guards. The remainder of the raiding party—8 to 20 officers—next moves in. The team then cuts down the crop and loads it in slings which are lifted by the helicopter and transported to a pre-selected site where it is weighed and burned. The actual execution of these raids, therefore, requires a good deal of planning, intelligence, courage, effort, and sweat.

YOUNG AMERICANS BATTLING POT

That August 6 raid, with which this chapter began, was typical of CAMP operations. It was viewed by its leaders not simply as part of a law-enforcement effort but as a part of a major national program. At the 7:00 A.M. briefing in the Mendocino County sheriff's office, Bill Ruzzamenti made it clear that he believed in the whole ideology of the war on drugs which President Reagan has proclaimed and which I had heard explained to me so often by high-ranking drug abuse officials back in their Washington offices. I honestly did not expect to hear it 3,000 miles away from a police officer just before a raid.

When I heard that litany repeated to reporters early on that clear California morning, I suddenly realized that however much I doubted its basis in reality, I finally came to believe that Bill Ruzzamenti truly believed it and so did scores, even hundreds and thousands, of officials throughout the country. Their belief is powerful, more powerful and important, in a sense, than my disbelief under current conditions. It is terribly important that those who agree with me understand that Bill Ruzzamenti and most of his brothers-in-arms (some of whom I have literally cross-examined on this point in Miami squad rooms, in Washington, D.C., restaurants, and in the training rooms of the FBI Academy in Quantico, Virginia, near Washington) accept that vision of the drug world with all their heads, hearts, and guts. If they are performing, in the end, evil deeds, they do not perceive them as evil nor can they now understand the value system that suggests there might be other strategies to deal with drug problems.

Once we had all reached the marijuana fields on that hot day, the press was allowed a photo opportunity. After the dozens of accompanying press and television people (several from other countries, intent on learning about American methods) had taken all of the photographs of the standing plants they wanted, one of the lead deputies called out, "Cut and count!" Approximately ten uniformed officers, some of them baby-faced kids who were working part-time during the campaign for ten dollars an hour, began slashing away, most with sanviks, a Swedish-designed tool (sometimes spelled Sandviks) that works well on sugar cane or pot plants. Barry Inman was the only one I saw with a machete, which he happily wielded on plant after plant, his hatless head now glistening in the mountain sun.

"I love it," Barry told a reporter in our group as he worked with his machete. "Being able to take something illegal from somebody and getting the dope off the streets is a good feeling," he explained. He said further that he hated marijuana although he had never smoked it and did not claim to know much about it. "Some of my friends smoke but I don't associate with them any more because of it. They get all screwed up and can't think straight," he said. Every one of the young foot soldiers in the battle that day seemed to share Barry Inman's feelings about his work.

Many of those troops had stayed, as had I, in the Lu-Ann Motel at the north end of Ukiah, just off Route 101, the night before, where I saw them walking about in fatigues and field boots, carrying what appeared to be rifles, flak jackets, combat knives, and a great variety of pistols, not a few in rakish holsters. Incongruities abounded. A group of mid-level officers sat grouped near the pool that evening and planned the next day's assault, peering intently over maps on small boards. When I asked where I could get ice for my beer, they immediately interrupted their strategy session and pointed politely to the proper room. Most of the soldiers were intent not on maps but on relaxing and having fun that evening. They seemed to be decent young Americans, happily prepared to carry out a combat mission anywhere. But this was not anywhere; it was Mendocino County, in the heart of some of the world's greatest wine country, in the United States of America. That military presence seemed jarring and out of place there.

They were not, technically speaking, soldiers, but rather civilian police officers, operating in military style. All three levels of civilian law enforcement—federal, state, and local—were committed in a coordinated fashion. CAMP claims that officers from 110 agencies are involved in its campaign. Many of them come for a brief tour of duty from local police agencies in other parts of California. For some of these officers such combat duty in the hills is touted as Special Weapons and Tactics (SWAT) team training. As of that day at the Lu-Ann Motel, a total of 1,020 raids had been carried out in northern California during three seasons. That degree of police persistence in one geographic area shows why CAMP seems to have set the record for the use of armed force in America to enforce civilian laws.

Laws prohibiting products that huge numbers of citizens desire have always created a lure for organized criminals. The American experience with alcohol prohibition was characterized by the rise of organized crime, especially the Mafia, to new heights of lawlessness and violence. Today, such criminals rarely deal in alcohol but in other proscribed though earnestly desired chemicals. Because they may defend their illegal enterprises with weapons and violence, a large-scale enforcement response—not simply a few police officers—is often necessary to control them.

For a short while on that Mendocino hill, I too was overcome by the conviction that this kind of massive police power was really needed, and I suddenly found myself cheering on the police officers. I was unprepared for the supportive feeling that welled up inside me as I accompanied them on this mission. I saw with my own eyes that they were dedicated, decent, and competent, and that the growers were criminals who had the effrontery to take over someone else's land (thus earning the label "guerrilla") and to cultivate an illegal crop on it. These actions by the guerrilla growers involved calculated, repeated invasions of the property of the Louisiana Pacific Lumber Company over a period of months. If those criminals could commit such acts of multiple trespass, I feared that they were capable of much worse. *Under current laws and social conditions*, then, this raid, and others like it, on guerrilla and commercial growers seem to make some sense.

That feeling of support, however, was soon largely overwhelmed by the contrary visceral feelings that welled up when I contemplated a small amount of the cut marijuana lying in a truck bed. For some reason, it had not been airlifted out. Two burly, young, armed officers sat proudly on the truck, looking like victorious gladiators. Had the truck contained the body of a wolf or a mountain lion or a deactivated bomb, I might have had a different reaction. Standing marijuana, I had just seen, is a beautiful dark green plant with a pleasant odor. Cut marijuana looks innocent and harmless. Even somewhat pitiful. Is this what these young police officers had just risked their lives to capture? While no violent growers were confronted and no booby traps were tripped, they might have been. Even in their absence, the movement of all of these people up hazardous mountain roads—the greatest danger, I am now convinced, that everyone faces in that region—and the whole process of cutting and helicoptering out the captured weeds represented hazards to the pilots, to the police, to the observers, and to the general public.

Following that raid, two California police officers and their pilot were killed when a small plane crashed while searching for marijuana. On October 29, 1986, moreover, a major disaster allegedly was almost caused by a helicopter on a DEA surveillance mission. The pilot of a United Airlines 727, trying to land in Los Angeles, claimed he was forced to fly over the top of the helicopter at an estimated 200 feet. The DEA claimed its pilot prevented the planes from even getting close. The incident occurred in the same general area where a private small plane collided with an Aeromexico DC-9 on August 31, 1986, killing 82 people.

In my scale of values, none of the risks involved in these raids, whether they be assessed as great or small, whether from violent growers or simple accidents, is worth the capture of innocent plants which could harm smokers only if they used the product repeatedly for many years.

Another jarring incongruity that day was created for me by the sudden appearance at the crest of the hill of John Ridenour. He was a gentle-spoken, 32-year-old local citizen in blue jeans, no shirt, long blond hair and beard, taking pictures of the scene with a 35-millimeter camera. Soon his wife appeared, carrying a small, well-fed baby. Apparently, they were trespassers since this was posted private property and Mr. Ridenour was not a lumber company employee. He was also in close proximity to that huge illegal garden and I wondered if he would have been arrested if we observers had not been present.

More surprising, he proceeded to give an interview to the press in which he admitted openly that he was a criminal, a mom-and-pop grower in the area. As he said this, heavily armed police were walking all over the trail, within earshot. When the press asked if he thought the police were acting properly, John Ridenour replied, "I haven't seen nothin' wrong this time or here. I thought all the guys and everything was fine. They didn't harass me. . . . I haven't seen any machine guns or that stuff that I'd . . . heard about." He was asked if he had heard of people moving out or ceasing to grow because of the police campaign, and replied that he had not but that many of them had changed the way in which they grew their plants; they were growing fewer of them and seeking to hide them better. "Everybody's out to make a living," he explained in his quiet voice, "I'm sure that they don't wanna have to grow pot. People like the country and this is a way to get money. They're just making a living."

"What do you find to be a bigger concern, the police or pot rip-offs?" a reporter asked. "Pot rip-offs," the grower immediately replied, referring to private citizens who steal other people's illegal plants. This was not a great vote of confidence in American police power, even when it was wielded in the fashion of an invading army. John Ridenour also provided this inside overall assessment about the potential impact on his neighbors of the major law-enforcement effort unfolding that day before his eyes: "They are wasting their money and time. There is dope all over these hills. They are putting on a good show but they will never get rid of it. They will never win."

Others have expressed the same ideas with a slightly different twist. After he served as interim district attorney of neighboring Trinity County, Weaverville lawyer William Neill observed in November 1984, "It would take two divisions to enforce the law in a meaningful way" in order to control "Trinity County's largest crop." The local lawyer concluded, "Aside from how any of us might . . . feel about the use of marijuana . . . personally, I'm not keen on having two army divisions wandering about the county." Mr.

Neill might have added that there is nothing in the record of drug-law enforcement to suggest that even two divisions would be successful in controlling marijuana in that or in any county.

HIGH-LEVEL PLEAS FOR MORE MILITARY FORCE

Unfortunately, too many leading officials do not understand the lessons of northern California as well as do Messrs. Ridenour and Neill, who have lived through them—nor does it appear that these prominent Americans have the vaguest idea of the reasons behind the historical repugance of America to the use of the military in civilian affairs. It had long been accepted in England that a magistrate or other leading law-enforcement officer of a country or shire, sometimes known as a shire reeve (later shortened to one modern word), could call upon the male citizens of the community over 15 years of age to assist him in the keeping of the peace or in apprehending felons. This "power of the county," one literal translation of *posse comitatus*, was to be used in the enforcement of civil laws. A related tradition grew up over the centuries, with roots as far back as the Magna Carta, that viewed with horror the use of the military to enforce those laws on local citizens. Whenever monarchs have called in military forces to enforce the law on a reluctant population, this usually signaled that there was massive defiance of some of those laws—and that a true civil war might be erupting.

Such was the case several centuries ago when the English living on the coast of the wild continent of America took up smuggling almost as a patriotic duty to defy the customs regulations of the government in London. The British responded by providing writs of assistance, which authorized general searches in homes for contraband, that is, goods smuggled from abroad without paying customs duties—and they brought in troops to assist in those searches and to whip these defiant citizens into compliance with the customs law. The results for King George III were less than successful. In the process of leading the appeal for the traditional rights of all loyal Englishmen, the fiery Sam Adams proclaimed in a speech in 1768 that "to be called to account by a common soldier, or any soldier, is a badge of slavery which none but a *slave* will wear."

Eight years later, Thomas Jefferson was moved to inveigh against the excesses of foreign soldiers as one of the reasons given to the world for the stunning, seditious action of secession from the lawful royal authority in America. While the constitution of 1787 did not expressly prohibit the use of the military to enforce the laws, it did place the civilian President in the position of commander-in-chief; and within a few more years, the Bill of Rights demanded narrowly defined searches, thus prohibiting general search warrants, which had warmed the cockles of the royal military heart.

After the Civil War, federal troops were used to keep order in the defeated South. As has so often happened throughout history, the troops were soon imposing a form of colonial oppression upon the people and their leaders. That moved Congress to pass the act of 1878 which made it a federal crime to use the military "as a *posse comitatus* or otherwise to execute the laws." While this had the desired effect at the time, it soon was a largely forgotten law—in part because the military was thenceforth rarely called upon to enforce the civilian laws in the scale and style seen in the mid-1700s and the Reconstruction Era. Moreover, there were recognized exceptions to the prohibition on the use of the military in American life. For example, the Coast Guard is exempt because, while in time of war it is the coastal defense force of the Navy, in peacetime it is considered a civilian law enforcement agency with the mission to enforce customs laws, control our borders, provide search-and-rescue services, and aid navigation. In the event of insurrection or major civil disorder, moreover, it was accepted that troops could be used on a temporary basis so long as the emergency lasted.

Current fears, however, have induced a significant cadre of American leaders to raise the specter of a permanent breach of the traditional wall between civilian and military affairs—and that breach is justified in the name of enforcing the drug laws. How sad that hard-learned lessons of democracy and freedom are ignored by those who should harken to them most. While there is a basis in fact for their concerns about controlling the vast amount of drug trafficking coming over our borders, there is an edge of hysteria to the ideas proposed by some of those leaders now most vocally urging that we call out the marines to save our kids from drugs. A major tenet of these military-minded drug fighters is that the vast commitment of the Reagan Administration is not enough and that a *real* war with a *real* military and allied diplomatic commitment is necessary.

Rep. Charles Rangel (D-N.Y.), the powerful head of the House Select Committee on Narcotics Abuse and Control, is one of the prime advocates of that position. He has consistently criticized the Reagan administration and the Joint Chiefs of Staff for not unleashing a major military assault on drug trafficking. The black leader has demonstrated how otherwise sensible and humane politicians of the major parties seek to outbid each other in being tough on drugs. When I wrote an article in the March 1984 *Justice Quarterly* calling for "Peace Without Surrender in the Perpetual Drug War," he responded with an article in the next issue, agreeing with me that this nation has never won a war on drugs because in the past all of the wars have been limited and uncoordinated.

Accordingly, Mr. Rangel called for a "total war" on drug abuse, which would involve a single federal director of drug strategy (sometimes called a "drug czar") a more aggressive war, and the elimination of foreign aid to countries, like Pakistan and Colombia, that do not take more effective action to curb drug production and subsequent exports to our shores. The congressman seemed unimpressed with my argument to him several months later on a network television debate that we lived in a glass house on the latter score because a virtual army of federal police officers had not prevented wholesale drug dealing on the streets of the nation's cities, including those of the capital city outside the very door of the television studio.

Edward Koch, the flamboyant mayor of New York, is often engaged in political imbroglios with the Harlem congressman, but on drug issues they are like blood brothers, although there seems to be sibling rivalry as to which of them will win the Rambo award in that arena. Mr. Rangel has made a good try, but my vote would be for the mayor. In a speech before the National Press Club in Washington, Mr. Koch actually asked why Mr. Reagan should not order the Air Force to use F-15 fighter jets for the purpose of "shooting down" suspected drug smuggling planes as they approach our borders. Under questioning from incredulous reporters he amended his statement to a suggestion that the Air Force pilots might put the wheels of their jets on the cockpits of the suspects and thus "force down" the bad guys. There are those, of course, who may be equally incredulous at the amended reply.

Mr. Koch noted in the same speech that most of the heroin that is smuggled into the country comes from either Mexico or Southeast Asia. Accordingly, he asked, "Why shouldn't every passenger coming from those areas be subject to a strip search?" Noting further that border officials were now overwhelmed with incoming passengers, he had a practical suggestion for aiding them in their duties: use military personnel to carry out the vast number of bodily searches that would be required under this new policy which would greet hordes of visitors as they arrived at the shores of freedom. The Koch plan could mean soldiers in uniform with side-arms or M-16s greeting each flight from dozens of countries, selecting hundreds or thousands of passengers each day, on the basis of intuition or hunch, to step aside into small, convenient rooms, take off all of their clothes, and be subjected to a search of their bodily cavities and perhaps their bodily wastes.

One is forced to wonder if drug fear has so clouded our national reason that more Americans do not see the supreme irony in two of the highest elected representatives of the Jewish and Negro people—both of which have suffered centuries of abuse from the arbitrary actions of the military and the police of many countries—united on the need for more armed force to deal with a delicate human problem, one that involves serious civil liberties issues. It would be in keeping with recent history to see them united on more gentle and peaceful approaches to dealing with drugs.

More gentle and more peaceful proposals on this subject might also be expected to come from female officials (unless I am being hopelessly old-fashioned). This expectation has not been fulfilled, as demonstrated by the harsh martial posture persistently taken by one of Mr. Rangel's chief counterparts in the Senate, Paula Hawkins (R-Fla.), chairwoman of the Subcommittee on Alcoholism and Drug Abuse. Like the gentlemen from New York, Senator Hawkins represents a constituency deeply troubled by drug trafficking and the violent crime and corruption that comes with it.* New York City and Miami have some of the worst drug trafficking and organized crime in America. Both are far more dangerous on those accounts than, say, northern California, Washington, D.C.,

---

* Ms. Hawkins was defeated in the 1986 election by former governor Bob Graham in a campaign dominated by the drug issue. By impartial local accounts, the mood of the electorate had been affected by the hysteria of the summer of 1986. Candidate Graham managed to convince the voters that Senator Hawkins only appeared tough on the issue and that he would be even tougher.

or many other communities with reputations for drug problems.

Moreover, as was pointed out to me on the wall map in his Miami office by James Dingfelder, staff director of the Vice President's South Florida Task Force, the entire state of Florida sits there in the calm, warm ocean like a giant dock or a string of safe harbors, just inviting the friendly neighborhood drug smugglers from South America to drop in. The huge sea of Hispanic people on the peninsula provides a haven for traders from the south. Once in that haven, they can easily connect with the established Hispanic drug-smuggling infrastructure. It is understandable, therefore, why some local leaders have issued a call for greater police and military force in the Florida area. Ms. Hawkins has loudly echoed that call.

In May 1984 she made the then seemingly outrageous suggestion of sending American troops to South America. This was in response to the unsolved murder of Colombia's justice minister, Lara Bonilla, apparently by cocaine traffickers. Ms. Hawkins wrote President Reagan: "I urge you to offer whatever resources necessary including U.S. military personnel to the government of Colombia in their war on illegal drug trafficking." The senator also suggested dispatching "helicopters, flame throwers, night vision equipment, radars, and firearms," explaining that "while the measures I propose are drastic," they are necessary "to fight these mass murderers."

The *Gainesville Sun,* in an editorial titled "Adios, Colombia," objected to the vision of our young people in uniform "skimming the Colombian mountaintops in armed gunships seeking out drug smugglers" because "the prospect of the United States employing its military might to intervene in another nation's domestic crime problem . . . is too chilling to seriously entertain. Americans certainly wouldn't tolerate the prospect of federal troops fighting domestic crime here at home." Senator Hawkins shot back a letter saying that "help from the military has been critical to the success of the South Florida Task Force," which assistance was made possible by the *posse comitatus* amendments which she claimed that she had introduced. "If we do not take some drastic steps to stop illegal drugs at their source, we can not only say 'Adios, Colombia,' but also 'Adios, Gainesville.' "

The dispatch of American soldiers to Bolivia by President Reagan in July 1986 showed that the proposals of Senator Hawkins were not so outrageous, after all. In the pursuit of the current drug war, what once seemed to represent extremism has often come to appear as moderation. Fortunately, the role of the American troops was to provide transportation and logistical support to the local forces and not to engage in battle themselves, as Senator Hawkins and others have suggested.

Those who agreed with two questionable assumptions—that drugs can be stopped at their source and that the military is an effective weapon in drug control—came out in support of a more far-reaching proposal introduced by another congressman from Florida, Charles E. Bennett, a Democrat, in 1985. The so-called Bennett Amendment called for expanding the exception to the *posse comitatus* restriction that had been voted in 1981 so that military personnel would be authorized to enforce directly the drug laws anywhere outside the territory of the United States. Even under the 1981 amendment, a Navy ship that spotted a suspected drug boat at sea, for example, could only inform civilian law-enforcement agencies such as the Coast Guard or DEA so they could later make the search and arrests. The Bennett Amendment would have allowed the Navy sailors to make the searches and arrests immediately on their own.

The amendment was also propelled forward on the legislative road by a good deal of emotion, some of it highly personal. Mr. Bennett recalled the rage he felt when he was forced to pay a drug dealer $100 for fear that the criminal would have his drug-dependent son killed if he did not pay. In 1977, his son died from a drug overdose. "I don't want to waste my pain," Rep. Bennett said. "There's hardly any limit to what I would impose on the big operators who would destroy America in making wealth for themselves."

The daughter of Congressman Stewart McKinney (R-Conn.) had been in serious trouble with drugs, a fact he mentioned when he urged his colleagues to allow the Navy and the Air Force "to interdict the greatest, slimiest, lousiest, cruddiest enemy we have got in this country, those people who would profit off of killing the kids of this country. . . . Drug dealers are killing our kids. Is it not the job of the military to protect this country, its future, its kids, for God's sake?"

Rep. Mario Biaggi (D-N.Y.) told on the floor of the House that he was fully allied with Mayor Koch's position on use of the military, including putting the Army to work policing ports of entry (a proposal not directly involved in the Bennett Amendment). The New York congressman furthermore specifically endorsed Mr. Koch's line of reasoning that (1) since the DEA director had said, in an offhand comment, that he would need 40,000 agents, added to the 2,000 now on the force, to enforce the drug laws adequately, (2) this would take an extra $1 billion, which was not forthcoming in a time of massive budget deficits; accordingly, (3) only the military could do the job of drug-law enforcement without any appreciable extra expenditures.

Remarkably, it took the conservative, hard-line Secretary of Defense, Caspar W. Weinberger, to make the point that there was a compelling need to keep the military out of civilian life. In a letter to the House Armed Services Committee, Mr. Weinberger declared that the Bennett Amendment would breach "the historic separation between military and civilian spheres of activity," which wall he described as "one of the most fundamental principles of American democracy." Therefore, the Secretary of Defense stated, "We strongly oppose the extension of civilian police powers to our military forces." More quietly, other Reagan administration agency heads involved in drug enforcement opposed the Bennett Amendment, to their credit. Even President Reagan and the First Lady have at times expressed doubts about going so far as to allow the military to get involved directly in drug policing.

The Bennett Amendment nevertheless passed the House on June 26, 1985, by an overwhelming majority, 364 to 51. However, later in conference committee with the Senate a compromise was worked out whereby funds would be provided to place more Coast Guard Tactical Law Enforcement Teams (TACLETS) upon Navy ships. This would meet several objections, including one which argued that drug searches and arrests would interfere with military effectiveness. There is much truth in this position because most service people are not trained in the law of search and arrest, nor do their normal duty assignments allow time for them to testify in court cases. To Coast Guard sailors, on the other hand, this is standard duty. The new drug-control act of 1986 contained a provision for at least 500 of such trained Coast Guard personnel to be placed on Navy vessels in drug-interdiction areas. Thus the emotional move to give American military people the full powers of search and seizure has been defeated for the time being. Nevertheless, it is clear that the pressure for greater use of the military in the enforcement of the drug laws is growing.

Despite the reservations about the use of the military sometimes stated by President Reagan, he has authorized its wider involvement in drug cases—in almost every respect but actually carrying out searches, seizures, and arrests. On April 8, 1986, the President took the extraordinary action of declaring drug trafficking a threat to the national security in a secret National Security Decision Directive. That directive authorized greater use of military equipment, troops, and intelligence resources in assisting domestic and foreign drug police, reportedly over the strong objections of Secretary Weinberger. The Anti-Drug Abuse Act of 1986 provided legislative support for most of these military initiatives. All of them should cause great concern in a democracy, especially the declaration that drug trafficking threatened the national security. One might argue more rationally that the drug laws and the wide-eyed drug warriors represented a greater threat. Throughout American history, we have seen that the depiction of a problem as a threat to the security of the country has often justified the most extreme measures in response.

If this hysteria continues, we may still reach the day when we will see American soldiers searching American citizens for drugs— and arresting them when contraband is found. It will be a sad day when that occurs, and we all should fervently hope—nay, pray, repeatedly, now that Mr. Justice Rehnquist heads the nation's judiciary—that such actions will be found unconstitutional by the courts.

SUPPLY INTERDICTION: WE NEVER DID IT

Powerful, vehement support for the intensification of the war on drug trafficking, whether through military or through civilian agencies, comes from across the political spectrum in Washington. Despite seven decades of failure, the litany is still stated by leading officials that only through interruption of the supply can eventual victory over drug abuse be gained. Drug-enforcement chiefs pay lip service now to the notion that they cannot win this battle without help on the demand side, but when they let their hair down, they truly believe not in the power of denial by users—unless it has been forced on them by the police and by fear of job loss—but mainly in the power of interdiction and denial of supplies.

A middle-aged federal drug-abuse official said to me in despair one day recently, "The ghost of Harry Anslinger hovers over Capitol Hill like a fog." He was referring to the head of the old Federal Bureau of Narcotics (FBN), the original bureaucratic ancestor of the DEA, who reigned from 1930 to 1962, longer than any federal police official in the history of the country, except the remarkable J. Edgar Hoover. The closest living legacy of Mr. Anslinger, to my knowledge, is to be found in the personage of Mr. Jack Cusack, the chief of staff of the House Select Committee on Narcotics Abuse and Control and one of the most respected people in Washington on drug-enforcement issues. Like his current boss, Congressman Rangel, the New York City native, now in his early sixties, has always treated me with unfailing politeness, which, I fear, might not have been my treatment at the hands of Mr. Anslinger himself. When I first met Mr. Cusack in the office of Congressman Rangel, he said words to this effect: Doc, its good to read your stuff, kind of warms my heart, brings back the old days; you know, we considered your ideas way back and rejected them because they don't work.

It was the voice of Jack but the spirit of Harry. For 32 years, the most remarkable accomplishment of the monochromatic FBN director was to convince America and the world that there was no other way to deal with narcotic addicts than harsh law enforcement and complete prohibition of the truly bad drugs, even in medicine for the organically ill, for any purpose. Whenever anyone, even highly respected authorities, such as the New York Academy of Medicine in 1955, suggested more gentle approaches to dealing with some addicts, such as British-style medical dispensation of drugs, he reacted predictably. Mr. Anslinger usually replied that "the British system is the same as the United States system," and besides, the so-called British system of decriminalization of drugs has failed, both of which statements were untrue at the time. Bureaucratic descendants of Mr. Anslinger—including Mr. Cusack and DEA administrators Peter M. Bensinger, Francis M. Mullen, Jr., and John Lawn, among others—have produced ideological progeny of the same twisted veracity.

Thus, the core of the dominant American strategy is still strict law enforcement and the core of the law-enforcement ideology is the old-time religious covenant: thou shalt not use bad drugs even to help dying patients lest the wall of prohibition be breached and our innocent children get the wrong idea about drugs. When, accordingly, Mr. Cusack tells me that my old ideas have proved not to work, he is simply repeating a key sermon in that old-time theology. To a seminar of journalists at Washington's Watergate Hotel in 1985, he added another essential principle of the enforcement creed: "we did it before and we can do it again." As I was sitting there listening, it occurred to me that most of the reporters in the room were too young to realize that this was a World War II slogan referring to the Germans. In this context it meant that America had deliberately cut off the supply of illegal drugs in the past and thus had reduced drug abuse; once we truly make up our minds that we are united in this new war, we could cut off drugs and then the number of drug abusers would plummet once again.

Mr. Cusack makes an impressive presentation. He has had years of experience as a DEA agent and supervisor and can talk on the basis of a long record in the field. He was the chief American narcotics agent in Paris during the early Seventies when the famous French Connection heroin ring was broken, and thus participated in making drug-law enforcement history. That success was coupled with an agreement between the United States and Turkey under which Turkey began exerting control over its opium fields, from which the raw material for the French heroin had come. In Mr. Cusack's mind, and in that of the leading drug strategists of the nation, those twin victories resulted in a drastic interruption in the illegal heroin traffic and a corresponding drop in American heroin abuse and related crime. That is why, Mr. Cusack later told a reporter, he did not want to hear any talk that the war on drugs cannot be won by law enforcement. Those victories were "a classic application of narcotics-law enforcement . . . When we cut availability, we eliminate drug abuse. It's just that simple."

How I wish that it were! We would gird our loins, unleash the military and the forces of law and order, make alliances with the good nations, and, World War II style, carry the battle to the bad, accepting whatever casualties were necessary to fight through to final victory. How simple the world *did* seem back in 1941, but now in all respects it is much more complicated.

A review of the factual record, and not simply accepted myths, leads one to the uncomfortable conclusion that American law enforcement has never created a long-term interruption in the supply of any illicit drug. I do not report this failure with glee because the lives of all of us might be infinitely better if the opposite were true, if the enforcement theology applied to the real world. But it does not. What does apply is the Iron Law of the Opium Trade, and not only to America and not only to the modern era: Whenever there is a demand for an illicit opiate, such as heroin, in time a supply appears; and when one source of supply is cut off, another soon replaces it in sufficient volume to satisfy the demand. (This law also applies to most other illicit drugs, certainly to marijuana.)

Official federal intelligence estimates indicate that the interruption of the French-Turkish supply line did, indeed, result in a drop in the percentage of the illicit American heroin market filled by Turkish sources: from approximately 53 percent in 1972 to 9 percent in 1974. Thus, one might conclude, Mr. Cusack and his allies are correct; law enforcement works. This claim would be correct only if we ignored the broader reality. Mexican Mud, or brown heroin, soon flooded into the gap, rising from 38 percent of the American market in 1972 to 77 percent in 1974, again according to official federal reports, which leading American government drug-abuse experts seem not to read. The total supply of heroin also was soon back at a high level.

This is not to say that the police officers who busted the French Connection were wasting their time. It is to say rather that the police should pursue major drug traffickers and organized crime leaders because so many of them are vicious, violent criminals who engage in a wide variety of destructive activities, ranging in recent years from terrorism to bilking governments of perhaps a billion dollars in gasoline taxes to murder—all in addition to selling vast quantities of illegal drugs. The FBI, the DEA, and all major police agencies should continue to assign courageous, competent officers to pursue these social jackals because they harm civilization in many ways, not simply by selling drugs. Moreover, even if 20 French Connections had been broken, this would not have solved the drug problem in America. A twenty-first ring would probably have soon come out of the criminal woodwork with an adequate supply of drugs, which are relatively simple substances to grow or to refine. It does not take a horticultural genius to grow hardy opium poppies or a chemical wizard to refine heroin from a morphine base. Therefore, the destruction of most of the current major criminal networks would have only a temporary impact on the use and abuse of drugs.

What about the claim that abuse and crime by addicts went down when that Turkish supply was interrupted in the early Seventies? There simply is no evidence to support this widely held belief. It seems certain that many addicts reduced their use, especially on the East Coast, where there was a severe shortage for perhaps several years. When addicts reduce their use of heroin, this is usually seen as the supreme achievement of government policy. In fact, when a heroin supply line to a community is interdicted, three types of addict reaction are probable.

First, one segment of addicts will increase their reliance on other drugs, especially alcohol. It could be argued that this is a good result because alcohol is less expensive and crime will therefore go down. Yet alcohol has a more criminogenic impact than heroin or any opiate on the emotions of users. Heroin usually cools the passions; alcohol heats them up.

Second, a significant group of addicts will simply try harder and use every bit of their native ingenuity to snare some of the smaller amount that is still available on the street. This pursuit will require more crime because the drug will be more expensive.

Third, a group of addicts might well leave the whole illegal drug culture, at least for a while. They might decide: to heck with it, I've had enough, my girl is fed up with me, I'm getting tired of the continual hassle, I am finally going to stop using smack—either through a treatment program or on my own—and start living a straight life. This group will be older, more mature, and near the end of their deviant careers. The most powerful "cure" for heroin abuse and related crime is not found in medicine or law enforcement but in age. In the trade, it is known as "maturing out" of addiction and deviance.

Thus it is never clear, on balance, how the interruption of a heroin supply line will affect a given community or a whole nation. While we may like the idea of pushing a segment of the addict population out of the black market, this is done at the price of pushing some addicts to more crime and others to different drugs. While conventional drug-abuse experts claim heroin drives users toward crime, I say hogwash; they have not done their homework. The scientific evidence demonstrates that we are all better off if the heroin addicts have a reasonably steady supply of the stuff rather than the other drugs they seek at a time of shortage. In particular, we should fear their actions when they turn to alcohol, barbiturates, methaqualone, amphetamines, and PCP. I would prefer they stopped using any of these chemicals, including heroin, but I have no idea how to accomplish such magical events for most addicts.

When I reviewed all of the official crime data, moreover, I was unable to find any persistent pattern of a drop in crime during the early Seventies. In 1971, the rates per 100,000 population for the seven most serious crimes, the FBI's Crime Index, was 3,136.7 in the Middle Atlantic states. In 1972, it dropped to 2,858.5, again seemingly proving the police-supply theories correct. Yet by 1973, when the heroin shortage continued, the Crime Index in those states went up to 3,690.3, and by 1974 it was up further to 4,267.7. National crime trends mirrored those of the Middle Atlantic states. These official figures might be used to support the argument that a police-imposed interruption of supply causes a temporary downturn in crime and later a huge increase as addicts are pushed into a crime frenzy.

A more moderate interpretation would be that the destruction of an illicit heroin supply line causes many unpredictable and often inconsistent results, not at all like beating the Germans in Normandy or the Japanese on Guadalcanal. One of the most cautious and sensible reports on drug policy in recent history, the Ford administration's *White Paper on Drug Abuse*, issued by a White House task force in 1975, came to similar conclusions. It made no claim that the heroin shortage produced a drop in crime. On the positive side, the *White Paper* stated that successful supply-reduction efforts may reduce the number of new users, increase the number of established users who cease use, and decrease the overall consumption of current users. On the negative side, "young, casual users of drugs are stigmatized by arrest; the health of committed users is threatened by impure drugs; black markets are created and with them significant possibilities for corruption of public officials; and crime rates increase, as users attempt to meet the rising cost of scarce, illegal drugs." The task force added, "Finally, no supply-reduction effort can be completely effective. Even if we were willing to drastically restrict civil liberties . . . some drugs would continue to flow into illegal markets."

In other words, this White House task force was telling the Anslinger disciples of the world, including those converts in the Reagan administration, that it just ain't so, that the war on drugs simply cannot be won, at least not on their terms. Even if we flood the world with drug police and their military auxiliaries, and even if we interrupt illegal supply lines, we may cause more harm than good. As now conceived, the mission of the drug warriors of America is demonstrably impossible.

That conclusion stares them in the face if they will only look, and is stated, sometimes indirectly, by street-level officers. On the same day in June 1982 that President Reagan went out into the Rose Garden to announce a new war on drugs, the District of Columbia Metropolitan Police Department announced that it had achieved a major success at a spot a few miles north of the roses: the largest heroin seizure in departmental history, 6.7 pounds of 90-percent-pure drugs, worth $15.4 million. Yet Lieutenant Carl Alexander observed, "There will be a shortage out there on the street. The price of dope will probably go up. Crime may go up because junkies will need more money to pay the prices."

MADDENING RESULTS

For those who believe in good old-fashioned American wars which reach predictable final satisfying scenes, dominated by demands for unconditional surrenders and total victories, such results are maddening. Conflict-ridden and unpredictable behavior lies at the heart of drug-human relationships, and strategies that ignore these complex relationships will always produce unexpected results. Several years ago, for example, the United States government led a national and international campaign to eliminate the abuse of methaqualone—known also by the trade name Quaalude and the street name "lude"—by prohibiting its use in medicine and convincing the sole U.S. manufacturer to cease production. Within a few months, every bit of information I encountered indicated that use and abuse of the drug was rapidly diminishing everywhere in the country. This remarkable event represented the second instance in American history wherein I have been able to identify a significant drop in the use of an illicit drug apparently through deliberately planned governmental action. The first involved that heroin shortage of the early Seventies, and we saw how that worked out.

For many months, it looked to me as if the prohibition of methaqualone would rate as the major exception to the consistent failure of prohibition policies in America. Then informants from the streets started to laugh at my naïveté on this matter. It was true, they said, that real 'ludes were hard to get, but the fakes were all over the streets and were being snapped up by the regular customers. In fact, many of the regulars liked the synthetics better than the originals. With good reason, for most of the counterfeit

'ludes were actually composed of Valium or other proven tran-
quilizers which had effects approximating methaqualone. During
my visit to the Miami front in September 1985, I was told by
streetwise experts that there was no great call for 'ludes in that
area because the regulars were quite content with the substitutes,
many of which were smuggled from Colombia and were sold at
reasonable prices.

In a similar vein was the success of the combined Coast Guard–
Navy–Air Force–Customs war against drug traffickers in the
southern approaches to America. In several operations, there have
been naval blockades of the Colombian coast—code-named Operation Hat Trick—which, as Coast Guard Lt. Commander Terry
Hart of the Vice President's office in Washington told me, "took
down everything that moved." Such operations under the Reagan
administration have been quite effective if we use the measure of
the amount of marijuana seized—at least a million pounds annually
in recent years. However, when I was in Florida in late 1985, I
was told that marijuana was more difficult at that time for young
people to buy than cocaine, which was plentiful and relatively inexpensive. One hopes that no Reagan strategist will applaud that
victory.

Indeed, during my entire time visiting the area covered by the
showpiece South Florida Task Force, I found precious little objective evidence of bottom-line success produced by the vast efforts
of the many competent enforcement leaders and officers I met.
Since 1980, the Miami Citizens Against Crime created a remarkable
movement to beef up enforcement, including convincing the Reagan administration to set up that task force. In addition, local tax
and bond monies were made available for more police and jail space,
as well as for education of young people. While the crime rate
dropped from 1980 to 1983, it started up again in 1984, and was
rising even more in 1985. Violent crime associated with the cocaine
trade, in particular, puts a blanket of terror over many parts of
Miami. These trends were reported to me by straight-arrow retired
Rear Admiral Van T. Edsall, director of MCAC, and now somewhat depressed over these results after so much work. I tried to
offer what comfort I could by saying that success in such efforts
was as rare as hen's teeth.

Street prices reflect this endemic lack of success. Illegal supplies of drugs have reached record levels while the massive Reagan
enforcement effort has been taking place. In 1981, when President

Reagan took office, the price of a kilogram of cocaine in south Florida was $60,000; by 1983, the glut had dropped the price to $20,000; during my visit in 1985, it had risen somewhat to $25,000–30,000, still half the 1981 price.

"It's dropping out of the skies," admitted Jack Cusack in 1985. "Literally. In Florida, people are finding packages in their driveways that have fallen out of planes." Federal intelligence estimates for the entire country are consistent with such incredible events. For 1980, analysts set the amount of illegal imported cocaine at 40 tons. For 1985, these experts place the amount at over 100 tons, worth enough to dwarf the entire treasuries of most countries.

The advent of crack in 1985 and 1986 was created in large part because of the glut in the cocaine market. In this sense, crack was a packaging and marketing strategy to deal with the economic problem of an excess of cocaine supplies.

Failure is also documented in reliable surveys of illicit drug use. While I have argued that the so-called epidemic had leveled off by the mid-Eighties, the total numbers of users and abusers of virtually all illicit drugs are at very high levels. During the two eventful decades since 1965, a period in which drug-law enforcement has been at record levels, the number of people who use illegal drugs has risen sharply. How can any pragmatic American look at all of these bottom-line numbers and deny that they add up to massive failure, not simply of individual officials, but of the fundamental principles of our entire drug-control strategy?

Seventy years of drug-warrior rule, of the chemical march of folly, have produced a situation for all Americans, including those who have no involvement whatsoever in drugs, in which illicit drugs are now more available than ever, our streets are awash with criminals, our sick are suffering needless pain—and our liberties, our sense of peace and privacy, our very personal dignity are all being greatly curtailed.

7

How the Warriors Invade Our Peace and Property

THE HONORABLE Rudolph W. Giuliani, U.S. Attorney for the Southern District of New York, was outraged at my remarks, and at those of several other academic dissenters participating in a forum. At one point he replied to me, "The freedoms of people arrested for drugs are very, very well protected in the United States." Later, even more emphatically, "We don't put people in prison because we like to but because we have no other choice." He then fairly shouted at me, "It's absurd to keep saying those silly things," a thought he threw out at least six times during an afternoon of heated discussion on a 100-degree August day at Manhattan's University Club.

SCORCHED EARTH: THE PROSECUTORIAL MIND-SET

The silly things I kept saying did not deal *primarily* with the matter of the protection of people once they are formally arrested for crime, but my concerns do include such matters because fear of drugs has induced American courts to approve of a wide array of irrational practices. Even though they have that stamp of judicial approval on them, our freedom in a real sense has been diminished by such court decisions. Indeed, one of the worst lines of court decisions in American history has been that which has approved ever-expanding police power in the pervasive search for chemical contraband. Drug prosecutions produce terrible judicial doctrines. Because they are based upon bastardized versions of scientific truth and democratic ethics, such decisions should be bound in separate volumes of court reports with a bar sinister (the ancient sign of bastard offspring) on the covers.

My concerns about freedom, though, go beyond perverse practices supported by judicial decisions or by statutes. The body of real American freedom has also been shrunk by a vast array of institutional practices that do not yet have the full legal stamp of approval on them. By "freedom" in this context, I mean the whole array of formal and informal rules that make for the personal dignity that is the birthright of a sovereign citizen in a democracy, whether or not that particular freedom has yet been articulated and protected by the legal system. Such freedoms range from the technical right to be free from unreasonable police searches in one's home (a traditional constitutional right) to the right to be free from being forced to urinate in a bottle at the whim of petty officials (a nontraditional and as yet undefined right). That full range of freedom, privacy, and dignity faces destruction at the hands of the drug warriors.

In addition, we must be concerned with the broad impact of our laws and policies on the number of Americans we place in our own prisons, not that, in one sense, they do not deserve to be there, but that in the longer run, we must inquire into what laws and policies we might change to lessen the number behind bars, to reverse the trend toward America becoming a prison nation. Thus, we should be concerned that conditions in America—created through a combination of bad luck and bad laws—have worked so as to produce the largest prison population in any democratic nation, in absolute and proportional terms.*

During the Reagan years, moreover, the total number of prisoners in major state and federal institutions jumped up sharply by

* The American prisoner rate per hundred thousand population in mid-1986 was 210. Recent rates for other Western countries are 111.5 in Austria, 99.7 in West Germany, 90 in the United Kingdom, 58 in Sweden, and 34 in the Netherlands.

60 percent—from 329,821 in 1980 to 528,945 on June 30, 1986. As White House drug-policy chief Carlton Turner has bragged, a significant part of that increase has been contributed by drug-law offenders.

It was my expression of such broad concerns about freedom that made Mr. Giuliani so upset, as did my challenge to his vision of the universal harmfulness of the illegal drugs. To see and hear the visceral reaction of Mr. Giuliani in this forum (an edited transcript of which was later published by *Harper's* magazine) documents again the great obstacles to reform of our drug laws and policies. This lawyer is a superb prosecutor who left New York in the early Eighties to become the Associate Attorney General, the number-three man in the Reagan Justice Department where he was allegedly the brains behind the drug war. He then returned to the city as the U.S. Attorney or chief federal prosecutor a few years later. He is precisely the type of person I want to see out in the front lines going after the Mafia and other organized crime syndicates. Every person of good will must applaud his brilliant ongoing work aimed at crippling whole Mafia families in New York. Indeed, several years ago many millions of people did applaud the portrayal of him as one of the heroic prosecutors in the book and the movie *Prince of the City*, the fellow who helped convict crooked New York City narcotics detectives who had turned into drug traffickers themselves.

Included in his gallery of supporters, in addition to this writer, is arguably the best drug journalist in the country, Dean Latimer, listed on the *High Times* magazine masthead as Executive Almighty Editor. Whenever I have mentioned the name of the federal prosecutor to Mr. Latimer, his praise has been unstinting (a badge of approval Mr. Giuliani may prefer not to display prominently). "Rudy Giuliani is the most honest, courageous, effective cop-type I have ever seen in action. He's great!" Dean Latimer once said to me with rare enthusiasm. The journalist even added the protective thought, "I wonder if he doesn't say all that silly stuff about drugs because he thinks he has to—in this political climate."

Mr. Giuliani, then, represents an important species of government official, who may be readily recognized by the following markings: highly educated, dedicated to the noblest ideals of the law, courageous, incorruptible, tenacious in pursuit of criminals, and either utterly hypocritical or utterly ignorant about the realities of drugs in society. My preference would be the latter, for honest education can remedy lack of knowledge. The fault of ignorance rather than hypocrisy, moreover, comports with the impression created by most drug warriors I have met. Whatever the ultimate truth, the result is the same in today's world. It is as if Mr. Giuliani, one of the most prominent members of this species, had two personas in the same human package, one highly rational and admirable, the other irrational and as scary as an ayatollah on the hunt for infidels corrupting the faithful with killer opium.

Or the killer weed. The difficulty with our system is that when such fine prosecutors as Mr. Giuliani are successful in convicting crooked cops or Mafia Dons, it is then assumed that they are competent to design broader drug control strategy for the nation, and the world. While serving as the Associate Attorney General, Mr. Giuliani once told a reporter, "I have trouble separating marijuana at one end from heroin at the other. If we liberalize our position vis-à-vis marijuana, we erode the position vis-à-vis heroin." He said then, and repeated at the New York forum mentioned earlier, that "we were wasting our time" talking about changing the drug laws or comparing alcohol prohibition to marijuana prohibition. The American people simply do not want to change the laws on marijuana as they did with alcohol. Moreover, while marijuana did not necessarily lead all of its users on to heroin, there was a definite connection, he continued, adding definitively, "Talk to drug addicts and they will tell you they started with marijuana."

A year earlier flamboyant writer Steve Chapple responded to that argument, after an interview with the then Associate Attorney General, when he fumed in *Outlaws in Babylon*, "I've met a few junkies and I can say that without exception every junkie starts his or her drug habit not with marijuana but with beer. Yes, beer. (And Budweiser or Schlitz, not even very good beer.)"

A split persona is also presented by Stephen S. Trott, who spent several years as Assistant Attorney General in charge of the Criminal Division at the Department of Justice, the man technically responsible for overseeing all federal criminal prosecutions, including those conducted by U.S. attorneys. In 1986, he was promoted to the job of Associate Attorney General, Mr. Giuliani's old position. Like Mr. Giuliani, he appears to be highly educated, articulate, honest, and steeped in the best traditions of the law. When Julius Duscha, the mild-mannered director of the Washington Journalism Center, asked Mr. Trott at a journalism conference, held at the Watergate Hotel in late 1985, why no E. F. Hutton official went to jail for what appeared to be massive check-kiting fraud by the prestigious brokerage firm, I heard Mr. Trott thunder back with an explanation based upon fundamental legal principles. The Reagan administration had not, despite what its congressional and press critics had alleged, gone easy on these upper-class criminals. Rather, the Justice Department had launched a massive investigation over a period of many months which had uncovered no evidence directly implicating any high executives in criminal conduct. Instead of sending a few low-level functionaries to jail, the government lawyers concluded it would make more sense to work out an arrangement under which guilty pleas were entered, no prison sentences were imposed, but important new rules were laid down for a whole segment of the brokerage trade that would prevent bilking of customers of billions of dollars in the future. It is a very complicated subject, and there *is* evidence that higher-ups knew, but the eloquence of then Assistant Attorney General Trott succeeded in convincing me, initially highly dubious, that there was a good deal of rational support for the finely balanced legal-social judgment made by the Reagan officials in the E. F. Hutton case.

On the matter of drugs, it was just the opposite—as if a near-hysterical demagogue, or indeed the ghost of old Harry Anslinger, had leaped into the finely tailored blue suit of this trim young lawyer with the earnest, winning manner. He talked war, plain and simple. "There's no peaceful coexistence with drugs," Mr. Trott trumpeted. He had just been on the CBS News "Nightwatch" program and debated with William F. Buckley, Jr., "who wants to surrender . . . like at Munich" (referring to the surprising position taken by the conservative columnist opposing the drug war and advocating complete legalization of drugs). Mr. Trott had also watched the television coverage of Mrs. Reagan and Princess Diana when they visited some drug-treatment program that showed a whole gymnasium full of kids and their parents. The stories they told about drug problems of our youth "tore my guts out!" He took this as further dramatic proof of the dire condition of our youth and the need for a war without quarter to save them. Neither Mr. Trott nor any of the journalists present seemed aware of the harm created by that very treatment program, which was not mentioned by name. It was Straight, Inc.

A reporter asked what leading government officials like himself specifically intended to do about the nation's drug problem. Mr.

Trott responded that we are going to use "a scorched-earth policy," which means that we are not simply going to send major criminal traffickers to jail but under the new laws we are going to seek forfeiture of "everything they own, their land, their cars, their boats, everything." Nobody asked if destroying organized crime would prevent kids from taking drugs or if the FBI was investigating the apparent kidnapping practices of Straight, which had been documented through sworn testimony in that federal case that had taken place just across the nearby Potomac River.

When I asked Mr. Trott how many of the 50–60 million illegal drug users in the country he wanted to send to jail, it was heartening to see a reflective, balanced response, almost in the same vein as the rational talk about E. F. Hutton. Of course, we cannot put all of those people in jail, or even a huge segment of them, the Justice Department leader explained. We would have to consider alternative sentences, like fines or community service. However, he has continued to call for a scorched-earth policy in the drug war and continues to cause deep concern in the minds of many rational citizens and officials.

Mr. Trott's boss, Attorney General Edwin Meese, has consistently called for attacks directly on users. The chief law-enforcement officer of the nation in 1985 sought to enlist the American press into that novel fight. In an address before a journalist's club, he declared, "I would like to suggest that there are no neutrals in the war on crime. The message must get through and that's where you and I can work together." The message: "to press hard on this story and connect the occasional cocaine user . . . with the governments that support this trade." Reporters should help drug users understand that they are not "just buying pleasure for themselves but . . . are supporting those who are dealing in terror, torture, and death." Mr. Meese's pleas drew a sharp response from Spencer Claw, editor of the *Columbia Journalism Review:* "That's exactly the role allotted to the press in socialist [in this case, meaning dictatorial] countries . . . to educate people and persuade them about the truth as the government sees it."

Mr. Meese has taken a similar position with the lawyers of the nation. In a speech before a lawyers' association in 1985, he declared that constitutional freedoms should not be used as a "screen" to protect "the evils of drugs." Moreover, "there are no bystanders, not even the lawyers" in the war on drugs. That also, of course, is the role assigned to lawyers in so-called socialist countries, to see to it that justice as defined by the party in power is carried out in court, unhindered by petty personal considerations such as the rights of individual suspects.

Prominent defense lawyers who openly defy the attorney general's curious view of the role of independent counsel report that many prosecutors are seeking to smear them as willing participants in their clients' alleged criminal behavior. "Governmental investigations of lawyers—including use of such tactics as informants, wiretaps, subpoenas, and office searches—have risen so dramatically in the last four years that they are almost common," reported *The National Law Journal* in late 1985. So also were requests by prosecutors that lawyers forfeit fees (that is, surrender to the government money they have earned) as the illegal fruits of criminal enterprises, a startling concept in a democracy, now supported by new legal provisions enacted by Congress at the behest of the Reagan administration.

"There's rampant paranoia among the criminal defense lawyers, and it's there with good purpose," declared Howard L. Weitzman of California, who successfully defended John DeLorean on drug-conspiracy charges and now claims that undercover "clients" have tried to set him up for prosecutors.

In October 1986, Mr. Meese went before the U.S. Chamber of Commerce and urged the nation's employers to help in the drug war by following the advice set out by former DEA administrator Peter Bensinger in a *Harvard Business Review* article. The Attorney General of the United States said in this major address, "Management must also indicate its willingness to undertake surveillance of problem areas such as locker rooms, parking lots, shipping and mailroom areas and nearby taverns, if necessary." The *Washington Post*, which has often waffled on drug-war issues, was sufficiently moved to label this suggestion "dangerous nonsense." The speech provided further telling insights into the minds of those who oversee the drug-enforcement effort of the nation, although up to now none of them had gone quite so far as to suggest spying on American employees in local taverns, an activity that would require, in some establishments I have visited, an uncommon degree of valor on the part of the spies.

SEIZING THE LANDS OF
FREE CITIZENS

As the most powerful government on the face of the earth flails about in its frustrated inability to control illicit drug use by one in every four of its citizens, its emotional reactions reach out and threaten rights and freedoms that few thought were involved in the drug war. Included are some freedoms so grounded in our very existence as a nation, so treasured by even our most conservative citizens that their violation would seem beyond the bounds of discussion, such as the right to own and enjoy property. That right was considered essential to the founders of the country who saw to it that it was amply protected in the United States Constitution.

Indeed, if there is anything that would seem to be an archetypal American value it is a vibrant and prickly repugnance at the invasion of a free citizen's right to own property and to enjoy the privacy of both home and lands. Yet that traditional value has been under assault by the drug warriors, as illustrated by events in the hills of northern California, where, as Mr. Meese suggested, there were few innocent bystanders, even among those who wanted to remain neutral. It is worth returning to that region for a further look at what impact massive drug-law enforcement can have on the peace, freedom, and personal dignity of entire communities of American citizens.

The plans for CAMP 1985 which struck the greatest notes of fear involved the confiscation of land under the 1984 federal law that some experts call the most repressive piece of legislation in American history. That rating of the law was one of the first thoughts voiced by Ronald Sinoway and by his colleague, Melvin Pearlston, when I talked to them in their Humboldt office. Both lawyers were appalled at the provisions of the Comprehensive Crime Control Act of 1984 (one of the proudest accomplishments of the Reagan administration prodded by the Miami Citizens Against Crime and the Florida congressional delegation) because it attempted to curb even more American freedoms in the name of winning the drug war. And the most galling part of the law to them was that which made land forfeiture much less difficult than in the past.

It has long been accepted in the law that a convicted criminal should be prevented from enjoying the fruits of his misdeeds and also that the instrumentalities or implements of a crime could properly be seized by the government. Thus, no significant issues of constitutional liberties were raised by seizures of rum runners' cash and boats during our earlier era of Prohibition nor are any raised now regarding such personal property of drug runners. However, the seizure of land, *real* property, has ever cut close to the bone of the freedoms treasured most by Britons and Americans since at least the time of the Magna Carta. Even a sovereign anointed by God would be wise to sleep lightly if he were in the habit of seizing the land of free citizens.

Nevertheless, the 1984 act adds a specific provision—the first in history, to my knowledge—to the American legal system that would allow the government to seize land on which drugs have been raised. Even before any criminal charges are filed, once an allegation of pot growing is made, it is now possible for government lawyers to commence a civil action for a "protective order" that will tie up the land for an initial period of ninety days. When the government is able to show "good cause" or produce an indictment, that cloud on the title will remain in effect almost indefinitely until the owner takes effective action to clear it.

Indeed, once marijuana is found, the presumption is now made by this law that the land was an instrumentality in a federal felony and that title should pass to the government. After conviction, an order can be entered conveying title to the government as of the time of the offense, thus voiding any transfer of the land that was made with the intent to avoid forfeiture. When this law was being rushed through Congress, there was no organized opposition, perhaps because few people really understood it or truly believed that it did violence to American traditions.

CAMP field commander William Ruzzamenti, with the most idealistic of motives, seems unaware of such traditions. He glories in the fear that will be produced up in the hills of Humboldt and Mendocino and Trinity counties among the growers, alone and in supportive communes, who themselves glory in their independence, defiance, and ownership of their own piece of those beautiful hills. Humboldt writer Ray Raphael told me that he was troubled about spelling out CAMP plans for 1985 in his book, *Cash Crop*, because he knew they would cause great fear and also because he knew that this was precisely what the DEA official wanted to happen—and yet Ray's objective was to tell the whole unvarnished truth, all of the conflicting sides and shades of it, about the role marijuana cultivation played in those communities.

Thus Mr. Raphael felt constrained to report in his revealing book these words of Mr. Ruzzamenti's: "The biggest focus of what we're doing is going to be on land seizures. Anybody who is growing marijuana on their land, we're going to take their land. It's as simple as that. It's done civilly through the federal system. Basically, people have to prove that they weren't involved and didn't even know about it. Just the act of having marijuana grown on your land is enough to tie it up; then you have to turn around and prove you're innocent. It reverses the burden of proof." Ray Raphael assured me that Bill Ruzzamenti's message either convinced some local citizens not to grow in 1985 or to reduce greatly the number of plants they risked putting on their land. Few of the people directly affected by these threats would fit the image of the fierce Mafia hoods which seemed to be in the mind of Associate Attorney General Trott when he declared that the forfeiture "scorched-earth" policy was to be a big weapon in controlling illicit drugs.

On October 12, 1984, five days after the law was enacted, a CAMP strike force was helicoptered to the 208-acre ranch owned by Rique Kuru and his wife, Natasha, in Mendocino County. The couple was arrested for growing 52 marijuana plants and for possession of a one-pound package of the herb—hardly evidence of membership in a major organized crime syndicate. Ronald Sinoway was retained to defend them. Mr. Sinoway had argued in the past that the exact forfeiture power of the government has never been settled and was not even done so by the 1984 law. In a series of cases dating back to 1870, he says, in which the government has tried to seize entire parcels of land because whisky stills were found on a part of them, the courts have always ruled that the government "could only seize the actual property where the still was, plus a little line of ingress and egress to it." In other words, Ron Sinoway's interpretation of the actual meaning of all the legal principles in this arena is that the courts have granted the government a very narrow power of seizure in actual cases.

Joseph P. Russoniello, the U.S. Attorney for the Northern District of California—the top federal prosecutor on the scene—takes the position that in the past the trend of the decisions was as the defense lawyer saw it, but that in large part this was due to the fact that "there wasn't any specific statute that permitted us to take the land." Armed with the 1984 act, the federal prosecutor started going after whole parcels of land.

These different visions of the 1984 law and of constitutional liberty were about to be tested in the Kuru case when Assistant U.S. Attorney Peter Robinson made the couple an offer that they found too good to refuse. They had lived on the property for only a year and had a total equity of approximately $20,000. If convicted of the charges against them, they faced the possibility of several years in prison and the legal maximum potential of thirty. Mr. Robinson offered to drop all charges if they would turn the property over to the federal government. They readily agreed. The assistant federal prosecutor then announced that the property would be sold at auction.

The auction was held on the courthouse steps in Ukiah on May 20, 1985. A somewhat unruly crowd was in attendance. Two offers were made. One was for ten cents. Another was for thirty pieces of silver, which a man flung on the steps of the courthouse.

During the 1986 CAMP campaign, the forfeiture weapon was used with a vengeance by federal authorities. California growers began paying unprecedented fines in order to prevent the government from taking all of their land. Mr. Robinson bragged in September 1986, "The fines are 50 times larger than we ever got before . . . and at least half the people paying fines will also go to jail." The government was taking the position that the discovery of 30 plants, hardly the mark of a major criminal, would trigger a move to forfeit the property. "We were using only about one acre out of 20 for pot," one outraged grower said, "but they tried to take the whole place, and we had to pay about $20,000 to save it. That's as much as our entire stake in the property."

ORGANIZED CITIZEN OPPOSITION

While many people will have little sympathy for anybody who grows even one marijuana plant, the CAMP program has produced widespread and organized citizen opposition to the war on drugs in that region, the greatest I have seen anywhere in this country or abroad. The opposition of those citizens has been aided by the involvement of a group of local lawyers, especially, as we have seen, Ron Sinoway and Mel Pearlston. The national NORML office and Director Kevin Zeese as well as lawyers affiliated with NORML in the San Francisco area have all put in a great deal of work in the many proceedings undertaken to control CAMP.

Ron Sinoway, now in his early forties, left a successful San Francisco practice and opened his office during the late Seventies in a small converted house nestled among the redwood trees on the Avenue of the Giants in southern Humboldt County. Soon after he opened the office, he started to share space and a small, competent and friendly staff with Mel Pearlston, who had been an assistant prosecutor in San Diego. Both men had come to the area for peace and space and had no particular interest in drug cases. Yet the two lawyers have become a focal point of opposition to the excesses of the war on drugs. They have become affiliated with NORML in their legal activities and have formed the Civil Liberties Monitoring Project, a nonprofit organization which operates out of their office. Local residents created the unique Citizens' Observation Group, which keeps a constant, nonviolent eye on the raiding activities of CAMP strike forces. Both lawyers, as well as attorney Edward Jay Moller of Redway, a few miles out of Garberville, provide legal advice to COG, which has many nongrowers among its members.

The gentle citizen opposition in these hills is usually expressed as opposition to the *excesses* or the *illegalities* of drug-law enforcement but I felt that an essential part of that organized dissent was a belief that the drug laws, at least to the extent that they prohibited marijuana, were irrational at their core. The opposition, moreover, was broader than the marijuana laws and was rooted in an overarching concept of a new, more private, and gentler culture than is now dominant in America.

Not all agreed on any one social philosophy, however. If there was one ideological point on which I encountered unanimity among the opponents in the hills it was that this was not a war on drugs at all but on much more important targets. Come on, these leaders can't be that stupid, I was told time and time again, whether in a law office or standing on the main street of Redway with a team of COG members. They can't be that excited over such an innocuous thing as pot. What were they warring over, then? To Mel Pearlston and Ron Sinoway it was over the Fourth Amendment and controls on police powers. To Barbara Arnold, "Susan," and "Oliver"—

members of COG, who sometimes use fictitious names for protection from the police they follow and report on—it was on a way of life that sought only contentment on the land and not the acquisition of goods and thus was a threat to the dominant capitalist system.

In these conversations, I felt like the fellow who told an acquaintance, "The boys at the bar were saying that you weren't fit to sleep with the hogs. But don't worry. I defended you and told them that, yes, you were." Thus, often I was forced into the position of saying, yes, those leaders are, too, that stupid! While some of them may believe the war might not work and are afraid to say so, most believe that this is a war on drugs and not a broader conspiracy; there is no evidence that this is a hidden war of the capitalists and imperialists against the socialists and peaceniks, as the hill-culture residents keep insisting to me. In no case was I able to convince anyone there that my view of the war's more limited goal was correct. However they defined their fears about the broader goals of the anti-drug crusaders, many of the opposition group believed that their whole way of life, and not simply marijuana cultivation, was threatened. They believed in their hearts that the authorities intended to eradicate not plants but the Valhalla Bill Ruzzamenti identified in that area, although sometimes he referred to it equally scornfully as a Nirvana.

On this point, Ron Sinoway recently responded, "It *is* nirvana—there are artists, craftspeople, dance companies, private alternative schools, a community center, festivals: basically, the realization of the dream of the people who grew up in the 1960s. Since people of this type do not hurt other people . . . , what is wrong with nirvana?" As to the argument that marijuana growing in that nirvana breeds violence, lawyer Sinoway's answer is that any time government intervention causes an agricultural product to be worth $2,000–$3,000 per pound in part because it is illegal, "one must expect some greedy people to try to take it and the people who have grown it for a number of months to try to stop the greedy people from taking it." Even with this occasional violence between growers and pot thieves, researchers of the Civil Liberties Monitoring Project documented that these hills are relatively peaceful places to live. Official statistics show that in 1983 Humboldt's total crime rate was 41 percent less than the average urban California county and eight percent less than the average rural county.

Mel Pearlston guesses that probably "there is more violence on a bad weekend in Oakland than in all of northern California since the advent of marijuana growing." This lawyer and parent observed on the basis of personal experience, "I feel so much safer here than I ever felt in the city [San Diego]. All right, I've worked there. I've lived there . . . and I'll raise my child in an area like this any day."

Arguments in opposition to the drug war are often thrown at the warriors by many of the denizens of northern California. Even during the day of that raid I witnessed, the reporters raised questions constantly not so much about tactics but about the wisdom of the basic strategy of keeping marijuana illegal. Although several helicopters were used in that raid, most of the police were transported in small passenger vans and trucks, along with the press. A day-long dialogue ensued in those vehicles and on the mountainside, even as the marijuana was being cut down and hoisted up in slings by the helicopters. That openness epitomized my entire experience in this charmed piece of the world and partially accounts for the fact that I felt less fear during my time there than the period I spent in the doctrinaire air of the drug-free youth conference in Atlanta earlier in that year—or, indeed, in the Deep South half a lifetime ago. The driver of our van was Larry Gobin, a soft-spoken officer of the California Highway Patrol, stationed in Garberville. Dressed in blue jeans for the day, he put his big six-gun in its worn holster and belt on the floor as he drove through the dusty hills. He listened politely on the way up the mountains to his passengers, three local reporters and a professor-writer from the east, who kept raising questions based on a value system that opposed the drug war.

Of course, Larry responded patiently: this raid and others like it under CAMP were worth the risk, effort, and money. The conflict between dope growers and those who opposed them was tearing apart the community which was so peaceful and calm when he came 15 years ago, he said. The presence of so much marijuana was seen as a threat to his family, especially to his two teenage sons, who happened to be employed by CAMP this summer to drive fuel trucks for the helicopters.

The most outspoken person in our group was Michael Koepf, a columnist and reporter for a highly respected Mendocino County newspaper, the *Anderson Valley Advertiser* in Booneville, perhaps 20 miles south, as the crow flies, from the spot where the raid was taking place. "There's been a very low level of violence, given the type of people who live in these hills," Mike Koepf declared. "The

red-necked deer hunters . . . pig hunters are growing dope . . .
and Vietnam vets who are scattered throughout these hills. Everyone carries, that is, everyone owns a rifle or a shotgun. Given the
type of people . . . the level of violence has been absolutely minimal.
They're playing it up to justify a large expenditure of tax monies
for this law-enforcement operation. This is political. We're at a
stage where now that Reagan and Meese are involved, [they can
say] if we can't win in Nicaragua, we got 'em on the run in Mendocino!

"I was a Green Beret, in the First Special Forces in Vietnam.
This is no way to conduct a guerrilla operation. This is a public
relations thing. There's no question about it," reporter Koepf continued. "This is no way to find dope. I find all sorts of dope—after
the dope has [supposedly] been removed—during the pig season
in the winter. . . . You don't need a helicopter to find dope." It's
everywhere, he claimed, in part because northern California had
been economically decimated in recent decades through the ex-
haustion of the salmon and the redwoods by those who ripped them
from the environment.

His neighbors grow marijuana because they have no other way
of surviving in a county with a 19 percent recorded unemployment
rate and a general economy with no visible means of support. All
those in his locality are the so-called mom-and-pop growers. "The
biggest grower in my neighborhood has eight plants. I walk in the
garden and he shows me his eight plants! . . . He's not going to
make a fortune on eight plants." In response to a statement by
Bill Ruzzamenti at the morning briefing that the normal height for
these plants is fourteen feet tall, he said, "That's preposterous.
. . . They get to about six feet. . . . He'll get three-quarters to a
pound of dope out of it . . . for each plant." If that grower sells
during the harvest season he will get $1,400 a pound; if he holds
on to a time when there is less available in the market, as much
as $2,400.

"After expenses, I would imagine he'd make eleven, twelve,
fifteen thousand dollars." The family, then, with the help of that
illegal income will just make it up to the poverty line. Should law
enforcement be going after growers like him? Mike Koepf says no,
"because you're going to go after half the population of Mendocino
County and destroy what little economic base there is left here."

Local citizen Koepf remembers training new troops in Vietnam
by playing the role of Vietcong forces. Reflecting on that training

experience, he says, "The growers are like Vietcong, in some ways. They know when these guys are coming. They hear 'em coming and they're gone. They're never going to catch 'em." (Mike Koepf seemed unaware that Bill Ruzzamenti had said that flight of the growers was one result he sometimes preferred.) The former Green Beret had come to see that the CAMP forces operated in the style of massive divisional movements in Vietnam. "They don't understand the enemy. They [the troops] have been kind of propagandized by the media . . . and by their own law-enforcement leaders. They have the same line: there's violence in the woods . . . and their kids can't go out into the woods anymore. That's a bunch of crap!"

We had been sitting in the van at the side of a road during one of the interminable waits that so often characterize the movement of large numbers of troops and vehicles. As he uttered that last word—at precisely that moment on my tape—a voice cut in, shouting, "Go home! Go home!" We looked up to see two girls, apparently local citizens in their early twenties, driving a station wagon down the long line of police vehicles, expressing sentiments that, according to Mendocino County sheriff Tim Shea at the briefing that morning, represented a distinct minority of local public opinion. The few citizens we encountered that day on the raid somehow all seemed to be in that minority.

Every citizen I asked during my entire sojourn in those hills agreed with Mike Koepf on the main point he was making at that moment: while there is indeed some danger from violent marijuana growers, it has been vastly exaggerated. Not a single person I encountered said that he or she was afraid to walk or drive anywhere there. Mike went out tramping through the woods while hunting for wild pigs as do many other local folks. Fear of marijuana growers has never interrupted a hunting foray, he says. Like many other local people, he does, to a degree, fear the police, but not because they are intentionally evil. "I'm looking at these guys, and they're all young. I can see how they're putting their guns on 'Miami Vice' style. I mean, they're wholly into this image of being a strong macho. . . . I talked to one guy and asked 'You ever been on an operation?' He said, 'No, this is my first.' He looked like he was 21 years old. Reminds me of a lot of guys in Vietnam. You know, you're bound to fuck up the first time in combat . . . and you'll probably fuck up the next six or seven times!"

Mike believed that huge raids by heavily armed police were

not the best approach to enforcing existing laws and that there were many options open to enforcement leaders if they were intent on curbing marijuana growing in the area—more gentle options in line with the friendliness often exhibited by the people and officials there. "There's a deputy sheriff on this raid today, all right, from a different area. And I think he was an effective eradicator. The local people would give him an awful lot of information about what was going on, especially about growers who had a tendency to violence. And he would go out and make a certain amount of arrests . . . but he also would go out and put his calling card on dope patches that he knew about. And he didn't worry about search warrants too much. He would just put his card on the fence. And, of course, as soon as the grower knew that the sheriff's department was aware of where his dope was, they'd cut it down." This may seem too lenient and completely incongruous to those who believe that contraband known to the police must be seized by force and destroyed by fire—after having been discovered by one of the helicopters that on some days seemed to be everywhere in the skies above the quiet hills.

LIFE UNDER THE HELICOPTERS

The complaints brought to the civil rights lawyers by outraged citizens in the region ran the full gamut from invasions of personal dignity to apparently clear violations of constitutional rights. A large number dealt with the strange, new, fearful impact of those helicopters. On August 16, 1984, for example, Charles Ervin Keys was at his home in the Rancho Sequoia area of Humboldt County with his son, Arthur, aged five. "At about 9:00 A.M., four helicopters in a diamond shape came within 100 feet of our home, shaking and blowing the tree tops. At about 9:30 A.M. the largest helicopter came back, put the nose of the helicopter about 100 feet away at my eye level (I live on a hillside) and hovered, watching me defecate [in] my outhouse. I didn't move so he moved right above me. He blew the toilet paper away from me and Arthur had to retrieve it for me."

This action seemed to be a clear violation not only of simple decency but also of the constitution. Even under the vast powers granted by the leading Supreme Court case on the matter, *Oliver* v. *United States*, the police have no authority to search the area close to a home, as opposed to "open fields," without probable cause. In that decision in 1984, the Supreme Court had greatly expanded police power when it upheld marijuana searches into private lands on anonymous tips—even when they were posted with "no trespassing" signs and when the officers had apparently violated state criminal trespassing laws—so long as the searches were confined to those open fields not within the curtilage or the area close to a homesite.

The police in the *Oliver* case had been on the ground. In 1986, the court faced its first appeal that dealt with the power of the police to search the homes and lands of citizens from a plane without a warrant on the basis of an anonymous tip. The Santa Clara, California, police had apparently used a small, fixed-wing aircraft to fly over the land of the suspect at 1,000 feet, within the accepted limits of navigable airspace. They spotted marijuana plants and later seized 73 of them. As has so often happened in the past, the power of the police to search for drugs was expanded and the rights of all citizens were diminished in the 5–4 decision of *California* v. *Ciraolo*. Even that grant of broad police power again seemed to have been exceeded by the low-flying helicopters that harassed Mr. Keys back in 1984.

Later that day, after Mr. Keys left his property with his son because he feared for their safety, the troops came on his property and took a .22-caliber rifle without a warrant. When he went to the sheriff's office and asked for the return of his rifle, Charles Keys was told that if he persisted, he would be charged with cultivation of marijuana, although he has sworn under oath that he is not a grower. The rural American citizen said he was angry at the invasion of his rights to privacy and freedom from illegal searches and seizures, in part because "I am an honorably discharged Viet Nam veteran, having served 17 months there in the marines, with 12 of those months in combat."

Marilyn Beckwith, 52, is a grandmother, the widow of a state park ranger, and a conservative Republican. She lived in the same area as Mr. Keys. Ms. Beckwith is blind and has a guide dog, Cameo. She also has the ability to "see" many events by instincts that keep sighted people wondering how a blind person could know such things. She reported on a series of raids in her vicinity, near Alderpoint, by keeping a journal, which read in part:

August 17, 1984. They came in again this morning about 8:00 o'clock. A large cargo-type helicopter flew low over the cabin, shaking it on its very foundations. It shook all of us inside, too. I feel frightened. . . . I see how helpless and tormented I am becoming with disgust and disillusionment with the government which has turned this beautiful country into a police state. I thought they were only going for large commercial gardens, but today they are flying low over this residential area with small helicopters and observation planes. I feel like I am in the middle of a war zone.

August 20, 1984 . . . They were out of earshot and I thought it would be a good time to take a shower in our wonderful solar-heated outdoor shower facility. I was surprised when one of the smaller choppers popped over the hill . . . circled the cabin slowly and was low enough to get a good look at me standing there showering in the nude. I was shocked and disgusted and embarrassed. . . .

September 10, 1984 . . . We had to leave the cabin early this morning because it was swaying from all the low-flying aircraft. . . . I had Cameo take me to our favorite spot deep in the woods under the big old fir tree. We spent the entire day there huddled, scared, crying while aircraft buzzed directly over our heads through the trees, shaking the ground.

September 11, 1984. I harnessed Cameo quickly and tried to get her to take me back to the old fir tree but she wouldn't go outside because of all the aircraft that were buzzing us so low and she crouched next to me on the floor trembling and shivering. [My adult son] Brian told me to hurry and get in the truck and we would spend the day in town. . . . As we left our property and started down the road in the truck one of the helicopters followed us, hovering low over the truck for a mile or so. . . . As we hurried along the bumpy dirt road Cameo lost control of her bowels. It seemed incredible that this was all really happening in America.

Allison Osborne of nearby Briceland wrote later that month, "It seems that we are in Viet Nam or Nicaragua. . . . The CAMP people have done 75 percent of their entire California operation in southern Humboldt. The people here are fed up." She and her young children live in a cottage in the woods. They had endured months of close overflights, which had deeply disturbed the children. On September 19, while busting a nearby parcel of land, the helicopters flew within 50 feet of her roof and the troops in them made clearly visible obscene gestures at her and her children.

When my 12-year-old daughter came home from school, this same day, she was terrified and ran up to a neighbor's house. The helicopters chased them (two 12-year-old girls) up Perry Meadow Road, for about 20 minutes. When my daughter and her friend would hide under the bushes, the helicopters would lift up; when the girls would try to run to the nearest house, the 'copters would come again and frighten them. . . . They saw guns, and thought they were going to be shot!

LIFE UNDER THE GUNS

Guns are often trained directly on local citizens on the ground of this war zone because CAMP officials have taken the position in writing that all persons coming near operations may be held and identified and that nearby structures must be searched to make sure they contain no one who might take hostile action against the raiders. In a standard military situation, this is plain common sense. In a civilian situation in a free country, it is a constitutional abomination. It constitutes warrantless invasions of American homes and detentions of American citizens without probable cause.

The raiders are often strangers to the area, young, terribly frightened, shocked at the sight of some of the clothes or bearing of hill dwellers, poorly trained, and led by field commanders suffering from the same drawbacks. Thus Hal Friedberg's experience on September 10, 1984, has become a typical, even mild, event for many hundreds of Americans who live in the region. A resident, like many others here mentioned, of the Rancho Sequoia community, he was driving down the road to work at 7:30 A.M. with a friend in the car.

As I came around a bend a CAMP troop with an M-16 rifle was standing in the road. He told me to halt. I kept moving and told him I was late for work. He told me to "stop or I will shoot your ass." I stopped. I asked him why he stopped me. He told me to put my hands on the dash. He then radioed someone else saying that "I have two suspects. What should I do?" He was told to let us go. . . . The whole time his weapon was pointed at us, and at some point he was joined by two other troops with weapons pointed at us. . . . I was highly shaken and totally nervous the whole day. I felt threatened and was scared the rifle might go off accidentally.

This type of military control reached new heights in the tiny crossroads village of Denny in Trinity County in 1983 and also in 1984. The residents of this area were considered so hostile to law enforcement that Mr. Ruzzamenti has said that it was necessary "to virtually occupy the area with a small army" for several days each year while eradication activities took place. That harsh action might have been justified if law and order had truly broken down, as police officials claimed. Local residents and their lawyers, on the other hand, insisted that the area was simply a typical rural community and that it contained no more violence than any other. There was no dispute, however, over the fact that a good deal of marijuana was grown in the area.

When a police officer believes that marijuana is being grown all over a community and that the residents might protect their plants with firearms, then it might seem perfectly rational to that officer to set up roadblocks for perhaps half a mile in either direction from the area being searched. That is how Sergeant David Laffranchini, the lead drug officer of the Trinity County Sheriff's Department, explained in a sworn statement why this piece of American soil was occupied in this small campaign in the war on drugs.

Residents were stunned and frightened to suddenly see strange men in combat uniforms, carrying military weapons, simply take over the entire area. At approximately 11:00 A.M. on August 24, 1983, for example, Eric Massett and his wife, Rebecca Sue, both in their thirties, were disturbed to see six men in camouflage uniforms pointing weapons at them as they pulled out of their driveway four miles outside of Denny. They were allowed to go into town and gathered with other frightened residents of the area. The Massetts did not leave town until the roadblocks were lifted at about 7:30 P.M., when the CAMP officials drove out of town in a convoy of vehicles. According to Eric, "Many of these troops pointed their rifles at us, and one man was waving a .45 pistol at us when they went by. They were shouting 'War on drugs!' 'War on drugs!' and they took our pictures and some said they would be back."

Many other local citizens, including Katherine Bauer, 34, reported roughly similar experiences. She was not accustomed to being impeded in her daily rounds since she was the local contract mail carrier for the U.S. Postal Service. Her status did not impress the drug warriors, who stopped her at gunpoint, demanded identification, forced her to return home to obtain it, subjected her to a weapons search and a registration check, and filled out a Field Interrogation Card about her.

At about 6:30 P.M. on the next evening, August 25, 1983, she was fixing dinner for herself and her five-year-old son at home when she heard "honking horns and yelling" out on the road. She walked about a hundred yards down her own driveway "to watch the parade," as the CAMP troops again left Denny. A friend and visitor, Michael Ulberg, was standing next to her on her own property. At that point a few gunshots were heard away up in the hills, which is not uncommon in the area. The convoy came to a quick halt and the troops piled out with their weapons. One armed officer yelled at Ms. Bauer, standing there in her own driveway next to her mailbox in her apron, to get moving, and she replied firmly that she was on her own land.

Next, Katherine Bauer stated in a sworn declaration, Deputy Sheriff "Chuck" Sanborn of Trinity County came storming up to her, stood within an inch of her, with his rifle next to her head, told her that she was an "asshole" and threatened that if he heard any more shots he would "open up" on her house. "As he was talking, saliva was spraying from his mouth. . . . I asked him to move back, and also asked him how he would like it if I spit in his face. He said, 'You do that and I will knock you on your ass.' " The officer of the law then turned his attention to Mr. Ulberg and threatened him with the muzzle of the rifle less than two inches from the citizen's mouth. Deputy Sheriff Sanborn fumed: "If there is going to be any shooting around here, I'm going to be the first son of a bitch to open up on all of you motherfuckers!"

CAMP helicopters often returned to this rural area, sometimes known as the New River Canyon. The constant noise and the obvious presence of armed men in the flying machines was a source of continuing fear. They often flew at or below tree-top level near homes. "By this time my son was afraid, saying 'Mommy, they are going to shoot me and they are going to shoot you!' " Katherine Bauer stated in October 1983. "He cried and lay down on the ground covering his head, repeatedly asking me to 'take me away from here where I can't hear them.' I tried to explain that the men were young with boys of their own, that they weren't going to hurt us, but he became hysterical and all I could do was go into the house with him and put on music to try to drown out the noise of the helicopters."

THE KILLING OF DUCHESS

Several years later, I observed firsthand the fear and trauma still lingering in the emotions of several other Trinity County residents. Judy Rolicheck's hands still trembled a bit, her eyes brimmed with tears that did not quite roll out, and her chin tightened up as she struggled to keep her composure. Her daughter, Deena, sat next to her and gently patted her back. "It worked on me. I'm terrified," said Ms. Rolicheck, even though it had been over a year since it had happened, at least the start of it. "Bill Ruzzamenti said he wanted us to be afraid of CAMP and I am," she explained. It was August 4, 1985, and we were sitting at the picnic table of their pleasant, well-kept rural home near the town of Ruth, on eight private acres within the borders of the Six Rivers National Forest, about 70 miles south of Denny.

In my eyes, the family seemed to be typical middle-class, suburban Americans who happened to be living in a rural area— definitely not hippies or members of any counterculture. At 45, sporting a hefty salt-and-pepper beard, and over six feet tall, Gary Rolicheck appeared a large good-natured fellow, with a strong streak of frontier independence in his bones, who did not drink beer or smoke marijuana but did occasionally drink whisky, usually neat. His great-grandfather had been a pioneer who had come to California in a covered wagon and Gary was thus a rare breed, a fifth-generation native of the state. He had always worked and was then employed by Trinity County in a good job that entailed maintaining the roads. Judy, 42, was a registered nurse who had worked steadily while they had lived in central California but had stopped when they moved to the hills in 1982. The Rolichecks' son is a student at the College of the Redwoods. Daughter Deena, 20, had a daughter of her own, Althea, 2, who kept crawling over the table during our discussion. The family claims that none of them has ever been arrested for any charge. All denied any interest or involvement in the cultivation of marijuana. "I didn't move out here to be a pot grower," Judy insisted. "That was the furthest thing from our minds."

That entire family loved Duchess, a Doberman pinscher, which Gary had given to Judy as a Valentine's Day present twelve years before the fatal incident. Deena had always played with her as a young girl and so had baby Althea. Duchess usually roamed freely, unchained, both at her earlier home in central California and here at this rural site. The dog played with other children such as those of Connie Cook-Riddle who lived on the Rolicheck property for most of 1983. She said that her two older sons, aged two and four, often ran "back and forth in front of and sometimes with" Duchess and never once were they bitten or threatened.

However, law-enforcement officers had a totally different image of this family and its dog. They believed that Gary Rolicheck was one of the hoods of the area and had a bad reputation in part because he was keeping bad company. Bruce Lee Hall, or Buffalo, was one of the worst of that bad company. He was the boyfriend of Kim, a niece of the Rolichecks. Buffalo and his friend, Joseph Boyer, were believed to have been members of a motorcycle gang and to have been hired as guards for local marijuana gardens. All three of the men were considered armed and dangerous by the authorities. Law-enforcement officers "knew"—in the words of an official report—that the "red Doberman pinscher . . . was vicious" and that the dog was being used to guard nearby marijuana patches. When confronted with these allegations, the family members simply shook their heads in wonderment. I have found no evidence to support the law-enforcement version of the facts.

As part of the CAMP campaign, a warrant had been obtained to search for gardens on nearby private land. None was necessary for the gardens seen on U.S. Forest Service land, which was in the Six Rivers National Forest, but one was not obtained for searching the adjoining private eight acres owned by the Rolichecks. A large force—15 to 25 men armed with rifles, shotguns, and sidearms—had been assembled for these raids. The lead officer was Sergeant Laffranchini of the Trinity County Sheriff's Department. Also in the large team were U.S. Forest Service law-enforcement officers Bobby Holdridge and Jerry Price. A helicopter and its crew were on standby in the event they were needed.

This military operation was planned for the morning of August 16, 1984. The Rolicheck residence was quietly surrounded by the armed men, and eradication activities started on one of the gardens far away from the house. "At this time Officer Laffranchini and Erwin Wade, CAMP leader," an official report revealed, "drove past the Rolicheck residence. They saw a red Doberman and a black dog about 100 yards from the residence. They reported that the dogs were vicious and they would have had to 'take them out' if they (the officers) had not been in a vehicle." The entire team was clearly scared at the potential of violence from the so-called dangerous marijuana growers and their vicious guard dogs. Thus, the stage for misunderstanding and tragedy was set.

In the Rolicheck house, as they started to rise and get breakfast that morning, were Judy; Deena; Althea, then aged one; Kim; and Bruce. Gary had already left for work at 5:30 A.M., several hours earlier. Judy looked out to see 15 to 25 armed men, pointing weapons, come toward the house. Some were in combat uniforms, others in sheriff's department outfits. Officer Bobby Holdridge yelled loudly, "Police! Step out where we can see everyone. I want to see your hands." Little Althea ran out on the porch and was quickly followed by the remainder of the stunned family. Duchess and a small black dog owned by Deena started running toward the troops and barking. The smaller dog retreated but Duchess kept barking. There was a good deal of confusion. Judy said, "Let me catch her and I'll chain her up." Some of the troops were saying "Get the dog!" and some were saying "Stay on the porch!" Judy shouted, "Don't shoot her! She's never bitten anyone!" Judy now reflects, "All she wanted to do was to be between us and them."

Bobby Holdridge did not believe that this was all this seemingly vicious attack dog wanted. The law-enforcement officer believed he was under attack and said, "Lady, call your dog. I do not want to have to shoot it." In the midst of this confusion, yelling, and fear on all sides, Officer Holdridge's apprehension became so great that he shot Duchess with his mini-14 Ruger semiautomatic .223 rifle. The dog went down and wailed, whereupon Deena pleaded that the animal be put out of its misery. Jerry Price complied and finished her off with a blast from his Model 870 Remington 12-gauge shotgun. A review of the scene now confirms Gary's bitter complaints that his wife and granddaughter, and perhaps his daughter, were in the line of fire and might well have been seriously harmed or killed by projectiles from these powerful weapons.

By now, both women were crying and Althea was howling hysterically. They retreated to the porch as ordered, started to contemplate their captors, and saw that many of them seemed to be scared young kids, strangers to the area, apparently from other parts of the state. Deena said they looked ready for a major battle, many of them had bullet-proof vests on, and it appeared, she said, that "they could have shot anything that moved." After showing identification to the officers, the family was told to stay on the

porch but was given absolutely no explanation for their detention
at gunpoint. During that detention, Judy had the presence of mind
to ask, "Do you have a search warrant?" One of the officers replied,
"No, but we can get one." Ms. Rolicheck responded, "I think you
had better leave, then." The officers did not and kept them under
guard, terrorized and ignorant of the reasons for their imprisonment on their own property, for approximately two and one-half
hours. (No member of the family was subsequently charged with
any crime even though Bill Ruzzamenti later claimed in a conversation with me that there was probable cause because of the paths
and water lines that allegedly led to the illegal gardens. Nor were
any samples of confiscated marijuana ever produced for inspection.)

Finally, one of the officers, indicating they had completed their
mission, said, "You can get your dog now." The family was left to
deal with the corpse of the family pet on its own. Judy and Deena
immediately picked it up and buried Duchess in the vegetable
garden next to the house. No apologies or explanations were offered then or during the months following this affair by any American official at any level of government, although the Rolichecks
have requested private interviews with officials. Even when James
L. Davis, Jr., forest supervisor, and Donald W. Bachman, forest
administrative leader, conducted an official investigation of the
shooting in the name of the Six Rivers National Forest, they managed the extraordinary feat of performing the entire inquiry without talking to the Rolichecks "because of the potentially dangerous
nature of the 'owners' of the dogs." It is not surprising that they
found the shooting fully justified.

So did Bill Ruzzamenti, who scornfully alluded to the case as
"the Benjy incident," referring to the gentle little dog which often
appeared on television. The very mention of this matter seemed
to energize him at the end of a long day in the field. I told the
DEA field commander that, after interviewing the family and observing the scene, I was inclined to believe the Rolicheck version
of the truth. He sincerely believed the police version and shot back,
"I am totally not concerned about that case! That dog was a guard
dog for the garden. . . . And the Benjy attitude they have about
that dog! They sicced the dog on the guys. The guy who shot that
dog . . . Bobby Holdridge . . . one of the nicest little-ol'-men-type
guys you'll ever want to meet. Loves animals. Loves kids. Loves
people. . . . He's a Smokey-the-Bear guy. . . . He doesn't even

like to have a gun! . . . He's into flora and fauna. He's not into Gestapo-type tactics."

Many other, more impartial observers have viewed these tactics, though, in those un-American terms during the course of court cases, discussions, and newspaper reports concerning the Rolichecks and Duchess in the months that followed. The events in this case have been a springboard for caustic criticisms of the basic assumptions of the American war on drugs and of the fearful situations it creates for our police and citizens, whether or not they are involved in marijuana growing. If the worst case is granted here, and if there was marijuana growing all around the Rolicheck residence, well-led and well-trained police officers would have handled this situation more peacefully. Even if the family had been directly involved in cultivation, which I doubt, they were not desperate gangsters so often conjured up by leading drug warriors. Moreover, the detention of American citizens at gunpoint without a warrant raises fundamental constitutional and legal questions, especially when that action was carrying out the specific written policy of CAMP and the executive branch of the United States government. It was no surprise then that Judy Rolicheck testified in the suit eventually brought against CAMP and that this incident was cited by U.S. District Court Judge Robert P. Aguilar of San Francisco in his historic and sweeping order placing judicial curbs on this phase of the war on drugs.

HISTORIC CONTROLS ON THE DRUG POLICE

Indeed, Judy Rolicheck's complaint was the first one mentioned and summarized by Judge Aguilar in his order that finally granted a far-reaching preliminary injunction on April 12, 1985. She had testified at the hearings as had a number of other local aggrieved citizens. Remarkably, the government did not put that Smokey-the-Bear guy, Bobby Holdridge, on the stand, even though it seems he would have made one grand witness for its side. Nor did the government produce any other police eyewitnesses. In a series of hearings before this judge in the nearby federal courts, the government seemed, as Ron Sinoway has said, to have adopted an attitude of "the king can do no wrong." It was either that ancient arrogance or appalling ignorance that affected the federal and state lawyers defending the interests of the government, led by Joseph P. Russoniello, the U.S. Attorney, and John Van De Kamp, Attorney General of the state of California. Those legal officials relied primarily on hearsay testimony from CAMP commanders.

The centerpiece of the legal counterattack on CAMP is an omnibus suit—*NORML* v. *Mullen*—which requests an injunction and also money damages in which the plaintiffs are NORML, the Civil Liberties Monitoring Project, and individual California citizens such as the Rolichecks. The defendants are various state and federal agencies and officers, starting with Francis M. Mullen, then administrator of the DEA in Washington, in their official capacities. A few officials, including William Ruzzamenti, are being sued in their personal capacities as well. One of the first actions taken by the plaintiffs in the matter was a request for a preliminary injunction in 1983 that would have stopped further CAMP activities. Judge Aguilar had stated at that time that he was "terribly troubled" by some CAMP tactics which seemed to violate traditional constitutional protections. As for the use of U-2 planes to spy on American citizens, he observed, "One cannot help but think of George Orwell's *1984*." Yet, the federal judge refused to issue even a preliminary injunction at that time because of the traditional reluctance of courts to enjoin the operations of police departments.

The basic legal rule on injunctions is that there must be a showing of irreparable injury, namely "a real or immediate threat that the plaintiff will be wronged again." It was on the basis of such venerable legal theories that Judge Aquilar had refused the original request in 1983 for a preliminary injunction in this case. Since then, the original 10 sworn complaints had been supplemented with 50 more. As any judge worth his salt in a functioning democracy would be, Robert P. Aguilar was distressed that the government had been so casual in its response to these complaints, at one time observing that law-enforcement officials had not offered to produce evidence from the agents directly involved and that they had put forth William Ruzzamenti, who could rely only on secondhand information. "He testified," Judge Aguilar wrote in his opinion, "that he never attempted to interview any of the declarants or inspect the private property at issue. As for the Rolicheck incident, he merely adopted the written investigative report of the United States Forest Service."

This impartial federal judge then came to some shocking conclusions about the behavior of American officials in the war on drugs. First, even if the hearsay produced by Mr. Ruzzamenti were given full credence, his testimony did not rebut the serious charges of constitutional invasions put forth by these citizens. Second, the written policies of CAMP provided concrete support for the charges of massive Fourth Amendment violations. The judge declared that such directives give "CAMP personnel virtually unbridled discretion to enter and search private property anywhere in the vicinity of an eradication raid, and to seize personal property and detain innocent citizens without probable cause or even reasonable suspicion of any criminal activity." Third, while the court was aware of the dangers to CAMP personnel, "such risks are no greater than that routinely faced by other law-enforcement officers." Fourth, these complaining citizens live in areas "where marijuana cultivation is rife. These are the areas where CAMP plans to return repeatedly each season until the growers throw in the towel."

Accordingly, Judge Aguilar concluded that there was the high probability of irreparable continuing harm to the plaintiffs. He then formally enjoined all CAMP agencies and personnel "from entering by foot, motor vehicle, or helicopter any private property other than open fields without a warrant" and "from entering adjacent or nearby property . . . unless exigent circumstances exist," which could not be deduced from "mere speculation." In recognition of the fact that helicopters had been used so as to violate the rights of citizens, the judge further enjoined the federal and local police "from using helicopters for general surveillance purposes, except over open fields. When conducting surveillance over open fields, helicopters shall not fly within 500 feet of any structure, person, or vehicle."

While this order may seem simply to restate the obvious and thus be only a polite slap on the wrist, actually it is one of the most sweeping judicial condemnations of the actions of specific American civilian police ever handed down. Since it came in response to a major campaign in the American war on drugs, it is of historic significance because courts have almost always upheld invasions of the rights of Americans when drug control is thrown in the balance on the other side of the scales of justice. Although this order has been upheld by the U.S. Court of Appeals, we cannot be sanguine that the current U.S. Supreme Court, led by Chief

Justice Rehnquist, will be supportive if it is appealed. When I was in California, moreover, I saw precious little evidence that the intrusive and harmful effects of the war on drugs were being curbed by the comprehensive order which had been in effect for months when I arrived. In the month after I left, Judge Aguilar took the further extraordinary step of appointing a monitor to ensure compliance with his sweeping injunction and to ensure "protection of civil rights." The monitor, a widely respected retired judge, Thomas Kongsgaard, was granted judicial powers. To my knowledge, this is the first time in the history of the country that police forces have been forced to operate under direct judicial supervision.

CAN THE DRUG LAWS BE ENFORCED IN A DEMOCRACY?

The new cases I encountered while in California raised the recurring question as to whether any major effort to enforce the drug laws can ever be consistent with American traditions of freedom and privacy in regions where there is massive defiance of those laws. This question may well be answered in the negative even where a judge issues a search warrant authorizing a particular search. On July 16, 1985, for example, Superior Court judge Timothy W. O'Brien of Mendocino County issued a warrant to search for six—yes, *six*—marijuana plants as well as inspect nearby structures that might contain evidence as to the identity of the growers. In all, the warrant seemed to authorize the search of at least a quarter of a square mile of American territory, including perhaps eight American homes, in the name of destroying a few offending plants.

The warrant was executed on the morning of July 18 in an area known as Gopherville, which lies at the northern edge of Mendocino County, two miles south of Whitethorn in Humboldt. The inhabitants were the roughest-appearing people I encountered in northern California. Many of them dress and live in a counterculture style, which often means in proud poverty. Within a short time of arrival, the heavily armed CAMP team had gone into several homes and assembled a dozen citizens in the front yard of the home of Steve and Sue Miller, a couple in their twenties, who are now being supported by welfare along with their two sons, aged 5 and 2.

Of the twelve people, some were marijuana growers, in my opinion, and some certainly were not. Five were veterans of service during the Vietnam era. Rick Thorngate had been a first lieutenant in the 101st Airborne Division and had been in combat for one year. The easiest way to describe him now is to say that he looks like a hippie dropout with his headband, long hair, and wide, piercing eyes. When I asked him what happened during the raid, as we sat in the Miller home on August 2, I was prepared to have him reply in some form of hey-man, far-out jargon. He sounded, to my surprise, at least as rational as your average college professor, even more so. He immediately recognized the military weapons, which he insists were potentially fully automatic M-16s, and was traumatized since he did not expect to encounter such weapons in this remote, peaceful area. The combat veteran knew how quickly five or six deadly rounds could be loosed by a nervous finger.

The soldiers and their commander seemed scared and barely in control. Rick saw that several of the young officers literally had white knuckles as they held their hands on the weapons. "Two guys with M-16s kept their thumbs right on the rock 'n' roll button [the safety and switch to automatic fire] the whole time," Rick Thorngate recalled. As is usual, the troops asked all of their prisoners for full personal information. When it came to the former airborne officer's turn, "I gave them my name, rank, and serial number. I told them I considered myself a prisoner of war. . . . They laughed. They thought it was a clever joke." Thorngate decided to simply sit in his car, around which these American prisoners were being held under the guns of the CAMP troops, and try to put himself in a trance that might help to keep the situation calm. For four hours, these men, women, and young children were held in the hot sun while the police searched the woods for six marijuana plants and the houses for evidence of this serious crime.

At one point, David Hill, a veteran of the Marine Corps during the Vietnam period, asked a young officer how long they were going to be kept and observed that he felt like a hostage in Iran. The policeman smiled and replied, "Yeah, Gopherville, Day One." Several of the officers took out small cameras and snapped pictures of the group being held at gunpoint, one saying, "The folks back home are not going to believe this!"

Rick Thorngate observed, "These were clean-shaven city people and they took a look at us with our long hair and beards and they were freaked out by us. They thought we were armed growers and guerrilla terrorists. . . . They were scared of us. I felt that I was . . . in some kind of a fascist state where I had done nothing wrong and I was held against my will . . . and I felt that unless everyone in the [prisoner] group . . . was very calm, cool, and collected something dangerous could happen." He felt that the prisoners maintained order and prevented violence from happening: "The people I was . . . held captive with . . . were better disciplined and acted more rationally than the police that were around us." Thorngate reflected, "I led troops in combat and I had to send people back sometimes. There were none of them [the CAMP troops] whose attitudes I considered to be even close to the professional attitudes of the eighteen-year-old kids that I served with in Vietnam." If his soldiers in Vietnam combat situations had acted the way these officers had in Gopherville, "I would have sent them back as dangerous to themselves and dangerous to the unit. . . . I wouldn't have taken them into combat with *me*."

Both veterans Hill and Thorngate later voiced no objections to the drug laws, but concluded that this was a horrible way to enforce them in the free country for which they had fought. Their sentiments were echoed by Steve Miller, who, like them, insists he is not a grower: "You want to get rid of pot? Okay. But not this way. . . . Just take the weed, take it all, and leave us alone."

When the heavily armed CAMP soldiers left, apparently they took with them several marijuana plants obtained somewhere out in the nearby field but made no arrests. I was assured by one of the growers in the group that there was an ample crop left behind in the area, from which I was graciously offered a sample (which I just as graciously refused). The officers also left behind a great deal of bitterness, even among those who insisted they were not involved in marijuana cultivation. It is of significance that Judge Aguilar's sweeping order did not directly deal with controlling detentions of citizens in those cases, like this one, involving the now locally famous Gopherville Twelve, where the officers are in possession of an apparently proper warrant. If that warrant made these detentions legal, then all innocent American citizens may be taken out of their homes in New York, Miami, Chicago, Los Angeles, anywhere, and detained at gunpoint because they happen to live near the site of a legitimate search for drugs.

THE DRUG WAR MAKES
AMERICA UNSAFE

If the government continues to press the war on marijuana planting, if the warriors are successful beyond their wildest dreams and
eradicate virtually all plants in California and elsewhere, the drug-
war leaders would have us believe that the use of drugs will decline
and public safety for all Americans will increase. In fact, quite the
opposite is likely to happen.

Until 1985, virtually the entire focus of illegal growers had been
marijuana and not some more harmful drug. Moreover, despite all
of the alarms that have been raised by CAMP officials, there had
been little solid evidence of real violence directed at police involved
in the drug war. On the other hand, there had not been one complaint made by any citizen of real violence directed at him or her
(as distinguished from an animal) by the police. In light of all the
emotions on each side, that had been an extraordinary record on
the part of both the police and the citizenry, and had provided the
best explanation possible of the difference between the Deep South
of my civil rights past and northern California in more recent times.
All of this is just starting to change.

On July 25, 1985, CAMP raiders discovered in a garden near
Ettersburg 1,200 marijuana plants and 400 opium-poppy plants.
The possibility of American farmers growing opium poppies has
never figured into the Maginot Line thinking of our drug-war strategists. When I wrote three years ago that such a horticultural
event was foreordained, there were some titters in expert drug-
abuse circles. However, William Ruzzamenti said that the Ettersburg garden was "a real sophisticated operation." Another CAMP
spokesman, Dan Roach, observed that the home-grown poppies
probably had been used already to make heroin. "The plants were
scored [cut] and looked as if they had produced the tars to make
the drug," he concluded.

If the war on drugs continues in intensity, there is no doubt,
to make another prediction, that opium-poppy production will spread
throughout the country. This, indeed, is another horticultural happening that has already begun. In August 1985, a major plantation
of 2,000 poppy plants was discovered by police in the remote town

of West Charlestown, Vermont. Many of the plants had already been slit to obtain opium for making heroin. There is also no doubt that both marijuana and opium plants will be grown indoors. In a 10-by-10-foot room, current legal and economic demand conditions mean that a skillful marijuana planter now can earn $15,000 to $25,000 per year. I will make no predictions on what a skillful indoor opium planter can make because the subject is so new but I would suspect that the potential income will be seductive to many Americans.

Violence by the authorities against growers has finally started to occur. U.S. Forest Service officers, operating independently of CAMP during the fall harvest of 1985, staked out a marijuana garden on public land in the Plumas National Forest near Oraville in northern California. One day they surprised the grower and in the ensuing confused gun battle killed the young man. This seems to have been one of the first killings of a marijuana grower by officials in the area and one of the first killings of anyone by Forest Service personnel in their history. Growers and local citizens are also starting to talk of violent reaction to the drug warriors and to act on that talk. On July 25, 1985, three shots were fired at a CAMP helicopter at the airport in the Hoopa Indian Reservation near the Trinity National Forest. On August 7, a carefully planned night attack in the same general area, at Willow Creek, nearly destroyed a CAMP helicopter with firebombs and rifle shots. A Humboldt County deputy sheriff told me that the attack had simply stiffened the backbones of the police involved in the campaign against marijuana.

When the federal government decided during the summer of 1985 to resume spraying marijuana plants with herbicides, either Paraquat or chemicals similar to it, concerns were expressed that this would trigger even more violent citizen reactions. In contemplation of the resumption of such spraying, "Uncle Sam," a marijuana farmer, told Ray Raphael, "And God forbid they spray Paraquat on our plants. If they spray the planes are going to get shot down. There'll be a level of violence around here that could set back the community a lot, almost like a civil war. I know that when they start spraying they're gonna get shot down—'cause I'm gonna shoot one down."

And the specter of past violence has not left the lives of those in the hills who want to forget it. As he was guiding me to his home from the Ruth store, Gary Rolicheck stopped his pickup truck and motioned me to get out of my car and look at something. Near the family home a few weeks earlier, someone had spray-painted a sign in white letters two feet long on the black asphalt road: "FUCK C.A.M.P." Several days later, Gary had happened upon a uniformed officer, apparently a deputy sheriff, standing near that sign, adding something else to it. The officer fled in his car at Gary's approach. What had been added was the painted outline, between the two words, of the figure of a dog, lying with its feet up and an X on its head, thus crudely reminding everyone who passed of the killing of Duchess.

There will be more contradictory and perverse results if drug-law enforcement continues along its present path. Many big growers and organized criminals will be imprisoned and thus taken out of the scene, a result which will please all decent people, except that our prisons will become even more explosively crowded. Yet many casual growers and small-time dealers will also be scared away by the threat of imprisonment. Many more adventurous, more hardened, and more criminal actors will be attracted to both the thrills and the rewards of the illicit drug business. The drug warriors will increase their pressure to catch them and will intensify the invasiveness of their searches, thus eroding the freedoms of everyone, not simply drug traffickers. None of the actions of law enforcement, however, will affect the level of demand. The price of many drugs may well thus increase and smaller packages of increasingly valuable contraband will be hidden in more ingenious ways in homes, in vehicles, in suitcases—and in bodies.

8

The Coming of the Body Invaders

WHEN TRACED to its logical extremes, the story of the relentless pursuit of drugs becomes a revolting tale. American law does not yet contain the general rule that failure to defecate on command of any police officer may be taken as reasonable suspicion of guilt and a basis for detention, but we are not far from the day when that obscene principle may be written into our legal structure. The reasons for this invasive trend are found in the nature of drugs and of how they are used and hidden. When the President stands in the Rose Garden and announces a new campaign in the war on drugs, the warpath from that garden in Washington ultimately must lead to the lands, the homes, the fields, the boats, the wallets, the pocketbooks, the bodies, the blood, and even the bodily wastes of millions of free citizens throughout our vast country. It is all such a logical progression and it is all done for the good of the nation.

MAKING TRAVELERS
DEFECATE ON COMMAND

Rosa Montoya de Hernandez was a cocaine smuggler. She was caught by a perceptive Customs inspector, convicted, and sent to prison. Good riddance, we all might say. But wait. In this democracy, rights and powers are ultimately defined by the appeals of convicted criminals to the U.S. Supreme Court. In those situations, the guilt of the particular defendants becomes irrelevant because it is recognized that the principles established will apply to millions of people only suspected of crimes, almost all of whom will be innocent. Think not, then, of this cocaine smuggler but of you, innocent traveler, and your mother and your spouse and your children as you next approach the Customs desk at an American airport. And think also of the precedents established in this case that might well apply in other situations throughout future American history.

Ms. de Hernandez reached the Los Angeles International Airport shortly after midnight on March 5, 1983, looking to all the unwary world like any other tired traveler. However, she had flown on Avianca Flight 080, a direct 10-hour journey from Bogota, Colombia. Questioning by a Customs inspector named Talamantes revealed that she spoke no English, had no friends or family in the United States, possessed $5,000 in cash, which she claimed was to be used for the purchase of legitimate merchandise for her husband's store, but that she had no appointments with goods vendors. Clearly, Ms. de Hernandez fit the standard "profile" of an alimentary canal smuggler which the Customs Service has developed for the guidance of its agents. (The alimentary canal is the tubular passage extending from mouth to anus.) Moreover, Inspector Talamantes had his own personal profile based on long experience since he had apprehended dozens of such smugglers on Avianca Flight 080 over the years. He knew that these foolhardy, or desperate, people would swallow balloons or condoms filled with cocaine or heroin and later, once safely in this country, excrete the small fortune hidden in their bodies.

On the basis of this knowledge and suspicion—but certainly without probable cause, that is, without a minimal amount of concrete evidence—the border officers asked a female Customs in-

spector to take the traveler to a private area and conduct a
pat-down and strip search. The female inspector felt Ms. de Hernandez's abdomen and observed a firm fullness. She also observed
that the lady was wearing two pairs of elastic underpants with a
paper towel lining the crotch area. No contraband was found. Yet
the inspectors remained suspicious and asked if the suspect would
agree to go to a hospital for an X-ray. She agreed but then withdrew her assent when she learned that she would have to go to
the hospital in handcuffs, protesting, "You are not going to put
those on me. That is an insult to my character."

The officers then offered their prisoner the option of returning
to Colombia on the next available plane, agreeing to an X-ray, or,
in the words of the U.S. Supreme Court, which eventually issued
a decision in this case on July 1, 1985, "remaining in detention until
she produced a monitored bowel movement that would confirm or
rebut the inspectors' suspicions." She chose the first option but a
flight could not readily be arranged. It was then decided by these
federal police agents that this traveler, still vigorously protesting
her innocence, would be kept in a barren room under constant
guard until their suspicions were satisfied. They told her, a Supreme Court justice further explained, "that she could not leave
until she had excreted by squatting over a waste basket pursuant
to the watchful eyes of two attending matrons." Ms. de Hernandez
responded, "I will not submit to your degradation . . . I would
rather die."

She was kept in that uncarpeted room, with no bed or couch,
for almost 24 hours. The Colombian citizen sat on the chair, clutch-
ing her purse, sometimes napping with her head on the table,
weeping, pleading "to go home," or to make a phone call to her
husband and children, and showing two small pictures of her children to everyone who entered. She was refused access to a phone,
and, on her part, she refused all offers of food and drink—and the
opportunity to use the toilet facilities. Not surprisingly, the de-
tainee soon showed symptoms of great discomfort and, as a lower
federal judge noted, "heroic efforts to resist the usual calls to
nature." Finally, the police went to a magistrate and obtained a
court order for a body search. A rectal examination in the hospital
revealed a cocaine-filled balloon. Then at approximately 3:15 A.M.
on March 6, almost 27 hours after she was first made a prisoner,
Ms. de Hernandez was formally arrested and advised of her Miranda rights. Over the next four days she excreted 88 balloons

containing a total of 528 grams of cocaine. Subsequently, the defendant was convicted of various federal narcotics offenses.

A review of the constitutional doctrines involved in the case of this Colombian traveler would find that the most important protection from unfair arrests and searches in the United States is in the Fourth Amendment, within the Bill of Rights, which declares that "The right of the people to be secure in their persons, houses, papers, and effects, against unreasonable searches and seizures, shall not be violated." The grand task of interpretation over the years, of course, has been to determine what forms of searches were "unreasonable." The controlling definition of unreasonable conduct is that of the U.S. Supreme Court in the *Katz* case (1967), where it was declared that henceforth the magic words would be whether or not the aggrieved person had a "constitutionally protected reasonable expectation of privacy." The high court, it was further explained, would not read the amendment as protecting individually conceived or subjective notions of privacy but only "those expectations that society is prepared to recognize as 'reasonable.' "

With very few exceptions, the high court in recent years has upheld that view of reasonable social expectations that overrode the individual citizen's right to privacy. In taking such repressive positions, the court is certainly reflecting the views of the dominant leaders of all elements of society, including the institutions of the law and police. Thus the pervasive factual distortions about the nature of the illicit-drug menace that dominate general public discussion are constantly being written into the laws and court decisions of our democracy.

One of the greatest judicial exceptions to that restrictive trend occurred relatively early in its development. The liberal decision was based on an incident that took place at about 9:00 A.M. on July 1, 1949, also, as it happened, in Los Angeles. Three deputy sheriffs, having "some information" that Antonio Richard Rochin, a heroin addict, was selling narcotics, walked in through the open door of his house and broke down the door to his second-floor bedroom. Rochin was sitting partially dressed on the bed, upon which his wife was lying. He immediately swallowed two capsules lying on the nightstand. The officers frankly testified that they jumped upon the man, in the presence of his wife and in his own bedroom, grabbed him by the throat, and squeezed his throat forcefully in an attempt to eject the capsules.

The men of the law failed in that endeavor. Deputy Jack Jones
then took citizen Rochin in handcuffs to the Angelus Emergency
Hospital and into an operating room. A doctor's assistant strapped
the handcuffed suspect to an operating table. Thereupon, a person
identified as Dr. Mier, presumably a physician, forced a tube down
the victim's throat and released a white fluid into it and thus into
Mr. Rochin's stomach. Through this method of search, which
everyone involved admitted and did not question on ethical or legal
grounds, victory was gained. The defendant vomited into a pail on
the floor and two capsules of heroin were found floating in that
pail. Mr. Rochin's conviction for illegal possession of narcotics was
based solely on those capsules.

On January 2, 1952, the Supreme Court broke new ground in
Rochin v. *California* when it declared that this search for drugs
was "conduct that shocks the conscience" and thereupon overruled
the conviction as a violation of due process of law. The justices
also viewed this behavior as equivalent to the coercion of a confession through methods "bound to offend even hardened sensibilities." In effect, the police action violated Fourth Amendment
restrictions on unreasonable searches and Fifth Amendment pro-
hibitions against forcing suspects to incriminate themselves.

Since that decision, it appears that the sensibilities of the American people in general and of Supreme Court justices in particular
have become more hardened and their consciences less shockable
whenever there is a case involving a search for drugs. In several
major cases since Rochin, the Supreme Court upheld the legality
of the taking of blood without consent in drunk-driving prosecutions. In those cases, though, there was probable cause and little
trauma to the individual from whom the bodily evidence was obtained. Those decisions, nevertheless, evoked ringing dissents from
liberal justices who saw them as proof of the continual shrinkage
of American rights, especially the right to personal privacy. There
have also been stories over the years which strongly suggest that
many of the practices condemned in the Rochin decision, or brutal
behavior in the same repressive league, continue to be practiced
in the byways and back rooms of American justice—in, for example, the little rooms where travelers who arouse the suspicions
of Customs agents are detained.

Ms. de Hernandez continually fought her conviction up the ap-
pellate ladder until it reached the Supreme Court, where then
associate justice William Rehnquist was assigned to write the ma-

jority opinion in the decision handed down on July 1, 1985, as drug-war fever was building in the nation. There can be no argument with his opening position that since the beginning of the nation, routine border searches have not been subject to "any requirement of reasonable suspicion, probable cause, or warrant." Border officials have never been controlled by the law to the extent that police within the country have been—and those border police may stop anyone and may inspect any *package* even on a hunch. However, the court had never delineated what was a reasonable level of suspicion that would justify the type of more drastic *personal* detention and searches that were visited on Ms. de Hernandez. The Supreme Court might have adopted the position of the U.S. Court of Appeals, which had thrown out the conviction because the custom agents lacked a "clear indication" of alimentary-canal smuggling.

Instead, the high court upheld the search and conviction and, for the first time in history, laid out a new test for such degrading searches which are now legal "if Customs agents, considering all the facts surrounding the traveler and her trip, reasonably suspect that the traveler is smuggling contraband in her alimentary canal." Therefore, the police at the border do not need evidence providing a "clear indication" of a crime but only a good hunch to go beyond a routine search. What about the long detention? The court stated that the nature of the offense and of the human system made it constitutionally justified. "In this regard the detention of a suspected alimentary-canal smuggler at the border," the future Chief Justice of the United States actually declared, "is analogous to the detention of a suspected tuberculosis carrier at the border: both are detained until their bodily processes dispel the suspicion that they will introduce a harmful agent into this country."

On the basis of such specious logic, formal and specific approval was given at the highest judicial level of the American government for the principle that when the suspicions of border police are aroused, even though they lack any clear evidence of crime, they may detain any traveler for an appropriate, though as yet undefined, period of time until that person dispels their suspicions by defecating in their presence and into a container of their choice so that the vigilant police may inspect the traveler's human waste for contraband.

Justice William Brennan wrote an outraged dissent, in which he was joined by Justice Thurgood Marshall, about this "disgusting and saddening episode." Justice Brennan declared that the court's decision would produce threats to the personal privacy of the great majority of innocent travelers who now might be subjected to shocking indignities by police searching for drugs. He wrote, "The available evidence suggests that the number of highly intrusive border searches of suspicious-looking but ultimately innocent travelers may be very high. One physician who at the request of Customs officials conducted many 'internal searches'—rectal and vaginal examinations and stomach-pumping—estimated that he had found contraband in only 15 to 20 percent of the persons he had examined. It has similarly been estimated that only 16 percent of women subjected to body-cavity searches at the border were in fact found to be carrying contraband.

"The nature and duration of the detention here may well have been tolerable for spoiled meat or diseased animals, but not for human beings held on simple suspicion of criminal activity," Justice Brennan continued. "As de Hernandez's counsel observed at argument, 'What if an innocent traveler just because they have had a long flight was unable to excrete and found themselves in a position where a border agent said well, we wish you to excrete [on] command so that we will be sure that you're not carrying anything internally. An innocent person might be unable to do that on command . . . but that wouldn't necessarily mean evidence of guilt.' "

Justice Brennan also observed that the reasonable expectations of privacy held by most international travelers do not include the possibility of being subjected to such indignities "all on nothing more than the 'reasonable' suspicions of low-ranking enforcement agents." He added, "In fact, many people from around the world travel to our borders precisely to escape such unchecked executive investigatory discretion. What a curious first lesson in American liberty awaits them on their arrival."

As of this writing, the de Hernandez defecation doctrine represents one of the most extreme invasions of rights that have been accomplished by the war on drugs. The decisions in few cases should cause such revulsion as that one, but all of these decisions are part of a broad interconnected network. The cases creating those invasions reach into diverse segments of American life and build upon one another's logic of repression. In each case there seems, by some standards, to be a perfectly sound reason for the apparently small incursion into the body of American freedoms.

MAKING STUDENTS STRIP
NAKED ON COMMAND

Such was the situation in the case of Diane "Doe." It arose in Highland, Indiana, a community of approximately 30,000 residents located in the northwest corner of the state in Lake County. Both the junior and senior high school buildings were located on the same campus, adjacent to each other, containing a total of approximately 2,780 students. From September 1978 to March 22, 1979, 21 instances were recorded of students found in possession of drugs, alcohol, or drug paraphernalia. This may seem, in retrospect, to have indicated a minor problem, but perhaps the nationwide growth of the parents' movement and of fears about student drug use had panicked this small county in the Midwest as they had so many other communities.

Meetings were held in the community to deal with this seemingly growing crisis. Having read of the use of dogs to sniff out marijuana in other Indiana schools, Superintendent Omer Renfrow decided to use the dogs to deal with the problem in his own school system. He contacted the local police for help and soon met with them and with Ms. Patricia L. Little, the owner and operator of the Edelheim Police Canine Academy in nearby Bunker Hill, Indiana. Ms. Little was engaged in the business of training dogs for purposes of attack, tracking, and detecting marijuana. She took the lead in providing 16 dog handlers, all local citizens with no particular expertise in drug matters, along with their dogs. But this was not all. Ms. Little also gave directions as to when strip searches were required.

This major quasi-military operation commenced at 8:45 A.M., March 23, 1979. Ms. Little, an unpaid deputy sheriff, was prominent during the entire operation, wearing a police-type poplin jacket displaying two badges on the arms. One read "Police Canine" and the other "Edelheim Canine." The uniform also displayed an American flag. The objective of the raid was to rid the schools of drugs and to discourage further drug use, but it was expressly agreed that no criminal prosecutions would result. All 2,780 students were kept sitting in their first-period classrooms. Through sealed orders left on the desk of each teacher, these young American students were—without warning, without advice as to their rights to object, and without a warrant—summarily ordered to sit with their books and purses and bags between their feet on the floor and their hands on their desks in plain view. Exit doors were sealed by teams of school employees. Any student wishing to go to the bathroom had to be accompanied and observed by an adult escort of the same sex so as to prevent drugs being flushed away.

Teams of searchers included at least one dog, one dog handler, one school official, and one uniformed, armed police officer. Because there was no evidence implicating any specific student, all were equally suspect. "Every single student was sniffed, inspected, and examined at least once," wrote a federal court of appeals judge. He continued, "The extraordinary atmosphere of the school was supplemented still further when representatives of the press and other news media, invited in by school authorities, entered the schoolhouses and classrooms during the raid and observed the searches while in progress. The raid lasted about three hours. After the sniffing and examining of 2,780 students, the searchers found fifteen high school students—and *no* junior high school students—in possession of illicit materials. . . . Four junior high school students—all girls—were removed from their classes, stripped nude, and interrogated. Not one of them was found to possess any illicit material."

One of those innocent girls was Diane, aged 13. Her teacher informed the class before the search began that the school had a "surprise" for the students. When the German shepherd dog reached her, it "alerted," sniffed at her body aggressively, and repeatedly pushed its nose and muzzle against her body and into her leg. The uniformed police officer then ordered Diane to stand and empty her pockets, which search produced no drugs. Yet the dog continued to sniff her body and to "alert." The shocked and embarrassed young girl, who did not use any drugs and who considered marijuana to be dangerous, was taken to the nurse's office where two adult women, one a uniformed police officer and the other a family friend, ordered her to take off all of her clothes. Diane did so although she was allowed to turn her back in the process. The women examined her body, inspected her clothing, and touched and examined the hair on her head. Again, no drugs were found, and the angry, embarrassed young citizen was allowed to dress and return to her classroom and to the curious comments and jokes of her fellow students. Subsequently, it was determined that the probable reason for the "alert" by the police dog was that Diane had been playing that morning with her own dog, who was in heat.

When I casually asked one mature woman of my acquaintance what her response would have been had this indecency been visited on her daughter, her reply was immediate: "Burn the damned school down that night!" However, Robert and Naomi Doe, the parents of Diane, opted for a more measured, legal response. They decided to sue, claiming that the young American's Fourth Amendment rights had been violated. Lower federal courts determined that the dragnet searches were constitutionally permissible as an exercise of the *in loco parentis* (in place of parents) power by the schools but that the nude searches were unconstitutional. Eventually, Diane collected damages in an out-of-court settlement for that strip search. Nevertheless, her parents pursued the case on appeal so as to obtain a ruling that the entire procedure, especially the dragnet search of children suspected of no crime, was repugnant to American constitutional traditions.

When the case reached the Supreme Court, it simply refused to hear the appeal. Technically speaking, no conclusions may be drawn from such an action, which means that the high court has not taken a position on the matter. It is fair to say, however, that had the justices been sufficiently disturbed by the searches of these young Americans, they would have found a legal basis to hear the appeal and to issue a resounding decision telling the world that such official behavior was unconstitutional. Only Justice Brennan *was* sufficiently disturbed, and he wrote a stinging dissent from the brief order denying the appeal on May 26, 1981, in the case known as *Doe* v. *Renfrow*. The justice agreed with the court of appeals in regard to its castigation of the strip search but he would have preferred that the high court summarily reverse that court's decision to the extent it upheld the dragnet search of all the students.

"We do not know what class [Diane] was attending when the police and dogs burst in, but the lesson the school authorities taught her that day will undoubtedly make a greater impression than the one her teacher had hoped to convey." The high court justice concluded that he would have granted the appeal to teach Diane and other students a different lesson, one that revealed something important about the grand traditions of American freedoms, that "before police and local officials are permitted to conduct dog-assisted dragnet inspections of public school students, they must obtain a warrant based on sufficient particularized evidence to establish probable cause to believe that a crime has been or is being committed. Schools cannot expect their students to learn the lessons of good citizenship when the school authorities themselves disregard the fundamental principles underpinning our constitutional freedoms."

Because the Supreme Court refused the opportunity to issue a full decision, it is not clear if the Constitution will be interpreted to protect American students from mass dragnet searches by police and dogs—or from commands by school officials and the police that they strip nude in front of strangers so they can be searched for drugs. In the only major case involving the search of a student since Diane's appeal, the high court approved the search, although it was much less intrusive than that of Diane.

The crucial incidents in the case took place one day in Piscataway High School, Middlesex County, New Jersey. A teacher discovered two freshmen girls smoking tobacco cigarettes in a restroom, and had promptly taken the two miscreants to the principal's office where they were confronted by the assistant vice principal, Theodore Choplick. One of the girls immediately admitted her guilt. The other, a 14-year-old with a stubborn streak, who is called T.L.O. in the court record, not only denied that she had been smoking in the lavatory but also that she smoked at all, ever. Mr. Choplick persisted in his investigation. He asked the defiant one to come into his private office and demanded to see what was in her purse. The public school official opened the student's purse, immediately found a pack of cigarettes, held it before T.L.O., and accused her of lying to him. Even though it was not against any law or school regulation for the young lady to possess the cigarettes, the school official believed that he had the power to inspect her purse for tobacco so as to determine if she was lying about smoking in the lavatory, which *was* against school rules.

As he had been reaching into the purse for the cigarettes, however, Vice Principal Choplick saw an item of even greater concern to him: a package of cigarette rolling papers. This was March 7, 1980, in one of the great urban areas of America, a time and place of public distress over the destructive use of drugs by young people, especially in schools. In his experience, Mr. Choplick had learned that the possession of rolling papers often meant that a student was using marijuana. He then searched the purse thoroughly and found a small cache of marijuana, a pipe, several empty plastic bags, a good deal of money in one-dollar bills, an index card listing the names of students who apparently owed T.L.O. money, and two letters—all of which evidence seemingly indicated that the freshman girl was not merely a pot user but also a pot dealer. The vice principal called the student's mother.

He also believed that his duty demanded that he do something else, which brings us over the threshhold of the major constitutional issue involved in this matter: he notified the police and turned all of the evidence over to them. At the request of the police, T.L.O.'s mother took her to the police station where the girl confessed that indeed she had been selling marijuana at the high school. The school authorities suspended her for several days because of violations of the school rules. After protracted court proceedings, T.L.O. was adjudged to be a delinquent by the local juvenile court and sentenced to a year's probation.

Most people would probably say, as they might about Rosa Elvira Montoya de Hernandez, so what? A mendacious, immoral little witch was dealing drugs in a school and got caught—thank heaven!—and anyhow she should have got some time behind bars. However, in enunciating the decision supporting the action of the principal and of the juvenile court, the U.S. Supreme Court in *New Jersey* v. *T.L.O.* for the first time sanctioned the use by a court of evidence which had been seized by a school official who did not have probable cause but only a good hunch that something was amiss. Up to the time of that decision, there was no doubt that school officials could make limited searches of students when there was a "reasonable suspicion" that they had violated school rules—and do so without a warrant or probable cause. Since the T.L.O. decision, however, school officials now have the power on the authority of the highest court in the land to make extensive searches of students—certainly their handbags and purses and also perhaps their lockers and desks—if there is a reasonable suspicion that they have violated even the most trivial school regulation; and if the officials discover evidence of a crime, *they may turn the material over to the police for prosecution.*

It is no surprise that in this tolerant judicial atmosphere school officials, urged on by parent and police groups, are acting today as if they have virtually unlimited power to search the possessions and bodies of all American students. Within the past few years, there has been a stream of reports from all over the country of school district after school district implementing a strip-search policy. As I read them, I wonder if I am in the right country or if my country has truly gone mad. I could not imagine any teacher suggesting such an idea when I was in public school during the Thirties and Forties—unless, of course, they were lechers or voyeurs or perverts of another sort. I am not joking about this. I suspect people who sit on pornography commissions looking at thousands of dirty pictures so as to protect the rest of us from them, and in the same way I suspect people who insist it is necessary to strip-search students to save them from drugs. I suspect them not only of fostering repressive invasions of American freedoms but also of pathological personal drives that make them want to feast their eyes on naked youngsters, who have been compelled to strip against their will, or to share the derivative thrill that they have made it possible for other people to do so.

URINE TESTS: THE FATAL FLAWS

I also suspect the personal pathology that drives leading American officials and drug-abuse experts to show so much interest in the bodily wastes of others, especially their urine, which has become the focal point of so much national attention today. Not long ago during dinner, moreover, I saw on national network news several congressional candidates walking sheepishly out of a small room holding bottles of their own warm urine, offered up for testing to show that they were clean. It was, in a word, revolting. To the list of suspected pathological traits of our leaders, then, must be added a desire to show off one's own bodily wastes to the world.

Urine testing is now flooding through every major institution, impelled by the same type of rationality that spawned the loyalty oaths during the McCarthy era and the religious oaths of belief during the prosecution of Puritan dissenters in the Star Chamber of seventeenth-century England (as well as the more recent attempts of the Reagan administration to commence random lie-detector testing of federal employees on grounds of national security). In the armed services, in law enforcement, in private industry, in the Olympics, and (is nothing truly sacred that deserves to be treated as sacred and exempt from such madness?) in major league baseball and football, leaders are lining up in patriotic phalanxes to be the first to say, Hand me a bottle, I'll take one right now, why shouldn't everyone else? To be opposed to such tests is seen, in some circles, as being opposed to a virtuous attempt to save the soul of America from chemicals. When I spoke in 1985 to a seminar of police chiefs at the FBI Academy, nothing I said evoked such emotional reactions as my observation that mass urine testing, even of police officers, raised serious issues of constitutional rights and invasions of privacy. One chief actually declared, I'll take one right now!

Like all procedures for detection of chemicals within bodies, there are positive functions for urinalysis. It is perfectly appropriate, for example, to say to a drug addict who has entered a treatment program under the care of a physician: a condition of staying in the program is periodic, unscheduled testing of your urine. Because prisoners have a special legal status, it is also appropriate in many cases to demand urine samples from them. Difficulties would arise, however, if an addict in treatment were automatically imprisoned on the basis only of a urine test—or if, as proposed by such experts as Drs. Nahas and Gleaton, suspected addicts were put into quarantine for forced treatment when they flunked a urine test. More legal difficulties would occur when people suspected of no offense were required to take urine tests on a mass basis, thus raising the specter of mass violations of the rights to be free from unreasonable searches and seizures and from being compelled to incriminate oneself. And that, of course, is what is happening today to millions of American employees.

In a nutshell, the fatal flaws in mass urine testing are that they take the fatal flaws of the anti-drug crusade of the last seventy years and drive them to further absurd extremes. The tests assume that there are rational distinctions between the legal drugs as a group and the illegal drugs as a group. The tests ignore the legal drugs—particularly tobacco and alcohol—and assume that traces of the illegal drugs—especially marijuana—in the urine should be taken as the sign of an impaired employee, or as a sign that the workplace is not drug-free, as all agree, including me, that it should be. At its most benevolent, the policy of the employer would then call for rehabilitation as a next step. But for what? The tests do not measure impairment. Yet a trace of any illegal drug is labeled "abuse." The absurdity is that it would follow that the employee would then be treated for the disease of drug abuse, which he or she might not have.

More often than not, however, the suspect would not be put

into treatment but into limbo, into disgrace, and into unemployment. In today's hysterical climate, one bad urine test can and has ruined many careers—as did suspicion of communism during the McCarthy period. As happened then, the legality of the tests is highly suspect. While the Supreme Court has not issued definitive rulings on them, many lower courts have blocked mass urine tests of public employees as violations of constitutional rights. Because the constitution does not apply so directly to private employers, the rights of their employees are less protected and the legalites are still being debated. Yet the essential irrationalities of the tests— and their scientific unreliability—may produce new legal doctrines and negotiated labor contracts that will erect new protections in the private workplace.

MAKING CHILDREN URINATE ON COMMAND

The leaders of the parents' movement and their technical experts, as we have seen, believe that there should be mass urine testing of students so as to ensure the goal of a whole generation of drug-free youth. In almost every case, a urine test is based not on evidence but on suspicion—or less, on the belief that the test is not even a search at all and that only by testing everyone in a given group can everyone in it be protected from the evil of drugs. Under the latter logic, neither evidence nor suspicion is needed because the procedure is seen in the same light as a preventive prophylactic or an inoculation.

Whatever the underlying logic, the urine test is becoming an all-American institution, like Mom and apple pie. Recipes for its proper formulation and use are traded across the country. Advice on how to obtain and monitor an accurate test is now standard fare in material prepared for parents' groups. Dr. Richard H. Schwartz, a professor of child health and development at George Washington University Medical School in the nation's capital and medical director of Straight, Inc., for the greater Washington area, wrote recently in a national parents' association newsletter of the values of weekly urine monitoring of rebellious teenagers who promise to abstain from marijuana. "It is best to collect the first voided specimen on a weekend morning, preferably following a night of suspected 'partying with friends,' " the medical school professor solemnly wrote, presumably to parents. "The urine should have a yellow or light orange appearance (this shows that the urine was not mixed with water), and the urine, if freshly voided, should impart a sensation of warmth to the container."

Such advice from a medical school professor raises an intriguing question. Are parents in danger of flunking a drug-war loyalty test when they declare that they would rather not know the color and temperature of their teenagers' bodily wastes, except in a clear case of a deadly organic illness?

This new era of parent-child love and trust was further epitomized in 1983 when Checkpoint Laboratories, Inc., of Manassas, Virginia, announced the mass marketing of the U-Care Kit, designed to enhance further the ability of parents to monitor the drug habits of their children. This kit, intended for sale over-the-counter without prescription in drug stores for $15, would have allowed parents to collect urine samples at home and send them by mail directly to Checkpoint, which would then send the results back to the parents, thus bypassing other commercial laboratories or medical doctors. At a press conference in November, the executives of the company seemed to suggest that they planned to cash in on parents' concerns about teenage drug abuse, and that they expected to sell 20 million to 30 million dollars' worth in the next year alone.

Such devices may help a few families but certainly they will tear many more apart. It is difficult to see how trust and love will survive continual tests administered in the home so that parents may be assured that their children are not lying to them. It makes sense that soon this company or another will market, and that some parents will eagerly purchase, a handy-dandy over-the-counter virginity testing kit. Then parents may be assured of having sex-free youth. The next family-trust invention will be an over-the-counter portable lie-detector kit. Next . . . ?

Only one organization on the national scene had the inclination to make a frontal assault on the marketing of the home drug-testing kit. Indeed, Kevin Zeese, national director of NORML, was interested immediately in part because the constitutional and fairness issues raised by urine testing now demand more of his attention than any other single subject. At that time, as it happened, one of my undergraduate students, Paul Shelowitz, was serving an internship with NORML. In part on the basis of Paul's research, Mr. Zeese soon filed a petition with the Food and Drug Administration, which regulates the marketing in interstate commerce of new medical devices under the Federal Food, Drug, and Cosmetic Act. In the petition, NORML raised a number of objections about the accuracy and effectiveness of the U-Care test, including problems that would result when urine samples were delayed in the mails for days and allowed to sit at unregulated temperatures. After several months of negotiations with the FDA by NORML and Checkpoint, the test was withdrawn from the market. Soon, the company ceased all operations. However, I thought at the time, there appear to be no insurmountable legal or scientific obstacles to the development of such a kit by an enterprising business, eager to reap the profits just sitting out there in the worried-parent market, at some time in the near future. I was unfortunately right. New tests for checking on children at home have since been put on the market by business firms.

A hint of the shape and size of the future national drug-testing market was provided in early 1985 when school superintendent Alfred Marbaise of East Rutherford, New Jersey, announced that henceforth all students would be given blood and urine tests for drugs and alcohol every year. Not only students suspected of drug abuse. Not only urine tests. Not occasionally. All students, every year, and both blood and urine tests. The superintendent seemed stunned at the national attention the announcement of this program received. (Today, we tend to forget that such radical notions have been on the scene for only a few years. Now there have been so many student search and testing programs implemented that they are no longer news, but they should be.) He also was unable to answer many of the questions that were asked, especially as to how the results of these searches might be used by school authorities and the police. Within a few months, the school board answered that the results of the tests would be made known to school authorities and, in certain cases, to the police, who could take whatever action they deemed appropriate. Students who refused to take such tests would not be allowed to attend school.

The school board insisted that its motives were helpful, aimed at rehabilitating youth with problems and at maintaining "a healthy school population," one "which is drug- and alcohol-free." The educational leaders did not seem aware of the question raised by Justice Brennan as to what lessons we are teaching our youth by these repressive and intrusive procedures. We must also wonder, with bated breath, what types of tests and searches for drugs the most paranoid of these students will devise when they become school leaders themselves. Fortunately, some students and their parents, aided by the American Civil Liberties Union, successfully fought this invasion of freedom. A local court stopped the program as an invasion of privacy. This decision has not cooled the ardor of school leaders and parent groups in other districts.

MAKING EMPLOYEES
URINATE ON COMMAND

In the American workplace, the most popular current test seems to be the EMIT system developed by the Syva Company of Palo Alto, California. It was the first relatively inexpensive, rapid, and seemingly accurate urine-screening test put on the market and intended for commercial use. A basic system cost approximately $3,500 and each test $6 in the early Eighties. Since it was first promoted nationally in 1981, the EMIT test for marijuana has been a huge commercial success, and was a large contributor to Syva's healthy gross sales of $100 million in fiscal 1983. The test measures delta-9 THC metabolites in the urine, that is, by-products of the process by which human beings break down and excrete marijuana in their systems. It also may be configured to test for a wide variety of other drugs, including heroin and cocaine. Syva literature states that the test measures only the presence of drugs, thus indicating "recent drug use," but warns customers that "no urine test method . . . can determine intoxication."

Syva also claims that its tests have proven to be at least 95 percent accurate, whether indicating negative or positive recent drug use. Nevertheless, the company literature also warns users that "positive results should be confirmed by an alternative method." One more comprehensive and reliable method is known as the gas chromatograph/mass spectrometer test, which takes more time and costs from $60 to over $100 for each use. In many cases, the responsible officials do not order any second, alternative test but instead simply repeat the EMIT process, or they quietly take action on the basis of the first positive finding. The problems of both administering the tests and making decisions on them are aggravated by the fact that the number of people subjected to them keeps rising every year, with perhaps five million Americans taking them now in connection with their employment either in civilian or military life.

Until I forced myself to review some of the stories of these ordinary human beings caught in the bizarre workings of the new urine Gulag, I confess that I had dismissed the problem as a relatively unimportant irritation, even something of a joke. The notion of peeing in a bottle to obtain or keep a job which has nothing to do with that particular function is, after all, somewhat ludicrous. Now I see nothing funny at all. The manner in which the tests have actually operated under the Reagan administration—remember, mass testing only began in 1981, the first year that Mr. Reagan arrived in the White House—demonstrates that they may create more victims of the drug war than any other single irrational weapon in this fundamentally irrational crusade.

Ann Chase was one of the first examples. In August 1981, the 61-year-old widow applied for a job at the Facet Filter Company in Madison Heights, Michigan. She was referred to a clinic where a medical doctor performed a pre-employment physical examination. Unknown to her, but in accordance with widespread current practice, her urine taken during that physical examination was sent to a nearby commercial laboratory which performed an EMIT test for drugs. Ms. Chase tested positive for marijuana. Without making any confirmatory tests, the laboratory so reported to the clinic, which reported to the company, which then informed Ms. Chase that she was being denied employment. Upon learning the cause, the suburban grandmother protested that in the entire six decades of her life she had never smoked any substance whatsoever, not even tobacco and certainly not marijuana. Her protests were rebuffed. The new technology had spoken and told the world she was a drug abuser.

The new technology, spurred on by the drug warriors, smeared another woman, 41-year-old Julie Medina, with the same defamatory label. She, too, applied for a job with the Facet Filter Company and was also denied employment because she tested positive on the EMIT test. Ms. Medina admitted later that she had smoked marijuana as a much younger person "years ago—not for a long, long time." Yet she was denied the opportunity to be gainfully employed at a time when jobs were scarce in that area.

Both victims eventually found that the only possibility of redress lay in bringing suit, which they did along with a third person,

Casey Triblo, who has become one of the most prominent fighters against the injustices of the urine test. Indeed, some journalists have taken to calling him the Ralph Nader of urine tests. In June 1981 Mr. Triblo, then in his late twenties, received word that a long-awaited dream had been realized. The Detroit Fire Department notified him that he was about to be appointed an emergency medical technician. The idea of saving people's lives in emergency situations had always appealed to him, and he had worked and trained for many years to reach this goal. He went to the physical a few days later and gave a urine sample. He was never told that it was to be tested for drugs, nor did he give his permission. Had he been asked, he says he might have gone along with it because in general he supported the idea of testing employees for drugs—if the test could show intoxication. After all, he did not want to work with "dopers" driving ambulances under the influence of any drug or alcohol. He believes that use off the job is none of the employer's business, however. It certainly had no effect on his performance.

An EMIT test showed him positive on marijuana use, although he was not told about it. In fact, Casey Triblo freely admits he was an occasional smoker, like millions of other Americans, and that he had a joint four days before the test. A second EMIT test also was positive, not only for Casey but for 11 out of 14 cadets in his class as well. The fire department then told them about the test but decided to let them all commence work on condition that they take another test after a month with the idea that all of the trainees would then have the opportunity to clean out their systems. In his opinion, everyone took the warning to heart. "Needless to say, we didn't smoke pot," Mr. Triblo later recalled. Certainly, he happily abstained for he did not want to see his dream slip through his fingers. Indeed, he used no marijuana at all during the entire period of his employment by the city, July 7 to August 27, 1981. The results of a private EMIT test he secured during this period showed him negative for marijuana. Yet the third test taken through the city came up positive and thereupon Mr. Triblo was fired, along with one other recruit who also flunked the test.

The tests had been done by Quality Clinical Laboratories in Wayne County, which had performed the same procedure on Ms. Chase and Ms. Medina. As in their cases, the lab had attempted no alternative tests and fire department officials claimed ignorance of the need for independent confirmation. Casey Triblo found himself unable to get an emergency medical technician's job because his reputation had been harmed by word of his firing as a drug abuser. He insists that his use of pot has always been moderate and that he would never report for any job in an intoxicated condition from any drug. His entire work record, including the brief time with the city of Detroit, was always at a high level of performance. Mr. Triblo now works as an ambulance driver at less than four dollars an hour. He also has spent a good deal of his energy and time, though, in his campaign against urine tests, especially the EMIT method. He secured a lawyer and brought a multimillion-dollar suit against the city of Detroit and Quality Clinical Laboratories on the grounds of libel, slander, loss of employment, and violation of constitutional rights.

Settlements were made out of court with Ms. Chase and Ms. Medina, perhaps because those defendants did not want the jury to hear their stories along with that of Mr. Triblo, the admitted current marijuana user off the job. In June 1986 a Detroit jury voted against Casey Triblo and thus upheld the current irrational claim that any person who smokes marijuana even occasionally is banned from working in many jobs. A saddened Casey Triblo wrote me about the jury, "I don't think the average lay person is motivated enough or intelligent enough to understand the pitfalls of the EMIT test or any other test for that matter. When you add the 'Reefer Madness' defense, as the city did, people tend to not take a chance of allowing a person who did drugs to take a public safety job." He added, "I've always maintained that if a test method was developed to determine marijuana *intoxication*, I would be willing to take a test before every shift."

One of the witnesses in the case for Casey Triblo was a prominent expert in the field, Dr. Arthur McBay, who was one of the originators of some of the techniques later used in the EMIT system and whose graduate students performed early assessments of the system. Dr. McBay in recent years has stated time and time again that he regrets now the role he played in its creation because of the "horror stories" and "dire consequences" that keep coming to his attention based on the irresponsible use of the test, as in the case of Ann Chase, Julie Medina, Casey Triblo, and tens of thousands of other Americans. Dr. McBay is the chief toxicologist in the Office of the Chief Medical Examiner, State of North Carolina, and professor of pathology and pharmacy at the University of North Carolina. He declared ruefully in November 1982, "The process was supposed to be for statistical research on use of marijuana and other drugs, not to crucify individuals. . . . I feel bad about it. People are being deprived of rights and privileges. People are being removed from jobs. Others are sent to jail. That's what I call some dire consequences."

The wide professional support for Dr. McBay's concern was shown a year later at a conference in Cincinnati. To 120 forensic scientists in the room, Dr. McBay asked a question: "Is there anybody in the audience who would submit urine for an immunoassay test if his career, reputation, freedom, or livelihood depended on it?" Not a single hand went up. That event was reported in *Clinical Chemistry News*, the official organ of the American Association for Clinical Chemistry, a publication that has consistently raised objections to the improper use of urine testing for marijuana in recent years. Despite Syva's claims, many clinical chemists argue that the EMIT test, like others, can produce many false positives, which may be caused by the nature of the urine, by medications, by the manner in which an individual metabolizes a drug, and by diet. "If you're doing a single EMIT, I don't know how you can tell whether you've got a wild one or not," Dr. McBay has stated. Simply repeating the EMIT test is a widespread practice, which was labeled "absolutely unacceptable" by Dr. Thomas Rejent, chief county toxicologist in Buffalo.

One example of the terrible dangers in the new chemical Gulag was brought to my attention by Dr. McBay in 1986. He sent me a notice he had received from the Syva Company advising users of EMIT that the company had discovered that three widely used medicines could come up positive for marijuana. One of those drugs was ibuprofen, taken for years by millions of people in Motrin, Nuprin, and Advil. "Cannaboid assay has been on the market for over five years. . . . This was discovered by accident this year. Who knows how many other substances might do the same?" Dr. McBay observed. Who knows, I ask, how many careers have been ruined by such small quirks of chemistry unleashed?

Dr. McBay also raised questions about the level of accuracy of the tests. He told me that 95 percent accuracy was the highest claimed by the Syva Company, and that was achieved when done by their own personnel. "It's like Babe Ruth saying, 'Here's a bat that hit .300' . . . and then handing it to me!" When Syva or any company hands its test kits out to less skillful technicians, the accuracy rate drops sharply to 90 percent, to 80 percent, and below.

If there *were* a false reading rate of 10 percent, with half false positives and half false negatives, this could mean that 5 percent of the approximately 5 million people tested this year in America were accused improperly of being drug users. Thus, there is a good chance that 250,000 employees were placed under suspicion or had their careers ruined for no reason.

Many clinical chemists are also greatly distressed over the most destructive myth attached to the new wave of chemical searches of American body wastes—that these tests measure impairment and thereby allow managers of major institutions to screen out potentially bad or dangerous employees. To those who will only take the time to hear their words of warning, the objective clinical chemists of the nation are saying, no, it simply is not true. The tests do not measure performance, past, present, or future. Of course, they know that Syva literature contains a caution in one paragraph about not measuring intoxication but they also know that much of the remainder of the promotional material on EMIT negates that warning. Even when an EMIT test is done properly, "You cannot gauge or judge impairment from a positive urine analysis of marijuana," stated Michael Peat, the co-director of the Chemical Toxicology Institute, Foster City, California. The high from marijuana may last a few hours, while traces could be in the urine for weeks or months.

However, the drug warriors are in the political saddle now and they are seeking to ride roughshod over all of the opposition, whether the objections are based on fairness, civil liberties, or science. Dr. DuPont, for example, has stated repeatedly in the national media that more urine tests are necessary to achieve zero tolerance for drugs and that current ones, such as EMIT, do not really need confirmation by alternative procedures because they are so accurate, a position which *Clinical Chemistry News* reported with apparent amazement. On the May 28, 1982, NBC-TV "Today Show" Dr. DuPont appeared with Casey Triblo and countered his criticisms of EMIT by declaring, "This particular test has not had a problem with false positives. And I would recommend people confirm it simply by doing the test again."

A brief summary of the ideological alignment on this issue was provided on national television by the "CBS News with Dan Rather" on July 16, 1985. Reporter Fred Graham said, "It's the American way. If blockades and drug busts have failed to stop drug abuse, try technology. Laboratory tests of urine samples, properly conducted, can now detect the smallest trace of narcotics and the Reagan administration is urging the nation's employees they must pass the test in order to hold a job. . . . Companies like IBM, General Motors, Greyhound, the Postal Service, and even *The New York Times* are using urine tests, mostly before people are hired." Chief White House drug policy adviser Dr. Carlton Turner then told the people of the country, "You have a choice: you give up your drugs, or you seek employment elsewhere. And one of the ways to do it [screen out drug users] is a urinalysis." J. Michael Walsh of NIDA added, "It will become, within the next year or two, very difficult for someone to get a job who is a current user of illicit substances." Fred Graham stated, "Some experts say 80 percent of all companies will be testing employees for drug abuse in five years. The question is: are the tests accurate and fair?" Casey Triblo appeared on the screen to answer in the negative, followed by Dr. McBay, who declared, "To me, it's . . . Big Brotherism. . . . It doesn't seem to be an American way of doing things."

TESTING SPORTS STARS: WHY?

Some of the most emotional calls for the spread of such Big Brotherism have come in regard to sports participants. For some years, international Olympics officials have demanded urine testing of all athletes. Yet in the early Eighties, American Olympic Committee leaders were dismayed when 15 U.S. participants in the Pan-American Games in Venezuela were discovered to have banned substances in their urine. The bad substances then were stimulants and anabolic steroids, which allegedly increase muscle size and strength. As a result, the American committee soon announced that every American athlete must be tested before taking part in both winter and summer Olympics for approximately 100 substances, not simply mind-altering drugs but also seemingly innocent medicines such as over-the-counter cold pills, nose spray, and eye drops.

The executive director of the U.S. Olympic Committee, F. Don Miller, announced in 1983, "I want to emphasize that this is a war on drugs and not a war on our athletes." Yet he then showed, once again, how that mythical separation is indeed simply that, by add-

ing, "Testing is not a choice. Any athlete who refuses is a positive."
The tickets for admission to competition, he made clear to our
athletes, were two bottles of drug-free urine.

When Peter Ueberroth left his triumphal accomplishments as
president of the Los Angeles Olympic Organizing Committee and
took over as the commissioner of baseball in 1984, he faced a problem not of legal nose drops but of illegal nose candy. The use of
cocaine by major league players made headline after headline in
1984 and 1985, including a sensational criminal trial involving players on the Pittsburgh Pirates. Soon, Mr. Ueberroth was proposing
various schemes of drug testing for virtually everyone in baseball,
save, strangely enough, for major-league players themselves. His
experience with advanced urine-testing techniques at the 1984
Summer Games convinced him, he confidently reported, that testing could be accurate and fair. "If you have the most sophisticated
equipment like we had . . . I've never heard of an argument that
the tests weren't foolproof," declared the commissioner of baseball,
who apparently had not listened to the arguments of Casey Triblo
or of Dr. Arthur McBay and his colleagues. The commissioner also
revealed, as both a comfort and a challenge, that he had taken the
test himself.

Mr. Ueberroth believes, like so many national leaders, that
major-league ball players have a special responsibility because they
are role models to the youth of the nation. He said he also saw
"another element in the darn thing," namely, "Baseball wants to
be a leader in setting an example in solving our drug problems.
. . . I think [FBI] director Webster would tell you that cocaine is
problem number 1, 2, and 3 in fighting crime in this country."
While the baseball commissioner's criminological theories may be
doubted, there is no doubt that, combined with the baseball cocaine
scandals, they soon led him to screw his courage to the sticking
point and actually propose mandatory periodic unscheduled testing
for the gods of the American pantheon, major-league baseball players themselves.

Tom Wicker came out against the idea in an editorial in *The
New York Times* titled "Say It Ain't So, Peter." Mr. Wicker proposed that individual players who reveal problems be dealt with
but that all should not suffer from a presumption of guilt. As for
the role-model notion, "Baloney. Do you want your son drooling
tobacco juice, kicking dirt on umpires, throwing at batter's heads,
spiking opponents?"

Another aspect of the role-model issue has been largely ignored. Virtually all of the players exposed as drug users had been doing well at their sports. They used drugs and won ball games, many times in championship style. There is nothing new about that juxtaposition. It has been very common in the history of American sports, except that the drug in the past has usually been alcohol. For example, Babe Ruth's exploits at bending an elbow off the field were as legendary as doing the same thing, with bat in hand, on the diamond.

On October 6, 1985, former star baseball pitcher Dock Ellis told Harry Reasoner and the country on the CBS television program "60 Minutes" that during each of the twelve years he played major-league ball, he was on drugs. The star had no problem getting drugs and no problem performing, sometimes under the influence of them. In fact, during the 1970 season he performed one of the most difficult feats in all of sports: he pitched a no-hitter. Before the game, he had taken LSD and was "tripping" during the entire nine innings. I wish that the leaders who want so much to make examples of our sports stars would wake up and look at the real content of those examples. Perceptive youngsters already see the hypocrisy in the current situation (one brought me the Ellis transcript from CBS at his own initiative) and are further turned off from believing anything said about drugs by authority figures, even so exalted a personage as the commissioner of baseball.

In July 1986 National Football League commissioner Pete Rozelle continued the dominant trend when he announced a plan for mandatory random urine testing for all players. This would have been the only major sport with such a comprehensive testing program. The players' union fought in court and a judge stopped implementation of the plan because it was in violation of the existing contract with the owners. There has been little opposition to the National Collegiate Athletic Association's new massive drug-testing program, which went into effect on August 1, 1986. I have severe doubts that it can be implemented without making college athletes second- or third-class citizens. As in Olympic competition, there are provisions for random urine tests before or after post-season and championship games. The detailed procedure for selecting athletes for tests, for supervision of the tests, and for control of "specimens" reads like a cruel parody of how to control political prisoners in a George Orwell novel. The list of "banned drugs" contains 81 names and all "related compounds." Most of the drugs are ordinary medicines, even some cold compounds and cough syrups.

Dr. Arthur McBay's reading of the program was equally critical but he also saw it to be technically impossible and useless in practical terms. In June 1986 he told me, "I am not aware of a single laboratory anywhere in the world that would be competent to do the testing as described in the NCAA rule. Certainly not within a reasonable time frame and not without great cost. Each test could cost at least one hundred dollars, perhaps two hundred dollars or more. That's five-to-ten thousand dollars a team for each game. Right after the test an athlete could go to his locker and sniff some cocaine. What good would these tests do?" That, of course, is the quiet question that no one in power is facing.

MILITARY TESTING: IS AMERICA SAFER?

However the issue of drug testing for athletes is resolved, the outcome is likely to have only marginal negative results for the country. This is not the case with the urine-testing program that has been imposed on the 2.4 million Americans now serving their country in the armed services. They have no union, no clearly established legal means of fighting back, and no true freedom of speech. Under current law, all 2.4 million of them can be and frequently are given direct orders to urinate in bottles at a given time and place. The irrational treatment of our service people provides a chilling vision of what civilian society could be in the future.

That is disturbing enough. More distressing are the repeated charges that the unbalanced search for drugs in the military has had the same chaotic influence on morale and group cohesion that Toughlove and Straight had on Fred Collins and the family he loved. It is, therefore, quite likely that the military effectiveness of some fighting units has been compromised. That is precisely what the tests were supposed to insure against, which again demonstrates that when unrealistic objectives are pursued in a hysterical fashion using flawed technology, human institutions will often produce perverse and destructive results. The story of urinalysis in the military under the Reagan administration is thus a major scandal.

During his administration, military commanders have often declared one major objective: zero drug and alcohol use. In fact, this sometimes is stated as, and always means in practice, zero *illicit* drug use. Both military law and administrative regulations surround that objective with protections for service people, including requirements that urinalysis results not be the sole foundation for punitive action, which is supposed to be based upon an impartial, wide-ranging review of all of the facts. In actual recent experience, one bad reading has destroyed tens of thousands of promising careers of competent and patriotic soldiers, sailors, marines, and flyers.

All of this did not start with Mr. Reagan, of course. In what appeared to be a commendable program in 1978, the Strategic Air Command declared that no marijuana use would be tolerated by any of its members at any time. We can all support the ultimate purpose of the SAC commanders and the Carter administration in making this sweeping declaration. No person in any country in the world can go to bed peacefully at night contemplating the nightmare that somewhere out there a drug-crazed B-52 pilot is aiming an armed H-bomb at a country that annoys him. There were reports at the time that the first urinalysis sweep turned up 2,300 marijuana users in SAC who were given the option of rehabilitation or discharge; 1,900 decided to leave the service rather than fight the irrationality.

If that harsh action had cleaned out even a few potentially drug-harmed pilots and crew, perhaps it was worth it. Yet the program did not deal with alcohol abuse nor did it distinguish between use and abuse of any drug. SAC leaders did not take into account the high probability of error in the testing process and thus took action on the basis of questionable laboratory reports on one of the least harmful drugs known to human beings. Critics at the time claimed that morale in some of these highly trained and vital units was greatly lowered.

When EMIT became available, the wide-eyed drug warriors in the Reagan White House found a serendipitous group of military warriors across the Potomac River in the Pentagon just as the war fever of the chemical crusade was heating up. The Pentagon chiefs were schooled in giving orders and receiving immediate obedience. It was in the American military, then, that the pressure for the

use of undemocratic methods to achieve the drug-free society—
the dream of using the Singapore model and to hell with this business about the rights of drug demons—has been given its fullest
play.

Within a few years, millions of tests were given to American
servicemen and women around the world, often on repeated occasions. Test tubes of urine by the tens of thousands, with accompanying paperwork, flooded into regional military laboratories. All
of the bottles, though, looked alike. Harassed and overworked
technicians complained that they could not keep up with the massive workload, that they were literally awash in urine, and that
sometimes they got the damned bottles mixed up. Commanders
kept up the pressure, took staff away from other duties and assigned them to the urine front, and demanded that the testing
continue. Thus repeated human technical errors were added to the
scientific unreliability of the tests and to the even more fundamental irrationality that this entire Byzantine effort was aimed at
marijuana. When complaints were made and reached the press and
Congress, the Army appointed a blue-ribbon commission which
dutifully reported that there had been no evidence of false positives
in Army and Air Force laboratories from April 1982 to November
1983.

Yet many cases of improper procedures and injustices floated
up on the tide and came to public attention. Major Carter C. LeFon,
head of the Brooks Air Force Base laboratory in Texas for most
of 1982, testified in one court-martial of a pilot accused by test
tube that the lab produced many false positives, to his personal
knowledge, while he was in command. If his estimate of 3–5 percent
false positives were accepted, as many as 1,185 innocent Army
and Air Force service people were put through personal agony for
no purpose by this one laboratory alone. Because of a backlog of
15,000 urine samples in early 1982, 25 inadequately trained technicians were assigned to the lab. The defenseless service people
were forced to work 12-hour days through weekends in unpleasant
working conditions.

"In one incident described by LeFon in court, lab technicians
were found heating tacos in the glassware drying oven, which is
supposed to be used to dry glassware after it has been washed.
LeFon said the lab tests probably had mistaken residual taco grease
for evidence of marijuana use, contributing to the disproportionate

number of positive findings made at the time," the *Army Times* reported.

Poppy seeds were the culprits when two Navy medical interns suddenly found themselves suspected of being morphine or heroin addicts in 1983. Both doctors, at the Navy Hospital in Balboa Park, California, denied taking such drugs. A second test again came up positive for opiates. Both clean-cut, straight-arrow young officers then took lie-detector tests, and both failed. It appeared that their careers were ruined. They suffered 15 months of anxiety and legal costs.

To their credit, Navy technicians discovered that both doctors liked the bagels topped with poppy seeds often served in the hospital cafeteria and that poppy seeds tested positive for morphine. The case illustrates the technical limitations of any testing method because, as Dr. McBay and other experts have explained, any one of a thousand foods or medicines might show positive for drugs on a urinalysis test because any one of them might be cross-reactive with the testing chemicals or with the drug. Lieutenant Dale Mitchell, one of the doctors, recognized his continuing peril for he still eats bagels topped with poppy seeds. After he was cleared, he observed, shaking his head, "I might come up positive again."

The sense of injustice created by the urinalysis mania permeated the services. Soldiers reported that the arbitrariness of the program brought out the worst in the military command system. Officers who were prejudiced against minority groups or women, I was told by one former infantry soldier, would simply tell a platoon sergeant to get a urine test, immediately, and the victim would be forced to comply. There were always half-decent odds that the target of prejudice would flunk the test. Whether or not these claims of bias were true, they were widely believed—and continue to be to this day, with destructive results for the armed services.

Other service people wrote bitterly in the early Eighties to NORML about their disillusionment and their own desire to leave such an unfair institution. One said, "On November 29, 1983, my second four-year enlistment in the military will come to an end. My plans are now to get out . . . even though I do not use marijuana, I will not subject myself to this kind of treatment . . . for four more years." Another: "The people that are being treated unjustly are the ones that will be fighting a war, our war, if it comes about.

Do you really think that they will fight for a country that has treated them so?" Yet another: "This test . . . is against the moral principles of every such person or any person having to humiliate himself by urinating in a cup."

The true humiliation should have been reserved for the honor and reputation of the commanders of the armed forces of the United States. Soon they were forced to admit the harm they had visited upon tens of thousands of citizens in uniform. The exact count of these victims is unknown, in part because their numbers have never been totaled and also because information about them has been revealed piecemeal in wave after wave. In June 1984 alone, the Army announced that it had begun mailing notices to 60,000–70,000 victims, soldiers and ex-soldiers, telling them that they could appeal personnel actions taken against them because drug-testing procedures had been found to be faulty. An Army spokesman stated that "probably the majority" of 9,099 soldiers forcibly discharged in 1982 and 1983 were punished on the basis of dubious evidence. The Navy and the Air Force made similar admissions about their drug-testing programs. Admissions of wrongful treatment of service people have never been made in such dimensions by commanders in past American history.

Yet the services continue to support the programs. Commanders point with pride to the drop in recorded drug use. Of course, that was to be expected because the innocent were punished along with the guilty. Navy leaders, for example, claim that illicit drug usage dropped from 48 percent in 1980 to 10 percent in 1985, on the basis of confidential surveys. The claim is also made that all of the technical and administrative problems have now been solved. In May 1985, Jarrett Clinton, M.D., Deputy Assistant of Defense for Health Affairs, was ebullient in reporting that advance: "Fortunately, these days, I am smiling."

There is precious little, though, for the rest of the country to smile about. While it may appear that the harsh program has reduced dangerous drug use in the military, all that is certain is that marijuana use has declined. Service people, like millions of their civilian counterparts, have learned some very practical scientific facts. Hard drugs, like cocaine, barbiturates, and opiates, are water soluble and tend to be excreted in two to three days, unlike marijuana which is fat soluble with the result that traces of pot may be found in the system for weeks or months. Even though the services sometimes test for these other drugs, many soldiers know that the odds of getting caught for, say, cocaine or heroin are much less than for marijuana. The lessons of that fact should cause no one to smile.

Abuse of alcohol has always been the major drug problem in the armed services. Anyone who was in the service before the Sixties and has a realistic memory knows from firsthand experience that soldiers often drank huge quantities of weak beer or cheap whisky, but were counted on as good fighting troops if after a night of such revelry they could be present at reveille, stand up, and count off, without in the process vomiting on the lieutenant of the platoon. While in infantry training at Fort Dix during the Korean War, my unit was admired by the officers because we could be counted on to supply them with ample doses of hard whisky while in the field on maneuvers. For some reason, I have never forgotten my platoon lieutenant with his .45 pistol on his belt who, one cold night in late 1952, made the rounds of the enlisted men's pup tents, sampled the supplies of most of the platoon's soldiers, stumbled into the large officers' tent, did a perfect somersault, landed on his back on his own sleeping bag, and was immediately off into a deep, drunken sleep. The latter events took place in front of the other company officers and one enlisted man, all of whom applauded the man's verve and style. Nobody suggested that we turn him in or test his urine. I suspect the same attitude would prevail today. He was, after all, only doing what soldiers have always done: he was getting blasted on alcohol.

At that distant time, marijuana in the army was unheard of— even though objective science might have told us that many soldiers would have been better off with pot than the alcohol they were guzzling. Since then, of course, soldiers have brought their new drug habits, especially marijuana, with them from civilian life. The advent of marijuana with the new troops could not have made that situation worse; indeed, pot offered a less harmful option to many service people. Now the American military commanders have achieved significant victories in the war on marijuana and virtually destroyed that more gentle option.

A few years ago, an American infantry soldier wrote in despair from Germany, "Mostly everyone here has quit smoking and turned into a legal alcoholic. Even today, I went and bought a half-gallon of Bacardi rum, myself, and I don't normally drink. I really hope someone, somewhere will realize . . . smoking marijuana does not make you a drug abuser. And no one ever O.D.'d on smoking the herb, you know." While we may prefer that this young trooper used no mind-altering drug, the American nation has never fielded a fighting force that did not partake of whatever drugs, including some wild varieties of alcohol, that the countryside afforded.

A particularly ironic example of the type of destructive injustice that is now being created commenced on November 13, 1982, when Chief Petty Officer Frederick A. Calkins was ordered to submit to a random urinalysis aboard the amphibious assault ship U.S.S. *Thomaston*. Calkins, an outstanding career sailor and deeply proud of his chief's rank, then went on emergency leave because of the death of his father. Upon returning to his ship, he was told that the urine sample, taken 54 days before, tested positive for barbiturates. CPO Calkins vigorously protested his innocence, but in a captain's mast proceeding, Commander Willard G. Chrisman relied on the urine test, found him guilty, and demoted him to petty officer second-class, which has cost the sailor approximately $6,000 in pay. Because the ship was at sea, a full court-martial was not available to the accused man.

A year later, Commander Chrisman was directing the movements of the ship when the *Thomaston* scraped bottom in a Pacific cove. Several of the ship's crew accused him of a series of offenses, including being drunk on alcohol. The Navy court-martialed him. Within a few years, the commander left the service under a cloud. The highly publicized urinalysis program had not provided any warning of the ship commander's potential for failure to perform his duty based in part on alcohol abuse. Calkins, though demoted, continued to perform as a superb sailor. In January 1984, he was chosen Sailor of the Quarter in an eight-ship squadron.

During the terrible summer of 1986, the Department of Defense released a 1985 survey of drug and alcohol use for all of the services. In a very revealing press briefing on August 5, Dr. William Mayer, the assistant secretary of defense for health affairs, claimed that overall use of illicit drugs had dropped 67 percent since 1980. He also claimed that there had been a significant drop in alcohol use. Another claim by the leading defense official was that, following the problems of the early Eighties with errors in urinalysis, "We have established a testing program which has never given a false positive reading." Cautious readers will take all of these claims with a grain of salt.

When asked by reporters exactly how many service people had been discharged because of bad urine tests, the Defense Department's top expert and his assembled staff of supporting experts could not or would not give clear answers. At one point in the briefing he stated that over the previous three years 51,000 people had been discharged for flunking the chemical test, and at another, 135,000.

On a few points Dr. Mayer was absolutely clear. For all commissioned and noncommissioned officers, "a single scientifically validated positive test for drug abuse results in the separation from service." Thus the armed services of the United States, with the guidance of leading medical experts, are using the urine tests in an improper manner. They are improper according to the express written reservations of the manufacturers of the tests (the presence of traces of an illicit drug in the urine does not measure impairment or abuse), improper according to the leading clinical chemists of the country, and improper according to common sense.

Dr. Mayer was also clear that alcohol remained a bigger problem in the military than any other drug. At the same time, confirmed alcohol addicts were not discharged from the service on that account because they were not violating any law and were "more treatable" than illicit drug users. There is little scientific support for the latter observation. The real reason for the distinction is that the armed services continue to perpetuate the myth that there is a scientific justification for the line between the illegal drugs and the legal drugs. One use of the former equals drug abuse and is the basis for immediate discharge from the service of the most competent, patriotic fighting men or women, who then carry an indelible stain on their records into civilian life. Use of the latter either in explosive bouts of periodic drunkenness on duty, like my lieutenant, or in a persistent addictive fashion may be treated with compassion and understanding. Thus it is probable that many thousands of occasional, nonaddicted marijuana users have been disgraced and thrown out of the service while many thousands of alcohol spree-drinkers and addicts have been kept on active duty at the bridges of fighting ships and at the buttons controlling nuclear weapons. On balance, I suspect that the security of the nation has been damaged more than it has been helped by the chemical assault of the drug warriors on the men and women of our armed services.

The truly important test of human worth throughout the history of our successful democratic enterprise has always been the quality of a person's performance in action rather than the nature of the chemicals that person ingested. Many of our armed services personnel who used, or even abused, alcohol have been splendid fighters. When congressmen urged President Lincoln to fire General Grant in 1862 because he drank too much whisky, the President brushed them off, declaring, "I can't spare this man—he fights!" Lincoln also said that he wanted to find out what kind of liquor Grant drank so that he could feed it to his other generals.

The matter is infinitely more complicated, therefore, than our military commanders, including the Commander-in-Chief himself, would have us believe. We cannot simply toss the process of selecting honest employees or brave fighting soldiers over to some lab technicians who inquire only into the condition of their urine. Science does not hold out the slightest hope that we can devise accurate tests that will allow supervisors and commanders to escape the responsibility of judging on an individual basis the worth and work performance of each individual. Even if the nation's leaders continue down the current path and use other clinical tests of urine, blood, saliva, or brain waves—all now being promoted by commercial businesses to the drug-war trade—this will mean even more invasions of the bodies, bodily wastes, and privacy of our free citizenry, but it will not predict which of the testees will fail in their civilian work or military assignments, or even identify accurately those who use prohibited substances.

JAR WARS: HAVE THE WARRIORS GONE TOO FAR?

The one good result from the epidemic spread of mass, random urine tests has been that they have helped create a spark of opposition to drug-war extremism in the solid center of American society. The first sign of that opposition was found in the general disapproval that greeted many of the recommendations of the report of the President's Commission on Organized Crime in March 1986. The commission took the most extreme ideas that have been floated during the Reagan era and gave them the imprimatur of a recommendation by a major presidential commission: greater use of the military; increased electronic surveillance; drug testing for virtually all employees, starting with government workers and those on the payroll of federal contractors; a prohibition on any government funds to programs that advocate the idea of "responsible" drug use; the repeal of all state laws which decriminalized marijuana; and large-scale prosecutions not only of sellers but also of users of drugs.

The commission made it explicit that this really was a "war on drugs—a phrase worn by use but nevertheless the only accurate description of what must be done." The presidential report continued, "We must identify the enemy." Included in that group were "friends, relatives, colleagues, and other 'respectable' people" who were small users of drugs and thus "the driving force behind the traffickers' assault on the country."

To me those words had a nightmarish quality. It was as if the presidential commission had read this book in advance and was trying to make its most frightening predictions come true. Deliberately, leading American judges and legal officials were calling for a war on our neighbors and children, just as I had been arguing. On us.

Even though some experts have argued that the war on drugs is not really a war in the American historical tradition of armed conflicts, it is clear that many leaders want to make it so—and are prepared to commit seemingly unthinkable acts, such as imprisoning hundreds of thousands of decent Americans, young and old alike, simply because they use disapproved chemicals. At least for a while, it looks as if the drug warriors have gone too far.

For the first time in recent history, a government report urging tougher drug-control measures was met with almost universal opposition, even from public figures who rarely speak out on such controversial issues. For example, on the NBC-TV "Today Show," host Bryant Gumbel asked a leading commission official, Rodney Smith, why the group adopted "this police-state mentality." Newspapers across the political spectrum from left to right castigated the commission for its extremism and callous disregard for constitutional rights. When I appeared on one of those Sunday television talk shows (CNN's "Newsmaker Sunday") with Mr. Smith, I pointed out to him that the commission report had produced more energetic unity in the sane center of American society for drug reform than all of my efforts in the past 14 years. (The clean-cut young lawyer took that as a compliment.)

It was the call for mass urine testing that produced the strongest reaction to the report of the high-level commission. On March 18, 1986, for example, Mr. Smith appeared before a congressional committee which was looking into the commission's recommendation of random drug testing for virtually all federal workers. Rep. Gary L. Ackerman (D-N.Y.), chairman of a House subcommittee dealing with human resources, shocked Mr. Smith by suggesting that he take a test before testifying. The congressman held up a small plastic jar, stated "I think a specimen is worth 1,000 oaths," and invited the federal official to go into the men's room right then and produce a sample "under the direct supervision" of a staff member, in line with the currently accepted degrading procedure for such searches. Rep. Ackerman informed the leading drug warrior that arrangements had been made with a laboratory to test the sample immediately. The crime commission official refused, later angrily calling the request a "cheap shot." After Mr. Smith's refusal, the congressman stated, "I thank you for very eloquently proving the point that we have set out to prove."

Heated opposition to mass random urine tests, without reasonable suspicion, continues across the country. Generally conservative unions are bringing suit after suit to stop them. Taking a lead role in this widespread opposition has been the National Treasury Employee's Union which, in an ironic twist of history, represents customs agents, the most intrusive group of body invaders in the country. It remains to be seen, however, if these sparks of centrist opposition to the interminable drug war can be fanned into a major reform movement in the years ahead.

PART THREE

The Saddest Victims

She (Dolores Koppinger) had a history of headaches which was controlled with Darvon. But her physician was worried about getting in trouble with the B.M.Q.A. so he was decreasing her medication. She tried to get by with aspirin or Tylenol. It's too late now for our mother, but please look into this case before anyone else dies such a death because they are denied pain relief medicine.

—THE KOPPINGER FAMILY

I have talked today to Dr. Stephen Hirsch, who tells me that Milton is well known to his committee, that he has manipulated many physicians and that I should not prescribe Dilaudid for him. I will comply. However, I view him as a pathetically ill patient with a poor prognosis who incidentally has a very rotten habit—and if we can take care of his other, organic problems, then we might make an attempt at treating his addiction. He is more likely to die of them than of his addiction.

—DR. SEYMOUR H. RUBIN

I have been victimized, but I am not a victim. Most of the people who call me for advice *are* victims. However, I win every day. I can still see. Seeing is winning.

—ROBERT C. RANDALL

9

The Sacrifice of Our Sick— by Denying Legal Medicines

DOLORES KOPPINGER and Milton Polansky died so that the nation could continue to pursue the impossible goal of making the rest of us drug-free. While they were quite different in many ways, they were alike in that their perceived drug addiction was used by the medical profession to justify the denying of currently legal medicines for the treatment of major pain due to organic illness. Although no doctor or official intended them to die, the results were the same: it is as if these grandparents were considered scapegoats and thus sacrificed to propitiate the gods of the drug war. The rationale for their sacrifice on this martial altar was that by denying medicine to ease the suffering of our sick the nation maintains the wall of prohibition that denies drugs to criminal addicts. On the basis of such delusions, of such hurtful myths, multitudes of our decent family members, friends, and neighbors have suffered, many of them eventually dying in agony.

These people are the saddest victims of our drug wars and deserve our greatest concern. If we do nothing else, we must implement whatever protections are necessary to insulate them from assaults by those drug warriors who haunt American medicine.

DOLORES KOPPINGER:
DEATH OF A GRANDMOTHER

Dolores M. Koppinger was a salt-of-the-earth, Middle-American, decent, loving wife, mother, and grandmother. She and her husband, John, a truck driver, worked hard together to raise two good children, a boy, named after his father, and a girl, Paulette, the mother of Mrs. Koppinger's much loved only grandchild. Mrs. Koppinger had great times with her family, especially her grandson, and was looking forward to the day when her son, too, would marry and when she would have more grandchildren to enjoy. She was also looking forward to the expected retirement of her husband within a few years. At 53 years of age, she functioned well, cooked a big meal every day, kept a clean house, was involved in several community organizations in the Sacramento, California, area, and attended a social function with her husband almost every weekend. There was not a hint of involvement in crime or illicit drugs about this lady or her family.

However, Mrs. Koppinger had a long history of painful illnesses, including bleeding ulcers and spinal fusion, which required numerous operations. Often, she needed the relief provided by analgesic (painkilling) medicines. It is also true that on one occasion many years earlier, she had developed symptoms of drug dependency, apparently after taking diet pills prescribed by a doctor, as was frequently done at the time. The patient was detoxified in a hospital and showed no further symptoms of amphetamine dependence. Her most persistent medical problems were created by recurring migraine headaches from which she had suffered for at least twenty years. Such headaches create disabling misery in the poor souls who have them and, if they are honest, humility in the most brilliant physicians. Medical science does not know their cause. In most cases such headaches produce nothing remarkable in chemical or electronic tests and there is no known cure or standard remedy. Every treatment involves much guesswork because science provides so little guidance.

Over the years, various physicians had tried different medicines to treat this puzzling condition in Mrs. Koppinger. Eventually, they had settled on Darvon. It appears likely that during her last years, the lady was taking approximately 195 milligrams of this drug every day, in three 65-milligram capsules. In fact, her Sacramento doctor provided her with slightly less than that: a once-a-week prescription for 20 capsules. This dosage seemed to control her pain most of the time. To the world and to her family, she seemed an ordinary sweet-natured contributing citizen, certainly not an addict or a social problem.

Her medicine had been created by Eli Lilly and Company and first marketed in 1957 as a safe treatment for mild to moderate pain. Originally, this wholly synthetic compound was controlled only loosely by federal law and was not even labeled a narcotic. Patients found the medicine very helpful and during its first 21 years of existence, physicians prescribed approximately 22 billion doses of the drug, which has the generic chemical name of propoxyphene hydrochloride. It proved particularly beneficial for patients who could not take enough aspirin or codeine to obtain relief without suffering disabling side effects. Because each person's organic and emotional structure is different, no scientist can predict in advance who will be helped by one analgesic or another.

There was comfort in the minds of physicians and patients in knowing that Darvon was a relatively mild painkiller. While comparing potency of drugs is not a precise science, it would appear that Darvon is approximately five times more potent, dose for dose, than aspirin, one half as powerful as codeine, 1/24 as powerful as morphine, and 1/50 to 1/100 as potent as heroin. While reasonable experts might dissent from some of these estimates, few would disagree that Darvon is in roughly the same league as the mild painkillers but wholly outclassed by the more powerful narcotics.

Yet, as always throughout the history of painkillers, this mild analgesic was soon being abused by some of its users, especially by those who took more than the recommended dosages or who combined it with alcohol. Even though no painkilling drug has ever been discovered that did not carry some risks of addiction and abuse, the company claimed originally that the drug offered the therapeutic advantages of the opiates, such as codeine, "without causing addiction or drug dependence." In line with past history, though, Darvon addicts soon appeared in doctor's offices and on city streets. So also did bodies in coroner's offices, whereupon autopsies determined that thousands of abusers were dying from the drug, often from suicide. In 1977, Darvon was finally placed in Schedule IV of the federal Controlled Substances Act, which limits prescriptions to five every six months and requires special records by druggists. Moreover, the Health Research Group, a Ralph Nader organization headed by liberal activist Dr. Sidney Wolfe, launched a crusade in the late Seventies to ban the drug totally or, failing that, to place it in Schedule II, along with morphine, where it would be strictly controlled.

On both counts the HRG failed, but on January 21, 1980, the DEA threw it the bone of classifying Darvon as a narcotic. This action tightened up controls somewhat, in particular by indirectly making it a crime to provide this drug to a narcotic addict for maintenance treatment of addiction, that is, to prescribe it for more than 21 days in a nondiminishing dose where the main disorder was dependence on any narcotic. Few doctors, though, were aware of the precise impact of the governmental action in this respect. Most simply started approaching Darvon with greater concern in the treatment of the organically ill, especially since the new classification had been preceded by warnings about possible misuse of this mild medicine from both the government and Lilly. The Food and Drug Administration cautioned the public and doctors, "Dependence may occur if patients take as few as 8–12 pills a day."

There was nothing essentially wrong in these actions—except that they went from one extreme to the other, treating Darvon first as virtually risk-free and then as a unique chemical threat to the public health, when all along it should have been approached as a painkiller that, like all others, carried benefits and risks. The hysteria promoted by a liberal organization fit into the mood of drug fear then permeating the political spectrum from left to right.

The California Board of Medical Quality Assurance, the state agency which polices doctors, had launched a campaign several years earlier against what it saw as improper prescribing by doctors. Within a few years, it claimed to have stopped the work of approximately 300 "scriptwriters," doctors who write prescriptions of controlled medicines purely for profit. After this, BMQA (pronounced "bumqwa" by some doctors in the state) turned its attention, in the words of the national professional magazine, *Medical Economics,* to "the next logical step—an effort to control physicians who might be inadvertently contributing to the drug-abuse problem by writing prescriptions that could be passed on to street addicts or could otherwise lead to patient harm." In 1979, as the fears about Darvon and other drugs began to spread throughout the country, BMQA investigators turned their attention to Dr. Harvey L. Rose, a physician who had practiced for 25 years in

Carmichael, the Sacramento suburb where the Koppinger family happened to live. Dr. Rose was faced with loss of his license and subjected to public humiliation for years, as will be explained in detail later. Fear of similar treatment spread throughout the medical community of the area.

In the midst of these public events, Dolores Koppinger was taking her medicine every day and minding her own innocent business. Her consumption of the drug was at a very low level, so low that some experts might say that it was functioning like a placebo. It was far below the minimum level of abuse listed in the warnings by the FDA. Moreover, no claim was ever made that the lady had ever diverted any of her medicine to improper channels. Then one day in the spring of 1983, her Sacramento doctor told her that he wanted her to cut down on the use of Darvon and to enter a hospital for drug detoxification. When a shocked Mrs. Koppinger pushed for an explanation, according to the version of these events claimed by the Koppinger family, the doctor could point to nothing in the conduct or condition of his patient that could justify it but rather indicated that his action was for the benefit of himself. "Look what happened to Dr. Rose" are the words John Koppinger now recalls the doctor saying.

The headaches returned with increasing frequency. Dolores Koppinger attempted to treat them with aspirin and Tylenol. It is likely that the aspirin caused stomach distress, brought on in part by previous stomach surgery. Because she was in pain and had perhaps lost count of the tablets, the sick lady took more of the only medicines available to her. Her husband pleaded with her to go back to the doctor for medicine to ease her misery. She would usually reply, "What's the use? He won't give me anything anyway." At 6:00 A.M. on April 11, 1983, when Mr. Koppinger was away on a truck-driving trip, her son discovered his mother unconscious and called an ambulance. Despite intensive care at the hospital, she died at 11:30 the next evening.

A report of a Sacramento County coroner's investigation stated the cause of death to be "Toxic Ingestion (Aspirin and Acetaminophen)," the latter being the generic chemical name for Tylenol. (The threat of these common, over-the-counter drugs is often not appreciated. Yet, according to the government's Drug Abuse Warning Network—DAWN—which covers perhaps a third of the country, 283 people died from overdoses of one or both of these two drugs that year; 221, from Darvon.) Because her blood showed indications of at least 35 tablets of the two drugs and also because of her prior medical history, the coroner classified the case as a suicide.

In a remarkable series of events, the family issued a public statement accusing the doctor of indirectly causing the death of Dolores Koppinger by withdrawing her medication for fear of "getting in trouble with the BMQA." The statement declared, "We hear of over-prescribing but never under-prescribing." Moreover, Dr. Rose, who had treated Mrs. Koppinger briefly for migraine several years before, and Mr. Koppinger convinced the coroner's office that Mrs. Koppinger was not suicidal and that she must have lost count of the pills she was taking due to her intense discomfort. An amended coroner's report concluded that Mrs. Koppinger had resorted to aspirin and Tylenol "because of the reduced availability of Darvon." On the front of the form the word "Suicide" was crossed out and in its place was substituted "Accidental overdose."

The doctor who cut off Mrs. Koppinger's medicine still has his medical license and practices in Sacramento. He has issued no public statements to challenge the charges openly made by the Koppinger family nor has he contacted them to apologize or to comfort them. The man's reputation as a competent, caring doctor seems intact. When I questioned him late in 1985 about his actions in this case, he painted Mrs. Koppinger as an addict who could not be trusted with medications: "I know she was abusing a lot of drugs." Therefore, the physician explained, "I didn't feel comfortable continuing to give her her prescription." Was not the withdrawal of the medicine actually based upon fear of the BMQA? The physician denied this allegation, declaring, "No one threatened me. I practice medicine as I see fit." He offered no information to support his charge that his patient was abusing a lot of drugs, nor has anyone else. In my opinion, Mrs. Koppinger had not been abusing any drug while she was being prescribed Darvon.

When I asked Mr. Koppinger why he had not gone back to confront the doctor over this tragedy, he replied that he was trying to put it all behind him, and also, "I was afraid that I would have punched him in the mouth." The officials of the board with the responsibility for assuring quality medical care to the citizens of the state had quite different emotions. An investigation of the death of Dolores Koppinger produced no action by the board. It would seem that the Koppingers were correct: under-prescribing is a safe course of action, at least for the doctor.

Moreover, when pressed for an explanation of the nonaction by the BMQA in late 1985, Assistant Executive Director Steven Wilford refused to talk to me specifically about this case for the very reason that no action was taken. "Speaking generally," however, the official suggested that it was quite possible that a patient such as Mrs. Koppinger was addicted to Darvon and that, in light of her past history, withdrawal of the drug was a proper medical choice—because in such cases, often there were significant problems of addiction. As for the headaches, the question would have to be asked, Mr. Wilford stated, whether "the Darvon caused the pain or the migraine." The state official thus viewed Mrs. Koppinger as quite possibly an untrustworthy addict, and seemed unaware that the creation of migraine symptoms by a narcotic would be a rare event indeed in the annals of medicine. Indeed, Dr. Barry Beyerstein, a leading Canadian researcher on opiates and brain functioning who operates a laboratory at Simon Fraser University, told me that the truth was quite likely exactly the opposite: "There is some evidence that the brain's endorphin [naturally occurring "opiate" or painkiller] system may be involved in migraine attacks. Because Darvon may interact with endorphin dynamics, Mrs. Koppinger's use of Darvon may possibly have had some beneficial effects over and above the analgesia she might have obtained from it."

It seems highly likely that Dolores Koppinger would be alive, functioning, and enjoying life today if her minimal prescription of this mild narcotic had been continued. The withdrawal of her medicine and her death were needless, and contributed nothing to the health and safety of America's surviving citizens. The number of such needless sacrifices to the drug war is unknown, in part because their existence is either denied or ignored.

HARVEY ROSE: TORMENT OF A GOOD DOCTOR

The torment inflicted on Harvey L. Rose suggests that not only are there far too many of these sacrificial lambs among helpless patients but also that when doctors come to their aid, those physicians may become victims themselves. Rose graduated third in his class from the University of Southern California Medical School and was a board-certified family practitioner. During 25 years of practice in the Sacramento area, he had developed a solid professional reputation and an interest in alternative medicine and holistic therapies—including acupuncture, hypnosis, and biofeedback—which involve virtually no use of drugs. "I have always tried to avoid the use of drugs in treating my patients," he stated recently, "but what do you do when all else fails?"

All else had indeed failed for a number of his patients. These were the chronic pain group, most of whom were suffering from nonmalignant and nonterminal organic diseases, and who required painkilling drugs for indefinite periods. While they constituted a small minority of his patients (approximately 20 out of 2,000, or only one percent), they required a good deal of his time and attention. Many of them had tried every conceivable nondrug and drug regimen without success—and were thus living in misery. Dr. Rose had listened to their needs and developed drug therapy for them, along with other treatments, that allowed almost all of them to function as productive citizens without needless or incapacitating pain.

In some cases, this involved prescribing drugs far in excess of commonly accepted medical standards, such as those contained in the *Physicians' Desk Reference*, the ubiquitous *PDR*. During the course of my research, I have discovered that in deviating from these norms, Dr. Rose was following a path trod by numerous perceptive physicians over recent decades in many countries. By observing the needs and concerns of their patients, these doctors found that many could function well only on higher dosages, in innovative combinations, and over longer periods of times than commonly accepted. In some countries and at certain points in history, this deviance has been viewed as a matter of rational professional disagreement, points of difference to be smoothed out perhaps at a medical seminar or decided objectively by controlled research. In, for example, the United Kingdom, when the authorities became concerned about a doctor by an inspection of pharmacists' prescriptions records, the situation was often handled by a quiet visit to the physician's office. All too often in the United States, however, medical detectives have read the lists of prescriptions and seen in them the smoke that reveals the presence of the fire of criminal abuse. Tally-ho. That is precisely how the BMQA read the records of Dr. Rose's prescriptions.

Based only on those records and not on interviews with any of the patients or with the doctor, the board concluded that the patients were addicts (meaning, in this context, dangerous, unworthy social deviants) and that the doctor was fueling their addiction. The officials then went to great pains to prove these accusations, which were founded, as is so much of modern drug control, upon numerous layers of fundamental misconceptions. Unknown to Dr. Rose, the investigation had started in 1979 when the state board had sent two undercover agents to his office for prescriptions of narcotics. They failed. The reason for their failure should have given pause to any halfway intelligent official on the hunt for an irresponsible prescriber: this doctor accepted new patients only on the basis of referrals. The agents could not even get an appointment.

Nevertheless, the investigation continued. Some of Dr. Rose's patients were contacted directly and were quite frightened by the investigators. Because he had nothing to hide, he urged them to cooperate with the officials, and did so himself by providing full records on patients when asked by the agents over a period of several years. The doctor heard nothing from the board for months and thought the matter was settled. His first knowledge that the board was launching a full-scale assault on his right to practice medicine and might even be trying to get him criminally prosecuted came from a newspaper reporter who called on August 4, 1981, to ask, "What have you to say about the charges the BMQA has filed against you stating you are prescribing to drug addicts without prior examination or medical indications?"

"What are you talking about?" the startled doctor shot back. "I don't have any drug addicts. That's a bunch of crap! I have chronic pain patients but they're not drug addicts. . . . By the way, I hope nothing of this is going to show up in the papers until I have a chance to know what's going on." His hopes were smashed the next morning, a few days before his forty-ninth birthday, when he picked up the morning paper outside the door of his house and saw the headlines: "Carmichael Doctor Faces State Charges." The state agency had gone to the press before informing the doctor. For the next four years, this caring physician and his organically ill patients were involved in an emotionally draining, gut-wrenching battle with decades of institutionalized ignorance as personified by the medical experts of BMQA.

The formal charges were that when Dr. Harvey L. Rose had prescribed medicines to six specified patients, identified only by letters A, B, and so on, he had not acted "in good faith," which is the standard set out in the Harrison Narcotic Act of 1914 and followed by all state laws. California law adds the requirement that physicians adhere to "community standards" in writing prescriptions for controlled drugs. Many doctors believe that none of these rules provides helpful guidance to a physician who truly deals with his patients' problems on an individual basis. It's one doctor's guess against that of another. One of those who expressed that position during this controversy was Dr. William W. Tucker, past president of the Sacramento–El Dorado Medical Society, who did not support the huge dosages Dr. Rose prescribed, but nevertheless observed, "It's like a driver being stopped for speeding by a highway patrolman. When the driver asks the officer just what the speed limit is, the officer answers, 'I don't know, but you were over it.' "

Dr. Rose seemed to be clearly over the limit, for example, in the eyes of investigators who read the records of Charles Grooms. On one occasion, Dr. Rose had written a prescription for 1,500 one-grain codeine tablets to tide this patient over a vacation in Mexico. (A grain is a venerable measure based on the size of an average small grain of old English maize or corn; it is now deemed equivalent to 64.8 milligrams.) This same patient regularly took 60 one-grain tablets, a total of 3,888 milligrams, of this natural derivative of opium every day. Dr. Rose himself admitted that Mr. Grooms's narcotic consumption was "huge, but necessary to keep the patient functioning well." And function well he did, even on the huge amount of narcotics he needed to control his pain.

Charles Grooms had been an airman in World War II, when his plane had been shot down over Italy, and he had suffered terrible burns and a broken back. After surviving the rest of the war as a prisoner of the Germans, much of the time as the treasurer of a prisoners' escape organization in the infamous *Stalag* depicted in the movie *The Great Escape*, he returned with his pain, especially from his back injury but also eventually from diseases of his heart and lungs and from diabetes. The war hero had been through a whole series of doctors and pain treatments, but his misery continued. Then he encountered Dr. Rose and for ten years before this investigation had become living proof of the effectiveness of the physician's methods of providing a meaningful quality of life and virtually normal functioning for his patients, many of whom had been bedridden in the past. Whether or not veteran Grooms was an addict, as the board charged, no evidence was ever put forth that he did not function well. Nor was there any indication that he ever sold any of his drugs, such sales being one common sign that a patient may be a criminal addict. Instead, there was every indication that Charles Grooms, who received the largest dosage of drugs of any of the accused patients, was a respected member of the community. He kept on working throughout his illnesses as one of the leading salesmen for Commerce Clearing House, a major national publisher of business and law books. Mr. Grooms had also served as president of the Sacramento Yacht Club and won his share of races.

No one knew about the medical problems of this prominent local citizen or about his drug intake. Before the accusations became public, he died in the hospital of a variety of organic problems, including heart and lung disease. Dr. Rose believes that his addiction to tobacco was a major cause of his death. There is no evidence that the opiates contributed to his demise. Quite the contrary, it appears that the huge amounts of drugs allowed him to continue to live a decent life much longer than he could have expected without them, and they soothed the agony of his last days in the hospital.

Despite the brave saga of Mr. Grooms and the humane efforts of his doctor, the memory of the war hero was slandered by the medical authorities of California, who included his case among the six patients to whom Dr. Rose allegedly prescribed in bad faith. His widow showed up to defend her husband and his doctor at Dr. Rose's formal hearing before the board, which began on May 10, 1982, in a Sacramento courtroom. More than 300 people, many of them Dr. Rose's supporters and patients, tried to jam into the room, necessitating a move to a larger room. Scheduled for five days, the dramatic proceedings took 13 days and stretched over three months. At every session, no fewer than 30 Rose partisans appeared; at the last one, each sat with a rose in hand.

In addition to the six patients in the original complaint, a group which included Mr. Grooms, Dr. Rose was later required to justify his action regarding yet a seventh patient. In this case, he had to defend his alleged lack of good faith in prescribing what one BMQA medical consultant labeled as "horrendous dosages" during a two-day period: 50 milligrams of Demerol and 2 milligrams of Dilaudid every three hours, plus at times one-half a grain of morphine. (Demerol is approximately 1/8 as powerful as morphine and Dilaudid five times *more* potent. Both are valuable synthetic opiates.)

Unlike most of Dr. Rose's patients, this patient, Mrs. Elizabeth Schildt, was bedridden and terminal. The board charged that Dr. Rose overprescribed for this patient without a medical indication, and a BMQA medical expert implied that it amounted to euthanasia.

During an emotional two-hour session on the stand, Dr. Rose testified that Mrs. Schildt was a close friend of his family, had been "like a grandmother" to his two daughters, and then at the age of 85 was suffering from the effects of a massive cerebral hemorrhage. She was nearly choking on a swollen tongue while going in and out of a coma, as death seemed to be approaching. One attending nurse had stated that the tongue was causing particular pain since it "was extremely swollen, protruding out of her mouth with her teeth imbedded in it," a condition she had never seen before in 22 years of nursing. That nurse, other testifying doctors, and the patient's family had all supported Dr. Rose's decision to seek to give Mrs. Schildt some measure of comfort in her last hours by prescribing those narcotic medicines. While explaining all of this on the stand, Dr. Rose broke down and wept, creating a scene which made headlines the following morning.

In regard to the other patients, who were ambulatory and receiving much smaller dosages of drugs than either Mr. Grooms or Mrs. Schildt, the board never denied that they were functional. Yet its experts maintained throughout the ordeal that they were addicts whose state of addiction was created or pandered to by Dr. Rose. Antony C. Gualtieri, M.D., chief medical consultant to BMQA, stated he warned Rose that "giving drugs to an addict might mislead you into feeling you're improving his quality of life." Dr. Rose resented such constant references to his organically ill, decent patients in such derogatory terms and bristled at such persistent misunderstanding of the nature of drug therapy by some of the most respected doctors in the state. Moreover, he recalls that warning by the state board's leading medical expert as having been couched in even harsher terms; Harvey Rose claims that in a settlement conference Antony Gualtieri had stated: "Doctor, we are concerned about your attitude. You've got to get over this preoccupation with the quality of life—you have to be concerned with the appropriateness of medication."

Dr. Rose also recalls the advice he got when he asked a prominent physician at a local medical society meeting, "What do you do with chronic-pain sufferers?" The reply from the physician, a past president of the California Medical Association, was, "I get rid of them."

In September 1982, the California Board of Medical Quality Assurance issued its judgment. It described Dr. Rose as "a competent practitioner who renders above-average patient care. He is very dedicated to his patients." Yet the judgment also declared that the physician was guilty of "unprofessional conduct," "gross negligence," and "incompetence" because of his prescribing practices, conceding, however, that "none of the violations . . . was motivated by personal profit or gain." The board placed Dr. Rose on probation for seven years and imposed severe restrictions on his prescribing powers.

The doctor fought back in the media and in court. He was joined by the patients originally accused of being drug addicts, none of whom had ever been even accused by the board of selling excess drugs. The patients filed a joint complaint against BMQA, demanding a halt to any further actions against their doctor. The Sacramento County Superior Court threw out the entire case on a technicality. BMQA stated it would bring the same charges again, and would add more complaints, including the charge that Dr. Rose was providing drugs to yet another alleged addict, a 73-year-old woman receiving three to four doses of Darvon a day for arthritic pain.

Eventually the parties met in the office of State Senator Leroy Greene and hammered out an agreement: all charges were dropped by the state; on his part, Dr. Rose consented to taking a new examination on drugs and to having a panel of three doctors monitor his prescribing practices for up to three years. The doctor continued to campaign against the irrationality of the drug war to the extent that it intruded into medical practice and made victims of innocent pain patients and their doctors. A new California law was enacted as a result of the case, which provides an educational option for well-intentioned doctors found to be misprescribing by the BMQA. This nondisciplinary review approach, Dr. Rose contends, was how his case "should have been handled from the outset." The harsh, secretive, punitive prosecution he suffered cost this physician dearly: $140,000 in legal fees so far and severe emotional trauma, which at times during his ordeal created such severe depression that he often contemplated suicide.

Out of the needless torment of this good doctor have come a few positive events. The doctor's patients and some of his medical colleagues rallied around him and contributed over $20,000 to his defense fund. There has been heightened awareness of the extent of destructive myths about drugs believed by leading medical experts. Those chemical misconceptions still dominate California medicine and that of the entire nation.

Yet there are many doctors who take a humane and rational view of pain medication, including the three who happened to be appointed to Dr. Rose's monitoring panel. The ultimate irony in this irrational story occurred at his final examination. A panel member asked how he would treat a patient who had certain chronic pain symptoms. Dr. Harvey Rose gulped and answered honestly that he would provide a wide array of treatment, including prescriptions of some narcotics over time—precisely as he had dealt with the original six patients. The panel seemed perfectly satisfied. On June 12, 1986, BMQA medical consultant H. H. Schwamb, M.D., sent Dr. Rose a letter saying that he was off the hook; he had passed the examination and would no longer be monitored.

To laymen this may seem unbelievable. It is disturbing to see how precise, predictable scientific principles play such a minor role in delineating the line between good and bad medicine when it comes to the use of drugs in treatment.

CHRONIC PAIN: YOU ARE BETTER OFF IN ENGLAND

Dr. Harvey L. Rose continues, in the midst of a busy practice, to seek new insights from American history and the experience of other nations into how to create ethical and effective guidelines for prescribing to chronic pain patients. It was in the course of that quest that he contacted me for information on a planned trip to England because he had read my writings dealing with that country and also knew of the periodic drug-policy institutes I have presented there. After his return, he wrote to his friends in his holiday greetings circular letter for 1985, "If you have chronic pain, benign or malignant, you are better off in England."

Chronic pain sufferers in England are comforted by the application of a set of simple and humane principles first fully enunciated by the famous Rolleston Committee Report in 1926. Its civilized advice regarding organically ill people is still largely followed in that country. The essence of that humane code is: *when a patient is suffering pain from a recognized organic illness, the use of any narcotic drug over a long period of time is presumed to be proper, even though the patient might already be an addict or might become addicted. If the person is functioning well and living a relatively decent life, the dosage and type of narcotic is considered a private matter between doctor and patient, not at all the business of medical societies or the police.*

The enactment of such a code in America—through laws and codes of ethical practice—is the most important reform that could be made to ease the suffering of the saddest victims of our drug wars. Its need is urgent in part because most experts are not aware of the extent to which we sacrifice our sick on the drug-war altar. Even the English are not fully aware of the importance of this commandment because it does not exist, completely fleshed out, in their law. It exists, rather, in a combination of custom and practice, barely understood as anything out of the ordinary by those enforcement officials and physicians most responsible for its application, day in and day out.

This can be seen by a brief glance back at the marvelous work of that committee of distinguished physicians, led by Sir Humphrey Rolleston, Baronet, president of the Royal College of Physicians. The main mission of the committee was to face up squarely to an issue with which we are not dealing at this moment—"the circumstances, if any, in which the supply of morphine and heroin . . . to persons suffering from addiction to those drugs may be regarded as medically advisable." They concluded that maintenance of addicts with these drugs was medically proper, first, where the patient suffered severe withdrawal pains without the drug and, second, where the patient could lead a fairly normal life with a steady supply of the medicine but not without it.

As a sort of preface to their answer to that continually vexing question of prescribing drugs to people *suffering only from addiction*, the committee dismissed out of hand any hesitation about the dispensation of these two powerful drugs to any patient, in or out of the hospital, "for the relief of pain . . . due to organic disease such as inoperable cancer." These physicians readily agreed that it was possible that the continual use of narcotics might produce a craving that would continue if the organic disease were cured. Yet they made the gentle, ethical decision, not dictated by medical science or the law, to ignore temporarily the possibility of addiction for such people in pain. The Rolleston Committee stated flatly that "there can be no question of the propriety of continuing to administer the drug in quantities necessary for relief of the disease, so long as it persists, ignoring for the time being the question of possible production of addiction."

In other words, this small professional group saw sixty years ago that the first duty of a physician in such cases was to relieve suffering. Later, the problem of addiction could be treated. The committee also gave implicit recognition to the fact that the same person might suffer from the intertwined conditions of organically based pain and addiction, both together requiring the long-term supply of powerful narcotics. It calmly accepted the possibility (1) that the controversial drug heroin might well be given to a person in pain from organic disease or from addiction withdrawal, and (2) that both types of pain might exist in the same person. One result of these principles was that all powerful narcotics, including the feared heroin, have always been used in the treatment of the organically ill in England.

Moreover, the committee gave credence to the existence of a certain type of human being whose authenticity is widely questioned by leading medical experts, especially in America, to this day: *the stabilized addict.* Many practicing physicians and drug-abuse researchers assume that the process known as tolerance—users needing more and more of a drug to obtain the same effect—operates like an immutable principle of physics. In fact, tolerance seems to affect some users and not others, or it affects users to different degrees. Some people take the same dosage of the same drug, day after day, year after year.

Thirty-five years later, another group of English physicians, the first Brain Committee, led by Sir Russell Brain, *explicitly* recognized the existence of stabilized addicts in England and provided typical case histories. In each case, the patient was middle-aged or elderly, had contracted some organic illness, was receiving one or more of a whole range of narcotic drugs in relatively stable doses, functioned reasonably well on the drugs, but suffered terribly when attempts were made to withdraw them. Like Dr. Rose's six patients, none of these was suffering from cancer pain and none was receiving heroin or morphine. In its report of 1961, the Brain Committee, in a further coincidence, described six patients by letter—as did the state board that attacked Dr. Rose in California, but with quite a different purpose and sense of ethics. For while each of the English patients was recognized as an addict, each was nevertheless regarded as a decent citizen and a patient in need of and entitled to painkilling medication.

Case 6, for example, was described as Mr. F., a clerical worker past middle age. "He suffers from a painful disease which has necessitated the amputation of limbs. . . . Over the last four years his dose of phenadoxone has been steady at the rate of 20 10-milligram tablets daily." The synthetic drug phenadoxone, sold in the United States as Heptalgin, is nearly as potent as morphine. Accordingly, our middle-aged clerk was taking a massive though steady dose of a powerful narcotic every day, the equivalent of nearly 200 milligrams of morphine. Yet the committee came to conclusions about him that directly contradict dominant American medical opinion: "On this quantity he appears to have shown no mental deterioration; on the contrary he continues to work responsibly. When other, nonaddictive drugs have been substituted from time to time, his pain has returned with renewed severity."

While Mr. F. was receiving the largest dosage of narcotics of any of the six Brain Committee patients, all were roughly similar to the six chronic pain patients whose treatment Dr. Rose was forced to defend. Had they lived in the United States, in some communities and at some points in time, all of the British patients might have suffered the agonies and humiliation visited upon Dr. Rose's patients and upon Mrs. Koppinger. And their doctors might have suffered the same fate that Harvey Rose did.

There is an additional powerful factor that would support a gentle approach to patients like Mr. F. or Mrs. Koppinger. It was not explicitly dealt with by any of the major British official addiction-study committees of this century and has been largely ignored by the medical-legal primitives who dominate most American policy in this arena, such as those who lead the California Board of Medical Quality Assurance. There is a high probability that, viewed in the proper light, virtually none of these patients should be considered addicts at all, either stabilized or otherwise. Indeed, it is quite possible that in the event that their organic condition changed, thus eliminating the basis for their pain, they would stop taking their narcotic drugs.

Thus it is always difficult to tell when a patient is or is not an addict—nor does the best of medical science contain a definition of addiction that is widely accepted. There is no accepted laboratory method by which addicts may be identified. The most humane, intelligent experts disagree on many specific cases. Some of the reviewers of drafts of this book, for example, urged me not to include Mrs. Koppinger and Dr. Rose's patients in the same chapter as people who admitted they were drug addicts and had ties to the streets and crime. I hope that I will be forgiven for keeping them in the same chapter. Because there is no definitive test for determining addiction, my test for deciding on the propriety of powerful drugs for pain is whether or not the suffering of the patient might be relieved. I apply that test usually without regard to moral qualifications or status of addiction. A patient in pain is a patient in pain, whether the pain comes from an organic illness, addiction, or a combination of them—and regardless of the morality of the sufferer.

Much American medical and legal folklore holds that many patients remain hooked on their medicine even when the underlying organic disease is cured and that therefore it is the irresponsible prescribing of drugs by American doctors over the decades that has been the main cause for the creation of huge numbers of dangerous addicts. My review of every scrap of the available historical record proves exactly the opposite to be true, and it is a pleasure to be able to expose a bum rap which has been placed at the door of our medical profession, but too often believed and perpetuated by its own members. A 1982 editorial in *The New England Journal of Medicine* confirmed the persistence of this myth among doctors and nurses and countered with the observation that "addiction among patients who receive narcotics is exceedingly unlikely; the incidence is probably no more than 0.1 percent."

Many American doctors use drugs and other treatments very well to control pain and anxiety. Even when they do not use drugs properly, the fears about the rate of addiction from medically prescribed narcotics is vastly exaggerated.

In part, this low incidence of addiction is due to the most ignored element in the entire field of drugs and medications, the expectations of the user and those nearby about its impact; in other words, set and setting. Most people in pain perceive themselves as patients taking a medicine. So also do their doctors and nurses. When their pain recedes, those users expect to stop taking the medicine. Such has been the pattern for centuries among over 99 out of 100 patients, in millions upon millions of instances. The most dramatic example I have encountered of the impact of that process of expectations upon the taking of narcotic drugs was reported some years ago at one of my London institutes by the famed research pharmacologist and hospice director, Dr. Robert G. Twycross of Oxford. The hospice patient was a 16-year-old girl suffering from bone cancer. The accompanying pain necessitated increasing doses of oral heroin over a period of weeks, dosages which plateaued during weeks 8 to 12 at 200 milligrams daily.

Thus this slight young person was taking daily the equivalent of roughly 600 milligrams of morphine, a dosage far in excess of each of Dr. Rose's patients and in excess of the great majority of all American patients known to medical history—as well as in excess of the actual potency of the drugs taken by most American street addicts daily in their highly adulterated doses. When, however, the young girl's cancer started to go into remission, the heroin dosage was slowly reduced over a period of weeks, and eliminated completely by week 15. She showed no signs of addiction or withdrawal after discharge from the hospital. For several years thereafter she was reported to be alive and well, and not seeking drugs of any kind. The young patient did not think of herself as an addict and did not act like one.

MILTON POLANSKY: WE PRONOUNCED HIS DEATH SENTENCE

Milton Polansky *did* perceive of himself as an addict. In fact, that's how he identified himself when he happened to get through my answering system early one morning a few years ago, and asked in a very direct voice, laden with a strong Baltimore accent, "Is this Arnold Trebach?" Braced for some form of verbal assault before I was fully awake, I said hesitantly that yes, it was. He immediately replied to my relief and surprise, "Well, God bless you! This is Milton Polansky. I'm a heroin addict. I've read your book, *The Heroin Solution*, and bought copies for my doctors." During the brief acquaintanceship that ensued, I returned his admiration, not because he was an addict who agreed with my view of the world, but because he seemed to be a *mensch* (Yiddish for a vibrant human being with integrity) who was honest about his weaknesses and who often laughed at the foolishness of the laws that made him a criminal. In an engaging way, he seemed to be saying that you can't let the bastards grind you down and one way to fight back is to joke about their utter stupidity and cruelty.

Thus Milton thought of himself as a heroin addict, nothing to hide, chin out, them's the conditions that prevail. "Who am I hurting?" he asked me defiantly one day over lunch. We both knew that, despite the views of many drug-abuse experts, there was no scientific evidence that the narcotics caused any significant organic harm to his body. Yet, there was sound medical research documenting the harm caused by persistent injecting of the skin, including abscesses and the many diseases that may be transmitted by dirty needles, such as hepatitis. Accordingly, I asked him if he was not hurting himself by the constant injections since 1940 when he started using heroin as a soldier. The look of disbelief that came over his face suggested that he viewed any person who did not use proper procedures in injecting as a fool. Once, "during the war" in about 1943, "I was at a long party with a jazz band and we shared a needle, in New Orleans, and I ended up in the hospital with hepatitis for a while," but that was the last time he remembered suffering from injections.

However, it would be misleading to portray Milton Polansky as simply a sweet old grandfather, a helpless victim of the drug laws, although that is how he appeared at the tragic end. He was also part devil, a scheming and successful manipulator of doctors and the drug laws and the prescription system. One of his fellow addicts, with long years of experience, told me that Milton was virtually without peer in his ability to "make" doctors, to convince them to "write" for him. In some cases, this was accomplished by pitiful appeals to the doctor's sympathetic nature; in others, by appeals to the physician's pocketbook. Milton would then fill these prescriptions, using some of the drugs and selling the rest to a small circle of fellow addicts. During recent years, it is likely that he took in tens of thousands of dollars every year in drug sales. Of course, when his supply ran low, he would spend roughly the same amounts to buy drugs for himself, often from within that same small circle of addicts. On some occasions, however, this would require venturing onto the mean streets of Baltimore, into rough neighborhoods such as one notorious area known as "the block." Unlike Dolores Koppinger, or Mr. F., or any of a multitude of innocent organically ill people who need analgesic medicines every year in America and in many other countries, Milton Polansky, doting father and grandfather, was a criminal narcotic addict.

It is important that his status as a criminal be recognized because that status puts him in the same category, speaking in broad terms, as some of the most destructive inhabitants of America. The manner in which we react to people who are both addicts and criminals is important. They are a challenge to our sense of ethics. Each of them presents unique problems and opportunities. If we can understand how we threw away the human opportunity in this case, if we can see the cruelty that we as a nation imposed on this one "criminal" addict, Milton Polansky, late of Baltimore, Maryland, there is some hope that we can commence evolving a more humane and effective approach to all of our unfortunate neighbors whom personal stupidity, fate, biology, or bad luck, separately or together, have pulled into addiction and some degree of related crime.

Milton's behavior as a criminal addict did not preclude his functioning in many ways as a decent human being. As far as can be discovered, he never committed a violent act or a burglary or a theft to obtain his drugs, which were not difficult for him to obtain for most of his addicted years. He was virtually unknown to police blotters, at least for serious offenses; the man did seem to get stopped often by the police for driving without a license. During much of his life, which commenced in November 19, 1918, Mr. Polansky was a successful Baltimore businessman, engaged in such fields as building renovation and real estate. He was a regular contributor to many charities. While he was not greatly successful in his marriages, he adored his children and grandchildren and I am told that they felt the same way about him. In most respects, he was a nice neighbor.

As the years passed, Milton Polansky developed a number of serious organic and painful diseases. None of them, to my knowledge, was attributable to his use of narcotics. Thus, like many addicts I have encountered, he was soon taking powerful narcotics as a form of self-medication to deal with both his addiction and his organic diseases. Also in line with the patterns of many of these dependent users, there were drugs he preferred and then there were those he found acceptable. In Milton's case, as with many addicts, his drug of choice was heroin and the acceptable substitute was Dilaudid, that legal synthetic opiate which may be several times more potent, dose for dose, even than heroin. He took methadone as a last resort but in general looked with disdain on the favorite drug of the addiction-treatment experts of America. There you have him, warts and all, a far-from-perfect being.

That flawed human package walked into the office of Seymour H. Rubin, M.D., in a Jewish neighborhood in the north of Baltimore, on October 20, 1982. Dr. Rubin knew a great deal about Milton and his family, having treated his brother, who had died 17 years earlier from diabetes and heart disease. He had not seen Milton since those days, and wrote in his notes, "I am shocked by his horrible and changed appearance. He looks thirty years older than his stated age." The patient, then aged 62, shuffled along haltingly and needed a cane. A medical examination revealed an even more shocking list of organic ailments. Dr. Rubin was especially concerned about the impending gangrene of both legs. Other serious conditions of the patient included diabetes, kidney failure, recurrent transient strokes, heart disease, and high blood pressure with congestive heart failure. Any one of these conditions, along with allied complications, could have rapidly fatal results, Dr. Rubin knew, especially if they were not treated properly. And, of course, those potentially terminal organic illnesses were being ignored by the patient because he was finding it increasingly difficult to find a steady source, legal or illegal, of medicines to treat his diseases—and thus his energies focused on an obsessive search for drugs to feed his addiction.

Seymour Rubin, a native of Baltimore and five years younger than Milton, is a graduate of the University of Maryland Medical School and board-certified in internal medicine. He has little experience, expertise, or interest in treating drug addicts. Yet, through a series of unrelated events, he has come to disagree strongly with the current medical-legal approach to them. While a frontline infantryman in World War II, he saw at a newly liberated concentration camp how harsh deprivation of basic needs can reduce decent, proud human beings to sniveling, conniving beggars. Later, at medical school in the late Forties, he heard Harry Anslinger of the old FBN tell the students in a guest lecture how to think about addicts: they are basically evil people; they'll do anything to get drugs; if they don't commit themselves to the Lexington hospital for detoxification, they should be put in jail and the key should be thrown away. "I feel that our medical profession is still guided by that attitude," Dr. Rubin now declares. "And yet I have found out that drug addicts are not all evil people. Many of them are pathetic people who have to be helped, to be led. . . . If, though, we treat any group of people badly enough, like what I saw at Dachau, we can turn them into whining puppy dogs. . . . If you just kick them out of the door, you may be protecting yourself as a doctor but you are not doing anything for the patient. . . . You're being a rotten doctor."

To avoid the common failing of being a rotten doctor in regard to a known drug addict, Dr. Rubin wanted to act rationally on his objective clinical assessment of Milton Polansky. That extensive evaluation concluded that the major threats to his health, indeed to his life, came from his multiple organic medical ailments and not from his incidental though "very repugnant" problem of drug addiction. He decided to provide periodic prescriptions of Dilaudid and then to seek to persuade his patient to go into a local hospital for treatment of his other major medical conditions. Milton refused to go into the hospital because he feared that the doctors there would attempt to detoxify him from Dilaudid and also perhaps put him on methadone, "which would tear me apart." He had been through 15 to 20 drug-treatment programs within the previous quarter-century and none had worked for him; he did not want to risk another attempt even if it was a prelude to easing his organic conditions. "I'll die of withdrawal!" he cried.

Seymour Rubin knew that every prescription of Diluadid he wrote for this known addict put his entire career at risk, and he knew also that the risk would continue even if his patient were to be hospitalized. It was all very chancy, though (as we saw with Dr. Rose and his final examination). Very often, doctors were not bothered by the medical or legal authorities; in other cases, they were and their careers destroyed. He called a leading state drug-enforcement official, who said he believed Mr. Polansky should be prescribed narcotic drugs, as had other law-enforcement officials over the years, according to Milton. But the physician was worried about his medical colleagues. Dr. Rubin told me that he wanted to be able to say, "Milton, I don't want any bullshit from you! You'll get Dilaudid but you must cooperate in this program of treatment." At that point, the doctor would have practically dragged his patient into a treatment slot he had ready at Baltimore's Sinai Hospital, especially for his limbs, which were becoming gangrenous. But Dr. Rubin knew that he could not assure his patient of a steady supply of Dilaudid, which he was then taking in dosages of about 40 milligrams per day (down from a high in the past of 240 milligrams). After several months of treating this difficult patient and agonizing over the case, Dr. Rubin finally concluded that he had to protect himself somewhat, and he called the head of the medical committee that polices doctors for the state medical society: Stephen A. Hirsch, M.D., Chairman, Committee on Drugs, Medical and Chirurgical Faculty of the State of Maryland.

Dr. Rubin's case notes for December 28, 1982, relate that in response to his call, Dr. Hirsch had emphatically declared "that Milton is well-known to his committee, that he has manipulated many physicians, and that I should not prescribe Dilaudid for him. I will comply with his wishes." Those wishes were communicated in writing a few days later, along with barely concealed threats: "Our very strong advice to you is that you not prescribe any controlled substances for Mr. Polansky, although you of course may treat him for conditions other than his addiction. . . . Mr. Polansky has been advised of the availability of drug-treatment programs in the community and that he should obtain treatment there for his addiction. Again, we appreciate your timely call. You have probably avoided much future difficulty."

Seymour Rubin was indeed out of difficulty with the medical powers who could obliterate his right to practice his profession, but not with his own conscience. He could not sleep well for weeks because he felt so ashamed at his weak compliance with the inhumane and ignorant decisions of the appointed state medical drug experts. There was no way to separate Milton's organic diseases from his addiction—and certainly no drug-treatment program of Dr. Rubin's knowledge that could cure his addiction. It was about this time that I called Dr. Rubin at Milton's urging, and while he agreed to talk with me, he asked that his name not be used because of his personal sense of shame. Since then, his sense of outrage has taken over.

"Even though I will prescribe no more Dilaudid, there is considerable conflict with what I consider the reasoned and compassionate practice of medicine," Dr. Rubin's notes stated. "Has Milton manipulated doctors, perhaps including me, because he is basically an evil person? No, he has done so because that is the only way available to him to obtain relief from his pains and agonies. Yes, he is at fault for having started his atrocious habit many years ago but do we treat chronic smokers and alcoholics in the same manner? . . . He is incurably addicted and more Dilaudid pills will do him no harm. . . . If we can take care of his other problems, his significant renal disease, his uncontrolled diabetes, etc., then we might make an attempt at treating his addiction. He is in far greater danger of the former than the latter, and is more likely to die of them." Operating on his own sense of medical science and ethics, Seymour Rubin had arrived at roughly the same humane point as had the Rolleston Committee some 56 years earlier. Yet he found himself unable to act on his convictions.

Dr. Rubin periodically responded to crisis visits and calls from his patient, to whom he would prescribe no more narcotics. He saw him deteriorate further before his eyes. On March 13, 1984, Milton showed up without an appointment at the doctor's office in a state of collapse. Dr. Rubin pleaded with him to enter the hospital immediately for treatment of all his conditions. Milton refused for all of his usual reasons. He was in enormous pain and shouted that he would lie on the examining table until Dr. Rubin gave him a prescription for Dilaudid. Even though he could barely walk because of the impending gangrene, he threatened to go out and rob a drug store if the doctor did not relent. The doctor did not. The elderly grandfather cursed and shouted and raved that Seymour Rubin was "just like the rest of the fucking asshole doctors."

After that incident, Dr. Rubin lost touch with Mr. Polansky. "I had heard rumors that these were agonizing times for him," Dr. Rubin told me. Almost a year passed. Milton somehow carried on although his doctor later observed, "It was a surprise he lasted as long as he did."

Milton Polansky, heroin addict, was pronounced dead by the medical examiner on March 8, 1985, at 3:50 P.M. Apparently, the old man died alone, perhaps in pain. His body lay undiscovered on the floor of his apartment for some time—since the medical examiner estimated on the death certificate that the date of death was March 3. The immediate cause of death was listed as "Arteriosclerotic Cardiovascular Disease." A contributing condition was listed as "Diabetes Mellitus." There was no mention of narcotic use or overdose.

Dr. Seymour Rubin shot off an angry letter to Dr. Stephen Hirsch and the state drug committee containing rare words of professional condemnation: "Your committee's concern with his drug addiction . . . was disproportionate and tangential. I thought it was more derived from sanctified dogma and bogus fears rather than from any true feelings about the quality of life or even the life itself."

Sitting in his office, alone with me on a quiet day during the holiday season at the end of 1985, Dr. Rubin was still ashamed and bitter: "In essence, I felt that we in the medical profession had pronounced his death sentence. If he had any chance of living, we took it away."

KENNY FREEMAN: THE NICE-NEIGHBOR JUNKIE

"A mature addict with a legal supply of clean drugs may well be a nice neighbor" was a thought I had put in a column that appeared in the *Washington Post* early in 1984. It had been written partly with Milton Polansky in mind, but I was also thinking of other drug addicts I had met since the early Seventies, many of whom were decent people. Drugs, I had found, were morally irrelevant. Some people who take narcotics behave immorally in other ways but not because of the drugs. Some people who are absolutely drug-free are also free of any morals. The truly important issues for me have become not so much whether people take drugs but rather how they treat those to whom they should be showing love and care. All of those thoughts were behind that sentence.

A copy of the paper ended up in a library in Jerusalem where the article was read and touched the heart of an American named Kenneth Freeman, who understood all of my underlying emotions, my unstated feelings, very well.

His letter in response touched my heart as well. He wrote: "I was really pleased by what you said, esp. about being willing to have a junkie live next door to you. That was sweet, and rare. You're absolutely right, as of course, you know; even the worst of us can get stabilized, and live normal lives. . . . On behalf of all of us junkies all over the world, thanks."

Kenny Freeman is a noncriminal, stabilized narcotic addict. He is not suffering from any other established disease or defect. To me he seems as healthy as an ox and a normal, stable, warm human being. Like many regular consumers of narcotics, he claims that "junk keeps me healthy." There may be some truth to that, at least in regard to respiratory diseases. The important point, however, is that Kenny represents still another group of confirmed drug users, distinct from any of those discussed in this section so far—mature, decent, noncriminal, addicted, and with no known organic health problem. Yet a "junkie," hands down, no excuses.

While living in a middle-class neighborhood in affluent Montgomery County, Maryland, in the beautiful Washington suburbs, Kenneth Freeman knew in advance that he was going to be a narcotic addict and bought himself a set of needles for injecting, which he stored, waiting for the inevitable day when they would be called for. At the age of fifteen!

Looking back on it all and now knowing about the discovery of endorphins, those natural painkillers in the body, he has made the diagnosis that he probably suffered from an endorphin deficiency, and still does. If he can make that scientific case, then, of course, he will have established an *organic* basis for his continuing need for narcotics, a theory only a few drug experts now support.

Even in the absence of strong scientific endorsement for his views, Mr. Freeman is quite certain of another unorthodox principle that may outrage even the most sympathetic observers. Far from decrying his involvement with drugs, or from urging young people to "avoid my mistakes," he believes that some youngsters, particularly those who would otherwise be suicidal, should be prescribed analgesic, mind-altering medicines from an early age. "I should have been medicated by doctors starting at age fifteen. As a teenager I was in a lot of trouble. The high school wouldn't let me keep coming unless I was in psychiatric care because I fought with the teachers. Also, the Juvenile Court ordered me to be treated by a psychologist. I was in five car crashes while I was in high school. I needed something then, and I didn't get it."

He now recounts that he has been using drugs heavily for a quarter of a century and for the past 17 years has been an addict. As of this writing Mr. Freeman is 43. For the most part, his internal needs, whatever their cause, necessitated self-medication and a good deal of agony. For the past 12 years, he has been on a stable, maintenance dosage of Darvon.

During many of these years, he has been a productive, contributing member of society. As a free-lance writer, he has been involved in one of the world's touchiest problems, Arabs and Jews in Israel. He lived for a year in Nazareth and also worked in the Gaza Strip. His articles have appeared in the *Jerusalem Post*, *Israel Review*, *Jewish Opinion*, and many other periodicals.

However, as a typical white middle-class college student and drug abuser of the early Sixties, he tried a staggering variety of chemicals, periodically getting in serious trouble with one drug or another. A life pattern of ups and downs emerged. Kenny did extremely well in college, graduating in three years with high grades and fellowship offers. Two years later, however, while in the graduate clinical psychology program at the University of Michigan, he was told by the faculty that he was "in danger of becoming another Timothy Leary" and was invited to transfer to the social psychology program. "To them, I was a Pied Piper of drugs who consistently proclaimed that psychology was full of lies. I was guilty of both charges."

Later, while at the University of North Carolina, he dropped out of graduate school and did nothing but inject amphetamines for eighteen months. Like thousands of other hippies (his own label), he found that being a speed freak was a full-time and destructive activity, for him "a total disaster." Friends convinced him that it would be much safer to inject another drug then quite easily available in Chapel Hill. Thus the young scholar found salvation by "becoming a simple heroin addict." He discovered, as have other, more objective experts, that compared to many drugs widely used and abused, heroin is a gentle chemical, although it is seductively addicting. "Heroin was much safer than Methedrine. It was much kinder to my body."

Then he went through a better period. Things quieted down and he went on with his education. He went back to school and eventually obtained a prestigious masters degree in public health from Johns Hopkins University in Baltimore. Mr. Freeman also obtained numerous professional jobs, doing research, consulting, and training in the drug-abuse field, often under contracts awarded to various firms by the federal government. To my surprise, he informed me that one was a firm I founded and headed for some years in the Sixties, where he had been hired as a research specialist. (To my embarrassment, I did not remember him.) In the years that followed, he became a professional journalist, an ardent Zionist, divorced, remarried, and the father of three children.

Kenny was a regular user of narcotics during this entire period. Upon reflection, he believes now that he was unconsciously involved in a process which he insists is common for many mature narcotic addicts: a search for the proper dosage at the lowest possible level of "his" proper drug.

The search had its risks. In 1969 Kenneth Freeman was arrested for possession of narcotics, along with his wife at the time, who was five months pregnant. This, coming on top of many trips to emergency rooms for injecting contaminated drugs and of the eighteen months of being too sick to work or do anything else, gave him the motivation he needed to start thinking about change.

Opportunity arrived in the form of a job as one of the first ex-addict counselors hired by the D.C. Department of Corrections. Kenny was given two weeks "to clean up," which he did, and was then placed on urine surveillance. For four months he ran encounter groups for addicts coming out of the Lorton prison complex.

Here he saw many of the clients in his group go on methadone. He also had friends taking methadone. Kenny's reaction was quite negative: "It scared me!" During 1969, while employed as an ex-addict researcher at my old consulting firm, he kept trying to stay clean and kept suffering severe pains, which seemed to be based at least in part on physical ailments, and in part on a good deal of anxiety. The leaders of programs he visited along with a friend, also working as an ex-addict, constantly raised questions: maybe they were keeping clean, but they "appeared sick."

A Washington physician advised both that they were headed for methadone, but an alternative might exist: propoxyphene or Darvon. They both tried it. For Kenny it worked. His colleague later went back to heroin, was arrested, disappeared.

Kenny insists that he always used Darvon as a medication to treat illness, not to get high. It was always prescribed by physicians for his "pain and sickness." Did the sickness exist before he ever used drugs? Did drugs cause the sickness? Does he suffer from a chronic withdrawal condition? Is it a physical problem or a conditioned reflex? No one knows.

Kenneth Freeman does know that Darvon worked. For years he used nothing else, no other narcotic, barbiturate, amphetamine. Nothing! He kept developing his "rules for surviving as a drug addict"—the smallest dose of the weakest possible narcotic. And, in his case, never injecting.

Over the years, he kept trying to reduce his dosage of Darvon but found that when his regular daily amount was reduced to approximately half, he became physically ill and felt harsh muscle cramps and leg pains, as well as mental depression. Nevertheless, he kept attempting to cut down. While a student at Johns Hopkins, he went into treatment with both a doctor and a social worker connected with the school, who took him on as a patient for several years. In the process they both came to the conclusion, at first against their own better judgments, that he should stop attempts at withdrawal because lessons from methadone treatment had taught them the value of regular, stabilizing doses. The Johns Hopkins experts accordingly advised their patient that he would be better off as a stabilized user of Darvon. That is precisely what Kenny Freeman became, with prescriptions for generic propoxyphene provided by the doctor, filled in bulk at wholesale prices directly from the manufacturer.

For several years, therefore, this narcotic addict had a legal habit costing $88 per *year*. Neither his regular use nor his possession of drugs in quantity—bottles of 1,000 pills four times a year—created a problem for anyone. Unfortunately for him, and the rest of us, the United States government in its majestic wisdom soon not only designated Darvon a controlled narcotic but, as we have seen, also made it a federal crime for any doctor to prescribe it to an addict except for detoxification, that is, for 21 days or less. At that point, like so many junkies, the young drug-abuse expert was heaved out into the borderland of the law and of society. He went from being a victim of his own internal needs to being a victim of the drug war. He was forced to go from doctor to doctor seeking relief. His doctor at Johns Hopkins fumed that the damned government was not going to tell *him* how to practice medicine but even he was aware of the new risks in his continued prescribing to this patient.

When that doctor left the country, Kenneth Freeman joined several group health plans and health-maintenance organizations. Out of fear of the law and often against their own sense of medical ethics and justice, the doctors in all of them eventually pushed him toward detoxification or oral methadone, the two grand choices of America's vast drug-abuse treatment empire.

He resisted methadone and opted for detoxification. Each time, that process dominated his life and threatened to tear it apart. Nothing else mattered but staying drug-free, not his wife, not his children, not his job. For him, as for so many addicts, detoxification was not a time of personal triumph, as the popular propaganda tells it, but of continual personal disasters. Detoxification never worked and he was soon back on his regular ration of Darvon. Because of the new legal restrictions, however, he was usually classified by his physicians as being in a period of detoxification. Therefore, he continued to receive legal prescriptions of his drug, but these were often stopped by various doctors.

In 1980, he went in despair to one of the country's leading medical experts on drug addiction, then practicing in the Washington suburbs, with whom he had had some prior professional association. The physician was quite uncomfortable to have this patient in his office, explaining that "of all the doctors in America, I am under the greatest public scrutiny." Even though the doctor recognized that Kenny was being harmed unfairly by an inflexible legal-medical system, he advised him, "Find a doctor who writes prescriptions for money and don't make a fuss. There are plenty of doctors out there who write scrips." Kenny turned down this cowardly invitation to commit multiple crimes. Indeed, since he became a stable Darvon addict, he has never used narcotics obtained illegally.

Somehow, the family stayed together during all of this stress and by late 1981 had emigrated to Israel. To his relief, Kenny discovered that Darvon in some forms was not a closely controlled drug there. The monkey suddenly was off his back.

Citizen Kenneth Freeman could walk into any drugstore in Israel and buy a weak Israeli-made compound of propoxyphene and acetaminophen over the counter without a prescription. For four years, this young professional man maintained himself—for the first time without medical supervision. Nothing changed, except that he did not think about it. "It was like insulin, a medication I took. No thrills. No highs. No sickness. No craving. Just ordinary, stable life."

While the Israelis were tough on hard-drug dealers and street junkies, and provided only methadone under the care of a doctor for addict maintenance, they seemed virtually to ignore addicts who could maintain themselves on the numerous less potent drugs available without a prescription. "In the U.S. I was a rotten junkie, being driven from doctor to doctor, while here I am a normal person," he wrote me. "And now, no one, but no one, treats me like a junkie."

From his newly secure position in Israel, addict Freeman urged me to begin work on a project I had mentioned to him: an international organization with the primary goal of securing more humane treatment for addicts. "We need it. Real bad. Why not start with me? Meaning, I think I've been treated awfully inhumanely, and my whole life has been turned around by what I consider to be an obvious endorphin deficiency that finally got treated correctly, only to have the treatment taken away. . . . I think that's

where the answers will lie in terms of treatment in the future.
. . . Someday, they'll figure out what each person needs to be
'normal' and that'll be that. In that more humane future. Please
do something for us poor junkies."

That plea took on a note of personal urgency when the family
came back to America in December 1985. They had returned primarily because Mr. Freeman's wife had been offered a very good
position with the federal government. When asked why in the
world *he* would return to the harsh drug-control system of America, he replied, "I was naïve. I thought that within a short time,
I'd get it all straightened out. It didn't even occur to me to take
extra Darvon from Israel, which I could have easily done—legally,
as far as I know."

Thus he was again caught in the limbo where America places
addicts who want to live within the rules. He created problems
for everyone, but by all rational lights he should have been treated
only with kindness and care.

For the previous 12 years, he had been living proof that addicts
can learn to live decent lives and to stabilize themselves, even on
low-potency drugs that rarely attract press attention. Kenny takes
three 65-milligram capsules of Darvon four times a day, a total of
780 milligrams each day, a dosage that has not varied, except under
pressure, since 1975. While on that dosage he has been a good
husband, father, journalist—and neighbor.

Nevertheless, it is now illegal in America for any drug other
than oral methadone to be used in the maintenance of addicts.
Doctors and patients who participate in a drug-maintenance plan
utilizing Darvon, or any other narcotic, in nondiminishing doses
for over 21 days are in violation of federal and state laws, and face
the possibility of severe sanctions, including prison sentences. There
is absolutely no scientific basis for this legal distinction among
narcotics (as I documented, I believe, in *The Heroin Solution*),
and thus the law is fundamentally unjust. Nevertheless, Mr. Freeman was now back on the fringes of society. His Darvon supply
from Israel was running low. A few caring American doctors prescribed for him but they became concerned about how long they
could continue. One suggested that he enter a methadone maintenance program.

As the days went by and his anxiety increased, Mr. Freeman
considered that option which he had hitherto resisted. The Washington, D.C., methadone program offered to put him on 50 milli-

grams of that approved drug a day. When he sought my advice, I said that it made no sense. Despite what one of his doctors said, these narcotics were not interchangeable. There were qualities in Darvon, as yet unexplained by science, that made that drug work for Kenny. The situation brought to mind an old American frontier maxim: if it ain't broke, don't fix it. Kenny Freeman was living a decent life on Darvon; methadone might tear up that life. Moreover, methadone was approximately 24 times more potent, dose for dose, than Darvon. Laws and allied medical principles that force a patient to needlessly substitute a drug that is both different in quality and also 24 times more potent than one now doing the job are obscene.

And what happens, he asks, if government funds for methadone are cut to balance the budget, or if the program is legislated out of existence? Kenny would be dependent on a narcotic 24 times more powerful than the one to which he is now addicted. What could he and other addicts do then? After all, when Kenny's doctor at Johns Hopkins put him on a maintenance dose of Darvon in 1974, it was perfectly legal and a standard treatment for patients with chronic pain. When Darvon was made into a narcotic by the magic wand of the law in 1977, no provision was made for patients like Kenny Freeman. "How can I trust the government now with an even stronger drug?"

In order to get on that more powerful drug legally and regularly, moreover, he would have to be treated as if he were a criminal, irresponsible, in need of daily supervision. After 12 years of continual, private maintenance, obtaining his medication every few months, he will be forced to go to a clinic every day, seven days a week, year in and year out.

Clearly, law and medical concepts must be changed so that the multitudes of decent, law-abiding, mature, stabilized addicts in America may be treated by their doctors with prescriptions of the currently legal drugs to which they are addicted. While such people may not necessarily be organically ill, they are all suffering from a widely recognized disease, that of narcotic addiction. This new freedom of treatment for such sick people must also include the right to all of these drugs in injectable form, along with a proper supply of clean needles, although Kenneth Freeman is not now interested in that option. Such reforms would save suffering on the part of many thousands of addicts and also of their neighbors— because fewer mature addicts would be forced to engage in crime or to buy in the black market. Accordingly, drastic reductions would take place in the profits for organized crime, in the temptations for police corruption, and in violence associated with criminal drug trafficking. If new statutes do not provide these freedoms for decent addicts, then lawyers must bring innovative lawsuits to establish them.

At this writing, Kenny Freeman is again going through withdrawal and he and his family are in pain. He is confronted with a drastic choice. To stay in America, he will have to give himself over to methadone, if detoxification fails. This will mean that he must act as if nothing happened in the last 16 years, that he is the same street addict that he was in 1968, and that he should expect to be treated like a junkie in a junkie clinic. Or he can return to Israel where, he says, "I would be treated simply as a normal person."

STREET ADDICTS: HOW IN THE NAME OF GOD . . . ?

Street addicts present a severe threat to society. Up to this point in this chapter, we have talked only of patients who are organically ill and of addicts who are, for the most part, now mature, noncriminal, and nonthreatening. However, it is much more difficult to imagine a truly compassionate treatment program for a predatory street criminal, whose drug taking is far from stable. Our initial approach to such addicts should be that they can expect to be arrested and punished for their predatory and violent crimes. I am not inclined to make excuses for their crimes because they are addicted—although I empathize with the pressure they feel. I empathize; I do not excuse. At the same time, medical treatment should be fully available to deal with their addiction, preferably in the form of detoxification and abstinence. If they survive an initial period of street criminality, and if they remain addicted while becoming more decent in their lifestyle, however, they should be treated along the lines proposed for Kenny Freeman, at least with a whole range of currently legal drugs.

At the same time, it should not be assumed that street addicts fit a single mold. Many of those who might bear that label are also pathetic, sick people, as was Milton Polansky, who at times was only one faltering step away from the street. For all of them, young and old, doctors must be allowed the option to attempt treatment with a wide range of drugs on a maintenance basis if necessary. It is difficult to look upon street addicts with anything but repugnance. I know from personal experience because my wife and I were once robbed by one in Rome, but at some points in their lives compassion is in order. They are also human and deserving of caring treatment. At the very least, we should increase the number and variety of gentle options we offer to such potentially harmful criminals, especially when they have reached the state of being social derelicts.

There are more heroin addicts, in all stages of health, in New York City than in most *countries* of the world. In a major report to the governor of New York in 1982, former HEW secretary Joseph A. Califano, Jr., now a leading Washington lawyer, declared that New York City was the heroin capital of the country. Of the 450,000 to 600,000 addicts in the country, he estimated that 234,000 were in New York State and 177,500 in New York City alone. Thus one out of every forty people in that city was a heroin addict! No expert has any easy solutions to the staggering problems presented by that concentrated horde of misery and criminality. To deal with many of those addicts, those involved in predatory crimes, the most appropriate methods involve policemen with guns and jailers with keys—at least initially. If, however, we analyze objectively who those addicts are, we would conclude that many of them, more than anything else, must be considered organically ill; accordingly, we should treat their addiction as a less important ailment.

Mr. Califano encountered just such an addict, in the company of many other fellow sufferers, on October 12, 1981. The prominent lawyer was being led on a tour of the addiction scene by police captain Philip Sheridan, the head of the Narcotics Division's Street Enforcement Unit. They entered a shooting gallery in a brownstone at 360 West 116th Street in Harlem. Perhaps fifty addicts, in various stages of despair, crowded the filthy floors of the building. Nobody ran away even though the police were coming in the building. Many of the addicts had arms and legs that looked like rats had gnawed at them because of constant injections with dirty needles. A policeman asked Mr. Califano to look at an addict sitting in a corner.

"I turned. He looked like he had elephantiasis of the legs. His ankles were swollen to the circumferences of thighs, his skin was so crusted with infection and so dried out that its dark color seemed faded to a worn-out tan. . . . His toes were so swollen they had all merged together. Like an elephant's hoof, I thought." In other parts of the building they found a young addict whose legs were so torn up by injections that he could not even walk. Captain Sheridan explained that most of these addicts got their money for their regular fixes by regular and extensive predatory crimes. Yet, as he drove away, the thing that bothered Mr. Califano was the image of those desperately sick people, all of them, lying about in misery. "I couldn't get the question out of my head," he wrote in anguish. "How in the name of God did the richest nation in the history of the world let any of its people get here?"

That was a worthwhile question. Yet a more important one is: how in the name of God can we allow those poor souls to *remain* there? That is what the lawyer and the police captain and the mayor and the governor and the President and everyone else has done. That, and recommending, as did Mr. Califano's report, more police and more courts and more jails to lock them up, because the criminal justice system of New York has reached the point of utter saturation with drug offenders. Nowhere in Mr. Califano's acclaimed report did he recommend that such obviously diseased addicts as the man with the elephant's hoof be offered what such a sick citizen would be allowed in England and what Dr. Rubin wanted to offer Milton Polansky, whose own legs were at the point of collapse: a place in the hospital for treatment of all of the organic diseases along with regular doses of powerful narcotics. Those medicines would have served that poor man a number of purposes, including maintenance of the addiction, even after he left the hospital. It is highly likely that the old addict in Harlem, like the old addict in Baltimore, would have happily accepted the legal Dilaudid in place of the illegal heroin, and stayed within the arms of legitimate medicine and off the backs of the rest of us.

In the end, therefore, the circle of concern runs from a Sacramento grandmother, who was probably not addicted and certainly not criminal, to a Baltimore grandfather, who was certainly both, to a Washington father, who was definitely addicted, had been a criminal and now was not, to an old man in Harlem, who may well have been somebody's grandfather and was also both addicted and criminal. The line that pulls the circle together is that all of these people were sick. All could have been helped by the more humane dispensation of *currently legal medicines* under the care of a doctor.

Those medicines were denied to these sick people because of irrational fears believed by leading professionals: The fear that narcotics in medicine may create hordes of street addicts. The fear that patients given narcotics will be unable to give them up when the sickness is over. The fear that once a patient does become an addict that person is doomed to a life of escalating doses of drugs and resultant degradation. The fear that providing drugs to a known addict will harm that person more than any other pain or infirmity suffered by that patient. All of these fears have a basis in reality for only a relatively few patients. For most, they are groundless and result in inhumane treatment.

One widely held fear is real. Doctors who treat patients with any type of narcotic in stable dosages for more than a few weeks outside of a hospital are in danger of professional destruction by supporters of the drug war.

10

The Sacrifice of Our Sick— by Banning Hated Drugs in Medicine

ANOTHER VITAL ISSUE was raised in the brief dialogue between the Washington lawyer, the police captain, and that sick old man in the wretched Harlem tenement. As they looked at the shocking condition of the man's legs, Captain Sheridan suggested to Mr. Califano, "Ask him what caused all this."

I did.

"The needle," the addict answered.

"What about the heroin?" I asked.

"No, no. The mix was dirty," he said, referring to the quinine or whatever white powder had been mixed with the heroin to cut its strength.

"Addicts'll never blame the heroin," Sheridan said. Then, turning to the seated addict, he added, "Isn't that right?"

"Oh, yes. Heroin is good. No heroin caused this," he monotoned.

HEROIN IS GOOD . . . IN MEDICINE

The incident reported by Mr. Califano provides additional insights into why we are in such catastrophic confusion regarding our drug problems. That poor old addict was correct. Volumes of scientific research, many of them listed in the appendix to Mr. Califano's large report, have concluded that no known organic damage is caused by the use of heroin. It is a physically benign, though powerfully addicting, substance. The organic damage does indeed come from injecting and from adulterants. Once again, we see how an important element of dominant social policy is based upon a hurtful myth—in this case, that heroin is organically harmful in and of itself.

The destructive impact of that myth forces us to reflect again on the irrational line between legal drugs, on the one hand, and illegal drugs, on the other. That line is a historical accident that bears little relation to science or reason. In the previous chapter, we looked at how sick people are harmed by the denial of drugs currently accepted as medicines. Here we look at the reverse side of this coin minted to support the drug war: the personal harm caused by the continued prohibition of hated drugs, especially heroin and marijuana, in the medical treatment of people acknowledged to be suffering from recognized diseases.

Let us start with heroin, the premier worldwide symbol of drug abuse, which is where my accidental involvement with drugs commenced in the early Seventies, when, full of drug innocence, I stumbled upon the prominence of heroin addiction in all major national crime-control strategy reports of the Nixon administration. My initial inquiries caused me a good deal of confusion. Heroin policy seemed to be based on half-truths and fears, not facts. Those distortions about heroin affected judgments, I started to see, about all illicit drugs. Eventually I came to agree with Edward Brecher, who declared in *Licit and Illicit Drugs* that until society understands and accepts the reasons for the failure of the massive drive against heroin, "it can hardly formulate sound laws and policies with respect to any drug." It finally dawned on me that unraveling the enigma of heroin would be like the discovery of a Rosetta Stone for the hidden language of drugs.

I decided to read everything ever written on heroin by medical researchers and other professionals and to speak to as many addicts, narcotics police, and treatment specialists as I possibly could. This simple chemical compound, I found, had been restricted to legitimate medical use only by the Harrison Narcotic Act of 1914. In 1924, prodded by public and professional hysteria, Congress passed a curious law that prohibited the importation of opium for the purpose of manufacturing heroin. The intent was to outlaw heroin, and, in fact, the legitimate use of the drug diminished greatly. Despite widespread beliefs to the contrary, however, heroin remained legal in American medicine until November 18, 1956, when it was totally outlawed.

My inquiry soon led from America to the United Kingdom because the calm English have always taken a different approach to this drug than we wide-eyed Americans. In 1974, I began organizing international seminars or institutes in England so as to provide a firsthand view of British heroin-addiction treatment methods, primarily for American professionals. During that first institute, while we were relaxing over a midday beer, a young physician in Welwyn Garden City, an hour's ride north of London, said matter-of-factly, "In the first hospital I worked in, we gave cancer patients a bottle of syrup containing heroin, gin, and cocaine, and we told them to take some when they felt pain." That remark provided an epiphany for me, a flash of insight, one of many I was to enjoy during the years that I have tried to understand this feared drug. My interest in heroin originally focused on how that drug affected heroin addicts and crime. Now I immediately understood that I would also have to understand how it affected cancer patients and pain. Moreover, I would have to understand how events had unfolded about both sets of issues in at least two countries, England and the United States.

HEROIN REFORM IN THE UNITED STATES

After many years of research and discussion with frontline participants in the heroin scene, I have yet to discover one sound scientific reason for banning its use in medicine for the treatment of the organically ill or the addicted. All of the reasons in support of the prohibition are in reality moral, political, ideological, or criminological. On those grounds also my argument has been that reason should support the use of heroin in medicine. I have made that appeal, based upon science and my view of the ethics of the matter, in print and in the electronic media throughout much of the Western world starting in the early Seventies. Others have joined, often independently and on their own initiative, in this legal-medical reform movement with the result that now there are campaigns in many countries to bring this dreaded drug, this symbol of degradation, back into legitimate medicine.

Heroin reform is becoming a respectable, even a popular, cause, an event seemingly impossible just a few years ago. To an extent, support for this reform has come in the form of a call for wholesale legalization of all drugs on the theory that the free market is the best regulator of all commodities, including addicting drugs. This position, which goes far beyond mine and thus gives me the delicious feeling of being a moderate today, has been expressed by such conservatives as economist Milton Friedman and columnist William Buckley. (When I first met Mr. Buckley, I was, therefore, able to throw out the clever thought that his new position had upset my equilibrium because, "for as long as I can remember, I knew that the sun would rise in the east, it would set in the west, and all the time, William Buckley would be on my right." He smiled indulgently.) Complete legalization is also the posture of many members of the Libertarian Party, a small but prestigious organization. Other public figures have come out for legalization primarily to take the profits, crime, and corruption out of drug sales. Such were the reasons expressed, for example, by both Hugh Downs and Barbara Walters when they recommended, "we should legalize everything" on the ABC television show "20/20" on March 14, 1985.

Reform focused on rehabiliting heroin alone has been spearheaded in the United States by the Committee on the Treatment of Intractable Pain, which I formed in 1977 with Judith Quattlebaum, a neighbor of mine at that time in Bethesda, Maryland. The committee has been concerned almost exclusively with making heroin available to cancer patients. Because my concerns were considerably broader, I soon left the committee to Ms. Quattlebaum's energetic leadership, but have remained a committed supporter of its good work. Within a few years the persistent lobbying efforts of the CTIP had produced an historical event, the first bill in modern times that proposed the reintroduction of heroin into legitimate medicine. Hearings were held in 1980 and 1984 by a committee of the House of Representatives.

The 1984 version of the bill was called the Compassionate Pain Relief Act, which would have made heroin available to cancer patients in hospitals under a four-year experimental program. Leadership on the bill was taken by Rep. Henry A. Waxman (D-Cal.), the feisty chairman of the Subcommittee on Health and the Environment. In working with congressional staff on this bill, I saw that the major issues had very little to do with science, as in past history. Accordingly, I prepared my testimony with crime and politics in mind. In that testimony at the hearing on March 8, 1984, I decided to place side by side, first, the highest amount of legal heroin that, I estimated, might be needed to treat all the cancer patients requiring it each year and, second, the lowest official estimate of the total amount of illicit heroin imported annually into this country. Those numbers were, first, 502 pounds of pure heroin and, second, 4.08 metric tons. Then I posited the worst-case scenario: assume all of the newly legal heroin were diverted and sold by criminals on the American black market. That diverted heroin would supply, at most, 5.6 percent of the illegal demand. Thus it would barely be noticed.

This argument had some impact on the subsequent debate and was repeated in various ingenious ways. For example, Rep. John Dingell (D-Mich.) declared on the floor of the House that the four tons of illegal heroin in the country each year were at least "the equivalent of two elephants in weight." The amount necessary under this bill for cancer patients was "the equivalent of a pimple on the posterior of one of those elephants."

In my testimony and in public statements I attempted to counter another obstacle put forth by the Reagan administration: heroin was no better than other currently legal medicines, in particular Dilaudid-HP. This concentrated form of Dilaudid was being touted by Health and Human Services medical experts and their professional allies as the new, safe, legal answer to the need for another high-potency narcotic for cancer pain. This was, I pointed out, simply a rerun of an old movie. In 1924, the representative of the American Medical Association had solemnly testified, in support of the opium-for-heroin ban, that heroin could easily be replaced by codeine. This alleged scientific fact from a high authority proved to be false. In 1980, the representative of the National Cancer Institute had solemnly testified, in opposition to the first version of this bill, that morphine acetate, a highly concentrated form of morphine, was a perfectly good substitute for heroin. And now it was Dilaudid-HP. While these were good drugs, they were not the same, obviously, as heroin. And each drug affects each person differently and individually.

When, moreover, I turned away from the historical record and asked an addict informant for an opinion, she pointed out that while she preferred heroin, her most common purchase on the streets at the time was Dilaudid. She offered to take me to at least four street corners, all within a few miles of the Capitol dome, where she often bought a "D"—a four-milligram standard pill of medicinally pure Dilaudid—for $35. She could buy the pills at that price because she has been purchasing them from the same reliable Washington street merchant for seven years. The regular price to the hundreds of customers who patronize those street sellers daily is usually $40–45. My adviser confidently predicted that when the more potent Dilaudid-HP was marketed, the pure pills would appear and be snapped up by eager buyers on the streets of Washington and other American cities.

No American government has demonstrated the ability to stop the illict use of powerful narcotics by so-called street addicts. Street addicts, I argued, were not the issue in this debate. That issue was how this society should deal with the 5 to 10 percent of terminal cancer patients whose final agonies are not eased by conventional drugs. I insisted time and time again that I could find no scientific justification for sentencing 20,000 to 40,000 Americans annually to a painful death without even the possibility of relief from this very effective painkiller.

When I had finished my testimony before the committee, Congressman Waxman picked up that theme and put two pointed questions to the other members of the panel appearing with me, all nationally recognized medical experts on the treatment of cancer pain: "Is heroin a safe and effective analgesic for the treatment of severe pain due to cancer? And do you believe the American medical profession is capable of administering this drug safely?" All three doctors, including two appearing in opposition to the bill, answered in the affirmative to both questions. One of these two, the distinguished pharmacologist Raymond Houde of the Sloan-Kettering Cancer Center, added, "If heroin were not banned, I would probably use it, too."

Despite this apparent endorsement, these doctors, like virtually all of organized medicine in America, opposed this humane bill for a whole variety of other reasons, the most powerful seeming to be fear of diversion into criminal hands. The AMA representative, Dr. Kathleen Foley of Sloan-Kettering, also objected to the extra attention being given to heroin, claiming that the proponents were misleading the public, particularly cancer patients, by hailing the drug as a panacea. Dr. Foley, moreover, argued against the ease with which heroin would be approved and made available to doctors under this "extraordinary legislation."

At this point in the hearing, I confess that I had become truly fed up with the demeaning attacks being made repeatedly on the proponents of the bill by Dr. Foley, who was sitting next to me at the witness table. I grabbed the microphone we shared and shot back, "I know of no misleading of the public by any of the groups supporting this bill. I think they have indicated that it is not a panacea and that it is a small part of the picture [of cancer pain control], but it is an important part of the picture. I think it would be unfortunate to suggest that this is an extraordinary piece of legislation. It was extraordinary that in 1924 we demonized a perfectly good medicine. I think this should be viewed as an ordinary bill returning us to a level of sanity."*

However, irrational fears, especially of diversion and pharmacy robberies, demanded that the chemical demonology continue. The National Federation of Parents for Drug Free Youth was quoted during the floor debate later in 1984 as warning, "to falsely legitimize heroin sends the wrong message about this devastating and illegal drug to our youth." Rep. Hamilton Fish, Jr. (R-N.Y.) proclaimed, "This bill will send a signal to the youth of this nation that 'heroin is ok.' "

Rep. Charles Rangel (D-N.Y.) fought against the proposed law during the debate with great passion, seeing the bill as the entering wedge for wholesale repeal of all the drug laws, the grand design of those who believed that enforcement had collapsed and was impossible to implement. Mr. Rangel claimed that behind this bill were a lot of people who would soon openly advocate that "we just start legalizing the entire illicit drug manufacturing and transactions in the United States," a movement that had to be stopped at this legislative pass.

---

* Dr. Foley is a caring doctor and a committed pain researcher. Our emotional interchange illustrates how there can be heated, honest disagreement over these issues of life, death, and human suffering. The doctor is also a courageous professional reformer in her own way. In 1986, Dr. Foley and Dr. Russell Portnoy of Sloan-Kettering published a seminal article in the professional journal *PAIN* reporting on an experiment with 38 patients. Among its radical conclusions: opiate maintenance of patients with chronic pain, not involving a terminal illness, was appropriate over the long term. The drugs were powerful narcotics currently available in American medicine. While some doctors and laymen alike may ask "so what?" the report was a breakthrough for American medicine, and the application of its recommendations would have saved Dr. Rose and many other doctors and patients much agony.

The Reagan administration launched a fierce battle to defeat the bill, using all of these arguments. It promoted a lobbying campaign by Department of Health and Human Services regional offices around the country, which, according to Congressman Dingell, was not only immoral but also illegal under statutes prohibiting the use of government funds for lobbying. In one form letter it had prepared, that department, which allegedly contains the best medical and scientific brains in the world, fairly screamed to that world, "This bill, in essence, legalizes heroin!!"

On September 18, 1984, I saw the bill go down to a decisive defeat in the House of Representatives, 355 to 55, but not before the most far-reaching and revealing congressional floor debate in recent American history on the ideological foundations of national drug policy. A dozen or so of his colleagues later came quietly, shamefacedly, up to Henry Waxman and confessed that no, they did not doubt the medical value of heroin, and, no, they did not worry about the small amount that might be diverted to the street. "They explained to me that with the November election coming up, a vote for the bill would allow their opponents to brand them 'heroin pushers,' " Congressman Waxman said.

On September 21, Harvey Elton Larsen, a 70-year-old cancer sufferer from the Eastern Shore of Maryland, wrote to thank me for my open support of the pain-relief bill. "I sort of feel that my death will be by cancer. . . . All should die with some dignity and if relief of pain can be done, it should be done, regardless of the drug utilized," he said. Then this sick old man added a very perceptive observation: "You must know that in some cases, it is being done. You certainly must know that some terminal patients are given heroin, legal or not."

At least I know of the stories, none of which I have been able to prove or disprove: The New York doctor who bought illegal heroin for his mother dying of cancer because the legal medicines he prescribed did not relieve her agony. The doctor who told the sons of another lady in her last painful days from cancer that they should cop some heroin on the streets of the Los Angeles *barrio* because the drugs he had given her did not work. I know also that many other people have threatened to do the same if the need arises. Whether or not the stories or the threats are actually true, they are consistent with one another and comport with my view of how I might behave in a similar situation.

There is no doubt of a broader, more optimistic reality. A historic shift has begun in American public opinion toward heroin and pain. In late 1984, *Common Cause* magazine summarized the major arguments put forth by advocates on all sides regarding the issue and asked its readers, most of whom are admittedly quite liberal, to send in a ballot. Eighty-six percent of those who responded came out in favor of allowing doctors to prescribe heroin to terminal cancer patients.

Clearly, the movement to bring heroin back into American medicine is not dead. Congressman Waxman has reintroduced the bill in the House and Daniel Inouye of Hawaii, a longtime advocate, has done the same in the Senate. All of the many American supporters in Washington and around the country will find a good deal of encouragement in the actions of some foreign medical associations and governments. They have listened to all of the arguments put forth on both sides of the American debate and come out for exactly the opposite course of action than that taken in this country.

In February 1979 the Australian Medical Association, for example, called for the lifting of the legal ban on the use of heroin for sick people in extreme pain, explaining that "to deny even a small number of patients a drug that may make their last days more bearable is not justified as a means of controlling drug abuse." In March 1985 the Human Rights Commission, an agency of the Australian government, formally recommended that all terminally ill patients, suffering not only from cancer but also other painful organic diseases, be provided heroin both inside and outside of the hospital. The commission based its recommendations in part on the novel grounds that international covenants on human rights might well be interpreted to mean that terminally ill patients should be considered "disabled persons" with a right to privacy, which could mandate that such patients have the privilege of choosing the painkilling medication that would best maintain their dignity during a time of severe pain and depression.

In its review of the medical evidence on the value of heroin, the commission adopted many of the conclusions of *The Heroin Solution*, including that which stated: "No scientific justification exists for continuing legal prohibition of the use of heroin in the treatment of the organically ill and the injured. Indeed, each patient in pain should be eligible to receive the drug in order to determine whether it provides particular benefits for him or her at that time."

THE SURPRISING
CANADIANS

To my pleasant surprise, Canadians have taken some of the most far-reaching steps of any people in recent history toward more humane and more rational heroin policies. My surprise is based upon several recent trips to that country, and discussions with addicts, doctors, officials, and lawyers, many of whom were affiliated with the anti-prohibition Concerned Citizens Drug Study and Educational Society of Vancouver. They told me that addicts often were brutalized by the police without regard to any civilizing legal restraint. They and their families lived in constant fear. In one 1980 case, members of the Royal Canadian Mounted Police testified during a coroner's hearing that they had grabbed British Columbia heroin addict Dennis John Williams by the throat and had been holding him, in the words of one of the famed Mounties, "as hard as I could." This was a "common occurrence" and "standard operating procedure" in order to conduct a "mouth search" for drugs often stashed there. In this standard case, as it happened, the subject of the search choked on the package in his mouth and died.

Coroner D. J. Jack had instructed the jury, "It's a war between certain elements of society and law enforcement. . . . The men involved from a police point of view . . . have to act with severity in combating this business. Draconian measures . . . [are] obviously a must." The jury took 25 minutes to return a verdict of accidental death regarding Mr. Williams, who had not survived this standard operating procedure.

Every level of the Canadian judiciary, up to the supreme court of the country, approves harsh approaches to drug users and addicts. Accordingly, I had concluded that the frontier roughness and puritanical attitude of Canadian officials had created a vision of the American system gone mad. My conclusions were supported by leading Canadian academic drug experts, such as Drs. Barry Beyerstein and Bruce Alexander of Simon Fraser University.

It did not seem possible that out of this harsh martial mentality could come a direct frontal assault on the basic ideology of the drug war. I was wrong and, as I said, surprised. Some of the most prominent leaders of recent reform efforts have been doctors, who have fought the drug-war mentality with appropriate frontier vigor and almost religious zeal. In 1979, Dr. Kenneth Walker of Toronto commenced a relentless campaign to bring back heroin for cancer patients. He founded the W. Gifford-Jones Foundation and published a syndicated column, "The Doctor Game," under the same pseudonym. In the column and in paid advertisements, he pushed his cause so well that soon he had much political and financial support from Canada's citizens. Dr. Walker gathered 30,000 signatures on a petition which he presented to the government in 1982. At the same time, 20,000 letters of support flooded government offices. One young girl wrote, "I'm sending this letter for my dead father. He suffered indescribable agony when morphine no longer worked." Major Canadian newspapers editorialized repeatedly in support of bringing heroin back, as had leading U.S. papers. In May 1983, health and welfare minister Monique Begin announced that clinical trials would be held comparing heroin to Dilaudid.

Meanwhile, the Canadian Medical Association had been investigating the situation. Another forceful reformer, Dr. William Ghent of Kingston, Ontario, led the CMA Council on Health Care in a three-year examination of the historical record. The authoritative report revealed how politics and deception had permeated the Canadian decision in 1954 to ban heroin totally in medicine, a submission to U.S. pressure in international health and narcotics organizations, including the World Health Organization. When, in the early Fifties, the CMA had been asked its opinion on the worldwide U.S. campaign, that body had responded that it opposed prohibition because heroin was better than morphine in some cases and also because the U.S. experience had demonstrated that absolute prohibition had not controlled street abuse. When the matter came up in the House of Commons on June 1, 1954, government ministers misled the entire legislature by giving the impression that the organized physicians of the country supported prohibition. One official stated on the floor of the House, "We discussed it with the Canadian Medical Association," but never mentioned the fact that the CMA advice had been against prohibition.

"Thus, with a degree of duplicity, . . . this useful drug was now criminalized and Canada joined the W.H.O., who had been persuaded by the United States that if all heroin was illegal, prosecution for possession would be easier and full worldwide control could be obtained and heroin addiction eliminated," stated the report of the Council on Health Care in 1984. The council recommended that heroin be licensed again immediately for medicine. In presenting a resolution to that effect to the annual meeting of the CMA in August 1984, Dr. Ghent observed, "We followed the U.S. like sheep and now, like sheep, we've got their manure to deal with." That fecal matter included, he explained, innocent patients in pain, a rising number of addicts, a criminal and corrupt black market, and many Canadian youth, who, far from being protected, were being enticed by the deviance of the heroin scene.

The debate at the CMA meeting focused primarily on the need to reverse the mistaken political decision of thirty years earlier so that addicts could be treated like sick people and not criminals. There was widespread support for that proposition because those doctors had concluded, as I have argued for years, that the fates of heroin addicts and cancer sufferers are inextricably intertwined when social policy is being decided. However, the resolution finally approved by the doctors of Canada was restricted to the need to approve heroin for treating pain. That overwhelming and historic vote on August 21, 1984, was soon followed by even more historic action by the Canadian government itself.

That government became the first of any Western democracy in modern history to take formal action in defiance of the American-led ban on a hated drug such as heroin in medicine. On December 20, 1984, the new conservative health and welfare minister, Jake Epp, announced in the House of Commons in Ottawa that heroin would soon be available to treat severe chronic pain whether due to cancer or another ailment. On September 19, 1986, the official *Canada Gazette* included four simple pages that contained an amendment that brought heroin formally back into medicine and set out the new regulations for its control. I later had a happy conversation about the historic event with Dr. Bill Ghent, who told me that he had already prescribed the medicine to a few patients, including one elderly lady whose pain was eased by a small amount of the drug taken infrequently. It was not a dramatic case. Indeed, it was a rather ordinary incident. But before the reform, the lady might have suffered more than was necessary.

The related issue of allowing heroin for treating heroin addiction has not yet been dealt with in Canada, although it was clear that the Canadians were thinking about it and were now also looking for guidance on that issue across the Atlantic rather than to their powerful southern neighbor, as they had done too often on drug matters in previous decades.

HEROIN IN BRITAIN: THE MYTHS PERSIST

Heroin in the United Kingdom has always been a subject of great controversy, even in regard to the most fundamental facts. American drug-abuse officials over the decades have consistently misstated those basic facts, not only about heroin but about the entire drug situation in England. They have often been aided in their deception by leading electronic and print journalists—and even worse, by leading scholars—who seem to take the official distortions at face value. During his 32-year reign as director of the Federal Bureau of Narcotics, Harry Anslinger sometimes had to argue down critics who opposed harsh law enforcement as the dominant American approach to drug issues and who proposed adopting elements of the more gentle British system. Director Anslinger often replied that "the British system is the same as the United States system," and, besides, the so-called British system of decriminalization of drugs has failed. Both statements have always been untrue.

Bureaucratic descendants of Mr. Anslinger have uttered pronouncements of the same doubtful veracity. In November 1984, then DEA administrator Francis M. Mullen, Jr., said he opposed the use of marijuana for medical purposes, adding the confusing thought that "decriminalization of drugs has been tried in a number of countries, England being one, and they now are aware that it has not worked." In November 1985, Mr. Mullen's successor, John Lawn, said in my presence to a seminar of journalists that marijuana, being much worse than alcohol, deserved to be kept illegal—and then immediately added the even more confusing thoughts (confusing to me, at least) that (1) "Great Britain tried heroin use for cancer patients and found it to be a failure"; and (2) the recent action of Canada allowing heroin for cancer patients had "the potential for a big problem. . . . I think it's a mistake."

Another major Big Confusion today, which I have heard in

allegedly factual news stories on major television networks and from scholars, is that the British now have a heroin epidemic that was caused by their curious custom of allowing doctors to give addicts virtually all of the heroin they wanted. The British, the story continues, have come to their senses and have moved almost fully in the American direction of control.

It is difficult to straighten out the strands of half-truth and full-lie contained in these various confusing accounts, but here is a summary of the actual situation in that island kingdom. Marijuana barely figures in this discussion of the current British scene because it has been illegal for decades, has been decriminalized in no part of the U.K., and is rarely used in medicine. There is little discussion or conflict in that country about the use of marijuana in medicine.

Nor is there any conflict about the use of heroin, or any other powerful narcotic, by doctors in the treatment of the organically ill. It is, accordingly, a simple falsehood for DEA administrator John Lawn, perhaps the leading drug-enforcement officer in the world, to state publicly that the U.K. has concluded that the use of heroin *for cancer sufferers* has failed or even that any serious questions are being raised about its use for that purpose. The truth is just the opposite.

Approximately 95 percent of all the licit heroin used in the world within recent history has been prescribed by British doctors, primarily for cancer sufferers. Official reports reveal that total annual legal consumption of heroin in all types of cases, usually organically ill and not addicted patients, has been rising consistently in the U.K., from 41 kilograms (90.2 pounds) in 1971 to 228 kilograms (501.6 pounds) of the pure drug in 1985.

It *is* true, however, that many physicians have decided to cut down on the prescription of heroin for the quite legal purpose of the medical maintenance of addicts. In 1969, the first full year in which some new restrictions were in effect on the power of most doctors to prescribe to addicts, 1,466 addicts were receiving maintenance doses of narcotics at year's end, of whom 34 percent were prescribed heroin alone or in combination with other drugs. By the end of 1985, only 2 percent, 140 addicts out of a total of 7,052 receiving narcotics, were being prescribed heroin. Along with reductions in heroin prescriptions came similar reductions in prescriptions of all injectables for addicts, especially methadone, which most British addicts preferred to receive from their friendly local chemists in ampules along with clean needles, a shocking and illegal practice in America. Soon British experts began to view that practice in the same light. Oral methadone became the preferred prescription of British drug clinic doctors. Some of the most ignored victims of the American drug war have been British addicts and their families, who have been personally affected by the importing of rigid attitudes toward treatment.

It was during this period—the mid-Seventies to the mid-Eighties—that there was a rise in crime by addicts and in the black market for drugs, and in concomitant cries by British leaders that the country had to get tougher with these deviants and adopt more American drug-war methods. What never seemed to dawn on opinion leaders—and on physicians and scholars—in both countries was that *the rise in addict crime and the drug black market took place in the wake of a tougher prescribing policy toward addicts regarding heroin and all narcotics*. I do not mean to say that the tougher policies directly caused the rise in addiction and crime because I have never claimed to understand mass swings in drug use. During this period, I also saw, while on frequent visits to the country, the suffering imposed on the society by economic malaise, massive unemployment, immigration from countries like Iran with a history of high opiate use, and the spillover of supplies from the huge American market. Whatever the causes, it is highly likely that addict crime and black market violence will continue to be incited somewhat by the new British habit of seeking to impose American martial methods on a troubling but still relatively peaceful drug scene.

Even with a modicum of American methods in place, the current English drug system remains a marvel of gentleness as compared to the American and to almost any other on the face of the earth. With all of its current defects, which I have pointed out repeatedly in print and in the electronic media of the U.K., it would be marvelous to see it implemented in America. Any doctor in England has the power to decide which drugs patients should receive. If the patient is organically ill, the police tend to keep a decent distance and almost never bother either doctor or patient, no matter what drugs are being prescribed. Even if the patient is addicted to one of a wide variety of powerful narcotics, any doctor in England has the power to prescribe the drug of addiction for long-term maintenance so long as the physician keeps accurate records and notifies the Home Office when a new addict is encountered.

However, in regard to three drugs—heroin, cocaine, and dipipanone, the last a powerful narcotic known as Diconal, suddenly popular with British addicts—a special license must be obtained from the Home Office by a doctor who wishes to prescribe them to addicts for the purpose of maintenance. Approximately 100 doctors now hold such licenses, most of whom exercise the power only rarely. Yet any one of those doctors may do so at any time. On the basis of independent clinical judgments, licensed British doctors decided to reduce heroin prescribing to addicts without being required to do so by law, and they may resume without interference by the police.

In short, so long as a British doctor follows relatively nonintrusive regulations, there are no restrictions on the dosage or the form of prescriptions for addicts. For example, any doctor, even one in general practice and without a special license, could prescribe to any addict injectable morphine, methadone, or Darvon, which could land any American doctor in prison, along with the patient. This is not to say there is no risk of prison or professional censure for doctors who deal with addicts. There is, but it is a minimal risk. It rises somewhat in cases where the doctor, working outside the National Health Service, is "private" and thus charges fees—and especially where a patient of such a doctor has been caught selling some of his prescribed drugs. Such events now disturb even the calm British.

Another feature of the British drug situation which disturbs many people there is that the number of drug abusers is rising throughout the country. Pundits claim that this problem also has been caused by the failure of the old indulgent British system. However, not only has the apparent rise taken place during a decade of hardening hearts but also no expert in England can tell why there has been a rise, a weakness all of us alleged experts share, if we are honest about it. Moreover, there is no certainty about the actual amount of the rise in drug abusers hidden out there in British society. All we know for certain is that there has been a significant increase in the number of addicts in treatment, that is, receiving a prescription for legal drug maintenance, a figure which, as I said, was reported to be 7,052 at the end of 1985 by the Home Office Drugs Branch. Moreover, the latest expert guess is that there may be 30,000–35,000 addicts or regular users of

narcotics in all of English society, a low number when compared
to America and other countries.*

Even if that guess is true, many English experts agree that
relatively few of them, unlike their American cousins, engage in
serious crime. For example, it is a rare event, indeed, for the
British police to arrest an armed addict-robber. In the great majority of cases, the British have accomplished the stunning feat in
this modern world of separating the status of being a narcotic addict
from the status of being a violent or predatory criminal.

If the current British drug-control system, warts and all, were
applied in America, there is the good possibility that the poor addict
in the Harlem tenement would be eligible for a warm bed and
injectable drugs on a number of grounds. First, since he was clearly
organically ill and visibly so, his doctors might have been allowed
to prescribe drugs for him, perhaps even heroin in a hospital,
without fear of being arrested by the police or defrocked by medical
societies. Second, since he was addicted, any doctor could prescribe
any drug, except heroin, cocaine, and dipipanone, for maintenance.
This would include Dilaudid or Darvon, and any drug in between.
A specially licensed doctor could also prescribe those three restricted drugs for maintenance.

Not only would that Harlem addict have been treated more
humanely, so also would Dolores Koppinger, Harvey Rose and all
his demeaned patients, Milton Polansky, and Kenny Freeman. All
of these sick people would suddenly have the option of being treated
as ordinary patients, with dignity and kindness. It is likely that
more addicts, including some of those who infest our streets, might
decide to accept those humane options if they were offered and to
treat the rest of us better for having offered them. If addicts were
being treated more humanely, so also would multitudes of patients,

* I am reluctant to push such comparisons too far because the items compared involve
such murky data. Some estimates talk of all "narcotic" addicts rather than only "heroin"
addicts. Since heroin is only one of the narcotics addicts often use, the comparisons become
quite imprecise. More imprecision is found in the fact that few people are willing to reveal
their bad habits to researchers and government officials. Thus, the estimates are based on
guesses about hidden activities. For what it is worth, however, official estimates state that
there are perhaps 500,000 heroin addicts in the United States out of a population of
238,900,000—209 per 100,000 of population. This is over three times the English rate of 62
per 100,000, based on 35,000 addicts and a total population of 56,400,000. I have made other
calculations over the years that have produced vastly higher rates of addiction in the United
States as compared to England. I have confidence in the precision of none of these calculations by me or anyone else—and believe that all we know with certainty is that the
addiction problem is much worse in America than in England.

numbering perhaps in the millions, *suspected* of being addicts or potential addicts. And the momentum for this vast reform movement in the United States could commence with the medicalization of heroin, that simple chemical compound first stumbled on by an obscure English chemist in 1874.

MARIJUANA IS MEDICINE

Humane advances would also occur if another feared drug, marijuana, were to be made available to treat organically ill patients who might benefit from its therapeutic effects under the care of a doctor. As in the case of heroin, there is no scientific basis for the ban on marijuana in medicine, only politics and fear.

Most of the public debate on marijuana deals with the wisdom of banning its recreational use by perfectly healthy people who choose to use the drug as an intoxicant. While the ban on recreational use makes little sense, the ban on medical use makes less. It creates needless victims of sick people whose pain and suffering might be eased by this venerable medicine. Starting at least as early as 2737 B.C., references have been made to hemp or cannabis as a therapeutic agent to treat a wide variety of illnesses, including nausea, convulsions, dysentery, malaria, cholera, dizziness, and the pain of childbirth, among many others. Modern medical research has sharpened knowledge about the precise impact of the drug in medicine and has confirmed some of the historical confidence of primitive healers.

That massive body of scientific research documents medical uses that rarely get discussed even in arcane professional journals. In 1973, Tod H. Mikuriya, M.D., produced a compendium of some of that research, *Marijuana: Medical Papers*. For example, Dr. Van M. Sim reported in 1971 after a major study, "Marijuana . . . is probably the most potent anti-epileptic known to medicine today." His conclusions were based in part on an earlier experiment that demonstrated that a substance related to THC, the major active ingredient in marijuana, controlled epileptic seizures in a group of children under study more effectively than did Dilantin, a commonly used and often beneficial anti-convulsive agent. However, the parents of epileptic children are rarely made aware of the medical value of pot primarily because the leading medical experts of the country have themselves been emotionally affected by the hysteria of the drug war. As in the case of heroin, the known and potential therapeutic benefits of marijuana are ignored by most medical scientists so that they cannot be accused of giving a wrong message to youth seeking an illegal high. It is a shameful story.

Even more shameful is the current record of the anti-marijuana crusaders, including a few in the White House, who continue to hound those who support the return of marijuana to medicine. Such reformers are consistently accused of simply using the medical argument as a cheap gimmick to slip pot to our schoolchildren—and sometimes of being marijuana addicts whose judgment is clouded with fumes of the deadly drug. I have personally observed such tactics directed against me and my colleagues. As a result of this type of irrational and harmful behavior, Americans who become organically ill are rarely informed, either by their doctors or by their government, that this medicine might ease their suffering.

Because mass social irrationality has been reflected for decades in government grants for scientific studies, almost all marijuana research funds have been devoted to the harm caused by the drug and how best to control it. Some years ago, for example, California police agencies were seeking to determine if they could discover pot-affected drivers by looking for dilation of their pupils, which would thus provide a legal basis for arrest. They asked a medical scientist to study this matter. In the course of his study, Dr. Robert Hepler, a neuro-ophthalmologist at the Jules Stein Eye Institute, University of California at Los Angeles, stumbled upon another important finding: cannabis lowers intraocular pressure and thus might well be important in the treatment of glaucoma, a dread disease that impairs vision and causes blindness in many people. Those unexpected though highly significant research results were reported by Dr. Hepler in the *Journal of the American Medical Association* in 1971. They were also duly noted in the collection of essays published by Dr. Mikuriya two years later.

ROBERT RANDALL: FIGHTING BLINDNESS IN AMERICA

When he started to lose his sight in the early Seventies, none of his doctors told Robert C. Randall about that article or about the vast body of scientific research indicating that there was a medicine that might help to stave off his impending blindness. That made him angry. What made him furious, and keeps his righteous outrage smouldering to this day, is the knowledge that government drug-abuse experts knew—*they knew !*—and they acted as if they had no responsibility to tell the millions of American glaucoma sufferers, many of whom were slowly going blind. At this point in his tale, the mild-mannered fellow becomes a steel-cold furious street fighter.

Mr. Randall starts telling his story, though, in the measured tones that reflect his education, a B.S. in political science and speech and an M.A. in rhetoric. In 1970, at the age of 22, he developed tension and what optometrists told him was "eyestrain" while writing a long research paper at the University of South Florida in Tampa. Sometimes he smoked a marijuana cigarette and on those occasions noticed that he was more relaxed and did not suffer so much from the eyestrain. He moved to Washington, D.C., in 1971 where he hoped to get a job as a political speechwriter. For a year and a half, as it happened, he smoked very little marijuana. In 1972, he noticed that he could not read a page with one eye because the print seemed shattered; it simply would not come into proper focus. He went to an ophthalmologist, who told him that the pressures in his eyes were double the normal level, that he had glaucoma, that the damage was 85 percent in both eyes already and that he was virtually blind in his right eye, and that he could expect to go totally blind in three to five years. On the day he received that news, Bob Randall was an otherwise healthy young man of 24.

He commenced studying his disease and eventually learned a great deal about it. Glaucoma is characterized by high levels of pressure inside the eyeball due to an impediment of the normal outflow of fluids within the body. All treatments, both through surgery and drugs, seek to lower that intraocular pressure by opening the blocked exit canal of the eye. None of these treatments constitutes a cure and the best medical science offers the victims of this disease is a holding action, the staving off of progressive blindness. A variety of drugs and medicines are used to carry out that holding action. What often happens is that they are tried by the physicians in series or relays. A patient will take several at once, develop tolerance to one, which will be diminished or eliminated, then have others prescribed in its place; then a new mixture is tried. Some patients try four or more drugs at once.

In many patients, the lack of control on the original disease is complicated by the side effects of the prescribed medicines. It took young Bob Randall a long time to learn about those harmful effects, which were often not fully explained by his doctors. He ended up doing research on the subject in medical libraries. The effects he discovered in the literature distressed him almost as much as the original diagnosis. Some of those medicines commonly used in glaucoma treatment, he found, could cause cataracts, retinal detachment, and death through respiratory, cardiac, or renal failure.

To add to his predicament, Bob discovered that most patients run through a number of drugs without exhausting the list of possibilities or suffering the worst side reactions because the great majority of patients are elderly when the disease is first diagnosed. Death, in effect, saves those older sufferers from having to face up to all of the complications of their medicines. In young patients, the disease often progresses toward blindness with fierce speed and as drugs are tried aggressively to retard the onslaught, the dangers of serious adverse drug reactions increase. To a young person like Bob Randall, then, glaucoma poses the danger of the rapid onset of blindness from the disease itself as well as further injury and even death from the standard medicines prescribed by doctors.

Of course, the many caring and competent doctors in the field felt the frustrations and tragedies of their patients. Those physicians knew that they were constantly balancing off the imponderables of nature and chemicals in the face of a relentless disease.

Bob Randall speaks fondly of the Washington doctor who discovered his disease and undertook his care initially. That doctor gave him a drug called pilocarpine. The young patient soon discovered that this standard medicine was "almost blinding" while it worked to prevent permanent blindness. Because he believed it to be a good medicine, and still does, Mr. Randall kept taking the drug, "but for about a year and a half, I lived, literally, almost blind." When pilocarpine proved inadequate, he was placed on a number of other drugs that did not cause additional, temporary blindness, but they had other side effects and dangers. "I was placed on all of the medications that were available at the time. They failed to work."

In the fall of 1973, at a time when he was seeing halos—a symptom of uncontrolled elevated pressure—and when his ability to see fluctuated daily, a friend gave him some marijuana to smoke. He went from the halos and haze "to clear vision, in 45 minutes." Mr. Randall was alone making an attempt to watch television and he suddenly realized, "Gosh, I can see well!" Then it clicked: "Marijuana's doing it; remember, in college, you used to smoke marijuana for eyestrain." The next morning, he began doubting the truth, and he then vacillated back and forth for months, now accepting the reality of the improvement and then doubting it. His resistance was based in part on his belief that marijuana was not a medicine at all but simply a social drug. How in the world could pot, a plaything, help him stave off blindness, a fate that all of medical science could not prevent? Then his marijuana supply ran out and with it his ability to see better. Randall found a new supply and soon his sight improved, again. He was convinced.

By late 1974, patient Robert Randall of the nation's capital city was regularly taking three standard prescribed glaucoma medicines plus his own prescription for three to five marijuana joints a day, which he smoked once every four hours. When he got high, he would stop smoking, since that seemed to indicate he had taken enough of his medicine. "My doctor was delighted because my eye pressure was suddenly under control for the first time since I'd been in treatment!" Yet he decided not to tell his doctor about his auxiliary treatment for fear of the legal and ethical complications this might present to the physician. (Despite falsehoods promulgated by anti-marijuana crusaders, Robert Randall has never stated that he saw marijuana as a cure or as the only medicine he needed to control his disease; on the contrary, he has always believed that he needed conventional medications as well. And he has always taken that position openly.)

To insure a continued quality supply of his new medicine he grew four marijuana plants on the sundeck of his apartment, which happened to be right across the street from the U.S. Marine barracks in southeast Washington, eight blocks from the Capitol. Everything in his life seemed to be settling down and he happily went away on vacation with his apartment mate, Alice O'Leary. During his absence, the police happened to see his plants, searched his apartment on the basis of a warrant, seized his plants, and left a surprisingly polite note suggesting he come down and turn himself in for arrest. "And so I came home from vacation and there was no marijuana to use. I immediately began having pressure problems."

Also, of course, he now had legal problems, since he had complied with the polite request and had turned himself in to be arrested for possession of marijuana. Instead of taking the advice of friends and simply pleading guilty and probably paying a fine, Bob and Alice decided to fight the case on grounds of medical necessity and hired local lawyer John Karr. The attorney said that his client had an interesting argument to use in his defense but that Mr. Randall would have to prove it first to him because "I'm not going to argue a looney case." Bob was thus faced with the urgent necessity of performing more in-depth research on the medical value of marijuana.

His search soon led to the NORML office, and he was pleasantly surprised that the founder and director, Keith Stroup, saw him immediately. Mr. Stroup told Mr. Randall of a suit by NORML in 1972 seeking to reclassify marijuana within the 1970 omnibus federal drug law, in which the Nixon administration had classified it in Schedule I, along with heroin, LSD, and other powerful drugs deemed so dangerous as to be unsafe for use in American medicine. NORML had been attempting for years to convince the government to come to its senses on this limited issue, and at least put marijuana into Schedule II, where it could be used in medicine but under tight controls; the government had been resisting this seemingly modest move bitterly—and has until this day in the late Eighties. Keith Stroup also gave him copies of articles supporting the proven value of marijuana in medicine, along with the names of federal drug officials.

IT'S REAL GOOD YOU'RE USING MARIJUANA

"I called five bureaucrats. . . . I said, 'Hi, my name is Bob Randall, and I am a glaucoma patient and I've just been arrested for marijuana.' Three of the people, two from the National Institute on Drug Abuse and one from the Food and Drug Administration, immediately said words like, 'Oh, it's real good that you're using marijuana, because we have lots of evidence which shows marijuana is effective in the treatment of glaucoma.' " Robert Randall now had two reasons to feel enraged and less secure about his life in this society. The first had been the arrest for possessing marijuana for his own use. While arrests for personal use of marijuana may seem trivial to some observers, they constitute the bulk of all drug arrests, now at least 400,000 every year, and are often traumatic and damaging. The second was the sudden knowledge that his government was, as a matter of high policy, deliberately withholding from him, a good citizen, a medicine that just might prevent him from going blind.

"I was already enraged that I had been arrested. . . . That made me feel insecure. . . . And when someone arrests you for something as meaningless as marijuana, you know they can get you for any reason. . . . It doesn't have to be rational. It doesn't have to relate to the facts," Bob Randall explained. And then there were all those other glaucoma victims sitting out there in society. (Eventually, Randall learned that there are at least two million glaucoma sufferers, that approximately 250,000 have serious sight impairment already, and that 75,000 are actually blind. Approximately 7,500 go blind every year from the disease owing to, in the opinion of government experts in the National Eye Institute, "inadequate medical therapies and surgical techniques." Perhaps 200,000 to 400,000 patients face the possibility of painful surgery to improve their condition. These patients seem to be prime candidates for trying a new medicine such as marijuana.)

It was at this point, in the year 1975, that this young man, originally from Sarasota, Florida, where his father owned a furniture store, and with no education in law or medicine, began to become one of the single most effective reformers of drug-control practices in modern American history. He faced the entire federal drug-abuse control establishment head on and beat it to its knees. Of course, he had a lot of help. But the story of Bob Randall must be seen in part as proof that one person can make a difference in the history of nations.

Even pleading the defense of medical necessity, which evolved out of old English common law, in a criminal case takes a good deal of courage. Few lawyers would even consider mentioning it because throughout the history of Anglo-American law it has so rarely worked. Its essence is that while the accused admittedly committed the act which ordinarily would be considered a crime, and was sane at the time, that should be excused because the actor was seeking to avoid an even greater evil. That may sound simple enough but if judges often allowed the defense, much of the criminal law could be eviscerated. One rare example of the successful use of the defense concerned a New Hampshire parent at the turn of the century who withdrew a child from school for health reasons and was deemed not guilty of violating a New Hampshire compulsory school attendance law. Bob Randall had to prove that he was going blind, that marijuana was not merely helpful but critical to prevent that event, that his violation of the drug law was an infinitely smaller evil than his going blind, and that this was one of those rare cases in which both the society and the law would benefit from the granting of the exception. This was a formidable and pioneering undertaking.

He contacted a number of medical research centers and underwent a variety of tests. His most significant medical adventure involved thirteen days of controlled experiments in 1975 under the direction of none other than Dr. Robert Hepler at UCLA, who was continuing his experiments on the effect of marijuana on eye pressure. Dr. Hepler had already expanded his data base to over 400 subjects. Marijuana provided by the doctor in the form of THC pills—generally favored by the medical establishment because they seem more like medicine and avoid problems of smoking—had no effect on subject Randall's eye pressure. Next, a single smoked joint had no measurable results. Both doctor and subject were confused.

"Finally, I said, 'Put me in a room, give me marijuana, and leave me alone,'" Bob Randall explained to me during an interview. After seven joints, enough perhaps to make an entire fraternity float off the ground, Bob Randall was high, but his pressure was down to normal. At every step, he had been using conventional medications as well. Thus the doctor and the patient had powerful proof of marijuana's value. For Randall, THC alone was not a sufficient additive to the mix of medications. That substance was different in some unknown way from a marijuana cigarette containing hundreds of other ingredients that, all together, must have accounted for the impact on his eye pressure. Based on the objective data developed during the tests, Dr. Hepler provided an historic affidavit to the effect that smoked marijuana definitely helped this subject's eye pressure and was the *only* remaining medical means which might stave off the progression of his disease toward blindness.

Bob Randall gained something else at UCLA: the knowledge that for years the federal government had been growing legal pot for experiments, such as Dr. Hepler's, at its farm in Mississippi. After discussion with his lawyer, John Karr, he decided to confront his government directly and to ask for legal access to the finished product of that unique southern plantation. He petitioned the DEA on May 20, 1976, for access to government supplies of marijuana for use as medicine that would help prevent him from going blind. DEA officials ignored him, and it was then that Bob Randall started his unremitting press campaign by going to reporters. He wanted the publicity not only to help himself and other glaucoma victims, but also to help cancer sufferers, because he had found that many of them were able to endure chemotherapy without vomiting by using marijuana. Not only that: he also found that many cancer patients actually got the well-known "munchies" from pot and thus regained their appetites for food, a wondrous event for so many people who recently could not even look a decent hamburger in the face. Sympathetic stories appeared, even though DEA officials let the word out to the press that this fellow was both a looney and a criminal.

His trial on the possession charge took place in July before Judge James Washington, Jr., a prominent black jurist and a former dean of Howard Law School, without a jury. Again, there was a great deal of press coverage. Because of the novel and important nature of the defense, Judge Washington took the case under advisement before issuing his decision. In light of the fact that the jurist pondered his decision for so long, the federal enforcement officials soon got the message that a pioneering marijuana decision was about to be handed down which would make them unhappy. Bob kept up the personal pressure on agency officials. Because NIDA controlled the Mississippi marijuana farm, his demands became focused on the officials of that agency, but he also kept up the pressure on staff at the DEA and the FDA, both of which have authority in this arena.

As it sank in on NIDA officials that this Randall person might well win that case in Superior Court on that necessity defense, they told him that they were giving in on his related petition for access to legal marijuana. The government would treat him as a research subject under an IND (an investigational-new-drug protocol) application. All he had to do was find a doctor willing to accept the drugs and to supervise the experiment. The government saw this as a method for sticking to its position that marijuana must remain a Schedule I drug, one formally prohibited totally in American medicine, except in rare and closely supervised experiments. Because the improper use of such drugs is considered a serious crime and also because the administrative red tape is strangling, few doctors want to be involved in such experiments. Nor do patients.

The NIDA officials made demands of Bob Randall, in sequence, that he be hospitalized in order to be a research subject; or that he go to the hospital to smoke; or that he buy a 750-pound free-standing safe or a 250-pound safe embedded in concrete to store his medicine. He rejected all of these, in sequence and in the sulphuric terms they deserved, as being utterly impractical. The NIDA officials backed down again. Then, Bob Randall explained, "The final bargaining point the government had was, in effect, 'We'll give you the marijuana if you never tell anybody. . . . You've figured out the game. You beat the system . . . and just between you and us, we'll give you the marijuana. You can keep your sight. We can keep our classification [on marijuana as a prohibited drug in medicine].' " He went to the press immediately after hearing this proposed "deal made in Hell." He was determined more than ever that every glaucoma patient, every cancer patient, constituting millions of his innocent fellow citizens, should get to know from his case that marijuana was a medicine that might help them at least to some degree.

Meanwhile, with the help of the government, he made arrangements with Dr. John Merritt, an eye specialist at Howard University Medical School a few miles from his home, who agreed to take him on as a patient and research subject. While Randall is white, Dr. Merritt, who is black, was particularly interested in his disease because black men have a much higher incidence of it than other people. At the same time, the physician cared about Mr. Randall as a human being in trouble and wanted to help him in any event. At about the time he found Dr. Merritt, Bob learned that the marijuana he had requested was on its way to Washington from that government farm in the south. Someone, somewhere in the halls of power had made the historic decision to breach the wall of marijuana prohibition. "So I walked into Merritt's office one day, November 12, 1976, and walked out with forty marijuana cigarettes. And went home."

THE RIGHT TO HEALTH

More important victories were to come, starting at the end of the month. On November 24, 1976, Thanksgiving Eve, Judge Washington issued a decision of profound importance in *United States v. Randall.* "The evil he sought to avert, blindness, is greater than [the evil] that he performed to accomplish it, growing marijuana in his residence in violation of the District of Columbia code," the judge explained, as he found the defendant not guilty of the charge of possession. Yet today leading government officials still conduct drug enforcement as if that historic decision did not exist.

Robert C. Randall has continued to make history and has continued to broadcast and broaden his victories over the drug warriors. He is the only person I have discovered in America who has received steady prescriptions of marijuana cigarettes for glaucoma over a period of years, with only one brief interruption. It has been a stunning series of victories. Yet none of them has ever been fully secure. Even the liberal Carter White House drug policy chief, Dr. Peter Bourne, threatened to cut him off because he kept appearing on television shows and in the press, telling the world and other sick people about the value of his medicine. Dr. Bourne wrote to federal research subject Randall on June 6, 1977, "Publicity in this case has forced consideration of tightening up the dispensing of your supplies." When Dr. Merritt took a new job out of the city in January 1978, the Carter administration terminated Bob's supply on the day the doctor left and told him that he would have to survive without his medicine until he found another doctor. Thus the United States government invited this patient to buy his blindness-prevention medicine on the street. He refused the invitation and managed to find a temporary alternate source through a network of contacts.

Bob saw that he might have to go through with a full legal suit to insure access to his medicine. Luckily, a leading Washington law firm, Steptoe and Johnson, agreed to take this new case on a *pro bono publico* basis. A young lawyer, Thomas Collier, was assigned to the case and he proved also to have an extraordinary impact on the course of events. But he also did not work alone, being helped at times over the ensuing weeks and months by at least two dozen of the firm's lawyers and paralegal assistants, all of whose time and expenses the firm contributed for the good of the public.

Tom Collier prepared a comprehensive suit against the DEA, NIDA, and the FDA that would guarantee formal approval of Mr. Randall's right to receive marijuana as medicine under an IND protocol. This new suit argued that there is a constitutional right to health and to the available medicines to secure it. The government did not have the power to deny a patient medicine when it knew that the denial would cause that person to go blind, Mr. Collier further claimed. While such claims make good ethics and simple common sense, they have never been fully established in the law. It was just possible that they were about to be, since the massive pleadings had been well prepared and bore the imprimatur of a major establishment law firm. Such a constitutional finding might have gutted the enforcement of whole sections of major drug laws. However, the full implications of this suit were not realized.

The Carter administration dragged its feet, demanded more scientific proof, and as a result the hapless research subject had to undergo yet another experiment with yet another new drug that had been discovered and yet another research doctor, this one at Duke University. For the first time in years, while in North Carolina under the care of that university research doctor, Bob Randall stopped taking marijuana for a long period, three weeks in this case; instead, he relied on the new legal medication, Timolol, and his regular regimen of conventional medications.

"Did you suffer withdrawal?" I asked. "From marijuana, no. I almost suffered withdrawal from vision," the patient answered. "The bureaucrats wanted to find out if I would really go blind," Randall insists. The government officials again had their answer: if this citizen did not have marijuana, he *would* go blind. (Often, these same officials had asked him in exasperation why he did not simply buy his marijuana on the street, like everyone else.)

The Duke doctor declared the experiment with Timolol a failure. The research subject came back to Washington on a Friday. On the next Monday afternoon, May 6, 1978, attorney Thomas Collier filed his powerful brief in federal court.

However, the case was never argued in court. On Tuesday, May 7, the United States government surrendered to Citizen Randall, telling him he could get his marijuana as a research subject under any reasonable conditions he suggested. Through the use of this tactic, the government prevented all of the assembled evidence and witnesses, including glaucoma and cancer sufferers, from appearing in court—and forestalled the probability of a major court decision upholding the rights of our sick to hitherto forbidden medicines.

Since then, on the basis of a negotiated out-of-court settlement, Randall has received a stream of monthly prescriptions from a Washington, D.C., doctor which are filled at a local hospital pharmacy. Mr. Randall refuses to divulge the name of either doctor or pharmacy—because the government insisted on nondisclosure in the settlement agreement. He receives a tin of 300 neatly rolled marijuana cigarettes from the U.S. government every month, and says matter-of-factly that he smokes ten a day.

"Ten? Every day?" I asked incredulously. He explains patiently, "I'm almost impervious to getting high. I marvel at social smokers, who pass half a joint around 20 people. . . . Everyone's high! . . . Ten a day without a break since May of '78." Then he adds that, of course, he no longer is dry in the throat or red-eyed, as are many regular social pot smokers, nor does he have a feeling of different consciousness or loss of short-term memory—or drooling from the mouth, as he believes some people suspect.

I can provide eyewitness testimony that this gentle man in his late thirties, who walks around with his neat government marijuana joints in an old cigarette package, talks and acts as naturally as any person I have ever known. He believes that the only impact that this massive ingestion of the smoke of a normally intoxicating drug has on him now is to reduce his eye pressure and thus prevent him from going blind. When pressed, however, he admits that he is aware that this steady intake of smoke may well cause organic damage such as cancer or heart disease somewhere down the line. Patient Randall chooses now to fight off his blindness and to face up to those other health problems later, if and when they develop. To each day the evil thereof.

Over a period of many hours of discussions, I saw him seemingly disoriented, even slightly, only once. That was when I introduced him to a large university class in April 1985. In my remarks I mentioned Peggy Mann's new book, *Marijuana Alert*, which had a foreword by Nancy Reagan and a good deal of discussion about how the movement to have marijuana brought back into medicine was a red herring inspired by the marijuana lobby to give pot a good name, particularly to our youth. I then read this section: "In

1979 Robert Randall, who suffers from glaucoma and who is on the advisory board of NORML . . ., sued NIDA. . . . He won the suit. . . . It is interesting to note that according to the FDA, despite his professed faith in marijuana as a cure for glaucoma, Randall continues to take traditionally prescribed medications for his disease."

When I read those lines to him, Robert Randall seemed momentarily stunned by the distorted and unkind picture they contained, especially since Ms. Mann had never even bothered to interview him. Ms. Mann was wrong when she implied that NORML had inspired his suit; wrong when she stated that he believed marijuana was a cure; wrong when she implied that he lied that he took only pot and not other medications; and she was even wrong on the date of his suit. At that moment, Bob Randall did indeed appear disoriented—but not as a result of smoking pot.

Those quoted lines were only a small part of a chapter which reveals the cruelty resulting from the drug-war mentality, even when expressed in the apparently loving language of the First Lady. The entire chapter is devoted to the proposition that sick people seeking to obtain marijuana as medicine are either faking or are being used by the drug lobby. It is replete with supporting statements from leading physicians such as Dr. DuPont, who declared, "Today, 'medical uses' has become the symbol behind which the pro-pot activists are marching."

LYNN PIERSON: CANCER VICTIM

Bob Randall continues—despite years of record ingestion of a weed that leading medical experts claim should have rendered him totally useless by now—to fight such cruel distortions with intelligence and patience on many fronts. One of his most loved comrades in this battle was a young man named Lynn Pierson, whom he met in Washington in 1977. Lynn was a Vietnam-era veteran who discovered one day in 1975 at the age of 24 that he had testicular cancer and perhaps only six months to live. He underwent surgery and then chemotherapy. The elemental idea behind these powerful anti-cancer drugs is that the body as a whole is more powerful than the cancer cells—since the medicines kill both cancer and healthy cells alike. The hope is that the total body will survive the onslaught while the cancer cells are killed. It does not always balance out that way. All that is certain is that many patients become terribly ill and nauseated from the medicine, some losing all of their hair or going into convulsions.

To convey the real human situation even more precisely, imagine if you will this scene. The cancer patient sits at the dining room table with the pill in front of him or her and thinks, sometimes out loud: I am feeling fine now, but I know if I take this damned pill, I am going to start to feel miserable again. Why should I take this poison for the next two weeks, when the doctor does not know if it will do any good? Screw it! I'll take my chances without it. And so the patient sweeps the pill off the table and flushes it down the nearest toilet, still agonizing about it.

That is what happened to young Lynn Pierson. He simply could not tolerate the harsh impact on his body of the medicines prescribed by his doctors. Then he discovered, at his doctor's suggestion, that smoking marijuana held down his nausea and made him feel able to tolerate the medicines that might, just might, save his life.

Bob is still emotional about Lynn. "The first minute I met Lynn I knew I had been waiting for him to come along," he says. Lynn was a true ally and a good complement to Bob's basically calm nature. Lynn was a fighter from the start, full of rage that he had to go out and buy his medicine illegally. They combined their anger and their drive. Soon, they were talking virtually every night on the telephone from Washington to New Mexico, where Lynn lived. Rather than petition DEA as Bob had done, they decided that Lynn should seek to get a medical-use bill through the state legislature. That would open up a new arena of drug-law reform.

New Mexico was ideal because it was a small state with a narrow media market. The gaunt six-foot-three cancer patient stalked the halls of the legislature, talking to every member, demanding that they pass the bill prepared largely by Bob and himself. The bill passed, and was signed into law on February 21, 1978, the first of its kind in the nation allowing the medical use of marijuana. It was a far-sighted law since it provided that the drug could be used not only for research but also as a simple medicine that would be available virtually to any organically ill patient, including those suffering from cancer, glaucoma, and other diseases. Federal administrative red tape proved more formidable than imagined, however. Lynn continued to smoke illegal marijuana and died in August 1978, never having obtained the medicine legally. He was 27 years old. Three hours after his death, an FDA official called to say that the state's plan had been approved. Even that approval was pulled back because of some technicality by federal officials, who sometimes create bureaucratic obstacles to such programs and always deny they do so. When the program finally went into operation a year later, state officials named it in honor of Lynn Pierson.

To continue the nationwide reform effort, Robert Randall created a new organization in 1980, the Alliance for Cannabis Therapeutics, or ACT. It has a single goal—to reclassify marijuana as a medicine. The work of ACT and Bob Randall along with NORML has produced dramatic results. Thirty-three states have approved the use of marijuana for glaucoma and cancer chemotherapy patients. Those state laws alone, of course, do not free up the drug. Federal approval is always needed for each state program, all of which are considered experimental exceptions to the national rule of marijuana prohibition.

On its part and to its credit, the federal government has made a major effort to provide THC pills to a large number of cancer specialists for distribution to those patients who might be helped. The entire program was begun by the Carter administration in the form of a giant research project. The Reagan administration has continued this humane effort and in 1986 went even further when it approved a *synthetic* THC pill, known as Marinol, for use in medicine as a Schedule II drug. This represented the first time in history that the government had down-scheduled any form of a drug that was originally in Schedule I. However, all other forms of marijuana and natural THC remain mired irrationally in the "prohibited" category. Each of the many thousands of patients receiving the natural THC pills is formally considered a research subject. Thus, even though there is compassion among the drug bureaucrats, the federal legal feet are still planted in the irrational concrete; technically, marijuana remains a Schedule I drug.

THE ONLY ONE IN THE
LIFEBOAT

The number of patients who have been able to obtain legal marijuana joints from the federal government for any purpose seems likely to total only in the hundreds. These are primarily cancer patients. While Dr. Edward Tocus, a key FDA decision-maker on this matter, has assured me that there are many glaucoma patients out there who are receiving legal marijuana cigarettes, as opposed to THC pills, and while I want to believe him, he could not name any, nor have I yet found one. I suspect that some glaucoma patients have received joints for a while in research projects, but did not use them for long, certainly not for a period of years. So far, Bob Randall apparently remains virtually alone in terms of long-term use, as he claims.

That bothers him. He told me that he keeps asking, "Why am I the only one in the lifeboat?" To enlarge that boat and to haul others into it, ACT has pushed a federal bill that would reclassify marijuana as a Schedule II drug. When Rep. Stewart McKinney (R-Conn.) reintroduced the bill on March 23, 1983, he estimated on the basis of federal data that at least 500,000 sick people would benefit from legal joints every year—50,000 chemotherapy and 50,000 radiotherapy patients who normally suffer intense nausea, plus 400,000 glaucoma victims.

Said one of those victims recently, "If we can find something better than my smoking ten joints a day, I am all for it." In the absence of that discovery Bob Randall continues to smoke his marijuana, to lobby for humane legal reforms, and to counsel many patients who call him for guidance and caring words from all over the country. When I asked him what reflections he had about his status as a victim of the war on drugs, he objected to my threshold thought. The manner in which he explained his objections raised my spirits as have few statements from people I have interviewed in recent years. He reminded me that he had beaten by a couple of country miles the medical prognosis of 1972 that he would be blind in three to five years.

Then Robert Randall continued: "I have been victimized but I am not a victim. Most of the people who call me for advice *are* victims. . . . However, I win every day. I can still see. Seeing is winning."

JOSEPH HUTCHINS: TRYING TO GET INTO THE BOAT

Joseph Hutchins is one of those people who have called Bob Randall for guidance on how to get into that lifeboat. Up to now, Mr. Hutchins remains a victim of the drug war. Mr. Hutchins's story explains why there is a need to establish explicitly the right of all patients to receive officially hated drugs in medicine for a wide variety of illnesses, including some that few drug-abuse experts have ever even heard about. Scleroderma, for example. I could claim total ignorance of the disease until early in 1985 when Kevin Zeese of NORML told me that the organization was trying to help a fellow in Massachusetts who claimed that marijuana was helping him fight off the ravages of a rare disease that affects few people, perhaps 250,000 in the entire country. I first met Joe Hutchins at the 1985 NORML convention in Washington, D.C. He is a tall, straight-arrow fellow, 41 years old, with a strong Bay State accent that reminds me of home. I learned that he was divorced and lived with his girlfriend a few miles from his ex-wife and three teenage children, with whom he had a good relationship, in the northeast corner of Massachusetts near Newbury and Newburyport. That day I heard Mr. Hutchins plead with the members of NORML to help get laws passed that would allow him to use the medicine that was keeping him functioning.

Joe Hutchins believes he contracted his disease while serving in the Navy in the Caribbean during the Cuban missile crisis of the early Sixties. Also known as progressive systemic sclerosis, scleroderma is a tissue disease that literally means "hardening of the skin." Neither the cause nor a cure is known, although it is known to be fatal to some sufferers. The Navy discharged Hutchins because of his illness but he was still able to work. From 1969 to 1978 he worked as a machinist at the General Electric plant in Lynn and had an excellent performance record. By 1978 his disease had progressed to the point where he had to stop working. The Veterans Administration then began paying him a 100 percent disability pension and he also commenced receiving Social Security benefits. Thus he had no great financial problems. However, his illness remained severe and he was placed on a wide variety of narcotics by his doctors, who were fighting a battle to hold back the unknown effects of the disease.

In November 1973, ten years after the initial diagnosis, his doctor, John G. Sullivan, chief of surgery, St. Elizabeth's Hospital, Boston, advised him that it was necessary to remove his esophagus and replace it with a segment of his intestine so as to restore his ability to swallow. His body was, in a word, disintegrating. So also was his mind, for he was disoriented by the array of legal prescribed drugs, including Darvon, Valium, and Ritalin, that he was taking every day. "I was a vegetable," Joe Hutchins told me. He considered himself a legal drug addict and a guinea pig for the Veterans Administration doctors who were attempting to treat him.

Some friends suggested that marijuana might help to relieve his symptoms, which included nausea, vomiting, loss of appetite, inability to swallow, hypertension, and anxiety. It did (which should have been no surprise to anyone with a knowledge of the history of the medicine). Accordingly, for a decade now, this American citizen has been obtaining illegal marijuana and treating himself more effectively than some of the best medical talent in the country had been able to do. Joe Hutchins found that he could lead a relatively normal life, that he had an appetite, and that he could keep his food down. The surgeon's knife was not necessary nor were narcotic drugs. All of those powerful treatments were replaced by one infinitely less drastic, marijuana—plus one regular prescribed medicine to control his blood pressure. His doctors have signed affidavits swearing that while they did not understand the precise process, marijuana seemed to have some relationship, in the words of Dr. Sullivan on June 25, 1985, to "Mr. Hutchins's remarkable remission."

His psychologist, Dr. Stephen Boy of Haverhill, has stated that it was impossible to draw any broad conclusions from Joe's case. Yet, he stated emphatically, "His emotional and physical situation are probably better than they have been in 20 years." Then Dr. Boy added a significant observation: "If I were diagnosed with scleroderma and had symptoms like Joe's, I would think about using marijuana."

None of this powerful human testimony or medical evidence has impressed the legal authorities of the sovereign Commonwealth of Massachusetts. On October 29, 1984, Newbury police chief George Riel led a raid that netted a claimed five pounds of marijuana, including two of high-grade sinsemilla, at the home of Joseph Hutchins. Although no buyers of his medicine have ever been produced, the chief lodged the felony charge of "possession with intent to distribute" and supported a $5,000 bond and the threat of a five-year sentence. Mr. Hutchins was kept in a cold cell all night without a blanket; the cold and his poor circulation left "my feet and hands black all night." He has consistently claimed that he had grown the marijuana in his backyard for his own use because his VA doctors had refused his persistent written demands that it be prescribed legally and because he did not want to purchase it on the illegal market. The police had taken, he said, his "entire winter supply" which he had just harvested.

The police action was consistent with the views of many medical experts who doubt the efficacy of Joe Hutchins's illegal medicine. The established medical opinion is that marijuana is a questionable treatment for scleroderma. One of Joe Hutchins's own doctors, Juan J. Canosa, then chief of rheumatology at the VA Medical Center in Boston, has stated he was "skeptical" of the beneficial effects of marijuana in dealing with the symptoms of his patient's disease. That skepticism accounted for the fact that Dr. Canosa never supported his patient's requests to him for access to federally grown marijuana.

At Hutchins's trial in Newburyport District Court on July 24, 1984, Judge Francis P. Cullen refused to allow the defendant to present the defense of medical necessity, which would have been supported by an impressive group of expert witnesses, including Dr. Norman Zinberg of Harvard Medical School. In a bench trial without a jury, the jurist convicted Mr. Hutchins of the serious offense of possession with intent to distribute. Judge Cullen also ordered him committed to a state psychiatric hospital for 40 days' observation because Joe had testified that he had been suicidal years earlier while on the VA medicines. The staff soon saw that this was unfair and unnecessary—and released him after 15 days. Shortly thereafter, a sentence was imposed: two years of probation and a $400 fine. The criminal appealed for a new trial—which is allowed in such cases under state law—in Haverhill District Court, whereupon in October 1985 Judge William Sullivan also refused to hear the defense of medical necessity and sentenced Joseph Hutchins to 30 days in the House of Correction.

During a brief stay of that sentence, Mr. Hutchins made urgent calls for assistance around the country, including one to Kevin Zeese of NORML in Washington. Mr. Zeese contacted one of the most prestigious law firms in the country, Covington and Burling of Washington, D.C. Lawyers David B. Isbell and Michael G. Michaelson, who is also a medical doctor, entered the case *pro bono* on behalf of Joe Hutchins, arguing in their first memorandum of law filed in November 1985 that the defense of medical necessity should be heard. A judge issued another stay of the sentence and the case is now on appeal.

The lesson of Joe Hutchins's torment is not simply that marijuana should be reclassified as a legal medicine for any sick person who might benefit from it. That indeed is part of the lesson but the narrowest element of it. The broader lesson is that his ordeal illustrates the immense amount of intolerance and ideological bias regarding all drugs and drug users that must be overcome even to begin to help the sick people who are victims of the drug war.

I saw face-to-face and felt directly a small piece of that inhumanity on October 30, 1985, during a live television show, "People Are Talking," in Boston on WBZ-TV regarding the subject of making so-called street drugs legal. Representatives of the drug-free-youth movement had been invited to sit in the audience. So also had been local resident Joseph Hutchins. As fate would have it, the quiet man, in suit and tie, was seated amidst the anti-drug crusaders, immediately next to a proper, middle-aged Massachusetts matron. During the show, I pointed out that one of the worst aspects of the war on drugs was that sick people were sometimes made to obtain their medicines illegally—and that one of these hapless victims was sitting in the audience.

I also observed that I sympathized with the concerns of the drug-free-youth movement and that I believed that many of the parents and leaders were quite decent people. "You say they're decent people, but they say—I've been talking to them during the break—that anyone who supports legalization is probably a drug user," countered host "Buzz" Luttrell. The implication was made clear by the anti-drug representatives present: users' minds and judgments were twisted as a result of the chemicals they took and thus they were not decent people, a category into which Kevin Zeese and I, sitting at the front of that audience, should also be placed.

Mr. Hutchins then was given the opportunity to explain his

disease and the treatment he received. "The Veterans Administration gave me a regimen of drugs for seventeen years which ruined my life. The side effects took my mind away," he explained. Mr. Luttell asked, "Marijuana doesn't do that?" Joe replied, "Marijuana doesn't do that." The people sitting around the sick man started to smirk, some to laugh openly.

Buzz Luttrell turned to that Massachusetts lady sitting next to Joe and asked, "Why are you laughing?" "Because marijuana is a mind-altering drug," she replied, seeming to imply that Mr. Hutchins was pulling a grand scam to obtain his recreational drug of choice; clearly, he also was not a decent person—and perhaps he was unable to think clearly due to the drug.

I interjected from the front of the studio, "Do you want him in jail, ma'am?"

The drug-free matron shot back at me, "That's a crock! In plain English. The major drug traffickers aren't in jail. Don't tell me people go to jail for using marijuana!"

"I just got sentenced to jail for using marijuana," Mr. Hutchins quietly told his neighbor.

She replied, "I don't believe it. . . . Anybody who needs marijuana for medicine can get it!"

One of the most important launching pads for the reform of American drug laws should be the reality underlying this Boston lady's disbelief. There should be no reason to believe that any sick person would face jail in America for seeking to obtain medicine. Nor is there any reason for that threat to continue to exist in a civilized society.

11

The Sacrifice
of Our Police

I SEE Barry Leibowitz as a victim of the war on drugs. The former federal prosecutor does not. And therein lies the moral of the story.

BARRY LEIBOWITZ: THE
PROSECUTOR AS VICTIM

Mr. Leibowitz is the only lawyer I know who was actually shot—with a cyanide-tipped bullet, no less—to stop his prosecution of drug dealers. When he had been an Assistant U.S. Attorney in Washington, the idealistic young prosecutor had been engaged in a long investigation of a murderous heroin smuggling ring led by a notorious international trafficker, Linwood Gray. On the morning of December 20, 1978, Gray shot Mr. Leibowitz just outside the federal courthouse in downtown Washington, within sight of the Capitol building. The first bullet sliced through the knot in his tie, the second lodged in the fatty tissue of his body, causing only a superficial wound. It was removed easily with the aid of a local anesthetic. A few days later, however, prosecutor Leibowitz developed severe and frightening cramps from what was discovered to be cyanide, most of which had fortunately been burned off in the barrel of the gun. He admitted he was scared, and began carrying a snub-nosed .32 pistol and wearing a bullet-proof vest.

Scared or not, he persisted in his work and eventually helped obtain convictions of the gang, but Linwood Gray received a sentence of only twenty months to five years for income-tax evasion. Because of insufficient evidence, Gray was never prosecuted, nor was anyone else, for the attempted murder of a federal prosecutor in broad daylight. Popular accounts stated that the prosecution team, including Mr. Leibowitz, were dismayed over the small social benefits obtained from drug-enforcement activities. After the trial, lawyer Donald Campbell, one of his colleagues in the U.S. Attorney's office, asked in despair, "What's the point of all this?" and added, "I'm not sure what good we do in narcotics prosecutions." It was reported in *The Washingtonian* magazine of May 1983 that even after the passage of several years, "Barry Leibowitz is still concerned for his life."

Thus I was prepared to find in Barry Leibowitz, now a private Washington attorney, a vibrant example of a warrior-victim who would exhibit fear and would offer me some persuasive personal insights into the futility of the drug war. I could not have been more mistaken on all counts.

Mr. Leibowitz turned out to be a very engaging young man of 38, wearing a dark blue lawyer's suit, silver-rimmed glasses, a welcoming smile, and a relaxed air. We strolled from his office through the muggy streets of Washington on a July day in 1985 to the Mayflower Hotel for a leisurely lunch. If he was still frightened, he hid it well.

Far from taking the position that the war on drugs was futile, Barry Leibowitz argued that the drug laws were proper and that they should be enforced more vigorously. "Why should murder carry a 20-year sentence and heroin trafficking only 15?" he asked across the white tablecloth. "They're the same thing. Why not the same sentence?" If there were any problems, then, with the drug laws, it was that they were not enforced harshly enough.

But did Mr. Leibowitz not see, I persisted, that he and other decent enforcement officials were at least in some ways victims of confused laws and policies that put their necks at risk—in his case, quite literally—for very little gain, in fact, for net social losses, something like the good soldiers we sent to fight in Vietnam? The reflective, intelligent former prosecutor simply could not agree with that line of argument. In this respect, he was like most of the warriors I have met in my wanderings across the front lines of the drug war in recent years.

These enforcers of the drug laws are rarely seen as victims by anyone, least of all by themselves. Drug police and prosecutors seemed trapped by their own rhetoric on the need to be tough in the face of the scum who are pushing drugs on our people. In the short run, their courage and toughness are sometimes effective, especially when it comes to dealing with the likes of Linwood Gray and his gang. In the longer run, it is up to the rest of us to rescue the drug warriors from themselves and to assist them in fashioning a new positive social role.

SUPERCOPS OR SUPERSCUM?

A major impediment to carrying out that social rescue mission is that many influential people view drug-enforcement police in one of two bipolar ways: they have almost supernatural powers to control drugs and could if they really wanted to but don't really want to, on the one hand; or, they are an army of pathological oppressors, on the other. Neither is correct.

An extreme example of the first view appeared at the beginning of the terrible summer of 1986, perhaps as an omen of what was to come. A respected veteran writer, James Mills, created this supercop vision in his massive 1,165-page book, *The Underground Empire, Where Crime and Governments Embrace*. The book was launched in a way calculated to make most writers, including this one, green with envy. Copies of the hardbound tome appeared on the desks of opinion makers all over the country with personal letters from the chairman of the board of the publishing company. Nelson Doubleday seemed to be looking readers earnestly in the eyes when he assured them, "Everything in this astounding investigative study is true; no names have been changed; there are no composite characters; no invented scenes or dialogue." Roughly similar words also were found at the beginning of the book.

The essence of Mr. Mills's allegedly true story was that during the Seventies, the federal government had created a superpowerful band of DEA and FBI superagents, named Centac (Central Tactical Unit), headed by a supercop leader, Dennis Dayle, who went out and knocked the stuffings out of major drug trafficking organizations all over the world. They did so not by going after white powder, the drugs, but instead after the leaders of the rings and imprisoning them. These brave agents were incredibly successful for several years but were stopped in their good work by the leaders of the FBI, which had been given jurisdiction over the DEA during the Reagan era. All of this had been kept secret until Mr. Mills let the cat out of the bag.

The federal drug-control agencies were putting on a sham drug war that was not truly meant to be won. Why?

Because the United States government is the largest narcotics conspirator in the world. This tired old grand deception theory was supported by these "facts": (1) since the narcotics trade is controlled by the corrupt leaders of third-world governments, such as Panama, Mexico, and Thailand, (2) the U.S. could stop the trade by simply telling those corrupt leaders to stop their criminal actions or else, and (3) our failure to do so is rooted in our desire to retain friendships and military alliances with those nations. Thus we crassly sacrifice the health of the world's people for military and diplomatic gains.

The amazing nature of the police revelations (believe me, I have summarized the whole thing: these supercops arrested leaders and not powder) and the veracity of the conspiracy theory were accepted with breathless belief by the major news organizations of the country. *Time* and *Newsweek* wrote supportive articles about the book and its revelations. The NBC "Today Show" devoted a rare five consecutive segments to it, during the week of June 9–13, with newsman John Palmer hanging on every word uttered by Mr. Mills. I watched and listened in awe as the literary scam of the decade unfolded before my eyes and ruined breakfast after breakfast for me. My breakfast times were not improved during the next week when Christopher Lehmann-Haupt, the lead book reviewer of the daily *New York Times*, gave the book a rave review on June 16. The prestigious reviewer admitted that he had an initial problem "of disbelief" but that he came to "ultimately trust what Mr. Mills reveals," a position taken by many of the major opinion leaders of the country.

As I watched all of this with a sinking heart, I realized how these incidents illustrated the extent of public and professional ignorance about the nature of the drug problem—and how much work we had to do in order to develop sensible policies. It was as if a major publishing house had put out a book telling how a lonely CIA agent and a few of his friends had developed a scheme to convince the leaders of the Soviet Politburo to defect with all of their code books—and how CIA director Casey had stopped the operation at the direction of the Reagan White House so as to support the defense industry. Had this occurred, I assume the book would have been immediately dismissed by the press and media as a silly fraud. That was my initial and continuing reaction to the Mills book.

I called the DEA public affairs office and asked the press officer who answered if the agency was issuing a reaction. Con Dougherty replied roughly along these lines: give me a break; you know us well enough to understand that if we had a unit that was that successful we would have kept it and bragged about it. He did confirm that there had been several such Centac units, that they had accomplished much good, that DEA had never kept them secret, that roughly similar combined units of agents from several agencies were still in operation, and that DEA had released information on their limited successes over the years. Mr. Dougherty had no comment on the other amazing revelations of the book.

On August 15, the FBI wrote to Doubleday, laying out many of the factual errors in the book. However, it took David Johnston, a reporter for the *Los Angeles Times*, to save the honor of the American press, and of much of the rest of society as well. In a front-page story on October 2, 1986, Mr. Johnston revealed the results of a major investigative effort which showed that the core of the Mills story was untrue. Of approximately 50 people mentioned in the book who had been also interviewed by reporter Johnston, 43 said the accounts of their activities were simply false, and four said their actions were distorted.

One of the most revealing comments was made by Douglas Chandler, a DEA official who had been head of Centac; he told David Johnston, "I found that he draws the conclusion that the DEA at one time had the solution to all the dope peddling problems and then abandoned it . . . that's ridiculous." Of course, it is.

On the other hand, it is not ridiculous to draw the conclusion that over the years police involved in narcotics investigations have committed some terrible deeds, as I hope I have already demonstrated. Documented stories of the excesses committed by drug-enforcement agents continue to come to light. In the December 1986 issue of *Reason* magazine, Stanford University policy analyst Dale Gieringer laid out a disturbing new indictment that lists an array of outrages. The article was titled "Inside the DEA" with the subtitle "In the murky world of drug enforcement, agents lie, cheat, and steal in the name of the law." I believe that Gieringer proved that claim and these related allegations: "When a drug law is violated, no individual rights are abridged. There is no murder victim to be avenged, no stolen property to be returned to its rightful owner. And there are no crime victims to complain to the police. So DEA agents must find, or create, their own cases. In doing so, they inevitably intrude on individual lives and liberties and twist the very laws they are supposed to uphold."

The most shocking cases in Gieringer's multiple-count indictment involve entrapment, where DEA agents went out and enticed susceptible individuals into trafficking in drugs. When they were prosecuted and claimed entrapment, very often the defense was rejected by judges on the legal theory that the defendants were "predisposed" to selling drugs in the first place.

In many of these cases, the DEA allowed some of its informants to traffic in drugs in exchange for turning in their friends and supplying other information. In too many cases, Gieringer claimed, DEA agents themselves directly engaged in trafficking. One of them was William Coller, an ace DEA pilot and a supervisor of DEA air operations. Bill Coller pleaded guilty to marijuana smuggling and got the relatively light sentence of three years in prison in exchange for full information on his many crimes.

Mr. Coller, now out of prison and working in the construction business, recently reflected on the type of day-to-day work world created for drug agents by the demands of the drug war: "It's a sad way to make a living, it really is, running around to bars and lying and seducing people into criminal acts. In the beginning it's just a game, but if you're a thinking agent, it really bothers you what you do. I seldom met a 'scarface' or violent-type criminal like on 'Miami Vice.' The vast majority of the ones I met were simply small-time entrepreneurs trying to make a buck. It really bothered me what I was doing to them, destroying their lives, their families. I look back at it and I'm really sorry."

While I am prepared to believe that Mr. Coller is truly regretful, I am not prepared to forgive him his personal transgressions; he deserved harsh punishment, perhaps harsher than he received. On a broader level, however, I am not ready to label all of the DEA or all of the police involved in drug enforcement as "The Real Scum of the Drug World," the description on the cover of the *Reason* magazine issue that contained the Gieringer article. Many of my friends and colleagues view the drug police in those terms and worse. On balance, I am more comfortable viewing most drug-enforcement officers, including Bill Coller, and indeed many of the institutions of American policing, as victims of the drug war. They are often not hapless or innocent victims but, like the soldiers who volunteered for Vietnam, in my eyes, victims nonetheless.

"BABIES!" I THOUGHT

Even though they resist the label, the prosecutors and, more often, the frontline police fit alongside the sick as the saddest victims of the drug wars. The sick come first, to be sure, but the police are second. They are caught in a mad series of social ambivalences and conflicts: between drug laws that at least one quarter of the entire population persistently flaunts and a rising political demand for enforcement; between a rising demand for drugs, a rising number of sellers, and a criminal justice system that is in a state of gridlock with room for comparatively few more offenders; and between their consciences and treasure troves of cash and drugs that amount to more than the salary of a brave lifetime. When police officers of integrity seek to enforce the laws in accordance with their oaths of office, they sometimes run into violent traffickers who are heavily armed and prepared to use their weapons.

On television shows such as "Miami Vice" the drug warriors seem to be glamorous, mature men and women who have weighed all the risks. When I recently sat in the office of a real Miami vice squad and saw the police prepare for an operation, I was struck by quite different emotions, as I had been a few months earlier on that Mendocino mountainside. The officers looked so young, so idealistic, so like my students—or children. One even had braces on his teeth.

"Babies!" I thought. They were good-looking, clean-cut young people, mainly Hispanic, in blue jeans and light shirts and jogging shoes. The young men and one young woman were enthusiastically gathering up their weapons, radios, and other equipment in nylon athletic bags, as if they were preparing for a ballgame. Yet, they were going out on the streets with a kilo of cocaine to meet a trafficker, risking their lives, I thought then, to protect me and my neighbors from drugs. I would rather not have the protection at that price. (I later reflected on how my concerns about the officers as human beings represented the other side of the coin to Bill Coller's concerns about the traffickers.) When I had voiced my reservations, their sergeant and one of the officers said flatly that they all believed in the value and effectiveness of the risks they took daily.

In carrying out the drug war, however, the reality is that our police are in danger of losing their decency, their personal and professional integrity, their physical and mental health, and sometimes their lives. A few insightful police officers have told me that they now recognize this danger. If more of them can be convinced of its reality and build up the courage to speak out, then the police and prosecutors could become powerful forces for reform. The public and politicians tend to listen much more closely to professional police officers than to liberal professors. The drug warriors, then, could save their own souls and lead in saving the soul of the nation—not from drugs but from the internal destruction being wrought upon the country, including its police, by the excesses of the drug war.

In March 1985, the brutally beaten bodies of American DEA Special Agent Enrique Camarena Salazar and his Mexican pilot, Alfredo Zavalar Avelar, were found near a rural road in Mexico. U.S. ambassador to Mexico John Gavin voiced the commonly accepted view when he declared that the murders of the two represented "losses in an ongoing war." I saw those men primarily as "victims" of a misguided policy in America and in much of the world. In my scale of values, I assign the same definition to the great majority of the other 55 American police officers killed in the last decade fighting the unwinnable drug war.

Many people seem to accept the death and injury of police officers as a painful though necessary cost in a just and virtuous campaign to save other Americans from poison. Officers slain pursuing drug violators are mourned by their colleagues but I have not encountered a single instance in recent years when a prominent police official or members of the rank-and-file raised public questions, in the wake of losing one of their own officers, about the wisdom of the laws or the possibility of rationally changing enforcement methods so as to reduce the number of police victims. In a religious crusade, the warriors rarely question underlying sacred doctrines.

When, for example, 27-year-old Ariel Rios was killed in Miami on December 2, 1982, he was mourned by the law-enforcement community. Concern was also expressed for his partner, Alexander D'Atri, 36, who was riddled with bullets, too, but miraculously survived. Both were U.S. Treasury Special Agents assigned temporarily to Vice President Bush's South Florida Task Force. The agents were involved in a buy-and-bust operation in Miami's Little Havana section when, in the words of the official newsletter of the Federal Law Enforcement Officers Association (FLEOA), "something went wrong." Something often goes wrong in such situations. These undercover drug operations are the most dangerous in the entire field of police work. Rarely are the risks to the officers worth the potential gain.

Many police leaders refuse to see that even within existing laws, they have a duty to do more to reduce the danger to their own officers, as well as to suspects and innocent citizens. While I argue for a wholesale revision of the drug laws, I accept the need to enforce existing laws, especially for large-scale and violent traffickers, who deserve only to be caught and punished. The existing laws, until they are changed, should be enforced, but with more restraint, caution, and concern for everyone involved.

None of this concern about pointless casualties came out in the FLEOA newsletter that carried the story about Ariel Rios, even though the association is dedicated to the professional advancement, health, and welfare of federal law enforcement officers. Indeed, another story in that newsletter demonstrates how the war mentality is so deeply ingrained in our law-enforcement structure that a good deal of consciousness raising will be necessary before the police can be recruited to play a role in seeking peaceful solutions to drug problems. In a letter to the editor, Frank T. Devlin, the Inspector-in-Charge of the Fugitive Squad of the U.S. Marshal's Office, commended two deputy marshals, John S. Boggia and Michael F. Witkovich, for their apprehension of Clyde Evans, a federal parole violator, who had originally been convicted for wire fraud and distributing narcotics. The marshals received confidential information in the early morning hours of October 7, 1982, that Evans was hiding in a Brooklyn apartment. They sought help from other officers, but no other police were available. They courageously went without additional assistance, knocked upon the door, and announced who they were. Immediately, they heard "the distinctive 'click' of the bolt going home on an automatic weapon." Nevertheless, they proceeded with their combat mission in Brooklyn.

The U.S. marshals kicked the door open, whereupon, almost as expected, Evans opened fire with a deadly .45 caliber submachine gun and with a pistol. The marshals returned the fire and killed Evans on the spot, although at first they did not know it. Deputy Boggia was wounded in the head whereupon Witkovich heroically rescued his partner, dragged him out to their car, and sped to a hospital. The entire neighborhood was soon cordoned off and large numbers of police and marshals flooded in with shotguns and automatic weapons. The police discovered that the fugitive Evans was dead. "It might be considered poetic justice," Inspector Devlin wrote, "that Evans's body was found with a tourniquet around his arm and a hypodermic needle stuck in his vein." Apparently, the police had interrupted the addict as he was taking an injection.

The inspector did not seem even to contemplate the possibility that other options of a more peaceful and more humane nature, for both the suspect and the officers, were available. Within current laws, it might be wise if all officers were trained to recognize, as indeed some do now, that the click of an automatic weapon is a signal for a courageous police person to get the devil out of the way, call for help, and negotiate with the suspect. And where, it might be asked, was the poetic justice in shooting a narcotic addict who was involved in the act of injecting? Even under current laws, that act is not a capital offense. Moreover, under another, more humane system there might at least have been the possibility that this addict would have been simply a peaceful patient injecting legal drugs prescribed by a doctor rather than a criminal shooting a deadly weapon at police officers in part to defend the drugs he had felt impelled to obtain through crime.

IN OUR SOCIAL CESSPOOLS: WHO'S CORRUPTING WHOM?

There are few calls by police or social leaders for changing the underlying policies that create the social cesspools into which we throw our police daily. Police failings are viewed as totally personal and in no way connected to the impossible conditions social leaders have helped to create. It is as if we hired police to work in our cesspools and then criticized them for smelling like they had just come from a cesspool somewhere. And most social leaders seem to accept the continued existence of those social cesspools.

Two popular books of the Seventies, both eventually made into major movies and both generally supported by other objective research, illustrate how widely these social conditions are known. The books exposed the situation in New York City, the center of hard-drug addiction and related crime in the country. Peter Maas's *Serpico* told the story of an idealistic, tough young policeman who believed that all the laws ought to be enforced fairly, even the narcotics laws and even the laws against corruption by his brother police officers in the New York Police Department. Frank Serpico took enormous risks to enforce both types of laws and became a victim in regard to both. His becoming a victim of drug-law enforcement was more sharply and immediately painful. On the night of February 3, 1971, Patrolman Serpico had been the point man in a buy-and-bust operation in Brooklyn. He had been standing in the half-open door of a dealer's apartment and was in the process of completing a heroin buy. Suddenly, a gun had appeared about eighteen inches from his face; it roared, and he collapsed with a bullet in his head.

When the word went out that Serpico had been shot, many in the department thought it had been at the hands of another cop; for months Serpico had earned the hatred of much of the force due to his anti-corruption work. He recovered from his wounds and continued his battle to expose systematic corruption in what is possibly the greatest police department in the world. The lessons of the book seemed to be that corruption was based upon internal attitudes and reward systems—and that it could not have continued unless it were at least tolerated at higher levels of the department.

However, I have yet to discover any mention in the book or movie, or in the related report of the famous Knapp Commission in 1972 on police corruption, that suggested that drug policies played a significant role in fertilizing the ground for corruption. Nor did anyone suggest that the young officer was a needless victim of a drug war that has been fought with the massive firepower of over 20,000 police officers and under the toughest state laws in this democratic nation—and which has continually failed. Even Serpico believed, "If the cops wanted to, they could eliminate a great deal of the narcotics business overnight." There simply is no factual support in the annals of police experience for this belief held by the idealistic and courageous officer, who reminds me in this respect of many others I have met in recent years.

A few modern police experts openly hold the view that the police are victims in the drug war. One is my colleague at the American University School of Justice, James Fyfe. Jim spent 16 years as a police officer on the streets of New York City, retiring as a lieutenant. While he is a respected scholar now and a critic of the excessive use of deadly force by American police, he is, in his heart of hearts, still very much a police officer. He winces when I mention Serpico and claims that many lowly police officers in the city were constantly forced to risk "a bullet in the face for a lousy nickel bag of heroin" just like Serpico. It was not unusual then and it continues to this day. Professor Fyfe is in good company, including that of the pioneer police practitioner-scholar, August Vollmer, who often lectured his colleagues in professional policing during the Twenties and Thirties about the corrosive influence of "vice" law enforcement on police institutions and on individual officers. Today, Vollmer and Fyfe and like-minded police experts are voices in the wilderness.

This was amply demonstrated in *Prince of the City* by former New York City deputy police commissioner Robert Daley, published several years after Frank Serpico had resigned from the force in despair and in continuing physical pain from his bullet wound. Daley's book dealt exclusively with the work of narcotics detectives and the agonies of enforcement in the city. It gave the inside story of the Special Investigations Unit, Narcotics Division. Detectives of the SIU operated with almost complete independence as virtually laws unto themselves in their ceaseless pursuit of high-level traffickers of narcotics, mainly heroin. "They chose their own targets and roamed New York at will. Someone once called them the Princes of the City, for they operated with the impunity, and sometimes with the arrogance, of Renaissance princes. They could enforce any law or not enforce it, arrest anyone or accord freedom," wrote Robert Daley.

The details of the drug-enforcement cesspool in New York City supported this broad statement of official decadence and defiance of laws, all in the name of enforcing impossible drug laws. Narcotics detectives made big cases and usually took part of the money and drugs simply lying around in the chaos. All the heroin seized as a result of the heralded law-enforcement triumph in the French Connection case by SIU detectives, for example, eventually disappeared from their office safe. They regularly violated laws meant to control their powers, such as those regarding wiretapping. At the same time, there was a touchingly humane side to these basically decent officers. If one of their addict-snitches ran out of drugs, some officers, such as the "hero," Robert Leuci, might leave their Long Island homes in the middle of the night and drive into the city to provide bags of heroin and relief. These were merciful acts, amounting to improvised heroin maintenance programs, which, as it happens, violated a fistful of laws, not the least being that the illegal heroin should never have been kept in the possession of the police in the first place. All told, in Brooklyn alone, perhaps 25 to 30 street addicts were being maintained by various police officers who regularly gave them illegal heroin because their informing activities had made it impossible for them to function openly on the streets anymore.

In the midst of a police department in the midst of a huge American metropolis, then, a medieval princedom operated in defiance of principles of ethical behavior—sometimes improving on them, usually falling beneath civilized standards, but almost always ignoring them. The book documents how the integrity, the lives, and the souls of most of these officers were destroyed while they tried to enforce the law from the base of that perverted princedom. To a large extent that included Robert Leuci, who went undercover and became an informer for the prosecutors investigating his colleagues. One of the key prosecutors was, of course, a young Assistant U.S. Attorney, Rudolph Giuliani. Detective Leuci testified against many of his old friends, helped send some of them to jail, and destroyed their careers. One of them committed suicide. Leuci stayed on the force but lived in terror and was often afraid to walk the streets of his own city.

I have never heard of any sensible lessons drawn from the tragedies documented by Robert Daley in writing about the activities of these often courageous and competent narcotics detectives in New York City—not by that author or by any of the key actors in real life. Even though he was shown to play a sensitive and caring role in the prosecutions, Rudolph Giuliani, now the U.S. attorney in New York, is as strong a supporter of the drug laws as ever. All the experts and participants involved seem to be saying that these were tragedies that happened because human beings are sometimes weak and deficient. Of course, that again is part of the truth but of less significance than the more ignored part—to an extent, these detectives were victims of the conditions created by the drug laws and the war on drugs.

My guess is that if we somehow convinced all of the professors, rabbis, priests, and nuns in New York to change uniforms with the SIU detectives, in a sufficient period of time the results would be roughly the same. And I suspect that no one would be talking about the new crop of corrupt police in any sense as drug-war victims, only as personal failures.

However, either we accept the idea that current conditions—a harsh drug war in the midst of a huge popular demand for illegal drugs—have created almost irresistible temptations for ordinary mortals, or we must accept another very harsh concept. That concept would be that the current generation of American criminal justice officials is composed of individuals who suffer from extraordinary defects of character.

Charges of corruption as well as illegal drug abuse have ripped through every level of government in communities throughout the country, and not simply in frontline drug policing, but it is in that enforcement arena that the greatest damage seems to have occurred. As the war on drugs took on increased intensity during the late Seventies and early Eighties, the charges came in continuing, growing waves.

One of the most notorious cases involved a heroic and successful DEA agent, Sante Bario. He had achieved star status for his skillful undercover work in arresting mobsters and racketeers while serving in the Internal Revenue Service and then later in the DEA. His wife, Joanne Bario, claimed that in Mexico City during the mid-Seventies she saw him slowly coming apart as a human being under the pressure of "making" (successfully investigating) undercover international narcotics cases; moreover, she saw a similar deterioration in other DEA agents, many of whom she believed to be alcoholics. Ms. Bario saw that it was difficult for her husband to know who he really was because he so often had to maintain at least two identities. In 1978, agent Bario was arrested for allegedly taking a bribe from a drug trafficker. One night while in jail, he went into convulsions and then into a coma from which he never recovered.

Sante Bario's death has never been fully explained. Some speculate he might have been poisoned. Nor has anyone explained how or why a heroic police officer became a criminal, the same type of criminal he had so courageously pursued throughout his career. Was it simply his personal failing? Was it the inevitable result of playing a criminal for so long? Was he framed by other corrupt agents? In any event, wasn't he a drug-war victim?

In the same vein, how do we explain the criminal behavior of the first FBI agent to be convicted of massive narcotics trafficking? Daniel A. Mitrione was the son and namesake of the American foreign aid official kidnapped and murdered by terrorists in Uruguay in 1970. At 38, he had become a respected 11-year veteran of the FBI, in recent years considered perhaps the most elite and the most incorruptible group of law-enforcement officers in the world. Under the powerful J. Edgar Hoover, who allegedly understood the harsh realities of the world of drug enforcement, the FBI managed to stay out of the field, a prohibition which ended when President Reagan demanded a full-court federal press in support of his drug war.

As part of the huge investment of federal officers from all agencies, Special Agent Mitrione was assigned in 1982 to Operation Airlift, a sting scheme to trap smugglers. In his undercover role, Mitrione was told to work with an informant who was cooperating with the police. In a familiar scenario that sometimes seems to flow naturally from the dynamics of the situation, one day the informer asked for the privilege of being a real dealer on the side while he was acting like one for the government. Agent Mitrione allowed the man to take a small load of cocaine to Miami and simply failed to tell his FBI supervisors about it. For this small initial courtesy, the appreciative informant-trafficker gave him $3,500 and a $9,000 gold Rolex watch. Soon Dan Mitrione was actively involved in the trade, skimming off small amounts from many of the illegal shipments he was supposedly capturing. Within a few years, he received in excess of $850,000.

To its credit, the FBI found him out, confronted him, and got him to plead guilty. In 1985, the disgraced federal officer was sentenced to ten years in prison. Commenting on the case, FBI director William Webster offered the usual banalities: "The corrupting power of drug money is one of the obvious reasons why this No. 1 crime problem must be conquered." This leading law-enforcement official had no new suggestions as to how to effect that conquest, or how to prevent his officers from succumbing to the lure of huge bribes, except to threaten other agents who might be tempted with a similar fate.

Greater insight into the dynamics of law enforcement in this new era of heightened temptations was later revealed by William C. Hendricks III of the Justice Department's Public Integrity Section. In 1985 he observed that over the previous few years these cases had been recurring time and time again. "Who's corrupting whom? Is the agent corrupting the informant, or is the informant corrupting the agent?" he asked in December 1985. At that point, many Reagan administration officials were openly dismayed over the extent of corruption of federal officials, especially in the drug area. Charges against DEA and FBI agents had become much more common; so were investigations of one group of agents by another in the same agency. In 1986, NORML did a study that resulted in a stunning chronological summary of cases of official corruption that were known to the public between January 1983 and December 1985. Approximately 300 justice officials at all levels of government were implicated. Because it was based only on newspaper stories, the report probably greatly underestimated the full scope of the problem.

Charges were even made against prosecutors who had graduated from the best law schools and had been recruited into elite Justice Department Strike Forces, the pride of the Reagan drug warrior corps. One of these was David P. Twomey, indicted in October 1985 for selling information to a major Boston-area marijuana smuggler whom the lawyer was supposedly investigating while serving as a federal prosecutor. Over an extended period Mr. Twomey allegedly received $210,000 in cash and a 30-foot sailboat. In March 1986 he was sentenced to 16 years in prison.

THE DRUG-USING ENFORCER:
A NEW DIMENSION

Another case that came to a head in the same month showed yet another dimension to this growing problem. Daniel N. Perlmutter was 29 and seemed to have started a brilliant career as an Assistant U.S. Attorney in New York City. Then it was discovered that he had been stealing cash, heroin, and cocaine from the office safe, where it had been placed as evidence. Attorney Perlmutter had broken up with his wife and admitted to being a cocaine addict. He stole the drugs mainly for his own use. After Perlmutter's guilty plea in October 1985, the head of the office, Rudolph Giuliani, commented sadly, "It was like a death in the family."

The use of illegal drugs by officials has been a subject usually mentioned only in whispers along the corridors of power. Yet government officials are not recruited from the moon, which might still be drug-free, but from a society in which illegal drug use is about as common as illegal sex. It should have been no surprise therefore when, in addition to Mr. Perlmutter, hard-drug users and addicts were recently discovered, for example, on the staffs of key Senate committees and in important federal executive agencies. It should also be no surprise to learn that a small but significant number of enforcement officials believe the drug laws to be hypocritical; some of those doubters include users of banned substances. In 1981, the former general counsel to the District of Columbia police department, Gerald M. Caplan, now a law professor, revealed that "a decade ago, more than 100 officers were taking heroin. How did we learn about them? Not because their performance was poor or because they were shaking down drug dealers. We took urine specimens. Those officers were users, not addicts, and they were not criminals, apart from their illegal use of heroin."

Add, then, to the complications of drug enforcement the fact that some officers doubt, with good reason, the rationality of the drug laws, the effectiveness of the war on drugs, the ethics of picking on drug users who commit no other crimes but possession— and that they use the substances themselves and observe in most instances that they seem to suffer less harm than if they had a beer or a shot of Scotch. That certainly thickens the plot, as could be clearly seen when D.C. police officer Bobby Walker was arrested for selling cocaine in 1983. The officer denied the charge but admitted that he used drugs as did many other officers, in part because, he claimed, they believed that it did not affect their performance on the job. Indeed, the 13-year veteran, who had received six commendations, claimed it helped him because "drugs calmed me down." Whether or not Officer Walker's claims about the impact of illegal drugs on police performance are true, it seems likely that his own drug use made him reluctant to vigorously pursue and arrest street drug users who, he observed, seemed to be hurting no one.

It is also likely that there are thousands of undiscovered Bobby Walkers in American criminal justice. For the great majority of nondrug-using officials, their continuing presence creates enormous stresses, contributing to the impotence and victimization of those "clean" officers who sometimes break under the resistance to the laws found both within and outside the criminal justice system. Therefore, the drug warriors are forced to work in such a twisted, schizophrenic world that it is a wonder that *any* of them keep their balance and their integrity.

THE PERSONAL TRAUMA OF UNDERCOVER WORK

Specialists in psychology are starting to document the harsh impact that drug-enforcement work, especially in undercover disguises, may have on the mental health of police officers. Dr. Michel Girodo, a University of Ottawa psychologist, reported in 1984 on the evaluations made of 270 American and Canadian undercover enforcement officers. He found that undercover agents were "psychologically at risk" three times more often than were agents before their first assignments, when they generally showed no unusual number of problems. By contrast, the undercover agents displayed abnormally high anxiety levels, depression, and major personality changes.

One agent had spent three years as part of a large community of drug traffickers, and had become accepted virtually as one of their extended family. While testifying on the stand for fourteen days in their prosecution, "his behavior reflected the schizophrenic life he had been forced to lead. One moment he would answer questions in the detailed, objective, and professional manner of a law-enforcement officer, and then, without warning, he would slip into the role of his other self." The officer would then take on the accent and body language of the targets, and was "apparently unable to control which part to display."

Another officer showed serious personality disturbances after living seven months undercover with a motorcycle gang. He developed paranoid delusions of grandeur and claimed to have evidence of massive conspiracies that would be of interest to both U.S. and Canadian enforcement officials. Those delusions operated so as to prevent him from slipping into a deep depression. "His case surfaced when he shaved his head, put a ring through his nose and attempted to board a U.S.-bound flight carrying three concealed weapons," Dr. Girodo wrote.

Yet another agent was discovered to have hidden drug purchases under the seat of his car in order to conceal his success in making the buys. It turned out that the three months he had spent with his targets had developed in him a genuine affection for them. The agent exhibited what might have been interpreted in other circumstances as decent, normal human behavior when he confessed, "I couldn't testify against them . . . they're my friends."

Success brought severe depression to a fourth agent in the study. During the six months following his victory over the targets he had befriended, the officer was unable to do anything but sit on his living room floor and talk to his dog.

THE SOUTH FLORIDA SYNDROME

In many cases of improper police behavior, there is no indication of an identifiable mental health collapse. All that comes through is bizarre and destructive behavior, often of a serious criminal nature. Such officers seem to act as if they lived in their own corrupt world unregulated by any law or ethical obligation. It is always a question as to whether the officers rationally and deliberately sought out the opportunities for illegal gains or if the temptations and stresses of drug enforcement simply happened to overcome their moral defenses.

Stresses on the police in the south Florida area seem to have exacted a huge toll in recent years. Indeed, simply to live in that area is to know daily that you are living in the middle of a war zone. Even after almost 10,000 arrests claimed by the federal drug task force since 1982, the *Miami Herald* observed in December 1985 that no matter where you live in south Florida, "chances are a drug dealer lives nearby." Chances are, too, that a corrupt police officer does also. Police officers have been implicated in a stunning array of offenses, most having some connection with the billions in drug money flowing through the community—drug use, drug sales, thefts of large sums of cash from police department safes, home burglaries, robbery, and murder. The question on the minds of many citizens was etched in a headline of the *Herald* in late 1985: "How many cops have gone bad?"

Far too many had, by that time and thereafter. The allegations of massive police corruption continued into 1986. However, I met a large cross section of the enforcement officials in that area—the staff director of the Vice President's task force, Customs agents, many Miami drug-enforcement police and prosecution officials, from top executives to street cops. And I have spoken to many experts in the area and reviewed a mountain of written material about that region and its police. If these people are somehow afflicted with mass defects of character, I did not observe them. In my opinion, many of the enforcement officers in south Florida rate among the best the county has. The entire structure of law enforcement and justice in that region, however, is being weakened by the harsh pressures of the drug war.

There is a message in the chaos of south Florida—and in the social cesspools into which we have thrown our prosecutors and police all over the country—that we cannot ignore. Even our finest enforcement officials face great risks of themselves becoming victims of the crushing pressures created by seeking to enforce the drug laws in the martial spirit demanded by the leading drug warriors at this time in America.

PART FOUR

Drug-peace

DEADLY MISUNDERSTANDING ON THE RANGE

The long and bloody range wars that pitted cattlemen and sheep herders appear to have been based on a misunderstanding.

There is new evidence that if either side had given in and grazed cattle and sheep together, ranchers would have made more money than they could by raising either species alone.

Studies by the Agriculture Department's Agricultural Research Service show that cattle and sheep have such different preferences in forage plants that they compete only slightly.

A rancher could produce more pounds of meat per acre by running cattle and sheep together than with either alone.

—*Washington Post*, February 9, 1986

12

Escaping the War Trap

LIKE most Americans weaned on Western tales, it was my belief that whenever sheep herders appeared on the horizon of a range, the cowboys were required, by the natural forces ruling the universe, to unlimber their weapons and fight the invaders to the death in order to save a precious way of life. It was a shock to discover recently that those perpetual small range wars were based upon a misunderstanding of basic scientific facts. Not only could cattle and sheep peacefully coexist on the same green pastures, but when left to their own devices, they formed social bonds. They actually liked each other. Each group grew bigger and stronger together than they had alone. It is quite possible that their human counterparts would have also.

The difficulty was that the human beings involved did not understand the basic facts. The sheep herders or nesters believed fervently in the need for fences and closed ranges; the cattlemen believed with equal passion in open ranges. Both groups thought that their way was the only way their vital animals could survive and that war on their opponents was thus unavoidable. They were dead wrong.

Similar unconventional and irreverent thoughts could be ap-

351

plied to many other costly American conflicts, those that are usually called "wars" in the history books. That rather grand conclusion stems not from pacifist principles, because I believe that armed force, regrettably, has a place in the world. It is instead based upon a reflective assessment of past major armed conflicts in terms of whether or not the issues were worth warring about, and whether or not there were peaceful options. Of all the American wars, in my opinion, only World War II, and perhaps Korea, seem to have been unavoidable. As for other conflicts, there have always been peaceful options, which were ignored in the heat of war passion. Either that, or our national actions were based upon greed or intolerance.

In particular, there was no need for wars to win the American Southwest or Cuba or the Philippines. These were acts of conquest, with no redeeming features, no cause worth celebrating.

It is highly debatable that there was a need for the American nation to enter the European war of 1914–18, the outcome of which was decided before we entered. The deaths of 116,000 American boys might have hastened the final result, but only by a few months.

In the seemingly unavoidable Second World War, there was no need to imprison 110,000 loyal Americans in concentration camps, a blot on American honor eagerly incurred because of the Japanese ancestry of the victims—and because of a fundamental error of fact based upon fear. The belief was that they were working for the enemy nation, that there was no difference among the Japanese wherever they lived. There was never any evidence of native Japanese disloyalty, a fact known to the FBI and duly reported but ignored by leaders in the passions of the times.

We tore apart American society for years and lost 58,000 American youth in Vietnam. There was no need for that horror, based upon a wide array of misconceptions, from which we have not yet recovered.

There is no need for the war on drugs, which is based on fundamental errors of fact, not least that it is impossible for users of hated drugs to live peacefully side-by-side with nondrug users, like cattlemen and sheep herders in the old West. I worry about how many of our boys and girls in uniform will have to die and how many basically decent American citizens of all ages will be imprisoned before our leaders understand the fundamental errors of fact upon which *this* needless war is founded.

The American nation can kick the drug-war habit but first it must realize that it is addicted to war in dealing with drug problems—in much the same way that too many of our citizens are addicted to drugs for coping with personal problems. Proof of that drug-war addiction among leading Americans appeared shortly after I read that news item on range animals with its evidence of yet another needless American conflict. It was the report *America's Habit*, by the President's Commission on Organized Crime. The report kicked up a storm of protest in the center of American society unlike anything I have ever seen. Even though the drug warriors are dominant, the opposition from both conservative businessmen and old-fashioned traditional liberals continues to this day. They constitute a minority voice but a strong one.

If our nation and our people are to escape the drug-war trap, we will be rescued by that sane, rational center of the political spectrum. Now is the time for it to continue that unity produced by revulsion to the vision created by the presidential commission report—a revulsion kept alive by the excesses of the scared summer of '86. Middle America's leaders must push for an open declaration by the government that the drug war has failed and that if we continue down the warpath, many of our most cherished national values will be torn to shreds.

Moreover, the government must recognize and admit that waging the war is the single greatest impediment to solving the problem around which it revolves: the abuse of drugs by our people. Thus, not only is the war unneeded, but also it prevents even modest solutions to the conflict and to healing its victims.

The two words "drug" and "war" are now so joined in the minds of our leaders that they tend to think of them as one, drugwar, something like damnyankee in certain regions of the country. A new word might be coined; perhaps "drugpeace" will do. That word and the ideas associated with it could form the foundation for the profound ideological change that must take place if we are to move down the road away from war and toward a vast range of peaceful options.

13

A Bundle of Peaceful Compromises

IF the idea of drugpeace were to be accepted, then everything is possible for the future. Great ideas and seemingly impossible compromises flourish where peace and love dominate.

We should start with the humble idea that no one has a complete solution to the drug problem. I certainly do not. All I can offer is what writer Peter Passell said in a *New York Times* editorial comment when he summed up my last book, arguing for a more tolerant view toward heroin and addicts, in these words: "How to turn a disaster back into a problem." That thought expresses the proper frame of mind with which to contemplate the peace process in the drug arena.

The U.S. Constitution of 1787 was a bundle of compromises which gave breathing space for the nation to work out a host of emotional issues peacefully. Similarly, we must begin work on a bundle of compromises on the law and politics of drugs now, before it is too late. We need a set of flexible proposals that can be adjusted over time on the basis of pragmatic experience, one of the better habits ingrained in the American character.

Here are some beginning steps, some pragmatic compromises that might take us into that calmer land beyond drug prohibition.

RECRUIT THE ENFORCERS
AS REFORMERS

It would be a major breakthrough—a minor miracle, some might say—if we could somehow convince the enforcers that they were, in a sense, victims, too, and that they had much to gain by becoming drug-law reformers. If I could arrange a quiet summit meeting of all of the major enforcement leaders and the loyal opposition at least to discuss such an apparently improbable goal, I would suggest several major new strategies. They would be aimed both at reducing the continuing sacrifice of our police in the drug war and at evolving a more positive role for all law-enforcement agencies in modern society.

Rather than treating the police like the enemy, like the scum of the drug world, the liberal critics would agree to join hands with them and support increased resources for the FBI, the DEA, and other enforcement agencies on the grounds that we all want violent criminals and organized-crime figures caught and imprisoned for as long as possible. There would be a unified campaign to support a major assault on organized crime, no matter whether the criminals were involved in drug trafficking or any one of a hundred other illegal conspiracies. That unified support would come at a frank political price.

To start with, law-enforcement leaders would have to admit that the role of all of their agencies is considerably more narrow than now claimed. Police and prosecution leaders would have to agree to stop claiming that their enforcement of the laws was saving our people from drugs. They would have to set their sights on a much more limited target: *American law enforcement would continue its responsibility to apprehend the often despicable people involved in the illicit drug trade but police leaders would admit publicly that even their best work had no significant impact on regulating the drug-taking habits of the citizenry at large.*

The military services would be restricted greatly in drug enforcement, and civilian police would stop using military tactics. Soldiers would concentrate on making themselves more effective fighters and police would seek to rejoin the ranks of a democratic civilian society in the function of friendly protectors. The role and budget of the Coast Guard in drug control would be expanded

because in peacetime it is the lead "civilian" agency with responsibility for enforcement of the smuggling laws. Coast Guard officers
and men know the rules of search and seizure; members of the
other services do not, and it makes no sense to spend time and
money to train them in that area.

All personnel involved in drug arrests and searches would be
instructed to go beyond the basic requirements in adhering strictly
to constitutional rights. In case of doubt, the officers would simply
come out on the side of individual freedom. This would mean that
military-style tactics in searching American homes and fields would
rarely be used, certainly not for a few marijuana plants. Even
where many plants were sighted, the police would consider peaceful options, such as asking the landowners to destroy them before
unleashing military assaults on American farms. Unless there was
no alternative, citizens found in the vicinity of raids would not be
searched or detained.

Greater concern would be shown for the physical and mental
health of law-enforcement officers involved in drug enforcement,
especially undercover work. Commanders would develop better
methods of support and guidance to reduce the possibilities of
corruption.

The FBI, the DEA, and all major law-enforcement agencies
would declare a moratorium on providing drug education for the
classroom. Police officers who provide drug-education classes usually propagate harmful myths about the nature of drugs. If police
want to tell students about the threats posed by drug traffickers
and the nature of drug policing instead of the dangers of drugs,
that would be quite appropriate. At the same time, I would hope
to see a great expansion in the number of honest drug-education
courses taught by trained educators who brought out all aspects
of the many conflicting facts regarding each of the most popular
drugs, legal and illegal. Drug education is vital and should be
carried out by professionals in the field of education who have the
knowledge and the guts to tell the whole truth.

The most painful part of this bundle of political compromises
for many enforcement officials would be the expectation that leaders of major police organizations would become leaders in drug law
and policy reform as part of the liberal-conservative alliance here
being proposed. Moreover, even if many drug laws were changed
and if some drugs, such as marijuana, were legalized, the police
should be made to understand that they will not be reforming

themselves out of jobs—as some of them, to my amazement, now fear. However liberal the drug laws become, there will always be limits and people exceeding them, and thus the need for good police officers.

Of course, the best of those officers might, at some happy time in the future when smuggling drugs *into* the country no longer makes any economic sense, be shifted to more important work—such as attempting to prevent the smuggling of American technology and military secrets *out* of the country to unfriendly foreign powers, an endeavor in which these officers might for the first time in their professional lives enjoy undivided public support.

SAVE OUR SICK FROM HUMILIATION AND PAIN

Most people of goodwill would agree that our sick must be protected from the excesses of the drug-war mentality. It would follow that this is a good centrist issue on which to focus major initial reform efforts, which might be divided conveniently into proposals to help, first, the organically ill and, second, the addicted. Both groups, remember, under American law are considered to be suffering from diseases.

If the millions of organically ill patients—those suffering from cancer, glaucoma, multiple sclerosis, and heart disease, for example—started to exercise their combined political power, they could move mountains. Even more could be accomplished if some of their friends and relatives took on the role of patient advocates and fought to represent the best interests of each disabled person. In many cases, the advocate would simply intervene with the massive medical bureaucracy so that ordinary civility and comfort were assured.

There are other, more aggressive tactics for patients and their advocates to undertake. These might deal with reform of the laws and practices that impose extra suffering on those who are already suffering too much. Some patients and patient advocates, alone or in organizations, may want to consider new forms of peaceful protest against the current system, which might be combined with lawsuits by committed lawyers. Such tactics have been used by civil rights and women's groups in recent history but never by organized advocates of the sick. Those government officials who have denied sick people access to marijuana, for example, should lose their anonymity and be treated with the moral opprobrium that would be appropriate for comparable deleterious criminal activity. The federal officials responsible are to be found primarily in the White House Office of Drug Abuse Policy; in the Department of Justice, which includes the DEA; in the Department of Health and Human Services, which includes the FDA and NIDA; and among the members and staffs of the key congressional committees that support the cruelty of the present system.

If tens of thousands of patients and their advocates flooded those officials with protests and demands for relief, their confident arrogance might be dented. I can testify that those officials believe that they have mass public support from the truly decent people of the country in denying sick people access to forbidden medicines. Only persistent protests can change their minds.

Even under current law, there is no reason why all patients suffering from cancer, glaucoma, scleroderma, or other diseases should not be immediately designated as a research subject and provided all of the THC pills or marijuana cigarettes their doctors are willing to prescribe. While the law would allow this, the federal officials do everything in their power to prevent it from happening except when some sick citizen makes such a fuss that he or she cannot be ignored. That, of course, is what Bob Randall did.

Ann Guttentag did so also. The New Hope, Pennsylvania, doll-store owner was suffering from terminal cancer and was one of those patients who could not be comforted by THC pills. In fact, she labeled those pills simply "laughable" as a means of dealing with the nausea brought about by her chemotherapy. "After chemotherapy, you can't even hold a sip of water down," she explained in 1980. This dying patient knew that marijuana cigarettes worked for her—like "a gift from heaven"—but her government in the form of the National Cancer Institute, the FDA, and other agencies insisted that a doctor test whether THC pills worked as well. Ann Guttentag made an emotional statement to the House Select Committee on Narcotics Abuse and Control in 1980 about how only the marijuana cigarettes helped her. After months of battling with many agencies of the federal government, the legal marijuana cigarettes arrived, but the patient died soon afterwards in August 1981 at the age of 50.

Almost all of the multitude of other patients like Ann Gutentag suffer and die in anonymity because few sick people want to go public with their illness and most are ashamed that they need a drug with such a bad reputation as marijuana. In some cases I have encountered, the victims suffered blindness or died while they were fighting and pleading with the federal drug bureaucrats for their medicine. I believe, therefore, that it would be morally justified now for a protest movement to start seeking living substitutes or patient advocates for victims who have died or who for other reasons are no longer in the fight. As it now stands, if the government officials are obstinate enough, their opponents melt away, almost literally. If, however, these officials knew that some advocate bearing the adopted name "Ann Guttentag" or the designation "Patient Advocate of Ann Guttentag" (of course, with the permission of her survivors) was going to keep pestering them to ease the suffering of sick people by allowing them access to hated drugs, as Ms. Guttentag herself would have done, it is possible that progress would be made in protecting our sick even under current laws. For the survivors, there would be the added comfort that this was one method of keeping the spirit and the memory of a loved one alive.

Bills should be introduced into the U.S. Congress and every state legislature that would declare heroin and marijuana "safe and effective" in the treatment of patients suffering from cancer, glaucoma, scleroderma, and other diseases, such as multiple sclerosis, where doctors and patients have found that it provides some benefits. Other feared drugs might be added if evidence of therapeutic benefit was produced. The bills should be drawn up along the lines of the one introduced by Rep. McKinney on the therapeutic uses of marijuana rather than like the Compassionate Pain Relief Act (CPRA) for heroin, an enlightened piece of legislation introduced by Rep. Waxman, which I have also supported. The McKinney bill, however, has the advantage of treating marijuana as a known and reliable drug with a proven history in medicine and placing it immediately into Schedule II of the Controlled Substances Act. No experiment is required, as in the case of the CPRA.

Humane legislators should formulate various versions of an omnibus bill that would be simple and direct in its purpose to reclassify heroin, marijuana, and perhaps other drugs as Schedule II medicines and thus available for any ill person, under the usual strict controls that apply to all medicines in this category, such as morphine. There should be no need for a legal sham that the patients are research subjects and no red tape holding back the healing hand of the physician who wants to help suffering people by prescribing them medicine whose therapeutic value has been demonstrated by long experience. Until such a law is passed, the lawyers of the country must take up the burden and bring suit after suit seeking to establish the right to health and to medical treatment for all of our sick citizens.

These suits often require a good deal of persistence on the part of the lawyers. NORML first sued the DEA in 1972 to force it to allow marijuana and THC to be used as regular Schedule II medicines (potentially addicting medicines used with stringent controls) for sick people. The case, *NORML* v. *DEA*, went through a seemingly endless number of appearances before federal administrative agencies and courts over the years, with the government officials continually resisting a hearing on the merits, that is, on the core issue of the medical value of marijuana, and thus obstructing the seemingly simple, compassionate step of allowing the categorization of the natural plant or its distilled essence, the pills, as medicine. The DEA and the FDA then became interested in encouraging the development of a *synthetic* THC pill, which was composed of a chemical named dronabinol, with the trade name Marinol. It was manufactured by Unimed, Inc., and approved by the FDA for use as a regular medicine to control nausea in cancer patients receiving chemotherapy. To their credit, as we saw, the drug officials made the historic decision to take a marijuana substitute out of Schedule I and for the first time in decades make it available to patients without requiring them to become research subjects. This was a great victory for NORML and for common sense.

NORML requested an administrative hearing on Marinol, however, for a variety of reasons, not least to determine why the natural marijuana could not also be rescheduled. In early 1986, the mountain came to Mohammed. DEA lawyers contacted Kevin Zeese at NORML asking that the hearing request be withdrawn, in return for which DEA would agree to place the core issue of natural marijuana in medicine before a federal administrative law judge. Mr. Zeese agreed. Thus a synthetic THC pill will soon be available to cancer chemotherapy patients, and there is hope for a new full and impartial review of the evidence on natural marijuana as a medicine in a wide variety of cases.

While serving as co-counsel with Kevin Zeese in this case, starting in 1986, I have seen with my own eyes how much work remains to be done to make that hope a reality. At one of the preliminary hearings before DEA administrative law judge Francis L. Young, on December 5, 1986, DEA lawyers argued that the process of actually taking evidence on the central issue of marijuana's medical value should again be delayed until the Food and Drug Administration had considered the matter—a proposal that might result in more years of waiting for the sick people of the country. Moreover, Joyce Nalepka, Mrs. Reagan's ally from the National Federation of Parents for Drug-Free Youth, appeared at the hearing, shooting daggers with her eyes at Kevin Zeese and me seated at the counsel table. She blurted out to Judge Young that he should consider the nature of the petitioner in the matter—that NORML got its money from *High Times* magazine and from sellers of drug paraphernalia. Judge Young made it clear that he would not be influenced by such talk. While Ms. Nalepka's remarks were deemed irrelevant and almost comical by some onlookers, I fear her cruel views still dominate the DEA and the American government: this suit to provide all forms of marijuana as a medicine to cancer and glaucoma sufferers is a red herring by drug pushers to seduce American youth into abusing pot.

Lawyers from major law firms can help overcome these hysterical views that are so harmful to our sick. In this case, it has been a comfort to see Frank Stillwell seated at the next counsel table, beside his client Bob Randall. Frank is a lawyer with Steptoe and Johnson, the firm which continues to represent Bob Randall's Alliance for Cannabis Therapeutics, also a party in the suit to reschedule marijuana.

LOVE THY NEIGHBOR EVEN IF HE IS USING HATED DRUGS

The essence of a war is hatred, hatred to the death of the enemy and of those who give him aid and comfort. To carry out a drug war successfully requires the persistent application of hate toward users of hated drugs. The principle could be stated thus: hate thy neighbor if he is using bad drugs.

The difficulty with that principle is that the majority of drug abusers are decent people who are often deeply troubled by their compulsion to take drugs so often. They are not helped by being treated with hate. The essence of dealing with people in trouble with drugs should be love, compassion, and care. The reverse principle, then, might be stated: love thy neighbor in spite of the fact that he is using hated drugs—especially if he is acting decently in other ways. Persistent application of the reverse principle by large numbers of people would undermine the drug warriors who are so harming our country and our families.

In fact, the first place for concerned citizens to begin making a contribution to drugpeace in the nation and even in the world is right in their own lives and own families. Parents and children personally interested in learning about drug abuse, however, must invest a good deal of time in study of this subject because the experts are in such conflict. There is no one source for unbiased advice. Certainly not the U.S. government, nor any single group of doctors or drug-abuse experts.

However, there are many experts now working in the country who advocate moderation, calm, and tolerance in dealing with drug abusers. They believe, as do I, that while the nation has serious problems of drug abuse, neither this generation of our adults or our children is in danger of being destroyed by chemicals. Individual citizens and groups of concerned parents should turn to the proponents of moderation and tolerance for educational information rather than to the alarmists who dominate national drug policy and the parents' movement today.

A group of mothers in rural Wasco County, Oregon, did just that in 1982 when they formed Mothers Against Misuse and Abuse. MAMA was created in reaction to the misinformation promulgated by the parents' movement supported by the White House. The group seeks to provide a full range of unbiased information about legal and illegal drugs to citizens of all ages, including the elderly, who often have trouble with prescription medicines. It has supported a school curriculum that teaches students how to make responsible decisions about important matters in their lives: managing stress, controlling time, and using drugs, among others. Led by an indomitable farmwoman, Sandee Burbank—who asserts, "It takes ovaries to do what we do!"—its members have become a powerful political and educational force in that state. Interest in the unique down-home, frontier honesty of MAMA has spread throughout the nation. It serves as one excellent model for rational community action by parents who are both concerned about drug abuse and turned off by the extremism and hypocrisy of drug-warrior educational programs.

Another model for guidance in approaching the subject of drug abuse may be found in the manner with which America has historically dealt with conflicting religious creeds: virtually all are accepted as decent moral options that ought to be available for those people who believe in them. The subject of drugs should be approached in the same spirit—more like religion than science. My wish is that law and medicine recognize the personal and nonscientific nature of the drug-abuse arena by enacting some form of First Amendment guarantee of freedom to select a personal drug-abuse doctrine, but limited somewhat by enlightened principles of medicine.

This freedom from an established ideology ought to be applied to the treatment arena so that the telephone directory Yellow Pages of any major city could contain listings for a full range of drug- and alcohol-treatment specialists. That legal list could include physicians who give no drugs whatsoever and rely only on psychotherapy; physicians who use oral medicinal opium for heroin addicts and Valium for alcoholics; social workers who believe in rapid detoxification and group or individual therapy; lay therapists who rely upon religious conversions and religious books as the answer to all addictions; and physicians who provide long-term maintenance with injectable drugs, such as heroin and Dilaudid, for narcotic addicts. Some of these approaches may be found today; some are still illegal, for irrational reasons.

In the absence of that wide freedom granted by law and practice, thoughtful people will seek to work out the greatest possible freedom within existing regulations. They will recognize that current Established Drug Abuse Doctrine makes little practical sense in another way—since some powerful members of that Establishment define drug abuse as involving even one use of any illicit drug or even the use of a licit drug, such as Valium or Darvon, outside of medical supervision. They might accept another definition, advocated today by many more sensible treatment experts, which comes closer to the mark: drug abuse is the use of any drug, including alcohol and tobacco, in such a way as to affect seriously health, work, or loving relationships. Having accepted that, or some other reasonable substitute, they will discover that there is no scientific method for even the most enlightened medical experts to determine if that condition exists in themselves or a loved one. While they can provide guidance, in the end thoughtful individuals must make a personal decision as to whether or not they or someone they love is in trouble with drugs and whether or not to start looking into treatment possibilities.

If they do decide that treatment is needed, rational citizens will beware of the popular cults like Straight or Toughlove or any institutional permutation that has hate and rejection at its core. I have cross-examined several recovering addicts on this point and just went over it again with Ned (who is doing splendidly now months after I first wrote about him). It has taken this fine young man years to get over "feeling like a junkie" in part because his body and emotions still remember the powerful narcotics that used to dominate them. That internal memory is almost gone but another lingers more powerfully: the lack of respect and the discounting of his worth as a human being that he felt from some physicians and also from some lay people who knew about his drug problem. Therefore, in seeking diagnosis and treatment of a drug abuser in the family, concerned citizens should look for professionals who seem to display compassion rather than disrespect toward that person. Such treatment professionals are to be found in every large community, but it takes personal effort to discover them because they do not walk around with "competent and compassionate" labels on them.

Never turn the alleged abuser over to a facility, as Fred Collins's parents did with him, breathe a sigh of relief, drive away, and simply leave the treatment of the so-called druggie up to the experts. The most important force in recovering from drug abuse is the maturing internal will and understanding of the patient, as the best treatment experts well know. Family members should play a role as both patient advocates and as caring members of an extended treatment team. They can see to it that the patient is not kept in an institution needlessly and at the same time they can help impose reasonable demands for responsible behavior. Moreover, they can also commence reflecting on their own behavior and on what piece of the action they had, if any, in setting the stage for drug abuse in the patient now in treatment.

If these guidelines are followed, then any one of a wide variety of existing programs may be chosen to help the drug abuser. None of them has a quick cure and relapse is the rule. There is no known doctor-induced cure for drug abuse. However, so long as the patient feels kindly treated and believes that he or she is being helped, involvement with a program should be continued. Preference should be given to programs, such as Alcoholics Anonymous, Narcotics Anonymous, and reputable individual professional counselors, where the participants can walk in and out at will, are not inmates, and thus bear full responsibility for their own fates. The imprisonment of alleged drug abusers, even in good psychiatric hospitals, should always be viewed with suspicion in a democracy.

Drug abusers and their families should seek to better understand the dynamics of addiction. Those dynamics are difficult to comprehend, even for experienced professionals. That search should be conducted by talking to drug users and reading about their experiences—and by quiet reflection on one's own inner feelings, especially by the drug abuser in question at the moment. The rewards of the search itself seem to be worth it for some people. Recently, a student came to me to say that for three years he had been a marijuana addict (the first such addict, by the way, I have ever met, although I have long claimed that abusers of this drug existed). He had taken my course, he told me, to come to grips with his problem.

At the beginning of the semester, we had discussed the dynamics of heroin addiction and treatment. Marijuana was barely mentioned. Yet the young man claimed that he started to understand how marijuana was dominating his life, how he had lost control, and how he might regain control through reflective insights into the role it played in his emotions. He was particularly affected, he said, when I talked about the positive power of heroin addicts to heal themselves when they, and not a doctor or a police officer or a judge, were "ready." Over a period of weeks, the student tapered off from five joints a day to the point where he quit totally; the day he came to me marked a month of being totally free of marijuana. In the previous few weeks, he said, he came to understand some simple truths: the drug played a powerful role in his life, as I had suggested in the case of heroin, because it was a form of self-medication for a variety of severe emotional stresses. Now that the medication was gone, he was more in touch with his feelings and had just made a decision to seek professional psychiatric help to deal with those stresses. The young student *knew* now in his guts that he had the personal power to do so. You could see it on his face: this kid was flying high, but without drugs.

Yet knowledge does not always lead to abstinence. With all of his knowledge, Kenny Freeman, and multitudes like him, believe they are better off with drugs. Remember, however, that the reverse principle should still be applied to alleged drug abusers: love them despite their drugs. While that principle may sound irresponsible, it is more in line with humanity's great traditions than current martial ideology. In a world dominated by drugpeace, we would approach users as decent, rational people and help them think out what was best for them, whether or not that involved continued drug use.

One of the great tasks of this new peaceful era would be to separate the status of being a narcotic addict from the status of being a predatory criminal. Crime and violence on the streets of America would be greatly reduced. We can start working on that task by adopting the new ideology about the essentially decent nature of addicts.

The most shining personification of that compassionate principle in action that I have ever discovered was the late Reverend Terence E. Tanner, a Catholic priest and director of a unique London association for the housing and care of narcotics addicts. He believed that perverse social biases had made such addicts "the scapegoats of our age." Being irrationally abused by society, they returned the favor. Terry Tanner believed, on the other hand, that if addicts were treated with trust and compassion, they would act as if they deserved that treatment. The outspoken cleric took a neutral position on the use of drugs—a heretical position in most expert drug-abuse circles—coupled with a strong moral demand that users live decently. "We do not encourage them to use drugs but equally we do not discourage them," Father Tanner wrote in 1976. "We encourage them to responsibility in every department of life and, as they begin to acquire responsibility, they limit their use of drugs or give them up altogether." Those addicts who continued the use of drugs, however, were treated with the same love as those who quit.

The implementation of Tanner's principles in America would require major changes of laws and attitudes, changes which seem to be much further in the future than legal reforms that would help only the organically ill. However, we should start working now toward a system under which doctors and their addict-patients would be left almost completely alone to work out ways of living responsibly with or without drugs. In those cases where drugs were chosen as part of the treatment, there is no reason why oral methadone should continue to be legally mandated as the only proper long-term maintenance medicine. If there is some scientific reason why addicts cannot be maintained on a wide variety of narcotics, including heroin, I have yet to discover it in the medical records of centuries.

What I *have* discovered is that many doctors and allied staff find it difficult to deal with addicts receiving so-called maintenance doses of drugs for long periods of time. There is no scientific manner in which to determine the proper dosage. Five milligrams of pure heroin a day will hold some addicts; a few need and function on 500 milligrams. Some addicts complain repeatedly that their current dosage is too low. Doctors and their staffs often find the whole business tiresome and frustrating. Their feelings properly reflect the nature of the disease of addiction—chronic, recurring, virtually incurable. A major task of the future is to come to grips realistically with issues of proper maintenance, issues which cannot be dealt with unless the initial legal right is fully established.

In the absence of statutes giving addict-patients the right to choose their medicine, and to commence working out ways of living legally with the drug, bar associations should encourage the lawyers of the country to bring suits to guarantee those rights. It is a violation of basic legal reasoning—and seemingly of the constitutional rights to due process and equal protection of the laws—to prohibit an addict to, say, Darvon from obtaining a legal maintenance prescription of that relatively weak narcotic while allowing access to the more powerful methadone.

We will know that the new era of drugpeace has arrived when police are trained to recognize that one of their most important duties is the protection of the rights of doctors and patients involved in legitimate drug-maintenance programs—and especially when addicts regularly start coming to DEA offices for help when their legitimate drug supplies are interrupted for some reason.

I NEVER SAID WE SHOULD LEGALIZE HEROIN AND ALL OTHER DRUGS

Up to now in this book, I have not argued that we should legalize *all* drugs nor that we should give heroin addicts *all* the heroin they want. However, if past experience is a guide, that is precisely how my position in this book will be summarized by scholarly experts and by journalists, friend and foe alike, as has occurred frequently in recent years. Allow me to state once again that I never have taken that position. Never. And I do not now.

Nor have I ever said, as claimed by *The New York Times* on September 14, 1984, that "the United States should give up on drug control." (I did say, as the newspaper reported, "We just don't have the power to solve the problem," and that some drugs, notably marijuana, should be legalized and taxed heavily, with the proceeds allocated to educational and treatment programs.) As so often happens in this emotional field, the twisted truth of the *Times* story was twisted even more in another harmful product of the awful summer of '86: a book by one of the leading drug-abuse scholars in the country, James A. Inciardi, the director of the Division of Criminal Justice at the University of Delaware. In *The War on Drugs*, Professor Inciardi presented the most complete scholarly apology for the modern war on drugs, including a call for greater application of police and military power, that has yet appeared in print.

To fashion that apology, scholar Inciardi found it necessary to demean the research and common sense of most drug-war critics in scathing terms, one being that they were "atavistic liberal thinkers." He dismissed out of hand any discussion of the British option in terms reminiscent of drug-enforcement leaders Anslinger, Mullen, and Lawn because that situation had "gotten out of control," a conclusion he supported with even new distortions. "Finally," Dr. Inciardi wrote, "there is legalization, or what might be called the *Trebach* model." He then went on to give a bowdlerized version of the misinformation that had already appeared in that 1984 *Times* story. To add insult to injury, he declared that this approach had failed in England.

I barely know where to begin to straighten out the mangling

of the truth contained in these few lines. The British have never legalized heroin nor have I, for the umpteenth time, recommended it. The Trebach model of legalization exists only in the imagination of some misguided reporters, scholars, and officials. As I have already pointed out in this book, I plead for moderation and compromise, for better laws, not wholesale repeal of them. Moreover, in my last book, *The Heroin Solution*, which I immodestly hope that Professor Inciardi and his allies will read, I argued that if the law relented and allowed medical doctors the option of providing narcotics, including heroin, to some addicts, this would open up the drug-abuse treatment field to the consideration of a whole range of new initiatives. I never said that the ultimate solution to virtually all problems of hard-drug abuse would be medically prescribed heroin. In fact my use of the term "solution" was a play on words because in old-fashioned American terms there is no way we can win total victory over heroin or any drug. I *did* say, and still believe, that real progress in breaking the vicious connection between addiction and crime is impossible without "medicalizing" heroin—allowing it to be prescribed by doctors for some addicts.

However, once that giant step is taken, we would have to confront a whole set of new issues that would emerge then, and only then. That is a long way from saying that heroin is the ultimate solution or that we should simply give up on all drug-law enforcement so that anyone who wanted a shot could simply put his money down on the bar and name his brand of poison. Medicalized heroin will get us through the gate and into a new, innovative ball park. It will not win the game.

The availability of prescribed heroin would mean that multitudes of addicts would be able to function as decent law-abiding citizens for the first time in years. Their health should be much improved because their drugs would be clean and measured in labeled dosages. The number of crimes they commit should drop dramatically. By implication, addicts to other narcotics, such as morphine and codeine, would also reap the same benefits. They would be eligible to receive maintenance doses of the drugs on which they were dependent. Hordes of potential crime victims would, accordingly, be denied the pleasure.

Many drug users, however, would not benefit at all—chippers or occasional users, for example. Since they are not addicted, they are not sick and would not be eligible for a prescription of medicine.

Of greater significance, many addicts tell me that they do not want to obtain prescriptions of legal narcotics. A significant proportion of the many addicts I have come to know in recent years view the very idea of drugs from doctors as obscene. "Here I am struggling, going through agony, to stop taking these damn chemicals and here you are telling me it's good for me to take them," they say.

Some even scream such remarks at me, like the woman from the Roxbury ghetto who was in the audience on a Boston television show in November 1982 and who shouted accusingly, "You want me to take drugs!" I yelled back, "No, I do not! Stop this instant!" More calmly, I added that I simply wanted her and her doctor to have the option of prescribed drugs if it helped her and if she felt it did not, she would, of course, never be forced to take them.

During the next year, on one hot day in July, Warren Weitzman, one of the American students attending my London institute, came into my room at the Imperial College of Science and Technology. Warren was in his thirties and had a long history of addiction to narcotics. In recent years, he had been clean. Warren paused, looked as if he had something important to say, and then said it. "You always told your classes that in cases of heroin addiction, permanent cure is the exception and relapse is the rule. [Actually, those were not my words but those of the British Rolleston Committee of 1926.] Well, I'm afraid I've relapsed."

After commiserating with Warren, I asked him what he wanted to do. He said he wanted to get locked up so he could kick, because he simply could not seem to rein in this run of drug taking. After a series of telephone calls around England, I managed to get him admitted to one of the best private psychiatric hospitals in the country, which happened to be only a few miles away in Chelsea. The addict was injecting hundreds of milligrams daily of pure heroin and Diconal, that synthetic narcotic much favored by English addicts. He desperately wanted to stop. It would have been the height of irresponsibility for me or anyone else, including his doctors, to have even suggested to him that he should take maintenance doses of heroin.

The option of medicalized heroin demands a complementary responsibility: the development of a finely tuned clinical judgment as to when to use that powerful option and when not to. That judgment demands the sensitive application of the art of human relations, which can rarely be delineated in a computer model or in inflexible principles of law and medicine.

In this case, what influenced me and the doctors I consulted was that Warren was taking a large amount of injectable drugs, he claimed that he was out of control, and he directly asked that he be institutionalized and withdrawn. He seemed quite in control of his mind and determined to seek help in staying away from drugs. All of these factors affected my judgment to support his request to be "locked up" in a closed ward. My decision was not based upon immutable principles of science but upon a weighing of a number of imponderable factors. In other circumstances, I might have suggested that an addict continue taking the narcotics until he had better thought out what he wanted to do. But not in this situation.

I took my suffering student by the hand, one might say, to that clinic where he was detoxified and treated with great kindness. He now claims that my intervention and the compassionate care of his doctor, the great Max Glatt, and of the clinic staff, saved his life. Now, several years later and back in the United States, I am still in touch with Warren, who has gone through eight months of treatment in a rigorous drug-free therapeutic community program. He has graduated and seems to be doing fine now without drugs. However, at times, I still hold his hand and tell him, yes, he can make it without heroin because he surely cannot make it *with* it. I remind him that he made a lousy junkie when he was using. He ruefully agrees.

My personal acquaintance with him and with dozens of other addicts during recent years has impressed upon me that they vary tremendously in their aspirations and inner emotional resources. Some want drugs. Some hate them, especially while they are compulsively seeking them. Some could lead decent lives with drugs. Many could never adjust to a steady supply of legal medicine. In these respects, addicts vary almost as much as nonaddicts.

Addicts to other drugs, such as alcohol and tobacco, which, though legal, are inherently more organically harmful, could never benefit from a steady supply. All they would receive would be more damage to their minds and bodies.

THE RIGHT TO AFFORDABLE TREATMENT AS OFTEN AS NEEDED

It is not simply a question, then, of providing drugs for addicts, but rather of creating a new right to treatment for addicted human beings that is affordable, suitable to the particular needs of each patient, and available to deal with relapses. This new right will require a vast infusion of government funds that will support treatment for the poor and also experimentation into more effective types of rehabilitation, utilizing new techniques often without any drugs whatsoever.

One of the ironies of the great drug war of the Eighties is that the Reagan administration actually cut treatment funds (from about $334 million under the Carter administration to a low of $225 million in 1982, rising slightly to $234 million in 1986) while it was pouring money into enforcement. At the same time, the drug-war hysteria gave great encouragement to the most venal elements of the drug-abuse treatment industry to increase their already huge fees to absolutely unconscionable levels. As medical writer Toby Cohen revealed in the *Wall Street Journal* in July 1986, at the profit-making Fair Oaks hospital group "the current cost of a hospital day is $1,000, which exceeds the cost of a full day in the coronary care unit of Massachusetts General Hospital. The cost of a full inpatient term of treatment at these centers—four weeks to six months—ranges from $28,000 to $160,000, with an average of $56,000." Two of the prestigious leaders of this highly profitable growth business are Dr. Arnold Washton, who argued with me on national television that it was time to get hysterical about crack, and Dr. Mark Gold, who founded the famous 800-COCAINE hotline, calls to which are taken at the Fair Oaks headquarters in New Jersey.

Fortunately, many good treatment centers for drug and alcohol abuse charge much less than Fair Oaks. The average at the Betty Ford Clinic in California is $5,000 and at Hazelden in Minnesota, $4,000. Even at the lower rates, as Ms. Cohen points out, the expense of drug-abuse treatment is beyond the means of most people in trouble with drugs and alcohol. Moreover, the total drug-abuse bill today drives up the costs of everyone's health insurance premiums. Based on typical current fees, projections as to the probable future cost to treat a large segment of all of our abusers—including those who abuse cigarettes and food as well as alcohol and narcotics—reach a staggering $240 billion a year. However, there are models in use today, such as one developed by Harvard Medical School, that could provide treatment to that wide variety of abusers of all substances at less than $6 billion per year, the amount now spent on health insurance. The Harvard model charges even less than Ford and Hazelden.

Operating in Cambridge and Somerville, it provides a wide variety of assistance, much of it delivered by nonphysicians, including a 24-hour walk-in clinic, outpatient groups, groups for families, women's groups, a detoxification unit, and three halfway houses. Over the past 16 years, it has treated approximately 20,000 patients a year at an annual cost of $1 million. The Harvard program also faces up to the likelihood of repeated relapses and expects patients to return on several occasions. As Dr. George Valliant, formerly at Harvard and now at Dartmouth Medical School, observed, "What's important is that treatment be available for everyone as often as they need it." That simple statement by Professor Valliant should be the major goal of the country in seeking to deal realistically with all types of addiction problems. To reach that goal will require a vast commitment of energy and resources—and a vision that goes far beyond conventional drug-war strategies, far beyond narcotics, far beyond any of the illegal drugs.

The right to affordable addiction treatment would mean, for example, that I might have provided some helpful guidance to the cigarette addict who called me from Baltimore several years ago. He was a construction worker who had found that he had difficulty climbing scaffolds because he had become so short of breath. The man also had some insights into the toll of tobacco on his body: "This stuff is killing me. I've gotta get locked up somewhere, soon! Where can I go?" While I suspect that there may be many facilities around the country, I knew of only one residential program that focused on tobacco addicts, and that was in the Far West. All of the other inpatient treatment programs I knew about dealt primarily with alcohol, cocaine, and other narcotic addicts, many of whom chain-smoked tobacco while experiencing the stress of attempted rehabilitation. The creation of a network of low-cost residential treatment facilities for tobacco users would, therefore, be a major advance in fighting drug abuse, would save billions in medical expenses for cancer and heart disease, would reduce a vast amount of human misery, and would in the end save countless American lives.

Yet this new innovation for tobacco addicts would be only one advance that the new right to comprehensive affordable treatment would involve. I do not claim to know the full dimensions of what is involved in implementing that new right. That is why I feel funds must be granted for experimentation and research on new methods. However, I feel certain that it will demand billions in federal funds and the imagination of our best thinkers in the treatment field—and that the rewards to the country and its people will be well worth the money and the effort. Also, I am morally sure that all forms of addiction will be dealt with more effectively than under the current drug-war regimen.

NEW PROTECTIONS FOR PERSONAL PRIVACY

The zeal of the drug warriors to search the homes, fields, property, and bodily wastes of free citizens for chemicals is unrelenting. Their zeal is being supported by powerful institutions across the land, from the Supreme Court to the White House to the executive offices of leading corporations. Opposition is slowly developing, but it will be a difficult fight for those who come down on the side of freedom.

A whole new fabric of personal protection will have to be created because the searchers are so numerous and so powerful. This fabric must contain many strands, including lawsuit challenges to invasions of personal privacy, state laws and local ordinances, provisions in collective bargaining agreements between management and labor, and the development of habits of restraint on the part of those in power. The fact, for example, that a Customs agent at the border has the power under a Supreme Court decision to conduct almost unlimited searches of bodies and bodily wastes does not mean that this awesome power should be used except in those cases where there are reasonable grounds to believe that a specific person is carrying illicit drugs.

Indeed, the basic rule should be that an invasion of privacy of any individual who lives under the protection of the United States Constitution should always be considered an exception to the rule which presumes innocence. This presumption of privacy and innocence should apply to everyone, to our children in school, to all employees, and to travelers in our airports.

Traditional democratic principles should guide the justification for searches and testing. There should have to be probable cause or some rational relationship between the search and the evil that ought to be prevented. Thus urine testing of airline pilots or addicts in treatment under proper controls might readily be accepted. Testing of baseball players or children in school seems much less reasonable. It is all a matter of sorting out our national priorities in the face of hysterical calls to fight an invasion by the chemical people.

If pushed to make a choice, however, I would argue that our society will be less harmed by the presence of more drug abusers than by the greater erosion of our freedoms. Moreover, there is little evidence that if we allowed the zealots of the urine test and the body search to realize their fondest dreams, the overall problem of drug abuse would be diminished. There are always practical limits to the impact of the most invasive methods of search.

FIRST EXPERIMENTAL STEPS

Those of us who see ourselves as members of the loyal opposition to the drug war should be shopping for any sensible compromise that will start taking the passion and hysteria out of the drug war. We should not demand the unconditional surrender or mass conversion of the drug warriors. But we must demand that some practical compromises be made now lest the drug war continue to erode American freedoms and to impose greater suffering on our people and those of other countries.

It might be wise to look into the experience of one of those other countries so as to get into the proper frame of mind to think peacefully about drug problems. While England is still instructive, these days I recommend Holland. It is the only country where the government itself calmly supports peaceful approaches to drug problems and openly opposes the very idea of a war on drugs. The Dutch seem to have dealt largely with the marijuana issue but have still not solved all of their difficulties with drugs. Yet, their spirit of moderation and experimentation is unmatched. They have tried a variety of approaches to supplying legal drugs to addicts through doctors and have kept adjusting their methods. A few years ago, the city government of Amsterdam came up with a proposal to experiment with medicalized heroin for addicts. The national government resisted and stopped it for the time being. When I was in Amsterdam in September 1986, however, Mayor Ed van Thijn sought me out at a reception he was holding at the Vincent van Gogh Museum to tell me that his government was going to propose the experiment again.

The city government is already showing its support for innovation in a variety of ways. I saw a small piece of that experimentation when I visited the Amsterdam chapter of the national addict union, or "Junkie Bond." The very existence of the union was breathtaking proof of how refreshingly different many Dutch leaders were in thinking about the fundamental nature of the drug problem. The union and another organization devoted to the interests of addicts, known by the initials MDHG, are greatly assisted by an annual contribution of approximately $80,000 from the city government. These related organizations, working side by side, provide a form of day hostel for addicts, along with information, advice, and friendly support of all kinds. On the day of my visit in 1986, members told me of a small book they were writing, which contained the reminiscences of addicts who had kicked the habit. The tentative title: "Each in His Own Way."

While at their headquarters in a decent-looking house not far from my hotel in downtown Amsterdam, I was seated in a room with three members of the group: Thijs van den Boomen, a nonuser and the organization's administrative director, and Willem and Mike, both drug addicts. As we talked about all of the services offered by the organization, I was surprised to see a picture of Martin Luther King, Jr., looking out over high stacks of big cardboard boxes. I was told that the organization was started by a Dutchman who was a disciple of King's because of the minister's great respect for human rights.

As for the boxes, they happened to contain "shooters," Mike told me. Many thousands of them. "Hypodermic needles?" I asked. Mike replied, "Yes, we call them 'shooters.'" All three then proceeded to explain that they conducted a major educational campaign to prevent disease among injecting addicts and prostitutes in the city. In addition, they provided free needles which could be obtained by turning in used ones. For the prostitutes, they also provided free condoms. I learned a few days later that the Dutch authorities were aware of only a few cases of AIDS among all of the 15,000–20,000 narcotic addicts of the country.

When New York City authorities suggested providing needles to prevent the spread of AIDS a few months later, the proposal met much resistance. However, this is precisely the type of pragmatic, humane compromise we should be experimenting with in America. It would not solve the drug problem but it would control some of its worst features and it would begin telling addicts that we view them as decent human beings.

We can look to the American experience for other examples of compromises, some of them on a grander scale. We should consider invoking a venerable conservative concept: states' rights, which was used to get this nation out of the disaster created by alcohol prohibition. In 1933 the federal government was backed out of alcohol control and each state allowed to determine its own policy.* In light of the abysmal failure of the federal government in the control of other drugs, a good basic principle would be to declare that in all matters pertaining to drugs, each state will have the power to make its own rules.

Federal laws and regulations would apply where national rules were absolutely necessary, however, such as the regulation of drug use during interstate travel. One of the worst forms of drug abuse, for example, is smoking tobacco on airplanes because of the health hazards for other passengers and crew—and also because of the danger of fires. Yet, strangely enough, the White House and the federal government lose their martial spirit when it comes to issuing a strict prohibition of the use of any smoking material on an airplane, which is the only logical step.

At some point in a more rational, peaceful future, the nation should consider enacting a federal drug-control statute similar to the Twenty-first Amendment regarding alcohol. This would mean

* The Eighteenth Amendment prohibited the manufacture, sale, or transportation of intoxicating liquors in the United States. It was proposed in 1917 and ratified in 1919. The Twenty-first Amendment repealed the Eighteenth and also provided that "The transportation or importation into any State, Territory, or possession of the United States for delivery or use therein of intoxicating liquors, in violation of the laws thereof, is hereby prohibited." In this convoluted fashion, a powerful coalition of sensible Americans in the center of the political structure managed to return the authority over alcohol to the states. The amendment was proposed in 1933 and, remarkably, ratified the same year. It was the only amendment ever to have been ratified by state conventions rather than by legislatures.

that federal law would generally defer to state law in regard to the control of all drugs, not simply alcohol, within the borders of each state. If conservative Utah, for example, wanted even stricter controls on marijuana and cocaine than now exist, so be it. If California and Massachusetts wanted more liberal laws, as they usually do, then again federal law would support those states in their sovereign decisions. This vision of future grand compromises entails a mix of conservative and liberal concepts, of old and new American ideals. It also provides the ground for social experimentation: the empirical results in one state may turn out to be superior, and thus set a constructive example for others to follow.

As we pulled the criminal law and the hard-line enforcers back to the borders of the drug-abuse arena, we would invite other, more tolerant thinkers and experimenters to come in. Drugpeace does not mean the absence of laws and morals but the creation of a more peaceful and effective system of laws and morals. We would call upon the ingenuity of lawyers, police leaders, political scientists, doctors, and enlightened lay people to devise new and more humane policies regarding drugs. I would accept any idea that made the situation more civilized so long as it met the pragmatic American test of creating more social gains than losses. If California wanted to expand the tough San Francisco ordinance controlling smoking tobacco in public places so that it applied throughout the whole state, then this would be an experiment worth encouraging. If Arizona wanted to allow experiments on maintaining heroin addicts on oral opium—an idea proposed by one of its most enlightened citizens, Dr. Andrew Weil—that effort should also be welcomed. If the District of Columbia, aware of the high incidence of cancer and heart disease due to alcohol abuse among its black citizens, wanted to ban all local media promotion of alcoholic beverages, this also should be followed with great interest and perhaps tried elsewhere.

The Oregon Marijuana Initiative was recently debated in that liberal western state. A persistent campaign by committed local citizens produced 87,056 signatures on petitions and a place on the ballot for the first statute that would have made fully legal the growth and possession of marijuana by adults for personal use. That proposition was defeated by about 70 percent of the electorate in November 1986. However, there still is a good deal of public support in Oregon and throughout the country for the legalization of this drug. Should that support grow to majority status, we would soon see both sale and use fully legalized in many states. At the same time, great support is growing for stricter controls on tobacco.

Because of this congruence of powerful historical, political, and scientific factors, therefore, some states might embark on an experiment in which the two drugs, both normally smoked, would be placed in the same category by the law. Both would be legal, highly taxed, pure, and sold in packages carrying a variety of explicit health warnings. Advertising of both would be strictly limited; some states might allow agate-print listing as with stock market prices today. Billions in new tax revenues would thus be raised, a major portion of which would go into special funds devoted to the treatment of persons harmed by the use of any drug, especially tobacco—and, as contradictory as it sounds, to publicity campaigns that provided realistic information to the public regarding the value of abstinence and of methods of achieving high states in life without drugs.

This proposal illustrates another principle of the drugpeace era: greater controls would be placed on the currently legal drugs, fewer on those currently illegal, especially marijuana, cocaine, and heroin, for both medical and recreational use. The civil law would, moreover, be used whenever possible rather than the criminal sanction.

The whole plan would seek out the middle ground between the extremes. As sages throughout the centuries have known, the truth is always in the middle.

More attention might well be paid in this new era to sound treatment programs for tobacco and marijuana addicts. Few such programs exist today, in part because of ideological conflicts. A true marijuana addict may well end up in a rigid institutional program run by one of the cults. Tobacco addicts seeking a well-run program will discover that most of their fellow patients are alcohol, cocaine, and other narcotic addicts who smoke tobacco incessantly. Rethinking our chemical ideology, therefore, may result in much more assistance to millions of addicts, especially those dependent on the deadly tobacco, now generally slighted by the professional treatment community.

The creation of good treatment programs for tobacco and marijuana addicts requires first that the need be recognized. Once that is done, then many of the ideas that have worked in other programs could be applied to those addictions.

Under a system of states' rights, some states might well fully legalize marijuana like alcohol while they medicalize heroin by allowing doctors to treat it as an ordinary medicine. What about cocaine? Should doctors be allowed to provide addicts with prescriptions, which is legal for specially licensed physicians in England? Should possession but not sale be decriminalized? Should it be fully legalized? I would authorize states to choose freely any of these options—medicalization, decriminalization, or full legalization—regarding any of the currently illegal drugs, including cocaine, rather than continue to risk the lives of our police and innocent bystanders in the war to control the lucrative and deadly traffic in drugs.

In this new era of legal and medicalized drugs, there is the risk that there would be greater abuse of previously prohibited drugs. If that occurred, the damage created would be balanced by the reduction in the abuse of the legal drugs, alcohol and tobacco, which might well result from a reduction in legalized pushing and in greater public education of the dangers of those substances. That situation would constitute an excellent social trade-off for the nation, and for those many other countries that will certainly follow the American example. The reduction in the per-capita use of alcohol and tobacco has already started. It is possible that we can continue to reduce use and abuse of those legal drugs, although we cannot prevent their use totally.

However, there is little likelihood that there would be an explosion of, for example, marijuana and cocaine use. Experience shows that there is a natural limit to the number of people who would try any drug no matter how easily available it might be. Easy availability is only one factor in personal decisions to use a drug. The largest reductions in the use of any drug by Americans have been of tobacco. The percentage of smokers in the population dropped from 41.7 percent in 1965 to 32.6 percent in 1983. During this same period, there was a dramatic drop in death rates from tobacco-related organic diseases. While tobacco remains our most addictive and destructive drug, all of this progress was accomplished without a war on tobacco, without locking up any tobacco users or dealers, but with education and persuasion that told the true facts about the drug.

When I was in northern California, the friendly citizens there would gladly have kept me knee-deep in world-class sinsemilla joints. I was no more interested in them than in rutabaga, which is also freely available there. The thought bored me.

If a pound of the best Colombian cocaine dropped out of an airplane in the Washington sky today and fell in my garden, I would wash it away with my garden hose, lest it affect my dog and the neighbors' cats. Even though millions of citizens use illegal substances, the great majority of Americans still share my attitudes toward these and other currently illegal drugs. Rutabaga. If the laws change, we are not going to become druggies or gorge ourselves on rutabaga, even if we retain our right to change our minds at some time in the future and sample some pot, cocaine, or turnips on occasion when the mood strikes.

In the end, we must rely on the wonderful old democratic faith. The role of government and of our wise men and women is to tell the truth, conflicting and full of warts as it is, so that the citizens may be fully informed. On balance, over time, we can rely on those citizens in a functioning democracy to make all sorts of stupid errors, but we can also be sure that in the final accounting, they will make more good decisions than bad.

That faith must now be applied to drugs as it has been to other areas of our national life. As we saw sheep living peacefully and happily with cattle, growing stronger together than apart, we could have seen sheep herders living peacefully with cattle herders in the Old West. Someday in the New America we may see American citizens, left to their own devices, working out ways either to ignore or to tolerate the peculiar drug habits of their neighbors, which, in any event, no power on earth can forcibly change.

All of the human species in our social pastures may well become more prosperous and happy under this peaceful arrangement.

Epilogue: My Proposals in a Nutshell

1. Stop talking about winning drug wars. In the broadest sense, there is no way to win because we cannot make the drugs or their abusers go away. They will always be with us. We have never run a successful drug war and never will. Our goal should be the fashioning of those methods of living peacefully with drugs that create the least possible harm for users and their nonusing neighbors.

2. Recognize that the line between illegal and legal drugs is a historical accident based primarily upon emotion rather than science. All drugs—including alcohol, tobacco, heroin, cocaine, PCP, marijuana, and many others—are dangerous. At the same time, all can be used in relatively nonharmful ways by many people.

3. Start thinking about drugs and abusers in new ways. Think drugpeace instead of drugwar. Think of drug addicts as potentially nice neighbors with a distressing problem instead of inherently evil criminals intent on robbing you because the drugs they take drive them crazy.

4. Protect our sick from the ravages of the drug war. They are its saddest victims. The great majority of them are innocent of any involvement with crime or the drug trade. If they are organically ill and suffering from diseases such as cancer or glaucoma, then

heroin and marijuana should be made available to them by prescription. If they are suffering from the disease of drug addiction and are dependent on heroin or cocaine, then those drugs should be made available to them by prescription. If they are injecting addicts, they should be provided with clean needles.

5. Demand of addicts in return that they live productive and noncriminal lives. Thus the social contract we make will be legal drugs in return for legal, loving lives. If some addicts continue to ignore their legitimate jobs, their loved ones, and the law, the deal, for them, is off.

6. Protect society from the ravages of the drug war—from criminal traffickers, from criminal drug addicts, and from criminal police and prosecutors. Much of this will be accomplished by reshaping our thinking and our laws concerning drugs, as was the case during Prohibition. Where the legal reforms do not automatically accomplish these happy results, we should add specific requirements, such as the contract with addicts.

7. Provide affordable treatment of all kinds as often as needed to everyone suffering from the disease of drug addiction. Tobacco addicts and alcohol addicts are drug addicts according to my definition. They will be harmed, not helped, by continuing to use their drug of dependence, unlike some narcotics addicts. All of these millions of people need treatment. It is not simply a case then of feeding drugs to addicts but of developing a network of treatment experts and facilities that meet the individual needs of each addict.

8. Curb the excesses of the venal elements of the drug-treatment business. The future of much of the new treatment network will come from the private sector. Yet too many of our leading experts, including prestigious physicians, are abusing and stealing from the public by locking up people needlessly and charging obscene fees. These medical jackals must be controlled and the best elements of the treatment profession encouraged to step in and help the addicted.

9. Convince the police that they are among the saddest victims of the drug war and that they should be in the leadership of the reform movement. In that role, they can be very effective. It is the equivalent of a conservative, communist-hating President making peace with a leading communist nation. This is not a fantasy. Remember President Nixon's historic initiatives with Red China.

10. Making peace with drugs and drug users is not the same as surrendering. (We did not surrender to Red China.) A peaceful

drug scene does not require the abolition of all drug laws but the creation of more sensible, more effective ones.

11. Give the police the financial, legal, and moral backing to escalate their courageous work against major organized-crime syndicates. If we reform drug laws, these social jackals will turn their attention to other illegal activities where they will continue to be major threats.

12. Back the federal government out of direct control of drug problems. Give the states primary responsibility. That is the compromise we devised to escape from the disaster of alcohol prohibition.

13. Create a bundle of peaceful compromises that will receive support from Middle America. Place greater controls on the sale and consumption of currently legal drugs, especially alcohol and tobacco. Place fewer controls on the currently illegal drugs. Examples: put health warning labels on every container of alcohol, including beer and wine; restrict all alcohol and tobacco advertising to agate-type listings in newspapers; prohibit all smoking on airplanes and in many other public locations; make marijuana use and cultivation legal for personal use by adults; medicalize heroin for addicts and pain patients by prescription but do not make them legal for casual recreational use.

14. Create new legal protections against the search for drugs in the homes, the lands, the bodies, and the bodily wastes of free citizens. Treat those drug warriors who want to display their own bodily wastes and to look at the wastes of others with the disgust they deserve. Perhaps we should even consider new and unorthodox methods of delivering the samples these perverts so earnestly desire.

Acknowledgments

Bruce Alexander, Barry Beyerstein, Eric Sterling, Kevin Zeese, and Norman Zinberg gave me much encouragement during every stage of this long project.

Many illegal drug users, some of them addicts still taking drugs, provided valuable insights into the realities of the drug scenes of the United States, Canada, England, and Holland. My knowledge of the addiction field would be incomplete without the hours and days they spent educating me. A few of them, such as Kenneth Freeman and the late Milton Polansky, agreed to be mentioned by name and thus to appear in these pages. Most of the others required anonymity. Even after all these years, I continue to be surprised when I discover yet another basically decent person addicted to powerful, illegal drugs.

A number of United States federal officials, with responsibilities in the drug policy field, have provided intellectual support and ideas to me over the years. A few of them, including Mr. X, who is quoted at length in the first chapter, have read and critiqued full drafts of the manuscript of this book. I offer them my thanks but cannot mention their names because of the ideological orthodoxy imposed on our government officials by the dominant drug-war extremists.

American drug policies have created a strange world: the two groups of people I encountered who needed anonymity the most were drug addicts and government officials who disagreed with policies that treated them as enemies of the state.

H.B. Spear, Jasper Woodcock, and Ann Dally continued their long service as mentors about the addiction situation in Britain. Jan van Dijk, Govert van de Wijngaart, Frits Rüter, and E.L. Engelsman provided helpful guidance on the unique Dutch approach to drug problems.

I have a profound debt to some of the modern pioneers of drug scholarship and law reform, whose writings helped shape my ideas when I first started inquiring into the field during the early Seventies. In particular: Alfred R. Lindesmith, one of the first of those frontiersmen, and his *Addict and the Law*, 1965; Rufus King, *The Drug Hang-up*, 1972; Andrew Weil, *The Natural Mind*, 1972, reissued in a revised edition, 1986; Edward M. Brecher, *Licit and Illicit Drugs*, 1972; David F. Musto, *The American Disease: Origins of Narcotic Control*, 1973; Thomas Szasz, *Ceremonial Chemistry: The Ritual Persecution of Drugs, Addicts, and Pushers*, 1974, revised edition, 1984; Horace Freeland Judson, *Heroin Addiction in Britain: What Americans Can Learn from the English Experience*, 1974; Lester Grinspoon, *Marijuana Reconsidered*, 1971, second edition, 1977; and the Drug Abuse Council, *Dealing with Drug Abuse*, 1972. While it may seem surprising, in the early Seventies I rated the two official reports of President Nixon's own National Commission on Marijuana and Drug Abuse as providing much of the factual ammunition for fundamental drug policy reform. I still do. Those reports are *Marijuana: A Signal of Misunderstanding*, 1972, and *Drug Use in America: Problem in Perspective*, 1973.

In more recent years, my thinking has been shaped by such works as: the Drug Abuse Council, *The Facts About "Drug Abuse,"* 1980; Andrew Weil and Winifred Rosen, *Chocolate to Morphine: Understanding Mind-Active Drugs*, 1983; Norman Zinberg, *Drug, Set, and Setting: The Basis for Controlled Intoxicant Use*, 1984; Stanton Peele, *The Meaning of Addiction*, 1985; Ray Raphael, *Cash Crop*, 1985; James B. Bakalar and Lester Grinspoon, *Drug Control in a Free Society*, 1985; and Steven Wisotsky, *Breaking the Impasse in the War on Drugs*, 1986.

Dominick Abel helped turn my original proposal into a book and served many kindly functions beyond that of a highly professional author's agent, which he is. Ned Chase wielded his editor's pen with skill, drive, and rare perception. My thanks go to Dominick Anfuso for helping to ease the progress of a manuscript through the intricacies of the publishing process—and for being graciously available to answer the myriad questions of an anxious author.

Deans Robert Cleary, Richard Apperson, and Rita Simon of American University provided grants of funds for research assistance at several points along the way. Catherine Sinclair and Paul Shelowitz directly provided that vital research support in the early phases—as did David Chipman, Beth Tarzia, and Robert Fitton in the latter stages. Derek DeVries was helpful in gathering preliminary information. Lyn Richmond and Joanne Sgro provided valuable editorial advice. Jenny McGough was a positive presence at the School of Justice in a variety of ways, which meant that my duties as both a teacher and writer were made easier by her many kindnesses.

—ARNOLD S. TREBACH

Washington, D.C.
January 1987

Index

Nancy Reagan's involvement in drug issues, 135; of PRIDE conference, 121

Pollin, William, 79–80, 89, 138

Portnoy, Russell, 206n

Posse comitatus, 164; amendments, 151, 167, 168–69

Pregnancies, teenage, 76–77

President's Commission on Organized Crime, 248, 353

Price, Jerry, 202

Prices of drugs, 177–78

PRIDE (National Parents' Resource Institute for Drug Education, Inc.), 118–23, 137–38

Prince of the City, Daley, 181, 340–42

Prison population, 180–81

Privacy rights, 195–98; and reform of drug laws, 374–75; urine tests, 231; and war on drugs, 217, 218

Prohibition, 3, 160

Property rights, 186–89

Propoxyphene hydrochloride. *See* Darvon

Pryor, Richard, 9

Psychological problems of undercover agents, 346–47

Punitive damages , 57

Pursch, Joseph, 19, 144–45

Quaalude, 176–77

Quattlebaum, Judith, 293

Quinine, deaths from, 80

Randall, Robert C., 308–24, 358, 361

Rangel, Charles, 165, 171, 296

Ransom, Goldfarb, 49

Raphael, Ray, 187–88; *Cash Crop*, 156–57

Ravin case, 102

Ray, Oakley, 107

Reader's Digest, 119

Reagan, Nancy, 21, 28, 30, 31, 40, 68, 77–78, 117–18, 121, 133–35; drug campaign, 135–38; visits to treatment centers, 142–46

Reagan, Ronald, 67

Reagan administration: drug policy, 3, 7–8, 16–18, 69, 108, 150–53, 177–78; funds for treatment, 372; and heroin reform, 294, 297; and marijuana, 78; and medical uses of marijuana, 322; and military drug testing, 241; and military forces for drug enforcement, 169–70; and reports of drug use, 14–15

Reasoner, Harry, 239

Reason magazine, 334–35

Recreational use of drugs, 108

Rehabilitation, and drug control, 5

Rehnquist, William, 208, 218–19

Rejent, Thomas, 235

Relapse, in drug addiction, 94, 110, 370

Renfrow, Omer, 221

Renner, David A., 154

Research funds, 308

Responsible drug use, 75, 108, 113, 119; parent's movement and, 139–41

Riddile, Melvin, 48

Ridenour, John, 161–62

Riel, George, 326

Right to treatment for drug addiction, 372–74

Rios, Ariel, 337

Risks in marijuana raids, 161

Robinson, Peter, 189

Rochin, Antonio Richard, 217–18

Rochin v. *California*, 218

Rogers, Don, 7, 8

Rolicheck, Deena, 201–4

Rolicheck, Gary, 201–4, 212–13

Rolicheck, Judy, 201–5

Rolleston, Humphrey, 267

Rolleston Committee Report, 266–68

Rose, Harvey L., 256–57, 258, 259–66

Rozelle, Pete, 239

Rubin, Seymour H., 274–78

Rudolph, Bill, 139, 140

Russoniello, Joseph P., 188–89, 206

Ruter, Frits, 104

Ruth, Babe, 239

Ruzzamenti, William, 154–56, 158–59, 187–88, 194, 198, 201, 204, 211; suit against, 206

Salazar, Enrique Camarena, 336

Sanborn, "Chuck," 200

SAT scores, 74–75

Schauteet, Arletha, 57–59

Schedule IV, Controlled Substances Act, 255–56

Schildt, Elizabeth, 264